THE MOST TRUSTED NAME IN TRAVEL: **FROMMER'S**

FROMMER'S EasyGuide to
COLOMBIA

By Nicholas Gill and Caroline Lascom

Idyllic San Andrés island.

CONTENTS

A colorful beach bar at Capurganá, on Colombia's Caribbean Coast.

A LOOK AT COLOMBIA

E merging like a sleeping jaguar and finally, definitively shedding its decades-long association with civil war and narco-bandits, Colombia is waiting to be discovered. The vibrant cities of Bogotá, Medellín, and Cartagena shimmy to the salsa music that pours from every bar and automobile. With splendid plazas and churches, haute and homey restaurants, and museums awash in looted gold, the nation is home to a diverse population that proudly keeps alive traditional Spanish, African, native, and Caribbean cultures and customs. Off-the-grid adventure beckons in the lush jungles of the Amazon and the Pacific Coast, or on challenging Andean treks. Paradise calls from postcard-perfect San Andrés and Providencia, while the mystery and magic realism of favorite son Gabriel García Márquez pulses through remote indigenous villages and once-forgotten colonial towns. Our Easy Guide presents the most authentic experiences in a country that defines "authentic." *¡Buen viaje!*

Seen here at Plaza de los Coches, colorfully clad *Palenquera* fruit-sellers are a fixture on Cartagena's streets.

BOGOTÁ, MEDELLÍN, EJE CAFE-TERO & THE NORTHERN ANDES

Colorful La Candelaria, Bogotá's colonial quarter, is home to most of the city's tourist attractions, as well as lively cafes and galleries.

A family of street musicians in Bogotá. Often called the "Land of 1,000 Rhythms," Colombia's rich musical traditions include countless variations of cumbia, vallenato, salsa and more.

The collections of Bogotá's Museo del Oro (p. 45) include tens of thousands of gold objects and pre-Columbian artifacts.

The Catedral de Sal, an underground church built in a 500-year-old salt mine, is the star attraction at Zipaquirá, a popular day trip from Bogotá (p. 68).

Colectivo microbuses provide transportation in Bogotá and throughout Colombia.

The cobblestone streets and centuries-old houses and churches around central Plaza Bolívar form one of Bogotá's most evocative neighborhoods.

A pushcart coffee vendor in Bogotá. As one of the world's largest exporters of coffee, Colombia takes its brew seriously.

Mountain bikers in San Gil. The 300-year-old Northern Andes town is a mecca for extreme sports enthusiasts (chapter 5).

The 1604 Iglesia Parroquial anchors Villa de Leyva's vast Plaza Mayor, one of the largest plazas—and one of the few to remain entirely cobblestone—in the Americas (chapter 5).

Eje Cafetero, Colombia's coffee-growing region, is a UNESCO World Heritage Site, with many traditional family-owned *fincas* now open to overnight guests.

Symbol of the city's urban renewal, Medellín's Metrocable gondola system connects once-blighted neighborhoods that are now home to flashy museums, parks, and municipal buildings.

Medellín's metro glides over Plaza de las Esculturas, also called Plaza Botero for the 23 bronze sculptures by native son Fernando Botero.

CARTAGENA & THE CARIBBEAN COAST

A woman knitting traditional handcrafts at Cabo de la Vela in La Guajira, ancestral home of the Wayúu people, a matriarchal society whose culture and customs still dominate the region (chapter 6).

The arduous 5-day hike to La Ciudad Pérdida ranks as one of the world's most exhilarating. "The Lost City" of the Tayrona culture predates Peru's Machu Picchu by 650 years (chapter 6).

A fruit vendor's cart in colonial Cartagena, whose history, exoticism, grit, and chaos inspired novelist Gabriel García Márquez's magic realism.

The 1600s Catedral Basílica de Santa Catalina de Alejandria (p. 94) looms over Cartagena's colonial Old Town.

Against the backdrop of modern Cartagena, the Church of St. Peter Claver (p. 95) memorializes Pedro Claver Corberó, a monumental figure in the abolition of slavery in Colombia and the Americas.

Expanded after Britain's Francis Drake pillaged Cartagena in 1586, labyrinthine Castillo San Felipe Barajas became a famously impenetrable fortress (p. 100).

Gilligan's Island fantasies nearly come true on Isla Mucura, part of the idyllic Islas de San Bernardo archipelago on Colombia's western Caribbean Coast (chapter 6).

Protected by the world's third-largest barrier reef, the waters of San Andrés make for great snorkeling and diving. Pictured here, shallow Cayo Acuario.

Coconut cocktails in San Andrés. Located nearly 500 miles from mainland Colombia, the tropical islands of San Andrés and Providencia have a laidback, ramshackle beauty.

A cow in paradise, Capurganá-style. Set at the edge of lush, dense Darién Gap, Capurganá is a sleepy haven for backpackers and a stepping off point for adventure travelers (chapter 6).

CALI, THE SOUTHWEST & THE PACIFIC COAST

A just-hatched sea turtle sets off from Playa Almejal beach in Bahía Solano. Turtle nesting season is September to December, when volunteers flock to the area to help protect the endangered creatures (chapter 9).

Dancers in the 500-year-old city of Popayán, where hotels fill up months in advance for the town's Holy Week festivities, among the most famous celebrations in Colombia (chapter 8).

The 30-minute journey to the tiny Afro-Colombian village of San Cipriano is worth it in itself, aboard a *brujita* (little witch), a jerry-rigged motorcycle that travels on old railroad lines (chapter 9).

Remote Tierradentro is known for its more than 100 *hypogeum*, underground painted tombs that date from the 6th to the 10th century. The culture that created them vanished and left little evidence of who they were (chapter 8).

Popayán's La Ermita church was built in the 20th century, but houses relics dating to the 1600s (p. 215).

Though not a tourist market, Silvia's Tuesday is one of Colombia's most authentic experiences (chapter 8).

Off Colombia's Pacific coast, Isla Malpelo is an uninhabited volcanic island that attracts divers—and a dazzling array of big marine life, including whale sharks (pictured here), hammerheads, grouper, and manta rays (chapter 9).

In their typical bowler hats, indigenous Guambiano women sell their produce and crafts at Silvia's weekly market.

The red hills of Tatacoa Desert. Because of the dry, clear conditions and little light pollution, the Tatacoa is an excellent place to see the stars of both hemispheres (chapter 8).

July through November, a blooming aquatic plant turns the river bed of the Caño Cristales, also called the "River of Five Colors," brilliant shades of yellow, green, blue, black, and red (chapter 10).

Bags full of produce, brought by boat from remote villages throughout the region, make their way along the Amazon River to the market in Leticia, Colombia's southernmost town (chapter 10).

On the Amazon River where it forms the border with Peru and Brazil, and with a population of fewer than 40,000, Leticia retains a frontier-town feel.

Friendly squirrel monkeys climb on for a snack in Leticia.

Reached only by boat, Puerto Nariño village is completely vehicle free, with paved footpaths instead of roads, and a few simple hotels and eco-lodge cabins (chapter 10).

THE BEST OF COLOMBIA

by Nicholas Gill

If there's a country poised to be the next big ecotourism destination, it's Colombia. Now with a lasting peace seemingly in place, pieces of the country long closed off to the wider world are opening up. With an area equal to that of Spain, France, and Portugal combined, Colombia has coastlines on the Atlantic and Pacific oceans, lush Amazon jungle, immense flatlands evoking the American plains, scorching deserts, and snowcapped mountains. Perfectly preserved colonial cities, Caribbean islands, and meandering rivers straight out of a Gabriel García Márquez novel are all here, not to mention 45 million residents that make Colombia second only to Brazil in human and ecological diversity among South American nations.

The capital of **Bogotá** is home to fine museums and pulsating neighborhoods, mixing the colonial past with the country's modern present. In **Medellín**, ride cable cars to architectural projects and rainforests high in the mountains. Take salsa lessons in **Cali** then to dance the beat of Afro-Colombian rhythms in **Cartagena**. Lie on the beach in national parks like **Tayrona**, then visit indigenous communities in **La Guajira** and **Puerto Nariño**.

Home to 10% of the world's plant and animal species, Colombia is one of the most biodiverse places on earth. Whales frolic just off the beaches of the **Pacific coast**, while monkeys and jaguars hide within the dense jungles of the **Amazon**. With more species than anywhere else, birding here is phenomenal. Plus you can hike in the high Andes, windsurf on mountain lakes, and help sea turtle hatchlings get out to sea.

Mysterious stone statues and burial chambers in Colombia's rugged southwest **at San Agustín** and **Tierradentro** date back more than 1,000 years, while the remote ruins of **Ciudad Pérdida** near

1 | The Best of Colombia

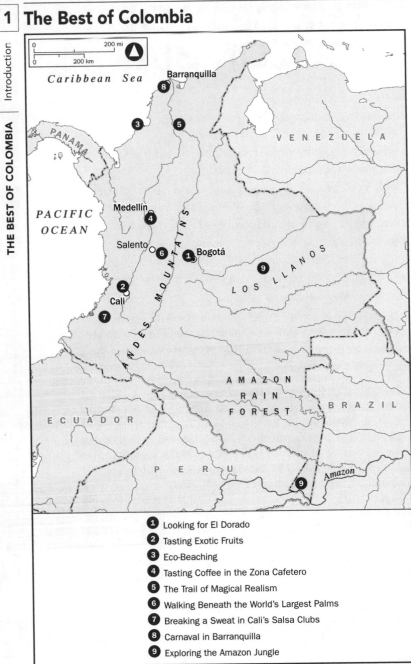

0 — 200 mi
0 — 200 km

Caribbean Sea

Barranquilla

8

3

5

V E N E Z U E L A

PACIFIC OCEAN

Medellín

4

Salento **6**

1 Bogotá

9

L O S   L L A N O S

2

Cali

A N D E S   M O U N T A I N S

7

PANAMA

A M A Z O N
R A I N
F O R E S T

B R A Z I L

E C U A D O R

P E R U

9

Amazon

1 Looking for El Dorado
2 Tasting Exotic Fruits
3 Eco-Beaching
4 Tasting Coffee in the Zona Cafetero
5 The Trail of Magical Realism
6 Walking Beneath the World's Largest Palms
7 Breaking a Sweat in Cali's Salsa Clubs
8 Carnaval in Barranquilla
9 Exploring the Amazon Jungle

the Caribbean coast are often compared to Machu Picchu. Colonial cities and fortresses dot the country, from **Cartagena** on the coast to **Mompós** in the north to **Popayán** in the south.

COLOMBIA'S best AUTHENTIC EXPERIENCES

o **Looking for El Dorado (Bogotá):** The myth of El Dorado began upon the discovery of a golden raft topped by tribal chieftains from the Muisca culture, which is now the centerpiece of Bogotá's Museo del Oro. The impressive collection contains more than 55,000 pieces of gold art created by pre-Columbian cultures like the Calima and Zenú. See p. 45.

o **Tasting Exotic Fruits (Cali):** Colombia has some of the most special tropical fruits you will ever see. At Cali's Galeria Alameda, see table after table filled with colorful fruits like *carambola* (star fruit), *curuba* (banana passion fruit), or the citrusy *lulo*. See p. 221.

o **Eco-Beaching (Caribbean Coast):** Opt between a hammock, tent, or a luxurious yet eco-friendly cabin while sunbathing on the sands of Parque Nacional Tayrona. When you tire of coconut palms, hike into the jungle to a pre-Columbian ruin or search for endangered wildlife. See p. 137.

o **Tasting Coffee in the Zona Cafetero (Medellín & the Eje Cafetero):** Colombian coffee is known all over the world, but in Colombia the best comes from the Eje Cafetero, a coffee-growing region located in and around the departments of Caldas, Risaralda, and Quindío. Aside from just producing the beans, many *fincas* in the region have also become country inns. See p. 204.

o **The Trail of Magical Realism (Caribbean Coast):** Immerse yourself in the world of Nobel Prize–winning novelist Gabriel García Márquez, who based much of his work on towns in Colombia. See the town of Aracataca where he was born; Cartagena, where he lived for many years; and the Magdalena River, which inspired some of his greatest work. See p. 126.

o **Walking Beneath the World's Largest Palms (Medellín & the Eje Cafetero):** In the Valle de Cocora, the *palma de cera*, or wax palm, stands as much as 60m high above the misty green hills. The setting for Colombia's national tree, amid grasslands and cloud forest, makes for a remarkable scene that you won't soon forget. See p. 201.

o **Breaking a Sweat in Cali's Salsa Clubs (Cali & the Southwest):** If you want to learn salsa, there's no better place the Cali, the world's capital. The dance originated here, and Caleños often dominate world championships. Test your game in the city's salsa clubs and schools. See p. 224.

o **Carnaval in Barranquilla (Caribbean Coast):** Outside of Rio, the biggest Carnaval celebration is held at this bustling Caribbean port town. The debaucherous 4-day festival includes masked parades, street dancing, and more *cumbia* than you'll be able to handle. See p. 116.

o **Exploring the Amazon Jungle (Amazon & Los Llanos):** Leticia, Colombia's tiny foothold on the Amazon River, is a jumping off point for isolated ecolodges, visits to indigenous communities, and wildlife-seeking expeditions. See p. 254.

COLOMBIA'S best ACTIVE ADVENTURES

o **Hiking to Ciudad Pérdida (Caribbean Coast):** The arduous 5-day hike to the lost city of the Tayrona is one of South America's greatest trekking experiences. You'll encounter indigenous Kogi villages and see rare wildlife. The feeling you'll have after climbing 1,200 stairs hidden on the side of a river to a setting that's as dramatic as Machu Picchu will leave you speechless. See p. 140.

o **Running Big-Time Whitewater (Northern Andes):** In San Gil, Colombia's adventure capital, you'll find all sorts of dare-devilish sports like mountain biking, canyoning, and bungee jumping. However, nothing will test your adrenaline as much as the Class V rapids on the Río Suarez. For a more mild experience, opt for the Río Fonce. See p. 81.

o **Surfing El Chocó (Pacific Coast):** Isolated towns like Nuquí and Bahía Solano make excellent bases for surfing the strong currents and tall waves of the Pacific Coast. Surfing guides and surf lodges are quickly becoming as common as howler monkeys. See p. 247.

o **Trekking and Climbing in the High Andes (Northern Andes):** Inaccessible a decade ago, Parque Nacional Cocuy, an Andean range of towering peaks and glaciers, is perhaps Colombia's finest high-altitude hiking destination, even with access into the interior being closed. For now, stick to short hikes from the town of El Cocuy. See p. 78.

o **Diving the Caribbean (San Andrés & Providencia):** PADI-certified dive centers can be found on these two paradisiacal islands, good places for exploring one of the world's longest barrier reefs. Manta rays, morays, sea turtles, and giant shoals of fish are all a boat ride away. See p. 269 and 278.

o **Swimming with Hundreds of Sharks (Pacific Coast):** The remote Pacific island of Malpelo is one of the world's most renowned dive destinations. It's here that divers can swim with 500 hammerhead sharks at a time, not to mention catch a glimpse of the extremely rare smalltooth and tiger shark. See p. 250.

COLOMBIA'S best RESTAURANTS

o **Leo Cocina y Cava (Bogotá):** Leonor Espinosa's eponymous restaurant has been redefining contemporary Colombian cuisine since opening in 2007. It's because of her that unusual ingredients like big-butted ants from

Santander and fermented yuca broth from the Amazon now appear in the realm of fine dining. See p. 57.

o **Cielo (Medellín):** With restaurants in Bogotá and Medellín, not to mention TV appearances, young chef Juan Manuel Barrientos has become one of the faces of Colombia's growing food movement. He adds molecular touches to native ingredients, so expect to have all of your senses tingled. See p. 181.

o **Cafe Pacifico (Pacific Coast):** Afro-Colombian traditions and regional ingredients are explored at this surprising Buenaventura restaurant. After a ceviche made with *piangua*, the local black clam, chase it down with a shot of *viche*, the regional aguardiente, which they have macerating with native herbs and fruits behind the bar. See p. 244.

o **Carmen (Medellín):** This lively Parque Lleras restaurant is run by two Cordon Bleu grads who like to pair Colombian ingredients with international cooking styles. Think pork belly glazed with tamarind or pig-cheek tacos with yuca tortillas. See p. 180.

o **El Boliche (Caribbean Coast):** What happens when a chef trained in three Michelin star restaurants in Spain opens a tiny, 16-seat cevicheria in Cartagena's Centro Histórico? Fresh seafood and other Colombian flavors are beautifully prepared for an always-changing menu. See p. 106.

o **Criterion (Bogotá):** Originally a French restaurant from the Rausch brothers, their flagship Criterion has increasingly moved toward Colombian ingredients. Their work with lionfish, an invasive predator, is helping save coral reefs in the Gulf from further deterioration. See p. 58.

o **Villanos en Bermudas (Bogotá):** Two of Latin America's most promising young chefs, one from Mexico and one from Argentina, join together in a three-level building to create Colombia's most ambitious restaurant ever. Food is strictly based on what's in season. See p. 59.

o **Andrés Carne de Res (Bogotá):** You don't know Colombia until you have spent an evening at Andrés Carne de Res in the town of Chia outside of Bogotá. Like a small city, the restaurant serves thousands of people every night, who come for steak and traditional specialties and to rumba until closing time. See p. 67.

o **Mora Castilla (Cali & the Southwest):** The colonial city of Popayán is one of the centers of Colombian gastronomy, and this unpretentious little restaurant serves classic recipes like *salpicón payanese* and *carantatas*. See p. 231.

COLOMBIA'S best HOTELS

o **Four Seasons (Bogotá):** The luxe international hotelier took over this emblematic property in the Zona G in 2015. Designed from pieces of colonial convents, the 62-room hotel's stone columns and hand-carved doors have been restored to their original glory. See p. 52.

o **Sofitel Santa Clara (Caribbean Coast):** In a converted 17th-century convent, this colonial gem in Cartagena's old city was the setting of the García

Márquez novel *Of Love and Other Demons*. Despite being the largest hotel in this part of the city, it manages to add modern amenities without losing the original architectural spirit. See p. 104.

o **Tcherassi Hotel + Spa (Caribbean Coast):** One of Colombia's biggest fashion designers enters the hotel game with a posh boutique hotel in a 250-year-old colonial mansion in Cartagena. There's an Italian restaurant, a spa, a vertical garden, and just seven immaculate rooms. See p. 105.

o **Charlee Hotel (Medellín):** It's modern and edgy and it towers over Parque Lleras—the Charlee is more than a hotel. With a ground-floor restaurant, rooms with hibachi grills, and a rooftop pool and bar, it's a place to see and be seen. See p. 177.

o **Eco-habs Tayrona (Caribbean Coast):** Crafted from native woods and thatched roofs from palm leaves, these cushy four-person Tayrona bungalows above Canaveral beach in Parque Nacional were inspired by ancient tribes that once lived here. A spa and gourmet restaurant are also on site. See p. 137.

o **Hacienda Venecia (Eje Cafetero):** Set on a working coffee *finca* near Manizales, this rural inn is designed with traditional Bahareque elements like bamboo-and-clay walls and red tile roofs. See p. 207.

o **Hotel Dann Monasterio (Cali & the Southwest):** In the white city of Popayán, this 16th-century Franciscan monastery is a colonial attraction as important as the city's famed churches and plazas. Elegant and classy rooms surround an atmospheric courtyard. See p. 229.

o **Portal de la Marquesa (Caribbean Coast):** In the long-lost colonial city of Mompós (aka Mompox), this 1735 home built for a rich merchant feels like a time machine. Hand-carved wooden doors, high ceilings, and original wood columns have all been restored by local artisans. See p. 160.

o **Cosmos (Pacific Coast):** What is this sleek, modern hotel doing standing over the bay in once-shabby Buenaventura? You'll never look at the Colombian Pacific's largest container port the same way after looking at it from a rooftop infinity pool. See p. 245.

o **Deep Blue (Providencia):** On the rainforest-covered hillside of this quiet Caribbean Island near San Andrés, this refined small hotel is popular with both honeymooners and divers. All of the 13 rooms have private ocean-facing balconies and some add private plunge pools. See p. 278.

COLOMBIA'S best
ARCHITECTURAL LANDMARKS

o **Barichara (Northern Andes):** Sometimes overshadowed by the adrenaline pumping going on in nearby San Gil, this colonial town dates to 1705 and is sometimes called the most beautiful in Colombia. Every single cobblestone street and terracotta-tiled roof here has been restored. See p. 79.

o **Villa de Leyva (Northern Andes):** Far from commercial routes, Villa de Leyva's stone plazas and colonial buildings have seen little development—outside of tourism—in 4 centuries. This is one of Colombia's first architectural attractions to receive attention. See p. 72.

o **Popayán (Cali & the Southwest):** The best preserved of Colombia's colonial cities, Popayán's whitewashed buildings have earned it the nickname "Ciudad Blanca" or "White City." Historic churches, monasteries, bridges, and university buildings have all been impeccably maintained. See p. 228.

o **Parque Biblioteca España (Medellín & the Eje Cafetero):** Installed on a hillside in the Santo Domingo neighborhood and reached by cable car, this modernist library complex has helped give a new face to Medellín. The three buildings, covered in dark stone tiles and resembling large boulders, have transformed one of the most dangerous neighborhoods in the city. See p. 175.

o **Monserrate (Bogotá):** The peak of this famed mountain hovering above Bogotá is noteworthy not just for the views, but for the Catholic Church balancing on top of it, The sanctuary was built in 1657 in honor of the Virgen Morena. See p. 44.

o **Salt Cathedral of Zipaquirá (Bogotá):** Two hundred meters underground, set in the tunnels of an old salt mine, is this dramatic cathedral and the Stations of the Cross. All of it is backlit with eerie mood lighting. See p. 68.

o **Castillo de San Felipe de Barajas (Caribbean):** Built to withstand pirate attacks, the imposing fort of San Felipe guards Cartagena from the top of the 40m-high San Lázaro hill. A complex network of walls and tunnels, this is the strongest fort the Spanish built anywhere in the Americas. See p. 100.

THE best UNDISCOVERED COLOMBIA

o **Mompox/Mompós (Caribbean Coast):** Set on an island in the Magdalena River, Mompós, or Mompox, is true García Márquez country. It was once one of the most important Spanish cities in the Americas, but faded into history until UNESCO named it a World Heritage Site in 1995. With its colonial core restored, it's now ready for tourists. See p. 155.

o **Tierradentro (Cali & the Southwest):** While Tierradentro is Colombia's second most important archeological site, it receives very few tourists because of its isolated location. Those who come are rewarded by more than 100 underground tombs, unlike anything else that has been discovered in the region. See p. 238.

o **Parque Nacional Natural Utría (Pacific Coast):** Halfway between Nuquí and Bahía Solano, this coastal park in El Chocó is home to mangroves and thick tropical forest. Its sheltered coves are where humpback whales come to raise their young. See p. 247.

o **Puerto Nariño (Amazon & Los Llanos):** Reached only by boat, this mostly Ticuna town on the Loreto Yacu River makes a good base for exploring Lago Tarapoto and the surrounding Amazon jungle. Keep an eye out for giant Victoria Regia water-lilies. See p. 258.

o **San Cipriano:** Set in a reserve amid wet, wonderful rainforest, this Afro-Colombian community can only be reached by *brujita*, a motorcycle-powered rail car from the nearest town. Once there, rent an inner tube to float in the adjacent crystal-clear stream. See p. 245.

o **La Macarena (Amazon & Los Llanos):** For a few months each year, during the wet season, an algae on the floor of a nearby river, Caño Cristales, turns a bright red, clashing with the green mosses and golden sand. Once impossible to reach, direct flights from Bogotá now allow for short trips. See p. 260.

o **La Guajira (Caribbean Coast):** This remote Caribbean peninsula near the Venezuelan border, home to sand dunes and scrublands, is emerging as an ecotourism destination. This is the land of indigenous Wayúu, weavers of the famous *mochilas* sold around the country, who have integrated cattle ranching into their traditional society. See p. 140.

COLOMBIA'S best BEACHES

o **Playa Almejal (Pacific Coast):** This legendary surf beach outside of Bahía Solano takes advantage of the strong currents and large swells of the Pacific Coast. There are also calmer waters for swimming, spotting whales, and just cooling off after a hike through the jungle. See p. 246.

o **Cabo San Juan (Caribbean Coast):** This is the most famous beach in Parque Nacional Tayrona, a place known for its many beautiful beaches. Essentially two beaches split by a rocky point, where there's good snorkeling off the reef and a trail that leads into the jungle to the ruins of El Pueblito. See p. 136.

o **Playa Blanca (Caribbean Coast):** Why settle for Cartagena's municipal beaches when this long stretch of white sand is on nearby Isla Barú? Come in the morning, lay down your towel, buy fresh fish and cold beer from the thatched beach shacks, then go back to the city in the afternoon. See p. 101.

o **Rodadero (Caribbean Coast):** For a straightforward and inexpensive all-inclusive vacation, this popular Santa Marta beach is your best bet. The water is nicer over in Tayrona, but if you have just a weekend to get away and don't want to overthink it, come here. See p. 121.

o **Johnny Cay (San Andrés & Providencia):** The idyllic white-sand beach, backed by just enough coconut palms, is perhaps the best reason to leave the main island of San Andrés. The tiny islet, a regional park, has no population outside of a reggae band playing for day trippers. See p. 269.

o **Cabo de la Vela (Caribbean Coast):** Near the far tip of La Guajira, a desert peninsula that forms Colombia's northeastern border, this remote cape adjacent to a fishing village is worth the effort. Just off the beach, American flamingos flock to the saline lagoons by the hundreds. See p. 144.

COLOMBIA IN CONTEXT

by Nicholas Gill

Once considered the most dangerous country in the world, Colombia, having implemented security improvements over the last decade, is slowly emerging from the internecine bloodshed of the 1980s and 1990s. Homicide rates in many Colombian cities, once among the highest in the world, have fallen below levels of many U.S. cities. Political kidnappings are a thing of the past. Since the early 2000s, a strong military and police presence have made land transportation reasonably safe again. With the conflict with the FARC coming to a close, expect things to get even better.

Thanks to this improved security situation, Colombia is a country ripe for discovery by foreign tourists. Though politically one nation, it is made up of three distinct regions, each with its own customs and traditions. The Atlantic and Pacific coasts, inhabited mostly by descendants of African slaves, are culturally linked to the Caribbean, rich in musical tradition and spectacular tropical scenery. The central and most densely populated portion of the country, crowned by the Andes Mountains, has managed to grow and prosper despite its unforgiving terrain. Dotted by most of Colombia's largest cities, it is the economic engine of the country. The sparsely populated eastern portion of the country is inhabited by tough, hard-working farmers and traditional indigenous tribes; it's a land of vast planes, thick jungle, unmatched natural beauty, and, unfortunately, high levels of guerilla activity and cocaine production.

Like most of the developing world, Colombia is a country of contradictions. Hip yuppies dress to the nines and sip $14 cocktails at über-upscale bars, while the poorest Colombians can barely afford life's necessities. Cosmopolitan cities offer luxury condos, theater, international cuisine, and all the amenities of the modern world, while many small pueblos seem stuck in the 19th century, stunted by high unemployment and old-fashioned attitudes. Despite all its woes—economic, social, and political—Colombia remains a fascinating country to visit.

Colombia

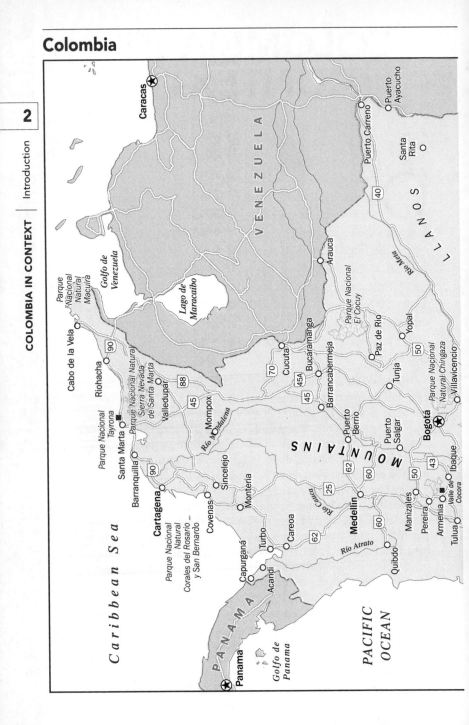

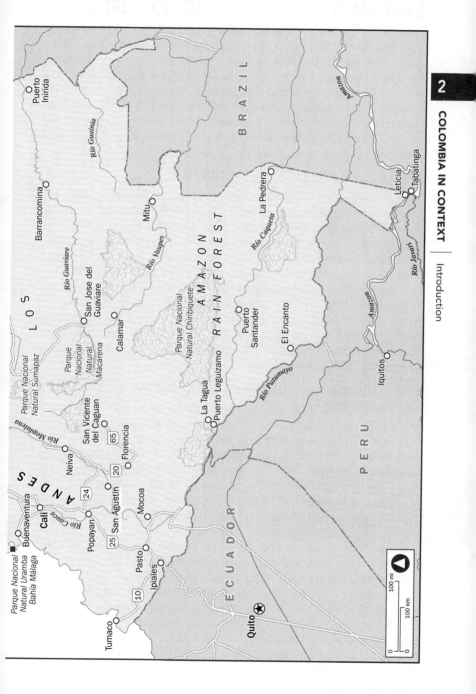

THE MAKING OF COLOMBIA

Colombia's vibrant, at times violent, history has shaped the modern society in ways that we may never fully understand. Simultaneously a romance and a tragedy, the story of Colombia is more complex and interesting than cable news would have you believe. Dating back tens of thousands of years, from when the first migrants traveled down through Panama, human history in the region has been shaped by waterways and mountains and thick forest cover. Natural forces like earthquakes and floods, not to mention the unexpected arrival of the Spanish and forced arrival of African slaves, have all contributed to the diverse society that inhabits the country today.

Prehistory (20,000 B.C.–1000 B.C.)

While Colombia does not have as extensive of an early history as other Latin American countries such as Peru and Mexico, it is located almost directly in between the two. Most historians think the first inhabitants crossed the Bering Strait in Asia during the last ice age, migrated their way down through North and Central Americas, and settled in the region around 20,000 B.C. They were nomadic hunter-gatherers who lived mostly along the coasts, river valleys, and highlands. In remote Chiribiquete National Park, archaeologists have uncovered cave paintings that date back more than 10,000 years. Images include jaguars, crocodiles, and deer, painted in red on vertical rock faces. The oldest pottery fragments, believed to be more than 6,000 years old, were found at the San Jacinto archaeological site. Still, very little is known about early human settlement in present-day Colombia.

Pre-Columbian Cultures (1000 B.C.–A.D. 1499)

While there were no colossal civilizations like the Aztecs and Incas to develop in Colombia, lesser-known cultures that were nearly as sophisticated did arise here, as archaeological evidence suggests. The country's geography often confined cultures to particular regions, such as the Andes or near the coasts. While these agrarian societies traded among each other, there were never conquering forces that took over vast pieces of the country, like there were in Peru.

A dozen or so cultures—like the Calima, Muisca, Nariño, Quimbaya, San Agustín, Sinú, Tayrona, Tierradentro, Tolima, Tumaco, and Urabá—left behind artifacts like intricate gold work and ceramics.

Several cultures left behind significant monuments, too. In the Sierra Nevada de Santa Marta and along the Caribbean coast, the Tayrona built settlements with roads, plazas, aqueducts, and stone stairways. Their signature achievement has become known as Ciudad Pérdida, or the lost city. Set high in the jungle-clad mountains, in a setting as majestic as Machu Picchu, the city may have housed as many as 8,000 people at its peak. In San Agustín in the southwest, past inhabitants left behind hundreds of megalithic sculptures of gods and mythical animals that date from the 1st to the 8th centuries. Not far away in Tierradentro, underground tombs dating from 600 to 900 A.D., some measuring as much as 12m (40 ft.) wide and unlike anything else in the Americas, reveal a complex social structure and belief system.

Spanish Conquest & Colonialism (1500–ca. 1800)

Columbus and his pals landed in the Americas in 1492, with the first European—Alonso de Ojeda—reaching Colombia in 1499. During a brief exploration of the Sierra Nevada de Santa Marta, he was impressed by the amount of gold he encountered with the local Indians, and they told him of more wealth in the interior. This gave birth to the legend of El Dorado, which would later be attached to the Muiscas, who tossed gold into the Laguna de Guatavita as a ritual offering.

Small Spanish settlements began appearing on the coast in the following years, though it wasn't until Rodrigo de Bastidas founded Santa Marta in 1525 that any of them were permanent. Eight years later, Pedro de Heredia would build Cartagena, which became the primary point of access into the continent and a center of trade. A massive fortress was built there to guard the growing collection of gold from pirate attacks.

In 1537, Jiménez de Quesada pushed into Muisca territory, which was split into two rivaling factions, the Zipa and the Zaque, allowing him to conquer the group relatively quickly. A year later, he founded Santa Fe de Bogotá at Bacata, the center of power of the Zipa. Around the same time Sebastián de Belalcázar, who deserted Francisco Pizarro's army while they were in the middle of conquering the Incas, founded Popayán and Cali. Various Spanish factions fought for power of the country until 1550 when King Carlos V of Spain established a colony under the control of the Viceroyalty of Peru.

In 1564, the Nuevo Reino de Granada was established, which included present-day Panama and most of Colombia. It was during this period that Cartagena was granted the privilege of being the exclusive slave-trading port in the colony, drastically changing the cultural make-up of what would become Colombia. Many of the African slaves worked in mines and coastal plantations. In 1717, the growing Spanish Empire in the New World pushed the colony's borders outward. Ruled from Bogotá, the Virreinato de Nueva Granada comprised the territories of present-day Colombia, Panama, Ecuador, and Venezuela.

The Fight for Independence (1793–1819)

As Spanish power grew in the region, mounting taxes and duties met with protests from inhabitants. The 1781 Revolución de los Comuneros in Socorro was the first major rebellion against the crown. When Napoleon installed his brother Joseph as monarch in 1808, many cities refused to recognize him and declared independence. After the collapse of the First Republic of Venezuela in 1812, Simón Bolívar joined the growing Colombia independence movement, winning six battles against Spanish troops before being defeated. After Spain wrestled the throne back from Napoleon, they quickly regained full control of the colonies. In 1816, Bolívar returned and formed a new army and marched over the Andes from Los Llanos, eventually joining forces with a British legion. They successfully defeated the Royalists and won a decisive battle in Boyacá on August 7, 1819. Bolívar and his troops then marched into

EL CONFLICTO ARMADO: who's fighting whom

Although security conditions have improved dramatically in the last decade, Colombia can still be an unpredictable place, with flare-ups between guerilla and paramilitary factions. To understand Colombia's half-century of civil war, it's important to know who the players were. On the leftist, guerilla side is the FARC (Revolutionary Armed Forces of Colombia), the country's largest guerilla army, with about 12,000 members. FARC signed a peace deal in 2016. The ELN (National Liberation Army) consisted of about 5,000 people and is in on-and-off-again demobilization talks. The M-19 was another deadly, mostly urban guerilla movement that demobilized in the late 1980s. On the far right are the paramilitaries; originally formed to combat the guerillas, they became major players in the drug trade. Las Aguilas Negras are a relatively new group, composed mostly of so-called demobilized paramilitaries.

To make sense of all the acronyms and ideology, not to mention the corruption, consider reading one of the following books, all of which provide excellent background: *Killing Peace* (2002) by Garry Leech; *Walking Ghosts: Murder and Guerrilla Politics in Colombia* (2005) by Steven Dudley; and *More Terrible Than Death: Violence, Drugs, and America's War in Colombia* (2004) by Robin Kirk.

Although the modern Colombian conflict didn't technically start until 1964, when the FARC was founded, Colombia has a bloody past almost as long as the country's history. The violence, always rooted in politics, pitted the Liberals against the Conservatives, resulting in both the Thousand Days' War, from 1899 to 1902, and, later on, La Violencia of the 1940s and 1950s. Combined, these conflicts took the lives of almost half a million Colombians. After the relative peace of the 1960s and '70s, violence

Bogotá 3 days later. He was named president of what would become known as Gran Colombia (Colombia, Venezuela, Panama, and Ecuador) and held the office until 1828.

Gran Colombia (1820–1921)

Right from the beginning, Gran Colombia was troubled. While President Bolívar was away fighting for independence in Ecuador and Peru, his vice president, Francisco de Paula Santander, held power. The territory was big and hard to manage. Laws were introduced to abolish slavery and to redistribute indigenous lands, but by 1830, the union was over. Venezuela and Ecuador broke away and a new constitution was written. Two political parties came to power: the Conservatives, who preferred centralized power, and the Liberals, who favored more power with the states. More than 100,000 people died in 1899 alone as a result of a liberal revolt that turned violent, called the War of a Thousand Days. Turmoil in the country allowed the United States to push a secessionist movement in Panama and in 1903; it too broke away and allowed the construction of the Panama Canal across the isthmus.

La Violencia (1948–1960)

After several decades of relative peace and stability, Colombia's most deadly civil war up until that point broke out, called La Violencia. After the flared up again during the '80s and '90s, mostly owing to the increased involvement of the guerillas and paramilitaries in the drug trade, as well as to Pablo Escobar, who had a hand in bombings, assassinations, and campaigns of terror.

Unlike most Latin American movements, the FARC, paramilitaries, and other nongovernment armed forces have had little backing among Colombia's poor, especially as these armed groups became more involved with narco trafficking. In fact, fighting for control of the lucrative cocaine trade appears to be the top priority for guerilla and paramilitary groups nowadays.

As a foreigner and a tourist, you are unlikely to face threats from any illegal groups, but it's still wise to avoid some remote rural areas, city slums, and other "red zones"—so declared by the government depending on recent guerilla and paramilitary violence. Your best bet is to stick to cities and heavily patrolled and visited destinations such as the Eje Cafetero, the department of Boyacá, and most of the Atlantic coast. Unless for some reason you'll be traveling to guerilla- or paramilitary-controlled areas, which are becoming fewer and fewer, you're fine to discuss the FARC, ELN, or paramilitaries with taxi drivers, waiters, receptionists, and other Colombians; everyone here seems to have an opinion, and this is a good way to interact with the locals and learn about the country.

Keep tabs on the ever-changing situation by reading *El Tiempo* (www.eltiempo.com), Colombia's most important and popular newspaper, and by frequently checking the U.S. State Department website regarding travel warnings (http://travel.state.gov). Although all this information may sound a bit ominous and discouraging, the bottom line is, unless you veer really far off the beaten path, you shouldn't face any problems.

assassination of Liberal leader Jorge Eliécer Gaitán, riots erupted all over the country. One of the bloodiest conflicts in the history of the Western Hemisphere, more than 300,000 people were killed in the fighting that followed. In 1953, the military, led by General Gustavo Rojas Pinilla, took over the country and ended La Violencia. By 1957, the two parties signed a pact, agreeing to alternate power every 4 years. The agreement outlawed other political parties, which planted the seeds of guerilla insurgency.

The Civil War (1960–2005)

Social and political injustices continued, and dissidents were unable to have their voices heard. In 1964, following the fraudulent election of a Conservative candidate, the FARC was formed by Marxist–Leninist Manuel Marulanda Vélez. The Ejército de Liberación Nacional (National Liberation Army/ELN) and more than a dozen other guerilla groups developed around the country during this period, each with their own philosophy. To counter the insurgency, paramilitary groups were created by landholders and even drug cartels, often using weapons supplied by the U.S. Murder and acts of terrorism became commonplace in Colombia. As communism fell around the world, the two major guerilla groups, the FARC and ELN, lost foreign support and turned to more desperate measures such as kidnappings, extortion, and threats.

The Cartels (1980–1995)

At the same time, the illegal drug trade grew more intense as newly wealthy drug lords fought with guerrilla groups, leading to more kidnappings and death squads. Under pressure from the U.S., the government began cracking down on the drug trade, even while Pablo Escobar's Medellín Cartel bribed or murdered countless public officials, founded its own political party, established newspapers, and financed public housing projects. Escobar and his crew lived a life of luxury, and his personal wealth was estimated at $2 billion. The turning point came in 1989, when the cartels killed presidential candidate Luis Carlos Galán. The government responded with the confiscation of cartel properties and a new extradition treaty with the U.S. The cartels called for all out warfare by detonating bombs in banks, houses, and an Avianca flight from Bogotá to Cali with 107 people onboard. After extensive negotiations with the government of César Gaviria, Escobar turned himself in and was put under house arrest, but later escaped. After a 499-day search, he was killed in Medellín in 1993. Around the mid-1990s, as the street price of cocaine fell, the cartels lost power and the guerillas took over the trade.

The Road to Peace (1995–2015)

From 2002 to 2008, right wing, Harvard-educated president Álvaro Uribe took power with an anti-guerilla agenda. Murder rates fell dramatically and highways became safer. In a risky mission, the military rescued high-profile kidnapping victims from FARC, taking away much of its negotiation strength. Uribe approved a risky bombing mission over the border in Ecuador that killed FARC

EATING & drinking

You won't be hungry in Colombia. Though every region has its own specialties, you're never far from a plate of beans, beef, plantains, and rice. Food is good, hearty, and generally cheap, if not particularly varied. For gourmands, major cities such as Bogotá, Medellín, and Cartagena offer a huge range of upscale, gourmet, and international options. Some typical dishes to look for on your menu include *ajiaco* (chicken soup with potatoes, avocado, corn, and capers), *bandeja paisa* (rice, avocado, salad), *chicharrón* (fried pork), *sancocho* (plantain, yuca, potato, and beef, chicken, or fish soup), *lechona* (stuffed baked pork), *arepa* (flat corn cake, often topped with cheese or butter), and *tamales* (corn dough, chicken, and vegetables cooked and served in plantain leaves).

Tinto, black coffee, is Colombia's most popular beverage and can be enjoyed at any time, just about anywhere. Other popular drinks are beer, *aguardiente* (firewater), hot chocolate, and soda products. Bottled (or bagged) water can usually be found at most stores and street stands. Thanks to its tropical climate and fertile soil, Colombia has countless exotic fruits such as *guanábana* (soursop), *lulo*, *maracuyá* (passion fruit), and *tomate de árbol* (tree tomato). Wine is not particularly popular in Colombia, and Colombian wines on the whole leave a lot to be desired. However, upscale restaurants and grocery stores generally offer high-quality Argentine and Chilean varieties. Colombia has an above-average beer culture, thanks to a growing number of craft breweries opening around the country.

leader Raúl Reyes, leading to a wider regional conflict. Despite a high approval rating, his administration was plagued by charges of violence and corruption.

Juan M. Santos was elected president in 2010, and in 2012 he began peace talks with the FARC in Havana, an effort that earned him the Nobel Peace Prize in 2016. They reached a bilateral ceasefire agreement in July of 2016, ending 50 years of bloodshed.

PRESENT-DAY COLOMBIA

While still fragile, a gradual peace has come to Colombia. The world's longest civil war has officially come to a close, and guerillas, paramilitaries, and drug cartels are no longer the threat they once were. A bigger issue now is re-integrating everyone back into a normal society. This is a country on the upswing. Now Latin America's fourth-largest economy, Colombia is in the middle of a historic boom. Poverty levels have dropped from 65% in 1990 to 24% in 2015. The GDP increased from $120 billion in 1990 to nearly $700 billion in 2015. Tourism is growing 12% a year, and new parts of the country are opening up.

Dining Customs

Restaurants range from the rustic and incredibly inexpensive to polished places with impeccable service and international menus. Set three-course lunch menus are usually called *comida corriente* and can be had for COP$2,000 to COP$5,000 in rural areas. The majority of restaurants include taxes and service in their prices, and your bill will reflect the menu prices. For others, however, you might see a subtotal, followed by a 16% IVA (general sales tax). It's primarily only higher end restaurants that do this. This is just a tax, not a tip.

Note: Dining hours are not much different from typical mealtimes in cities in North America or Great Britain, except that dinner (*cena*) is generally eaten after 8pm in restaurants. Colombians do not eat nearly as late as Spaniards. Although lunch (*almuerzo*) is the main meal of the day, for most visitors, it's not the grand midday affair it is in Spain, unless it is the weekend and you are dining at a rural *parrilla*, where most locals linger over lunch for a couple of hours.

Music & Dance

Often called the "Land of 1,000 Rhythms," Colombia is one of the most musically rich nations on earth. The combination of geographic features and influences of indigenous, African, and European cultures have resulted in the full spectrum of musical expression. While many international visitors might already be familiar with Shakira and salsa, even quick visits will expose other layers of the country's musical portfolio.

One of the most popular musical genres in Colombia is *cumbia*, a combination of indigenous, Spanish, and African musical styles that originated on the Caribbean coast. In cumbia's original form, performed by African slaves and their descendants, only percussion instruments and vocals are used, and the accompanying dance evokes the shackles once worn by slaves. The modern form of cumbia began to appear in the 1940s and '50s, when it moved from the countryside into urban areas. It was then that brass instruments and keyboards were integrated into the cumbia sound. This more big band strand of cumbia is now called *porro*.

Gabriel García Márquez once claimed that his prize-winning novel, *One Hundred Years of Solitude*, was just a 350-page *vallenato*, a musical genre that developed on the Caribbean coast. The style dates back more than 200 years and songs are mini-epics, with poetic stories and characters. It's said that the genre grew out of oral tradition, carrying news from village to village. Vallenato is played on three instruments: the *caja* (drum), *guacharaca* (scratcher), and accordion. In 1993, musician Carlos Vives released *Clásicos de la Provincia*, a modern vallenato album that brought the genre a brief moment of international attention.

Champeta grew out of various African, Colombian, and Caribbean styles in coastal cities like Cartagena and Barranquilla in the early 1980s. Electric guitars, synthesizers, and *picós* (speakers) were added in the 1990s, while recent years have seen influence from *reggaetón*. On the Pacific, *curralao* is most representative of African rhythms. It's played by groups of four musicians, one of whom who plays the Colombian *marimba*, a wooden xylophone resembling the African *balafon*.

While *salsa* was created in New York City by Puerto Ricans and Cubans, it quickly spread to Colombia, where it developed more Caribbean-esque rhythms. The fine footwork of Colombian salsa dancers regularly puts them at the top of world competitions. In the 1980s, an abundance of cash from the cocaine trade helped fuel new salsa clubs and a new wave of salsa orchestras in Cali, paving the way for it become the world capital of salsa. Influential artists include Orquestra Guayacán, Grupo Niche, La-33, and Jairo Varela.

Textiles

Colombia's textile tradition dates to pre-Columbian times. On the Pacific Coast and near the border with Panama, the Kuna culture is renowned for their *molas*, cotton panels featuring geometric figures and animals, meant to reflect the heavens and the natural world. The Guambiano, in the Valle de Cauca around Silvia, are known for the striking blue and fuchsia dresses that they weave themselves, as well as blankets. In La Guajira, the Wayúu have an extremely complex crochet technique used for making bags, hammocks, and traditional costumes.

Books & Literature

Colombia's literary pedigree ranks it among the world's finest. During the colonial period, Spanish settlers wrote chronicles of conquest and religious devotion. Gonzalo Jiménez de Quesada, who founded Bogotá and led a disastrous expedition to find El Dorado, wrote of the conquest of the Muiscas in *El Antijovio* (1567). Juan Rodríguez Freyle, a Spanish priest, wrote extensively about colonial life in early Bogotá in *El Carnero* (The Sheep) in 1638.

Post-independence, Juan José Nieto wrote *Ingermina, o la hija de Calamar* (Ingermina, or the Child of Calamar) in 1844, a novel about the conquest of the

Calamar Indians. In the late 19th and 20th century, the *costumbrismo* genre, a colorful depiction of peasant life and criticism of the government, was led by authors like Eugenio Díaz, Candelario Obeso, and Jorge Isaacs. In *Risaralda* (1936), Bernardo Arías Trujillo explores the lives of Afro-Colombians, their connection with the land and struggle with white dominance.

Perhaps Colombia's greatest contribution to the literary world is the invention of *magico realismo* (magical realism). This is the form of writing where elements of magic or fantasy appear in otherwise realistic fiction. The 1967 publication of *Cien años de soledad* (One Hundred Years of Solitude) by Gabriel García Márquez changed Colombian and Latin American literature forever. García Márquez went on to win the Nobel Prize for Literature in 1982, and he is credited with kicking off the Latin American boom that exported literature from the region around the world. Other notable works closely examined life, love, and politics in Colombia, such as 1975's *El otoño del patriarca* (The Autumn of the Patriarch), 1981's *Crónica de una muerte anunciada* (Chronicle of a Death Foretold), and *El amor en los tiempos de cólera* (Love in the Time of Cholera), 1985. Other notable modern Colombian writers include Laura Restrepo, whose novel *Delirium* (2004) describes the effect of violence on the individual and a society, and Juan Gabriel Vásquez, whose novel *The Informers* (2008) is a thriller about corruption in the second half of the 20th century.

Travel writing has also made its mark here. *The Fruit Palace* (1986) by Charles Nicholl is a true account of a journalist's quest for a great story about cocaine, based primarily in Santa Marta. Wade Davis details two generations of Amazon explorers in *One River: Explorations and Discoveries in the Amazonian Rain Forest* (2010). And Ramon Chao's *The Train of Ice and Fire* (2010) chronicles his son, musician Manu Chao, and his band as they reconstruct an old passenger train and journey into Colombia's violent countryside.

Film

Colombia's film industry is one of the strongest in the region, with several films getting international attention in recent years. In 2016, *El abrazo de la serpiente* (Embrace of the Serpent), a film about an indigenous Amazonian shaman who is the last of his people, was nominated for an Oscar for the Best Foreign Language Film. The 2004 drama *María Llena Eres de Gracia* (María Full of Grace) follows the story of a pregnant, 17-year-old girl working in a flower plantation who quits her job to become a drug mule. The film earned Catalina Sandino Moreno a Best Actress nomination at the Academy Awards.

Nominated for the Palme d'Or prize at Cannes, *La Vendedora de Rosas* (The Rose Seller, 1998) depicts life on the streets of Medellín in the 1980s. It's based on the story "The Little Match Girl" by Hans Christian Andersen, and shows children hawking at streetlights in areas filled with poverty and drugs. The 2009 film *Los Viajes del Viento* (The Wind Journeys) was shot in 80 locations around Northern Colombia, using four languages (Spanish, Palenquero, Wayuunaiki, and Ikun) while telling the story of a *vallenato* singer who stops playing after his wife dies.

Several of Nobel Prize–winning novelist Gabriel García Márquez's books have been turned into films. Filmed partially in Mompós, *Crónica de una Muerte Anunciada* (Chronicle of a Death Foretold) tells the story of a murder in a small Magdalena river town, while *Amor en los Tiempos de Cólera* (Love in the Time of Cholera), released in 2007, was a big-budget Hollywood production in English, with actors Javier Bardem and Benjamin Bratt. *Del amor y otros demonios* (Of Love and Other Demons) was released in 2009, though it was less successful.

Colombia's cocaine years have been well documented in film and television, as the over-the-top Netflix series *Narcos* will show you. Several more honest portrayals have also been attempted. *The Two Escobars* (2010) is a sports documentary about a soccer star with the last name Escobar who could not have been more different from the drug kingpin. Juan Pablo Escobar fled Colombia after his father's death in 1993, becoming an architect and living in anonymity until the release of the documentary about his own life, *Sins of My Father*, in 2009. *Killing Pablo: The Hunt for the World's Greatest Outlaw* (2002) is the film version of Mark Bowden's acclaimed 2001 book following Escobar's capture.

WHEN TO GO

Because of its proximity to the equator, Colombia's temperatures vary according to altitude rather than season. In high altitudes, days are cool and nights can dip near the freezing mark. In lowlands, expect a tropical, humid climate with little difference between daytime and nighttime temperatures. As a general guide, the average temperature in Bogotá is 57°F (14°C), in Cartagena 87°F (31°C), and in Medellín 75°F (24°C). The rainiest months are October and November. In the Andean region, the dry season falls between December and March and July and August. If possible, avoid Colombia in October and November, as these are the rainiest months, and flooding and poor road conditions are common.

Christmas is a particularly festive time in Colombia, though prices often rise and hotel rooms fill up quickly in Cartagena and the Atlantic Coast, as well as in other popular tourist destinations. During the Christmas holiday, Easter, and summer vacation, you'll have to book hotels in advance and be prepared to pay a bit extra.

Climate

Bogotá's Average Temperatures & Precipitation

	JAN	FEB	MAR	APR	MAY	JUNE	JULY	AUG	SEPT	OCT	NOV	DEC
Avg. High (°F)	66	66	66	66	66	64	64	64	64	64	66	66
Avg. High (°C)	19	19	19	19	19	18	18	18	18	18	19	19
Avg. Low (°F)	42	44	46	48	48	48	46	46	43	45	45	42
Avg. Low (°C)	5	6	7	8	8	8	7	7	6	7	7	6
Wet Days	10	11	13	20	22	19	19	17	15	21	20	14

Cartagena's Average Temperatures & Precipitation

	JAN	FEB	MAR	APR	MAY	JUNE	JULY	AUG	SEPT	OCT	NOV	DEC
Avg. High (°F)	87	87	89	89	92	92	89	92	89	89	87	87
Avg. High (°C)	31	31	32	32	33	33	32	33	32	32	31	31
Avg. Low (°F)	74	74	74	76	76	76	76	76	76	74	76	74
Avg. Low (°C)	23	23	23	24	24	24	24	24	24	23	24	23
Wet Days	2	7	10	6	7	13	14	8	2	6	4	1

Cali's Average Temperatures & Precipitation

	JAN	FEB	MAR	APR	MAY	JUNE	JULY	AUG	SEPT	OCT	NOV	DEC
Avg. High (°F)	74	74	74	72	72	74	74	76	76	72	72	72
Avg. High (°C)	22	22	22	21	21	22	22	23	23	21	21	21
Avg. Low (°F)	52	52	55	55	55	52	52	52	52	52	52	52
Avg. Low (°C)	11	11	12	12	12	11	11	11	11	11	11	11
Wet Days	17	16	17	20	19	16	13	10	14	24	25	24

San Andrés's Average Temperatures & Precipitation

	JAN	FEB	MAR	APR	MAY	JUNE	JULY	AUG	SEPT	OCT	NOV	DEC
Avg. High (°F)	83	83	83	84	85	85	84	85	86	85	84	83
Avg. High (°C)	27	27	27	27	28	28	28	28	28	27	27	27
Avg. Low (°F)	78	78	78	80	80	80	80	80	80	79	79	79
Avg. Low (°C)	25	25	25	26	26	26	26	26	26	26	26	26
Wet Days	19	13	8	9	14	20	24	23	22	23	22	23

Leticia's Average Temperatures & Precipitation

	JAN	FEB	MAR	APR	MAY	JUNE	JULY	AUG	SEPT	OCT	NOV	DEC
Avg. High (°F)	85	85	85	85	85	84	84	85	86	86	86	85
Avg. High (°C)	30	30	30	30	30	29	29	30	31	31	31	30
Avg. Low (°F)	71	71	71	71	71	69	70	69	69	71	71	71
Avg. Low (°C)	22	22	22	22	22	21	20	21	21	22	22	22
Wet Days	24	21	22	22	23	19	16	16	17	19	21	23

CURRENT WEATHER CONDITIONS The best place to head online for a detailed weather forecast is www.wunderground.com.

WHEN YOU'LL FIND BARGAINS The cheapest time to fly to Colombia is usually during the off season: from late August to November and in May. Though that mostly coincides with the rainy season in the highlands and coast, it rarely rains all day. Remember that weekday flights are often cheaper than weekend fares.

Rates generally increase in early December, then hit their peak in high travel season from Christmas until the end of January. In mid-June through August, when most Europeans take their holidays, there are more crowds and limited availability for the best hotel rooms.

You can avoid crowds, to some extent, by planning trips for the shoulder season, from about February to April, though you should be mindful of the uptick during *Semana Santa* (Holy Week). In general, the shoulder season offers the best combination of fewer crowds and good weather. Be mindful of major Colombian holidays, particularly at places like Cali and Cartagena, which are major destinations for Colombians as well as international travelers.

Calendar of Events

For additional information on major festivals, see www.colombia.travel/en/fairs-and-festivals. For information about regional festivals, see individual destination chapters.

JANUARY

Carnaval de Negros y Blancos, Pasto. Dating to indigenous groups celebrating the lunar calendar, this Carnival of blacks and whites is one of Colombia's biggest festivals. Music, food, dancing, and parades with enormous floats put the town in party mode. January 4 to 6.

Feria de Manizales, Manizales. Essentially a bull fighting festival, Manizales annual fair attracts some of the top toreros from around the world. The weeklong event becomes a giant party with parades and pageants. Early to mid-January.

Hay Festival, Cartagena. Originally from England, this literary and arts festival branched out to Colombia more than a decade ago and now attracts tens of thousands of visitors. Nearly 150 events are set up in venues all over the city during the 4-day festival. Late January.

FEBRUARY

Carnaval de Barranquilla. The second-largest Carnaval celebration outside of Rio de Janeiro is as wild as they come. Days are filled with dancing *cumbia,* masquerade parades, pageants, and concerts. The weekend before Ash Wednesday.

MARCH

Cartagena Festival Internacional de Cine (Cartagena Film Festival), Cartagena. Getting bigger each year, this film festival attracts stars from around the Americas. Screenings and judging take place in theaters around town, including at Teatro Colón near the Centro de Convenciones. Founded in 1959, it is the oldest film festival in Latin America. Early March.

Festival Iberoamericano de Teatro de Bogotá, Bogotá. More than 100 performing arts companies from more than 80 countries around the world come to Bogotá. They perform on stages, in the bullring, in shopping malls, on plazas, and elsewhere around the city. The event lasts for 2 weeks and occurs every other year. Late March to early April.

Semana Santa. Handsome and spectacularly reverent processions mark Easter week, particularly in the city of Popayán. Other important celebrations take place in Mompós, Pamplona, and Bogotá. Late March/early April.

JULY

Rock al Parque, Bogotá. South America's largest rock festival takes place in Simón Bolívar Park, attracting the biggest bands on the Colombian music scene. The annual 3-day festival was launched in 1985 and attracts hundreds of thousands of concert-goers each year. It is free of charge. Early July.

Festival de la Confraternidad Amazónica, Leticia. A festival of cultural integration among communities in the Tres Fronteras region, which includes Colombia, Peru, and Brazil The event is marked with dances, music, pageants, and food. July 15 to 20.

Fiestas Patrias. A series of patriotic parties mark Colombia's 1810 independence from Spain. Major events include a Grand National Concert and a 17-day hike to relive the journey liberator Simón Bolívar took several hundred years ago. Major celebrations occur in Bogotá, Medellín, and Cartagena. July 20.

AUGUST

Petronio Álvarez Festival, Cali. Named in honor of a musician from Cascajal, this annual festival is a celebration of the native music and culture of Colombia's Pacific Coast. Nicknamed "el Petronio." Early August.

Feria de las Flores, Medellín. This weeklong event is one of Colombia's most important festivals, attracting visitors from all over Colombia and the world. Festivities include orchid exhibitions, *paso fino* horse parades, a pageant, concerts, and awards. Early August.

Alimentarte, Bogotá. The capital's biggest culinary festival attracts some of the best chefs in the world, and more than 150 restaurants. The 3-day event includes demonstrations, deals in restaurants, food stands in Parque Virrey, and a showcase of Colombian ingredients. Late August.

Congreso Nacional Gastronómico, Popayán. The national culinary festival includes conferences and workshops, as well as the preparation of traditional foods. First week of September.

Festival Mundial de Salsa, Cali. This global salsa competition brings together more than 5,000 dancers from all of the salsa schools in Cali with dance academies from other cities and abroad. September.

Festival de Jazz, Mompós. This annual jazz festival attracts an array of national and international musicians to this Magdalena River town. Early October.

Concurso Nacional de Belleza, Cartagena. This 4-day event celebrates the annual contest to elect Miss Colombia, with pageants and an awards ceremony on the final night. Early November.

Feria de Cali, Cali. One of the largest parties in Colombia, the Cali fair celebrates bullfighting, salsa dancing, pageantry, and basically anything that makes Caleños happy. December 25 to 30.

Public Holidays

Colombia has more public holidays than any other nation except Brazil. Usually, if a holiday falls on a Saturday or Sunday, it is celebrated the following Monday. Public holidays are New Year's Day (Jan 1); Epiphany (Jan 6); St. Joseph's Day (Mar 19); Maundy Thursday and Good Friday (Mar/Apr); Labor Day (May 1); Ascension (May); Corpus Christi (May/June); Sacred Heart (June); Day of St. Peter and St. Paul (June 29); Independence Day (Aug 7); Assumption (Aug 15); Discovery of America (Oct 12); All Saints' Day (Nov 1); Independence of Cartagena (Nov 11); Immaculate Conception (Dec 8); and Christmas (Dec 25). Bogotá and other major cities empty out during holiday weekends, and many businesses close early or don't open at all.

SUGGESTED COLOMBIA ITINERARIES

by Nicholas Gill

Many first-time visitors to Colombia are overwhelmed by the sheer amount of things to do in the country. Not only is there plenty to explore, it's a big country. Even if you have several months to spend in Colombia, you won't come close to seeing all of it. Destinations tend to be spread out and require some advanced planning to get to. Bus and driving routes between major cities can take entire days, and transportation to remote towns and villages might only be possible on certain days of the week. An extensive air network will help shave some time in transit and might be your only choice for reaching some isolated attractions. Keep in mind that as modern and sophisticated the country might appear in some places, it's still Colombia. Once you leave the cities things move at a slower pace. Sometimes when the sun is out or rain is beating down on you, they don't move at all. Planning too tight of an itinerary is never a good idea here. The itineraries that follow are meant to be suggestions of what is possible—with flexibility to shave off a day or take an extra stop when needed. Relax, and take some time to stop and smell the coffee!

REGIONS IN BRIEF

Colombia is a country with much to offer the adventurous tourist. Whether you want to enjoy the sophisticated city atmosphere of Bogotá or swim in the clear Caribbean waters of San Andrés or Providencia, Colombia has what you're looking for.

BOGOTÁ Situated at an elevation of more than 2,630m (8,600 ft.), and bordered by the Andes to the east, Bogotá is the third-highest capital in the world. Its nearly 8 million residents make it

Colombia's largest city by far, and one that has some of South America's best museums, universities, and restaurants. Bogotá is quickly taking on an international character as more and more multinationals invest in and set up headquarters there.

MEDELLÍN & THE EJE CAFETERO   Colombia's main coffee-growing region is blessed with magnificent mountain scenery, coffee-terraced slopes, and old-world small towns. But Antioquia and the Eje Cafetero aren't all country: Armenia, Manizales, and Pereira are thriving cities with a coffee-based economy, and Medellín, Colombia's second-largest metropolis, is one of Latin America's most progressive and innovative cities.

THE CARIBBEAN COAST   Cartagena, the pride and joy of Colombia, has the most impressive old city in the Americas, dating all the way back to the 16th century. Its many plazas and restaurants come alive at night, and its colonial architecture is unmatched anywhere on the Western Hemisphere. North of Cartagena, check out the modern city of Santa Marta, a good base for exploring the Sierra Nevada Mountains and pristine jungles and beaches of Parque Tayrona.

SAN ANDRÉS & PROVIDENCIA   Some of the safest and most accessible travel experiences in the country are found here. San Andrés, long popular with Colombian tourists, has beautiful white-sand beaches and sprawling, all-inclusive resorts, while less-developed Providencia is famous for its Caribbean-English architecture, dense jungle, and scuba diving.

CALI & THE SOUTHWEST   Cali, the salsa-music capital, claims to have the most beautiful women in Colombia, and its nightlife is unrivaled anywhere in the country. Popayán, second only to Cartagena in terms of colonial architecture, is a beautiful whitewashed city with an active student and cafe life. Farther afield you'll find the archaeological sites of San Agustín and Tierradentro, home to stone statues and burial chambers that date back roughly 1,500 years.

THE PACIFIC COAST   The Pacific coast and El Chocó, inhabited almost exclusively by African descendants, is one of the wettest regions in the world, known for its dense jungles and unnavigable rivers. This magnificent landscape is still unexplored, though towns like Nuquí and Bahía Solano are seeing growing numbers of eco-tourists, surfers, sport fisherman, and whale watchers. Even the once dreary port city of Buenaventura has some cool restaurants and hotels now.

LOS LLANOS & AMAZON JUNGLE   Most of Colombia is composed of sparsely inhabited plains and jungle. Los Llanos, as they are known in Colombia, are physically similar to the American plains, and inhabitants have a definitively independent, relentless spirit. Los Llanos, Colombia's agricultural heartland, is known for its magnificent sunsets and beautiful *fincas* (farms), which fill up with tourists from Bogotá during holiday weekends. The Amazon covers 33% of Colombia but contains only 1% of the country's population, consisting mostly of traditional indigenous tribes. Except for Leticia and its surroundings, this area is inaccessible.

THE BEST OF COLOMBIA IN 2 WEEKS

Two weeks in Colombia should provide you with a good feel for the country and give you enough time to see some of the major sights and cities. Keep in mind that road conditions can be unpredictable, so it's best to fly between the far-flung destinations.

Days 1–4: Bogotá

On your first day, arrive and get settled in the city. Stay at the amazing Casa Medina (p. 52) or Hotel de la Opera (p. 50) and eat at one of the many gourmet restaurants in Bogotá's "gourmet district." Spend your first full day (**Day 2**) in Colombia exploring **La Candelaria** and the historic center. Have breakfast at La Puerta Falsa (p. 57), Colombia's longest-running business and restaurant. Take the cable car up to **Monserrate**, Bogotá's highest peak, and admire the view of sprawling Bogotá. Stop at the **Museo del Oro** (p. 45) at Santander Square, and visit the **Museo Botero** (p. 45) for an overview of Colombia's most famous artist. Recharge your energy by having lunch at any of La Candelaria's quaint eateries, popular with college students. In the afternoon, head to **Plaza de Bolívar** to feed the pigeons and be awed by Bogotá's eclectic architecture.

On **Day 3**, if you're around on a weekend or holiday, hop on the **Turistren** (p. 48), the only remaining steam engine in Colombia, or visit a few more of Bogotá's 50-plus museums—those interested in Colombian history will enjoy the **Quinta de Bolívar** (p. 46). Also explore some of the city's most popular parks, such as **Parque de la 93**, **Usaquén**, and **El Parque de Bolívar**.

Dedicate **Day 4** to shopping. If you're looking for handicrafts and cheap clothing, shop to your heart's content at **Plaza Santander** (p. 64) or, if you're around on a Sunday, head to Usaquén (p. 65). If you're looking for posh designer clothing, leather goods, or jewelry, head to one of the upscale malls in the city's northern districts. Also spend some time exploring some of the city's funkier neighborhoods, like **La Macarena**, home to some of the city's strangest (and most entertaining) bars and restaurants; **El Centro**, with its many universities and cafes, gallerias, and vibrant bar scene; or the north, home to the city's best malls and restaurants.

Days 5–7: Villa de Leyva

Take a 4-hour bus to the perfectly preserved town of **Villa de Leyva**, and spend **Day 5** exploring the cobblestone streets and handicraft shops. Stay at the Hospedería Duruelo (p. 74) for a luxury experience, or Hostal Renacer (p. 75) if you want to get away from it all. On **Day 6**, learn a bit about the Colombian independence movement by visiting the **Museo de Antonio Nariño** (p. 73) and see one of Colombia's most complete collections of religious art at **Museo del Carmen** (p. 73). Spend the evening people-watching in the main plaza from one of the many open-air cafes bordering the plaza. Alternatively, book a tour with one of the numerous

Columbia in 2 Weeks

Week 1
- 1-4 Bogotá
- 5-7 Villa de Leyva

Week 2
- 8-9 Medellín
- 10-11 Cartagena
- 12 Islas del Rosario
- 13 Cartagena

Caribbean Sea

PACIFIC OCEAN

Cartagena

Medellín

Villa de Leyva

Bogotá

Cali

ANDES MOUNTAINS

LOS LLANOS

0 — 200 mi
0 — 200 km

companies offering adventure and nature activities around Villa de Leyva. Go rock climbing, go horseback riding, visit a vineyard, hike in a nearby desert, or explore one of the many waterfalls around town.

Spend your last day in Villa de Leyva rappelling, hiking, mountain biking, and exploring the area's many natural attractions. Outdoor enthusiasts will enjoy horseback riding through the Villa de Leyva desert and visiting the area's many waterfalls and rivers.

Days 8 & 9: Medellín & Antioquia

Fly into Medellín and spend **Day 8** exploring the city center. Hop on a Turibus to visit the **Catedral Metropolitana** (p. 173) and other major sites. In the early afternoon, take the free cable car up to the *comunas* (municipal districts) for great views of Medellín. For dinner, dine at one of the many classy restaurants around **Parque Lleras** before heading to **Vía de Las Palmas** for a night of dancing. For a change of pace, on **Day 9**, book a tour of the surrounding Antioquian countryside with Aviatur (p. 168).

Days 10–13: The Caribbean Coast

Fly from Pereira, Armenia, or Manizales to the magical city of Cartagena. On **Day 10**, spend the morning sunbathing and swimming in the warm Caribbean waters. In the afternoon, book a chiva tour (p. 90) of the city for a brief history and overview of the city's major sights. At night, dine alfresco at a table overlooking one of the city's lovely plazas.

On **Day 11**, head to the **Old City** to explore its many plazas, museums, and shops. Have lunch in **Santo Domingo Square**. In the evening, book a spot on a rumba *chiva* (p. 90), a typical Colombia party bus, or, if you're feeling a bit more romantic, take your special someone on a carriage stroll through the Old Town.

Spend the next day in **Las Islas del Rosario**. Visit the **Aquario de San Martín**, and go snorkeling and swimming in the bright green waters of **Isla de Barú**, 45km (28 miles) from Cartagena. If you still have energy left, head to Getsemaní for a night of fun and dancing. On **Day 13**, depart Cartagena, flying either directly home from there or connecting in Bogotá.

BOGOTÁ & THE HIGHLANDS IN 1 WEEK

For those flying in and out of Bogotá, a weeklong regional trip into the highlands is quite manageable. You can add an extra day or two in the city if desired, though this trip emphasizes getting out of the city and into the countryside to visit quaint colonial villages, hike in some spectacular Andean terrain, and partake in some adventure sports like whitewater rafting and paragliding.

Day 1: Bogotá & Zipaquirá

Rent a car at the airport and drive straight to **Zipaquirá**, a colonial town just 30 minutes or so outside of Bogotá. After checking in to the **Hotel Camino de la Sal** (p. 69), visit the **Catedral de Sal** (p. 68), a Catholic church built in an old salt mine. Afterward, explore the town's main plaza, surrounded by colonial architecture. For dinner, drive to the nearby Chía for the famed steakhouse and crazy party at **Andrés Carne de Rés** (p. 67).

Days 2–4: Parque Nacional El Cocuy

Wake early and drive to **El Cocuy**, a whitewashed colonial town that will be your base for hiking in **Cocuy National Park** (p. 78). Spend the first evening acclimatizing and hiring guides (and horses if desired) for short hikes through the mountainous terrain. While there, keep an eye out for condors, which are often spotted soaring overhead. If access into the interior of the park improves, you can spend an entire week here on more extensive treks in the park and ice climbing on glaciers.

Bogotá & the Highlands in 1 Week

Zipaquira
2-4 Parque Nacional El Cocuy
5 San Gil
6 Barichara
7 Bogotá

Days 5 & 6: San Gil & Barichara

From Cocuy, get back in the car and drive to **San Gil** (p. 80), the adventure sports capital of Colombia. While rafting the Class V rapids on the Rio Suárez reigns supreme, almost any X-Games style sport you can imagine can be done here. There's paragliding, caving, canyoning, and hiking. Don't forget to ride the cable car over **Chicamocha Canyon** (p. 83) either! Spend your nights in the colonial town of **Barichara** (p. 79) to explore the tree-lined plazas and charming cobblestone streets lined with whitewashed houses topped by clay-tiled roofs.

Day 7: Back to Bogotá

Spend your last day driving back **Bogotá** to catch your red-eye flight home. Otherwise make another stop in the colonial town of **Villa de Leyva** (p. 72) on your way to break up the journey even more.

THE COLOMBIAN CARIBBEAN IN 10 DAYS

For many travelers to Colombia, the Caribbean Coast is their entry point into Colombia. They came for a day on a cruise ship or a wedding and return realizing that there is so much more to see. After the colonial city, there are islands with palm-fringed beaches, national parks home to eco-friendly hotels, and plenty of opportunities for things like windsurfing and fishing.

Days 1 & 2: Cartagena

Cartagena's **old city**, a UNESCO World Heritage Site, is one the most-visited destinations in all of Colombia. There's a reason that hundreds of thousands of cruise ship passengers stroll through these 16th-century streets each year. Begin at the **Plaza de las Coches** before moving to **Plaza Santo Domingo**, stopping for lunch at **La Vitrola** (p. 108), and watching the sun set into the ocean from the old city walls while drinking a mojito at **Café del Mar** (p. 94). On **Day 2** visit the **Castillo de San Felipe de Barajas** (p. 100), an imposing hilltop fortress built by the Spanish. In the afternoon go to **Plaza de la Trinidad** in the once-gritty Getsemaní neighborhood, where you can take a break with a drink and some tapas at **Demente** (p. 106), followed by live music and dancing at **Café Havana** (p. 111).

Days 3–6: San Andrés & Providencia

Catch a flight to the postcard-perfect island of **San Andrés** (p. 263), a popular honeymoon destination and the home to large all-inclusive resorts from the chain **Decameron** (p. 271) or small beachside properties like the **Posada San Andrés** (p. 272). Spend your days snorkeling the coral reefs of the seahorse-shaped island **Providencia** (p. 274), a catamaran ride away. After enough sunbathing, rent a scooter and ride around the island to the villages of **San Luis** and **La Loma** (p. 265).

Alternatively, instead of catching a flight to San Andrés, you can take a boat to **Las Islas del Rosario**, an archipelago of tiny islands not far from Cartagena. go snorkeling and swimming in the bright green waters of **Isla de Barú**, 45km (28 miles), where you can stay at the **Agua Azul Beach Resort** (p. 101).

Day 7: Barranquilla

After returning to Cartagena, rent a car or hop on a bus to **Barranquilla**, a bustling port town and Shakira's birthplace, situated about an hour and a half up the coast. See where the Magdalena River meets the ocean and dine on fried bocachico, but save some time for a soak in the pool at the **Hotel El Prado** (p. 115). If you happen to be there during Carnaval, second in size only to the one in Rio de Janeiro, don't go anywhere!

The Colombian Caribbean in 10 Days

Map showing Caribbean Sea, Providencia Island, San Andrés (3-6), Santa Marta, Parque Nacional Tayrona (8-10), Barranquilla (7), Cartagena (1-2), NICARAGUA, COSTA RICA, PANAMA, Gulf of Panama, COLOMBIA, VENEZUELA.

Legend:
- 1-2 Cartagena
- 3-6 San Andrés & Providencia
- 7 Barranquila
- 8-10 Santa Marta & Parque Nacional Tayrona

Day 8–10: Santa Marta & Parque Nacional Tayrona

Continue up the coast to the city of **Santa Marta**, South America's oldest surviving city. At night, wander around **Plaza de Bolívar** (p. 98), hitting up the city's excellent crop of bars and restaurants. During the days, take trips to the fishing village of **Taganga** (p. 133) and **Tayrona National Park** (p. 132), where you will find unspoiled beaches. Choose between boutique colonial hotels like **Casa Carolina** (p. 122), or a green hotel like Tayrona's **Eco-habs** (p. 137). Take a flight home from Santa Marta, or return to Cartagena.

ALTERNATIVE COLOMBIA

Getting to some of Colombia's most remote destinations has gotten easier as security concerns have lessened, and commercial flights on small planes now fly to many places that could once only be reached by driving for days down bumpy roads. There are red rivers, indigenous villages, and long-lost colonial cities in the jungle that seem straight out of a García Márquez novel.

Days 1 & 2: Caño Cristales

From Bogotá, catch a flight to the town of **La Macarena** (p. 260), the jumping off point for exploring **Caño Cristales** (p. 260), a river in the Serrania de la Macarena. From September through November, plants in the river turn a bright red, sticking out of yellow and green sand and various shades of mineral in the rocks. Guided tours from La Macarena will lead you to different parts of the river on foot and horseback. Open to tourists only since 2009, few Colombians even realize this exists.

Alternative Colombia

Days 3–6: The Amazon

Fly back to Bogotá and immediately hop on another flight to **Leticia**, Colombia's outpost on the Amazon River near the borders of Peru and Brazil. You can check into the cushy jungle resort with a pool, the Decameron **Decalodge Ticuna** (p. 256), or a rustic ecolodge far from the city like **Yoi** (p. 260). While there, go on day trips and hikes with guides from your hotel, using the river as your highway. You can fish for piranhas, go on jungle walks in search of monkeys and native plants, or visit indigenous Bora and Ticuna villages. While in town, have a meal at **Tierras Amazónicas** (p. 257) for grilled pirarucu and *mojojoy* (palm weevil grubs).

Days 7–9: Mompós/Mompox

From Cartagena, catch an early morning bus—and later a ferry—south into the interior, where the tropical grasslands dance with the Magdalena River. **Mompós**, a beautifully preserved colonial city, was once one of the most important in Colombia. It's now a UNESCO World Heritage Site, and over the past decade tourists have been rediscovering it, as security issues that once prevented travel there have subsided. Check into the cozy **La Casa Amarilla** (p. 160), right on Plaza Santa Barbara facing the river, and spend the intensely hot days ducking in and out of colonial buildings and drinking *limonada* sweetened with panela. You can also visit rural fishing and agricultural villages by canoe. Have pizza from a wood-fired oven at **El Fuerte** (p. 161) then hang out with a cold beer on **Plaza de la Concepción**, watching for bats. When ready, return to Cartagena for your flight home.

COLOMBIA FOR FAMILIES

If you listen to some media reports (and friends who have been living under a rock for the past decade) it would seem that Colombia would be the absolute worst destination for a family vacation. Don't listen to them. The whole country is family-friendly. Families can bond over the pristine nature of the Pacific Coast, sample exotic fruits and shop for handicrafts in the markets of Cali, and learn about ancient cultures in San Agustín.

Day 1: Cali

Get your children's attention right from the start of the trip by going straight to the **La Galeria Alameda market** (p. 221) for exotic fruits like lulo, pitahaya, guanabana, and granadilla. Swing by the **zoo** (p. 219) where kids will appreciate native species like the spectacled bear and a butterfly garden with more than 800 different species. After lunch at **Hacienda del Bosque** (p. 222), sign up for a salsa dancing lesson. Keep the fun going at night with a visit to **Container Park** (p. 222), a gourmet food court with six restaurants serving food out of recycled shipping containers.

Days 2 & 3: San Agustín

Rent a car (or take a bus) and drive south through **Puracé National Park** (p. 232), keeping an eye out for orchids and unique wildlife such as mountain tapirs or cougars. Continue until you reach **San Agustín**, home to South America's largest collection of monolithic and megalithic sculptures. In the easily accessible main archaeological park (p. 235) you'll visit three sites with a total of about 130 statues that date back more than 1,000 years. You can visit other archaeological sites on horseback, but save time to sample *cerdo ahumado* (smoked pork) at **Donde Richard** (p. 237) and coffee from area fincas at **Macizo** cafe (p. 238). On your way out of the

Colombia for Families

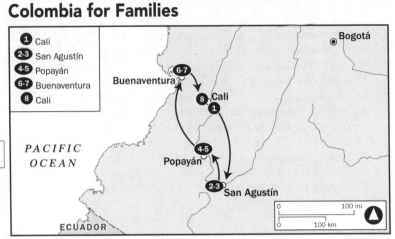

1 Cali
2-3 San Agustín
4-5 Popayán
6-7 Buenaventura
8 Cali

village, pass the **Salto del Mortiño**, a 200-meter-high waterfall, and stop at **Alto de los Idolos** (p. 235), another archaeological site.

Days 4 & 5: Popayán

Spend a few days exploring the city of Popayán. Founded in 1537, it has some of the oldest and best-preserved colonial architecture in all of Colombia. Begin at **Parque Caldas** (p. 228), the city's main plaza, before moving to historic churches like Iglesia de San Francisco and Iglesia la Ermita. Cross the Roman-style bridge, **Puente del Humilladero** (p. 229), and spend an afternoon in the **natural history museum**, which has a collection of more than 3,000 native species. Keep in mind that Popayán is known for its traditional gastronomy, so make stops for classics like the tiny, fried empanadas de pipian at **La Fresa** (p. 231) and Salpicón Payanés at **Mora Castilla** (p. 231).

Days 6 & 7: Buenaventura

Instead of going straight back to Cali, continue on toward the coast, making a stop at **San Cipriano** (p. 245), an Afro-Colombian village deep in the jungle with a crystal-clear river perfect for floating on inner tubes. There are no roads there, so the family will need to hop on a *brujita*, a rail cart powered by a motorcycle, to zip through the lush green forest. In Buenaventura, check in at the **Cosmos** hotel (p. 245), with views of the port and bay. Have a dinner with of fare at **Café Pacifico** (p. 244). The next morning, sign up for a whale-watching tour (when in season) or just a lazy beach day at **Ladrilleros**.

Day 8: Cali

Allow everyone to sleep in before the drive back to **Cali**. Make any last gift shopping stops, maybe visiting **Loma de la Cruz** (p. 224) for handicrafts. Transfer to the airport and head home.

BOGOTÁ

by Nicholas Gill

Your first encounter with Bogotá may not be love at first sight. The constant rain, chilliness, and surrounding pine-forest mountains make London seem downright sunny. But give Bogotá time, and you will discover a sophisticated city of skyscrapers, glitzy upscale shopping centers, restaurants to satisfy even the most discerning palates, and nightlife that will leave you needing a vacation from your vacation. Colombia's capital and its largest city by far, Bogotá is a sprawling metropolis, home to eclectic and experimental architecture, a bohemian university crowd, a lively cafe scene, and attractive city parks. It is a city bursting with energy and culture.

Bogotá is, more than anything, a city of contrasts. Class differences are still very much apparent, with the wealthy, modern northern section a world apart from the slums, poverty, and high crime rates of the southern part of the city. Though security has improved dramatically in the last few years, the city center can still be dangerous at night, so you're better off not wearing expensive-looking jewelry and clothing when visiting these areas. Still, Bogotá is one of Latin America's safer cities, and it's unlikely you'll encounter any serious problems.

HISTORY   Prior to the arrival of the Spanish, the land that is now Bogotá was the southern capital of the Muisca culture, called Bacatá. While little evidence of the Muisca exists today, much of the early colonial period remains in the form of cobblestone streets and centuries-old houses and churches around Plaza Bolívar and throughout La Candelaria.

SIGHTSEEING   Most landmark buildings—like the capital, neoclassical Teatro Colón, and the 17th-century Iglesia de San Francisco—sit within a few blocks of each other. Take the tram to Cerro de Monserrate for the best views of the city, then head to the northern suburbs to see the capital's more contemporary side, with glitzy skyscrapers and posh red-brick residential towers.

EATING & DRINKING   Bogotá seems to have more restaurants than it does people. In some areas, like the Zona Rosa, entire streets

Bogotá

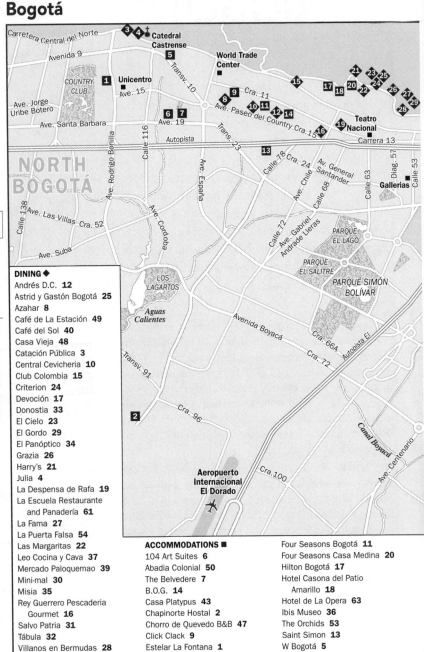

Carretera Central del Norte

Avenida 9

3 4 † Catedral Castrense

5

World Trade Center ■

Transv. 10

COUNTRY CLUB

1 Unicentro ■

Ave. 15

Ave. Jorge Uribe Botero

Ave. Santa Barbara

Calle 116

6 7

Ave. 19

Cra. 11

9

8

Ave. Paseo del Country

10 11

12 14

Cra. 15

15

17 18 20 22

21 23 25

24

26

27 29

28

19 Teatro Nacional

16

Carrera 13

Autopista

Trans. 23

13

Calle 78

Cra. 24

Av. General Santander

Ave. Chile

Calle 68

Calle 63

Diag. 57

Calle 53

■ **Gallerias**

Ave. Rodrigo Bonilla

NORTH BOGOTÁ

Calle 138

Ave. Las Villas Cra. 52

Ave. Suba

Ave. Córdoba

Ave. España

Calle 72

Ave. Gabriel Andrade Lleras

PARQUE EL LAGO

PARQUE EL SALITRE

PARQUE SIMÓN BOLÍVAR

LOS LAGARTOS

Aguas Calientes

Avenida Boyacá

Cra. 664

Cra. 72

Autopista El

Transv. 91

Cra. 96

2

Aeropuerto Internacional El Dorado

Cra. 100

Canal Boyacá

Ave. Centenario

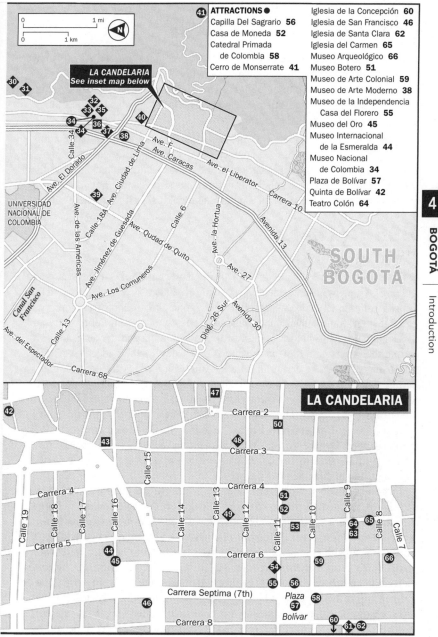

ATTRACTIONS ●

Capilla Del Sagrario **56**
Casa de Moneda **52**
Catedral Primada
de Colombia **58**
Cerro de Monserrate **41**

Iglesia de la Concepción **60**
Iglesia de San Francisco **46**
Iglesia de Santa Clara **62**
Iglesia del Carmen **65**
Museo Arqueológico **66**
Museo Botero **51**
Museo de Arte Colonial **59**
Museo de Arte Moderno **38**
Museo de la Independencia
Casa del Florero **55**
Museo del Oro **45**
Museo Internacional
de la Esmeralda **44**
Museo Nacional
de Colombia **34**
Plaza de Bolívar **57**
Quinta de Bolívar **42**
Teatro Colón **64**

4

BOGOTÁ | Introduction

LA CANDELARIA

are lined with restaurant after restaurant and bar after bar. Start your day with a cup of fair-trade coffee from a local roaster, snack at streetside *arepa* stalls and juice stands, and then have an elegant dinner with 10 courses and a wine pairing. Cap off your night with pints of craft beer or adventurous cocktails on a rooftop bar.

ARTS & CULTURE   The city is home to Colombia's best museums, from the vast collection of pre-Columbian gold at the Museo del Oro to the chronological artifacts that explore Colombia's past at the Museo Nacional. Art is ever present here, with graffiti-lined streets in La Candelaria and a blossoming gallery scene in districts like La Macarena.

SHOPPING   Although you will find better—and less expensive—handicrafts in the provinces, Bogotá has the country's best shopping. Edgy urban designers have boutiques in trendy districts in the north, while sophisticated malls with the latest designer labels have cropped up all over the city. The finest jewelry stores (think in terms of emeralds and gold) are all found here.

ESSENTIALS
Getting There

BY PLANE   Planes arrive at **El Dorado International Airport** (airport code: BOG; www.eldorado.aero/en; ☏ **571/266-2000**), located about 13km (8 miles) from the city center, which has undergone a $1 billion expansion program that has transformed it into one of the busiest airports in Latin America. It accounts for nearly half of all air traffic in Colombia and the demand is so strong that a second airport in the city is under development (see box p. 47). Most major North American and Latin American airlines fly here. Primary airlines include **Avianca** (www.avianca.com; ☏ **800/284-2622**), which handles a sizable percentage of national, regional, and international air flights, as does **LATAM** (www.latam.com; ☏ **800/435-9526**). Both fly to major cities within Colombia, as well as to Lima, Cusco, São Paulo, Rio de Janeiro, Quito, Santiago, and Buenos Aires. Within Colombia, **Satena** (www.satena.com; ☏ **1/605-2222**) flies to small, out of the way airports on the Pacific Coast, Amazon, and highlands.

From El Dorado you can get to the city center by taxi or bus. Alimentador (feeder) buses are parked next to the El Dorado Terminal and connect to Portal El Dorado, where passengers then transfer to the Transmilenio mass transit system that runs all over the city. If you have a lot of luggage and don't feel ready to deal with crowded Colombian mass transit, your best bet is to take a taxi, which costs between COP$45,000 to COP$55,000 from the airport, depending on where you need to be dropped off. Be sure to obtain a computer-printed slip at the airport exit before getting into your taxi. Make a sharp right upon exiting the airport to obtain your computer-printed slip. This slip indicates how much your route will cost and prevents you from being ripped off by dishonest taxi drivers. Give this slip to the driver and pay upon arrival at your destination. Do not accept rides from solicitors at the airport exit; these drivers are not associated with the airport, and you don't want to be the one to test their honesty. An alternative is to use the airport's free Wi-Fi and order an Uber, as cars are always there waiting. Getting to the city center or northern Bogotá from the airport should take about 30 to 60 minutes, depending on traffic.

BY BUS   Bus travel around Colombia has improved dramatically in the past decade as security concerns have lessened. Virtually every city and town has a bus service to Bogotá. Most buses to Bogotá drop you off in the main bus terminal, Terminal de Transporte, at Calle 22 B no. 69–59, depending on the bus company and where you are arriving from. From the terminal, you'll need to take a taxi to your hotel. It's important to obtain a computer-printed slip here as well, and take a bus-terminal-associated taxi or request an Uber.

Visitor Information

Tourist information in Bogotá is mediocre at best. Most of Bogotá's tourists are Colombians, so any brochures you manage to get will probably be in Spanish only. The most helpful and informative tourist office is the Instituto Distrital de Turismo y Cultura (www.bogotaturismo.gov.co; ✆ **1/327-4916**), at Carrera 8 no. 9–83, right across from Plaza Bolívar. The office is open daily between 8am and 6pm, but hours can be reduced, especially on Sunday. Other tourist offices can be found at El Dorado Airport (at both the national and international decks); the main bus station, Transversal 66 no. 35–11, Local Module 5–27; and the International Center, Carrera 13 no. 26–52. The bilingual Bogotá Turística is a decent city guide sold at Panamericana shops throughout the city. Your hotel should also be able to offer some information, maps, and a few pointers such as how to get to Zipaquirá. Personally, I find Panamericana stores to be the best place to find tourist information, as they always have maps and sometimes sell English-language guides. Some popular Panamericanas are located on Carrera 15 no. 72–14; Unicentro mall; Calle 92 no. 15–37; Carrera 13 no. 59–69; and Carrera 7 no. 18–48.

City Layout

Although Bogotá is a massive city covering over 1,555 sq. km (606 sq. miles), almost all tourist attractions are concentrated in the historic center and La Candelaria, while many of the best hotels, restaurants, nightspots, and stores are spread out in northern neighborhoods. There are good mass transit options connecting La Candelaria and El Centro to the north. Gridlock can be frustrating, and you can feel at times as if you're entire trip is just sitting in traffic. Try to explore entire neighborhoods at a time and save extra time getting in between. Laid out in a grid, *carreras* run north to south and *calles* run east to west. Streets and avenues are almost always referred to by number rather than by proper name. La Carrera Séptima is Bogotá's most important avenue, running the entire length of the city. If you're ever confused about whether you're heading east or west, remember the mountains are on the east of the city. Most tourists stick to the northeastern and central-eastern parts of the city. The south is the poorest and least visited section of the city.

Neighborhoods in Brief

La Candelaria Bogotá's semi-restored colonial quarter is home to most of the city's tourist attractions. For many tourists, La Candelaria is the most interesting part of the city. The sector has a definitively intellectual feel, home to half a dozen universities, several museums, galleries, cafes, the famous Teatro Colón, and La Biblioteca Luis Angel Arango, once considered the most important library in the country. La Candelaria, with its many pedestrian-only cobblestone streets, is the perfect place to spend the day exploring, enjoying a leisurely lunch, taking in the colonial architecture and atmosphere, or visiting a museum or two. Most tourist and cultural attractions are between Calle 7 and Avenida Jiménez, and Circunvalar and Carrera 8. This sector has a long history with writers, artists, and journalists, and you'll probably spend most of your sightseeing time here.

Plaza de Bolívar Just South of La Candelaria, this is a great place to people-watch and admire examples of Bogotano architecture. Unfortunately, you have to keep an eye out for the thousands of pigeons that make the plaza their home. See p. 43.

Downtown & El Centro Internacional This is a chaotic, noisy, and vibrant area—not the kind of place you want to end up lost at night, but you should be all right during the day. Some of the city's best bargain shopping can be found here, particularly around Plaza San Vitorino, though you may feel a bit overwhelmed by the sheer number of shops and the somewhat seedy atmosphere. The international zone starts at Calle 30 and is home to many of Colombia's most important companies, high rises, restaurants, and cafes.

La Macarena Behind the Plaza de Toros between calles 22–26 and carreras 2–6, you will find the edgy, bohemian neighborhood of La Macarena, with its many cafes and bars frequented by a hip crowd that likes to stay out late. Some of the city's best art galleries are here too. As one Colombian put it, La Macarena is the equivalent of New York City's Lower East Side, on a much smaller scale. There aren't many hotels here other than the Ibis, but it's a great place to base yourself because it's convenient to both ends of town.

Usaquén Like La Candelaria, Usaquén is one of Bogotá's most picturesque neighborhoods. Home to a pleasant plaza, a colonial-style church, and many restaurants and bars, Usaquén is also famous for its proximity to the Hacienda Santa Bárbara, a beautiful courtyard mall of upscale stores and boutiques that was once the home of a wealthy family. Usaquén really comes alive at night when the lively university and post-university crowd fills its restaurants and bars. This residential sector feels like a quaint small town and, in fact, it didn't become part of the city until 1954. Be sure to check out the impressive Sunday flea market, where you'll find everything from handmade clothes and one-of-a-kind jewelry to souvenir-style knick-knacks.

La Zona Rosa Located between carreras 11 and 15 and calles 79 and 85, near the upscale Andino mall, La Zona Rosa is Bogotá's most exclusive nightlife center. Home to many clubs, bars, and restaurants, La Zona Rosa is where you'll drop COP$10,000 to COP$30,000 for a cocktail or COP$100,000 for a bottle of rum. However, keep in mind that cocktails in La Zona T are a lot bigger than what you get in North America. La Zona T, a cobblestone pedestrian walkway, makes for a pleasant nighttime stroll. Just a few steps away, on Calle del Sol, you can window-shop at the stores of famous Colombian designers.

Parque de la 93 Located between calles 93A and 93B and carreras 11A and 13, Parque de la 93 is another exclusive area, popular with the city's worldly and elite. It's home to many international and gourmet restaurants as well as to several clubs, bars, and cafes; the park itself often hosts musical events and is beautifully decorated at Christmastime. During the day, families bring their children to the pleasant green park for ice cream and fresh air, and at night the area comes alive with music and energy. The bars and clubs here attract a slightly older crowd than those in La Zona T.

Avenida Chile Also known as Calle 72, Avenida Chile was once home to Bogotá's wealthiest families, where they built their European-style mansions in the beginning of the 20th century. Over the years, the area has become a bustling, vibrant commercial area with dozens of skyscrapers and some of the city's top hotels. This is the city's most sophisticated cosmopolitan area, and its side streets are filled with English- and Swiss-style mansions.

La Zona G Also known as the Gourmet Zone, La Zona G is adjacent to the Centro Financiero and is home to some of the city's best restaurants. If you're looking for world-class dining, this is the place to come.

Getting There & Getting Around

Navigating Bogotá isn't necessarily difficult, it's just time consuming. The city sprawls northward from downtown, essentially one neighborhood after another, but because of persistent heavy traffic it can take a long time to get across the city. While the mass transit Transmilenio was meant to alleviate some of that congestion, your journey time may still only be slightly better than a taxi.

BY TRANSMILENIO One of the fastest and cheapest ways to get around is the Transmilenio, Bogotá's decade-old bus system that runs on its own road lane. Think of it as a subway network on wheels. The Transmilenio runs weekdays and Saturdays between 5am and 11pm and Sundays and holidays 6am to 10pm. A single ticket will cost you COP$2,000. Some 1,500 buses cover 112km (70 miles) and move, on average, 2.2 million people a day. You'll probably have to study the maps at each Transmilenio for quite a while to understand how the system works. If you speak some Spanish, you're best off asking one of the many Transmilenio workers, who can tell you what line and bus to take to your destination. Be sure to keep an eye on your personal belongings because robberies do occur, particularly hands diving into bags, purses, and pockets during rush hour.

BY BUS Hundreds, if not thousands, of buses service Bogotá. You'll pay a flat fare—usually about COP$1,500 to COP$2,000—no matter how far you're traveling. Get off and on buses as quickly as possible, because drivers are unlikely to be courteous enough to come to a complete stop or make sure you get off safely. When going from the north to La Candelaria, take buses marked GERMANIA. Don't take buses marked LA CANDELARIA, which will leave you in a bad part of town. When going to the north, buses that say UNI-CENTRO will generally drop you off a couple of blocks from where you want to go. Don't expect a bus to stop for you just because you're standing at a bus stop; you'll have to flag it down.

BY TAXI OR UBER Perhaps the best way to get around the city, taxis are relatively inexpensive. Many foreigners choose to get around this way to avoid Bogotá's sometimes confusing bus and Transmilenio system. You can get from the north to the city center for about COP$8,000 to COP$16,000. It's wise to call a taxi from your hotel or restaurant, especially at night, or use the Uber app, which tends to be just as secure and cheaper. Your biggest risk is that a taxi driver will take an out-of-the-way route to your destination and thus charge you an unfairly inflated fee, so just make sure the driver turns on his meter. However, there have been cases of robbery, assault, and even rape reported involving mostly unlicensed taxi drivers, particularly at night, so make sure to call a

The World's Largest Urban Bike Route

Called *Ciclorutas de Bogotá* in Spanish, the city's network of bike paths is one of the most extensive on planet earth, totaling some 300km (186 miles). Bike parking was even added at Transmilenio stations to integrate bikes into the system. Additionally, every Sunday and on public holidays from 7am until 2pm is the cyclovía, where many main streets around the city are closed to cars so more bikes, as well as joggers and skaters, can use them. While there have been rumors of a bike share program coming to Bogotá, for now your best option is to rent a bike or take a bike tour with **Bogotá Bike Tours** (www.bogotabiketours.com; ℂ **1/342-7649**).

trusted taxi company. If you call a taxi, your driver is likely to charge COP$1,000 to COP$2,000 in addition to your fare. Recommended taxi companies include **Auto Taxi** (ℂ **1/366-6666**), **Radio Taxi** (ℂ **1/288-8888**), **Taxi Express** (ℂ **1/411-1111**), and **Taxis Libres** (ℂ **1/311-1111**). If you're not used to getting around Latin American cities, I recommend you take Uber to avoid the hassle of telling your driver where to go, especially if your Spanish is limited.

BY CAR   Driving in Bogotá is not for the faint of heart. Almost 50,000 Colombians a year are killed in traffic-related accidents, meaning your chances of being hurt or even killed in a car accident are far greater than your risk of being kidnapped or killed by guerillas or narco-traffickers. Be prepared for honking cars weaving in and out of traffic, reckless drivers, and many near-collisions. Pedestrians often cross despite the presence of oncoming traffic, and vendors and beggars often congregate around traffic lights. If, after hearing this, you are still convinced you want to drive in Bogotá, I recommend you do so only upon getting in and out of the city or exploring the region.

BY FOOT   La Candelaria and El Centro can be easily explored on foot. Usaquén, La Zona Rosa, and Parque de la 93 are also easy neighborhoods to explore on foot as well, but you'll have to get to these places by taxi, Transmilenio, or bus. Because Bogotá is essentially a grid, it's relatively easy to get around without getting lost. Theoretically, you can get anywhere on Bogotá on foot, but long distances make taking a taxi more practical.

[FastFACTS] BOGOTÁ

ATMs/Banks   Colombian and international banks with currency-exchange bureaus and ATMs are plentiful throughout Bogotá, especially in El Centro and the northern neighborhoods such as Chapinero and El Retiro, which are full of malls, hotels, and restaurants.

Doctors & Hospitals   As prices tend to be inexpensive compared with North America and Europe, an increasing number of travelers are coming to Colombia specifically for surgeries and dental work. The U.S. and British embassies (see "Embassies & Consulates," p. 293) provide lists of English-speaking doctors, dentists, and other healthcare personnel in Bogotá. English-speaking medical personnel and 24-hour emergency services are available at the following hospitals and clinics: **Hospital Universatario**, Carrera 7 #117-15 (www.fsfb.org.co; ℂ **1/603-0303**), **Clinica del**

Country (Carrera 16 no. 82–57; www.clinicadelcountry. com; ☎ **1/530-0470**), or the **Marly Clinic**, Calle 50 no. 9–57, Chapinero (www.marly. com.co; ☎ **1/343-6600**).

Emergencies In Bogotá, the police emergency number is ☎ **112**. Another emergency number that works throughout the country is **123**. Other good emergency numbers to know: the Security Police (DAS; ☎ **153/0180-0091-9622**); the Tourist Police (☎ **1/337-4413** or 1/243-1175); and the police station in Bogotá (☎ **156**). The fire department can be reached by calling **119**, and information can be reached by dialing **113**.

Internet Access Public Wi-Fi has overtaken Internet *cabinas* (booths) and cyber-cafes as the most common form of Internet access in Bogotá. There is free Wi-Fi

access almost everywhere if you have a smartphone, laptop, or tablet. You'll find it in shopping centers, public parks, restaurants, cafes, and nearly every hotel in the city.

Mail & Postage You can send mail from the post office 4–72 (www.4-72.com. co; ☎ **1/770-0380**), at Av. 6 no. 34A–45. The DHL and Western Union offices all over town are a more secure option.

Pharmacies There are a number of pharmacy chains in Bogotá, most with 24-hour locations, including **Droguerias Olimpica** and **Farmacity**. Ask at your hotel for the most convenient location.

Safety Most areas of Bogotá that tourists frequent are as safe as average North American cities. However, in downtown, La Candelaria,

and some of the city's residential areas, the risk of street crime remains, particularly late at night. Although carjackings, assaults, and armed robberies are not routine, they're not unheard of either. Armed attacks at ATMs have also occurred. Use ATMs during the day, with other people present. Most thefts occur on public transportation, such as buses and the Transmilenio. Be very careful with your belongings; leave your passport and other valuables in the hotel safe, and use a money belt. Public street markets are also frequented by thieves, as are parks (especially at night).

Telephone Bogotá's area code is 1. It need not be dialed when making local calls within the city, but it must be dialed when calling Bogotá from another city.

EXPLORING BOGOTÁ

Many visitors to Bogotá are here only for a few days, usually as a part of a larger trip to Colombia that might include Caribbean beaches, eco-lodge stays in the Amazon and Pacific, or colonial towns in the highlands. However, once you've had a taste of the city's nightlife and cultural offerings, it's hard to stay away, and many end up returning. There's plenty to do for those who stay longer than a day or two and enough museums and restaurants to keep you going for weeks. Most visitors are torn between two primary areas of the city: the center and La Candelaria, and the northern suburbs. In the center and La Candelaria are most of the best museums, historic architecture, and attractions; the best restaurants, hotels, and shopping are in the north. Most visitors sightsee in the center during the day and eat and sleep in the north at night. For those with a bit more time, day trips into the countryside in Zipaquirá and Chía offer some respite from the fast pace of the city.

Created in 1539 by Bogotá's founder, Gonzalo Jiménez de Quesada, the **Plaza de Bolívar** has changed substantially over the last 5 centuries but has remained the sentimental center of Bogotá. The square was remodeled to its current appearance in 1960 as a tribute to 150 years of independence. Plaza de Bolívar provides a good insight into the eclectic architectural styles of

Bogotá: Here you'll find the colonial-style **La Casa del Florero**; the 19th-century **Catedral Primal**, which evokes the Renaissance churches of Europe; the neoclassical **Capitolio**; and the palace-like **Casa de Nariño**. On the northern side, the **Palacio de Justicia** is an abrupt, monumental building with a tragic history: It has been burned down twice, first by a mob in 1948, and then by M-19 guerillas in 1985. The statue of Simón Bolívar in the middle of the square was the first public monument in Bogotá.

The majestic **Teatro Colón**, Calle 10 no. 5–32 (www.teatrocolon.gov.co; ✆ 1/284-7420; Transmilenio: Museo del Oro), in the heart of La Candelaria, took its present form by 1895 under the direction of Italian architect Pietro Cantini. Check out the fresco-covered foyer; the wooden, beautifully engraved boxes; and the opulent chandelier marking the center of the theater. With a five-level, 938-person capacity, the theater is home to Bogotá's symphony orchestra and is still used for Bogotá's most important performing arts. For tickets, call ✆ 1/341-0475. Individual or group guided visits are from Tuesday to Saturday between 10am to 5pm and Sunday from 1 to 5pm. Admission is COP$4,500; COP$8,000 for character/costume tour.

At an altitude of 3,048m (10,000 ft.), the **Cerro de Monserrate ★★** (www.cerromonserrate.com) offers spectacular views of Bogotá. It's also home to two very good restaurants, decent souvenir shops, and the **Santuario de Monserrate**, with its 17th-century figure of a fallen Christ, which attracts hundreds of pilgrims every weekend. You can see them climbing the slopes of Monserrate to pay their homage. The top of Monserrate can be reached by cable car or funicular, beginning at Carrera 2E no. 21–48, Paseo Bolívar, **Estación del Funicular** (✆ 1/284-5700). The funicular costs COP$16,400 Monday to Saturday and COP$9,600 on Sundays; it runs 7:45am to 11:45pm on weekdays, 6am to 6:30pm Saturdays and Sundays. The newer *teleférico* (cable car) has the same price and runs from noon to midnight on Monday through Saturday and 9am to 5pm on Sunday.

THE TOP ATTRACTIONS

Casa de Moneda ★ MUSEUM   In 1622, the building that houses the Casa de Moneda was Colombia's first mint, issuing the first gold coins in all of the Americas. The vast collection includes roughly 8,000 pieces, ranging from coins, medals, and banknotes to machinery used for minting coins and bills.

Calle 11 no. 4–93. www.banrepcultural.org/museos-y-colecciones/casa-de-moneda. ✆ **1/343-1111.** Free. Mon, Wed–Sat 9am–5pm; Sun 10am–5pm. Transmilenio: Museo del Oro.

Museo Arqueológico ★ MUSEUM   Set inside of a mansion that once belonged to colonial viceroy the Marquís de San Jorge, this fine museum has an extensive collection of pre-Columbian artifacts. A compliment to the Museo del Oro (see p. 45), the pieces here are mostly ceramics, primarily from cultures from within Colombia, as well as Peru and Ecuador.

Carrera 6 24 no. 7–43. www.musa.com.co. ✆ **1/243-0465.** COP$4,000. Mon–Fri 8:30am–5pm; Sat 9am–4pm; Sun 10am–4pm. Transmilenio: Museo del Oro.

Museo Botero ★★ MUSEUM   When Colombian artist Fernando Botero Angulo donated about 200 pieces of art to Colombia from his personal collection in 1980—including 123 pieces of his own art and the rest from the likes of Picasso, Chagall, and Renoir—he stipulated that there would be one condition: it could be visited by the public for free. While the collection of Botero's work is not as extensive as the one in Medellín, there are many important pieces. The work is spread out over two floors in an elegant colonial building that once housed the archbishop. Audio guides are available in English for COP$6000. The museum is part of a larger art collection from the Banco de la República, and other exhibitions halls can be accessed within the same complex.

Calle 11 no. 4–41. www.banrepcultural.org/museo-botero. ✆ **1/286-0466.** Free. Mon–Sat 9am–7pm; Sat–Sun 10am–5pm. Transmilenio: Museo del Oro.

Museo de Arte Colonial ★ MUSEUM   Set inside Las Aulas Cloister, an ex-Jesuit university that's one of the oldest buildings in Bogotá and a national monument, the Museo de Arte Colonial has an extensive collection of 17th- and 18th-century art, including paintings, sculptures, silver, furniture, and coins. The highlight is the largest existing collection of works by the New Granadan painter Gregorio Vasquez de Arce y Ceballos, including paintings and a complete set of drawings. After being closed for several years for an extensive renovation, the museum re-opened in 2016.

Carrera 6 no. 9–77. www.museocolonial.gov.co. ✆ **1/341-6017.** COP$5,000. Tues–Sat 10am–5:30pm; Sun 10am–3:30pm. Transmilenio: Museo del Oro.

Museo de Arte Moderno ★ MUSEUM   Bogotá's modern art museum, better known as the MAMBO, opened in 1979 and was designed by notable Colombian architect Rogelio Salmona. Spread out over four floors are more than 4,000 pieces of modern art from both Colombian and international artists.

Calle 24 no. 6–00. www.mambogota.com. ✆ **1/286-0466.** COP$5,000. Tues–Fri 10am–6pm; Sat–Sun noon–4:30pm. Transmilenio: Calle 22.

Museo de la Independencia Casa del Florero ★ MUSEUM   Located on the northeast corner of Plaza Bolívar, La Casa del Florero (the House of the Vase), also known as the Museo del 20 de Julio, dates back to the late 16th century and was built for the eldest son of one of the founders of the city. It was here that a dispute over a vase, between Spaniard José González Llorente and Colombians Antonio and Francisco Morales, led to the War of Independence. The museum's 10 rooms, which feature independence memorabilia, are fine examples of early Colombian colonial architecture.

Calle 11 no. 6–94. ✆ **1/334-4150.** COP$3,000. Tues–Thurs 9am–5pm; Sat–Sun 10am–4pm. Transmilenio: Avenida Jiménez or Museo del Oro.

Museo del Oro ★★★ MUSEUM   This is the pride and joy of Bogotá. It's home to one of the world's most impressive collections of its kind: more than 34,000 pieces of gold and 20,000 other pre-Columbian relics. The museum makes a great base from which to learn a bit about the pre-Columbian cultures that inhabited Colombia and South America before the Spanish conquest and the extent of their sophistication. Be prepared to be wowed by the top-floor, 8,000-piece "gold room" and the Muisca gold raft found in Lake Guatavita, which is tied closely to the legend of El Dorado. English-language tours are available at 11am and 3pm. If you can't make one of the guided tours, there are also English-language audio guides available—just ask at the front desk. With the success of this museum, it has branched out with six other smaller, regional locations in cities like Cartagena and Santa Marta.

Corner of Calle 16 and Carrera 6. www.banrepcultural.org/museo-del-oro. © **1/343-2222** or 343-1424. COP$3,000. Tues–Sat 9am–6pm; Sun 10am–4pm. Transmilenio: Museo del Oro.

Museo Internacional de la Esmeralda ★ MUSEUM Most emerald mining in Colombia takes place along the Eastern Andean ridge, to the north of Bogotá. The 45-minute guided tours (in English and Spanish) offer a good intro to the process, an exhibition of different types of emeralds, how quality is determined, and the different mines in Colombia where the best stones are being mined. There's an emerald store, of course, at the end of the tour, though you're better off buying elsewhere. This museum is on the 23rd floor of the Avianca Building.

Calle 16 no. 6–66. www.museodelaesmeralda.com.co. © **1/482-7890**. COP$5,000. Mon–Sat 10am–6pm. Transmilenio: Calle 19.

Museo Nacional de Colombia ★ MUSEUM Founded in 1823, this is Colombia´s oldest and longest-functioning museum, providing a good overview of Colombian culture and history. It is currently home to over 20,000 historical and archaeological items, dating from 10,000 B.C. to the modern era. Most impressive is the pre-Columbian exhibit of tools, handicrafts, and jewelry produced by Colombian indigenous communities before the Spanish conquest. You'll also find a modern-art collection here, as well as a pleasant cafe.

Carrera 7 no. 28–66. www.museonacional.gov.co. © **1/334-8366**. Free. Tues–Sat 10am–6pm; Sun 10am–5pm. Transmilenio: Estación Calle 26.

Quinta de Bolívar ★ HISTORIC SITE In 1820, the government of Nueva Granada donated this house to Simón Bolívar in gratitude for his quest for independence. Bolívar owned the house for 10 years, though he was off fighting other campaigns in Peru and Venezuela for much of that time. Colombian government acquired the house and turned it into a museum in 1922. It was recently restored to its original state, the way it was when Bolívar lived in the house. Many of El Libertador's personal belongings can be found here.

Calle 20 no. 2–91. www.quintadebolivar.gov.co. © **1/336-6419** or 336-6410. COP$4,000. Tues–Fri 9am–5pm; Sat–Sun 10am–4pm. Transmilenio: Calle 22 or Calle 19.

COLONIAL CHURCH ROUNDUP ★★

Church lovers are in for a real treat in Bogotá. The city's colonial origin means that there are some excellent, fully preserved churches in La Candelaria and El Centro Histórico. Though Bogotá's many churches may be staid on the outside, their insides are often opulent examples of colonial religious art. Below is a list of some of the city's best churches. Except where noted, admission is free (though donations are accepted).

Everywhere you look in Bogotá there is something being developed. New buildings, from shiny steel skyscrapers to posh brick condo towers, are popping up. There's money here, lots of it, and more is coming. The government is doing everything it can to handle the growing population and make business development easier.

While the world average air passenger growth is 2% to 4%, the rate in Colombia is growing at around 18%. Currently 27 million passengers fly each year to Colombia, and by 2019, that number is expected to reach 40 million. While El Dorado airport has undergone a major expansion, there are plans to add a second airport in Bogotá, in the west of the city, by 2022 to handle the surging air traffic.

To help alleviate Bogotá's horrendous traffic, a metro system is in the works. While cost concerns probably axed a possible underground system, the first phase, entirely elevated, should be ready some time in 2017, running from Portal Américas on the north to Calle 6 in the city center.

4

BOGOTÁ

Exploring Bogotá

Capilla del Sagrario ★ Built between 1600 and 1700, and restored after the 1827 earthquake, the Capilla del Sagrario is an excellent example of colonial architecture with Mannerist, Moorish, and even indigenous influences.

Carrera 7 btw. calles 10 and 11 in front of Plaza de Bolívar. ℂ **1/212-6315.** Mon–Fri 7:30am–12:30pm and 3–5:30pm; Sun 4:30–5:30pm. Closed holidays. Transmilenio: Avenida Jiménez.

Catedral Primada de Colombia ★ Finished in 1823, this cathedral stands in the same spot as the first church of Bogotá, which was finished in 1539. Inside are paintings and carvings dating from the 17th and 18th centuries, the tomb of Gonzalo Jiménez de Quesada (the founder of Bogotá), and one of the largest organs in all of Latin America.

Carrera 7 no. 10–11 (at Calle 11). www.catedraldebogota.org. ℂ **1/341-1954.** Mon–Sat 8:30am–1pm; Sun 8:30am–2pm.

Iglesia de la Concepción ★ Construction on this church began in 1583, making it one of the oldest in Bogotá. It is another good example of colonial and Moorish architecture.

Calle 10 no. 9–50. ℂ **1/284-6084.** Mon–Sat 7am–6:45pm; Sun and holidays 7am–1pm.

Iglesia del Carmen ★ Built in 1938, my favorite church in the city looks like something out of a Candy Land game. The Iglesia also serves as a prestigious private school—your best bet is to visit Sunday morning.

Carrera 5 no. 8–36. No phone. Transmilenio: Museo del Oro.

Iglesia de San Francisco ★ This church once belonged to the Franciscans and was rebuilt after the 1785 earthquake. Check out its beautiful (and very gold) high altar, yet another excellent example of 17th-century church architecture.

Carrera 7 and Avenida Jiménez. ℂ **1/341-2357.** Mon–Fri 6am–7:45pm; Sat–Sun 6:30am–12:30pm and 4–7:45pm. Transmilenio: Avenida Jiménez.

Iglesia de Santa Clara ★★ The single nave here is decorated entirely with painted motifs, and the adjoining monastery, home to the **Museo de Arte Colonial** (see p. 45) is considered one of the most architecturally rich in all of Colombia. The church, built from 1629 to 1674, is one of the best examples of colonial architecture in Bogotá.

Carrera 8 no. 8–91. www.museocolonial.gov.co. ℂ **1/341-1009.** COP$2,000; COP$1,000 for guided tour. Tues–Fri 9am–4:30pm; Sat–Sun 10am–3:30pm. Transmilenio: Avenida Jiménez.

Organized Tours

Bogotá is a large, spread-out, and confusing city, so if you want to make quick work of a visit, an organized tour of the major sights might be the best option. Standard city tours are offered by innumerable agencies.

Destino Bogotá (www.destinobogota.com; ℂ 1/753-4887), an arm of Via Travel, runs numerous standard day tours in and around the city. Their most popular tour is a 3½ hour tour of La Candelaria, hitting many of the main sites like the Museo Botero and Plaza Bolívar, and includes little extras like a glass of *chicha* and warm *pan de bono*, for COP$146,000. Departure times are flexible. Additionally, they offer guided museum visits, 30-minute helicopter flights over the city, and day trips to Guatavita lake and the Zipaquirá salt cathedral. A company that's appropriately named **Bogotá Free Walking Tours** (www.bogotafree walkingtours.com; ℂ 1/281-9924) offers 3-hour walking tours of La Candelaria on Tuesdays, Thursdays, and Saturdays at 2pm with an English-speaking guide.

Turisbog (www.turisbog.com; ℂ 1/250-6225), is a hop-on, hop-off style double decker bus that circles the city with seven stops including Parque 93,

---

BOGOTÁ turistren

The **Tren Turístico de la Sabana**, as it's officially known, is Colombia's only remaining steam train and is a great way to see Bogotá's picturesque (if cloud-covered) countryside. The train departs from La Estación de la Sabana at 8:30am on Mondays through Fridays, 8am on Saturdays, and 7am on Sundays and holidays, or you can hop on board at the Usaquén train station about 40 minutes later. Passengers are dropped off at the same station they boarded at about nine hours later. The train ride is popular with families, and on board you'll enjoy an authentic "papayera" band playing vallenatos, as well as an Andean band playing typical music from the Cundinamarca region. A small on-board restaurant serves typical Colombian snacks such as hot chocolate accompanied by fresh cheese, tamales, and *aguapanela*, a sugarcane-based hot beverage. You have the choice of disembarking at the salt mines of Zipaquira, where, for an extra fee, you can visit the famous, one-of-a-kind underground salt cathedral; or you can get off at Cajica, a typical Cundinamarca pueblo, with a pleasant plaza, cute stores, and tasty pastries. For more information about the **Bogotá Turistren**, visit www.turistren.com.co.

Note: To purchase tickets, go to the Sabana station, Calle 13 no. 18–24 (ℂ **1/375-0557**) or the Usaquén station, Transversal 10 no. 110–8 (ℂ **1/629-7407** or 629-7408). Tickets cost COP$52,000 for adults, COP$38,000 for children, and COP$25,000 seniors over 60.

El Retiro, and Quinta de Bolívar, as well as some of the more out-of-the-way places like the Jardín Botánico and Maloka that would make for expensive taxi rides. Tours run Wednesday to Saturday and cost COP$56,000 for 1 day, or COP$78,000 for 2 days.

There are a growing number of less traditional tours focused on niche interests as well. English language graffiti tours of La Candelaria are offered twice a day by **Bogotá Graffiti** (www.bogotagraffiti.com) at 10am and 2pm. Tours, which last about two and a half hours, are guided by street artists and those directly involved in the scene and are free, but donations are accepted.

Street food tours are another way to get off the beaten path, and a number of operators now have trips. **La Mesa** (www.delamesa.com) has 3-hour-long street food tours in La Candelaria every Monday, Wednesday, and Friday morning, departing at 9:30am for US$49 per person. Groups are kept to a maximum of eight. American Karen Attman and Colombian Peter Corredor, who write the blog **Flavors of Bogotá** (www.flavorsofbogota.com), run coffee-shop tours of the city, bringing clients to the city's best cafes and to meet with some of the better known baristas and roasters. Tours depart at 9:30am from La Candelaria on Thursdays and the Zona G on Fridays and costs US$35 per person.

Outdoor Activities & Spectator Sports

BIKING Bogotá is a biker's city, especially on Sundays and holidays when the city hosts Ciclovía, an event where many roads are closed to automobiles and opened to bikers, walkers, and joggers; thousands of Bogotanos take to the streets between 7am and 2pm. It's one of the city's greatest communal experiences. **Bogotá Bike Tours** (www.bogotabiketours.com; ✆ 1/342-7649) rents bikes and leads bike tours around the city.

BULLFIGHTING Bullfighting season is in December, January, and February at La Plaza de Los Toros Santa María. A number of smaller events are held here throughout the year. For information about bullfighting, contact the Corporación Taurina de Bogotá, Calle 70A no. 6–24 (✆ **1/334-1628**) or La Plaza de Toros, Carrera 6 no. 26–50 (✆ **1/334-1482**).

FUTBOL (SOCCER) As in most of Latin America, soccer is popular in Bogotá. The two local teams are: Los Millonarios, Carrera 9 no. 70–09 (www.millonarios.com.co; ✆ **1/347-7080**), and Independiente Santa Fe, Calle 64A no. 38–08 (http://independientesantafe.com; ✆ **1/544-6670**), both of which you can contact for tickets. Games take place at El Estadio Nemesio Camacho El Campín, Carrera 30 no. 57–60 (✆ **1/315-8726**).

TREKKING & ROCK CLIMBING Several trekking and adventure groups function in and around Bogotá and can also arrange hikes in other parts of the country. Try **Caminantes del Retorno** (www.caminantesdel retorno.com; ✆ **1/285-5232** or 1/245-0518), **Clorofila Urbana** (✆ **1/616-8711**), or **Colombia Ecoturística** (✆ **1/286-3369**). For rock climbing, your best bet is **Roca Solida**, Av. 19 no. 133–23 (✆ **1/600-7480**) or **Rock Climbing**, Carrera 13A no. 35–66 (www.rocasolida.com; ✆ **1/245-7284**).

Especially for Kids

A surprise to some, Bogotá is an excellent city for traveling with the entire family. The major museums are unique and stimulating enough that even young children can appreciate them. Rooms of glittering gold artifacts at the **Museo del Oro** ★★★ (p. 45) rarely disappoint, while kids may giggle at the abnormally rotund figures from Fernando Botero's work at the **Museo Botero** ★★ (p. 45), yet still gain an important lesson in perspective and Colombian history. Not far from Parque Independencia, the **Planetarium** ★, Calle 26b no. 5–93 (www.planetariodebogota.gov.co; Ⓒ **1/281-4150**), was remodeled in 2011 and also features a space museum and cafe.

You can take kids on a trip to **Parque Jaime Duque** ★ (www.parquejaimeduque.com), which is like a Bogotá Disneyland with five different zones that include rides, a zoo, and restaurants. It's open Wednesday to Friday (COP$26,000) from 9am to 5pm and Saturday and Sunday (COP$34,000) 10am to 6:30pm. **Maloka** ★ (Carrera 68 D No. 24A–51; www.maloka.org; Ⓒ **1/427-2707**), Bogotá's interactive science museum, features nine different halls with themes including the solar system, human body, and water. Admission is COP$15,900. There's a 3D theater with an additional fee.

Dining out, especially for long weekend lunches, is often a family affair in Bogotá. On the northern outskirts of town there's **La Granja de Tenjo** ★ (www.lagranjatenjo.com), a country-style restaurant on a working farm. Not far away in Chía, there's not a kid in the world who won't love eating at the zany, whimsical steakhouse **Andrés Carne de Rés** ★★★ (p. 67), which is the size of a small city and covered in kitsch. The restaurant turns into a giant dance club on weekend late nights, so it's best to come early and leave before it gets too rowdy.

WHERE TO STAY

Most hostels and budget establishments are located in La Candelaria and El Centro, near the majority of the city's attractions, while large international chains and trendy boutique hotels tend to cluster in the northern half of the city, closer to the best shopping and restaurants. *Note:* Colombian hotels use the New Year's holiday as an excuse to raise their rates by up to 10%.

La Candelaria

La Candelaria is relatively safe and a good place to stay if your budget is tight and you want to save time and money on getting around. Many of the city's best museums and cultural attractions are here, as well as some of the most historic architecture, which is reflected in the hotels here. However, everything seems to close down when the sun sets; the nightlife that does exist here tends to be slightly bohemian and student-centered. Avoid accommodations in El Centro, because this area can be loud and unpleasant at night.

EXPENSIVE
Hotel de La Opera ★★   One of the top spots to stay in La Candelaria, de La Opera is on a lovely cobblestone street adjacent to the Teatro Colón.

The hotel was created from two restored colonial homes, each with an original courtyard. All guest rooms are decorated with Italian furniture. The spacious, beautifully decorated suites are well worth a splurge. The terrace restaurant, El Mirador, offers great views of La Candelaria, as do most of the hotel's rooms. Enjoy live-music shows on Friday and Saturday nights, as well as complimentary use of the pool, Jacuzzi, and sauna.

Calle 10 no. 5–72. www.hotelopera.com.co. © **1/336-2066.** 42 units. COP$335,000–COP$500,000 double; from COP$555,000 suite, includes continental breakfast. Transmilenio: Museo del Oro. **Amenities:** 2 restaurants; hot tub; pool; spa; free Wi-Fi.

The Orchids ★★ Set in an 1892 Neoclassical townhouse in the heart of La Candelaria, this was the first high-end hotel to open in the neighborhood in years when it began taking reservations in 2013. More intimate than the Hotel de la Opera, every piece of woodwork at Orchids has been immaculately restored, and spaces have been updated with contemporary pieces of art. It's like 19th-century bourgeois crossed with a 21st-century gallery. Details old and new mesh seamlessly with the vertical gardens and a glass elevator in an interior atrium. Salons and libraries—named after Marcel Proust and Oscar Wilde, with collections of leather bound books and pre-Columbian ceramics and even a few Achuar shrunken heads (recreations of course)—are ideal for browsing, while the Les Pêcheurs de Perles hammam, with a Jacuzzi and steam room blanketed in mosaic tiles, completely cuts you off from the world outside.

Carrera 5 no. 10–55. www.theorchidshotel.com. © **1/745-5438.** 8 units. COP$550,000 double, includes breakfast. Transmilenio: Museo del Oro. **Amenities:** Art gallery, restaurant; steam room; free Wi-Fi.

MODERATE

Abadia Colonial ★ Another good choice in La Candelaria, the Abadia Colonial has 12 rooms organized around three small courtyards and a pleasant dining area. The hotel is well-maintained and spotless, with a fully restored Spanish-style exterior complete with wooden balcony. The simple but elegant guest rooms are comfortable, spacious, and tastefully decorated. Located right in the heart of La Candelaria, the hotel is close to the Museo Botero and dozens of cafes and restaurants.

Calle 11 no. 2–32. www.abadiacolonial.com. © **1/341-1884.** 12 units. COP$200,000 double, includes breakfast. Transmilenio: Museo del Oro or Las Aguas. **Amenities:** Restaurant; free Wi-Fi.

INEXPENSIVE

Casa Platypus ★ At the edge of La Candelaria, Casa Platypus has the feel of a boutique hotel with some extra amenities that are more like a hostel, such as a communal kitchen, a book exchange, and a roof terrace filled with guests exchanging travel tales. The colonial building features simple, smallish rooms with creaky wood floors and private bathrooms. Owner Germán Escobar is a world traveler with a wealth of information about what to do in Bogotá.

Carrera 3 no. 12–28. www.casaplatypusbogota.com. © **1/281-1801.** 17 units. COP$150,000 double; COP$45,000 dorms, includes continental breakfast. Transmilenio: Museo del Oro. **Amenities:** Shared kitchen; roof terrace; laundry service; book exchange; free Wi-Fi.

Chorro de Quevedo B&B ★ This small hotel is set in a renovated colonial house where rooms range from cozy to large. The upstairs rooms are a real bargain for families or those traveling in a large group. Though simple, rooms are tasteful, elegant, and, at this price, a good bang for your buck. The hotel is located in ultra-bohemian Chorro de Quevedo, where plenty of cafes, restaurants, and bars are nearby. You should be warned the plaza fills with hippie-esque bongo players all day and night Friday and Saturday, though the hotel rooms do a pretty good job of keeping the noise out.

Calle 13 b n. 1–53. ℂ **1/439-7575.** 6 units. COP$149,000, includes continental breakfast. Transmilenio: Las Aguas or Museo del Oro. **Amenities:** Free Wi-Fi.

In North Bogotá

Ever since multinationals started moving in by the droves a few years ago, four- and five-star hotels in Bogotá are often booked at full capacity, and despite the seemingly endless selection of high-end lodging, finding a hotel in the northern part of town is no easy feat. I suggest booking at least 15 to 30 days in advance and calling a few days before arrival to confirm your reservation; guests have sometimes shown up only to discover the hotel is overbooked and they've been moved to another nearby hotel. *Tip:* Hotels in north Bogotá are business-oriented, so they often drop their rates (by as much as half) on weekends—be sure to ask about special deals.

Aside from the hotels listed below, **Hotel Casona del Patio Amarillo**, Carrera 8 no. 9–24 (www.lacasonadelpatio.net; ℂ **1/212-8805**), is a pleasant bed-and-breakfast with rates starting at about COP$188,000 per night. One of the cheapest options in the North is the unpretentious **Chapinorte Hostal** (www.chapinortehostelbogota.com), a 10-minute walk from Zona T and about a 15-minute taxi ride from the city center. The hostel is as simple and plain as it gets: Rooms are tiny, bathrooms are shared, and you'll have to rent a towel for COP$2,000, but doubles start at COP$88,000 and the location is relatively safe.

EXPENSIVE

Four Seasons Bogotá ★★★ After quietly taking over the Casa Medina in 2015, renowned luxury hotelier Four Seasons made a big splash on the Bogotá hotel scene by building an entirely new property in the Zona T a year later. The subtly chic rooms—nearly half of which are suites, with dark leather headboards, pale wood floors, and hand knitted carpets—are straight out of the classic Four Seasons playbook. Additional amenities include a full spa and two restaurants: the Japanese BBQ spot Kuru with two-story glass windows and the more casual Biblioteca. Service and detail are impeccable.

Carrera 13 no. 85–46. www.fourseasons.com/bogota. ℂ **1/325-7900.** 64 units. COP$1,110,000–COP$1,310,000 double; from COP$1,600,000 suite. Transmilenio: Calle 85. **Amenities:** 2 restaurants; bar; spa; free Wi-Fi.

Four Seasons Casa Medina ★★★ Built in 1945 by the wealthy Don Santiago Medina, this well-located hotel in the Zona G joined the luxe international chain Four Seasons in 2015. The property, which was designed using the remnants of a colonial convent, has immaculately decorated rooms with hand-carved dressers and leather armchairs, plus all of the modern amenities you would expect at a Four Seasons hotel. The building was declared a national monument in 1985 for its unique Spanish- and French-inspired architectural style. All rooms are slightly different, but each has a spacious marble bathroom, a comfortable work area, and double-paned windows to keep out noise. Every floor has elegant sitting areas and balconies, and guests can enjoy a cup of coffee in any of the many terraces and courtyards. In this home away from home, you can dine in style in the intimate, atmospheric restaurant or on the beautiful rooftop terrace.

Carrera 7 no. 69A–22. www.fourseasons.com/bogotacm. ℂ **1/325-7900.** 58 units. Superiors from COP$1,110,000; suites from COP$1,600,000. Transmilenio: Calle 72 (about 3- to 4-block walk). **Amenities:** 2 restaurants; small gym; spa; free Wi-Fi.

Hilton Bogotá ★   Despite being a big international chain, Bogotá's 15-story Hilton has done a good job of not feeling like one. There's a heated outdoor pool, a first-floor bar, plus a 24-hour gym and a branch of cult coffee roaster Devoción near the valet. The cushy rooms have 400-thread-count sheets and are equipped with the latest electronics. Suites add separate living rooms, while Club rooms include lounge access with free breakfast and drinks. The location is on a busy avenue in in the heart of the city's financial district, though a 10-minute walk from Zona G restaurants and shopping.

Carrera 7 No. 72–41. www.hilton.com. ℂ **1/600-6100.** 245 units. COP$728,000 double; from COP$1,050,000 suite includes breakfast. Transmilenio: Calle 72. **Amenities:** Restaurant; bar; cafe; outdoor pool; concierge; gym; free Wi-Fi.

W Bogotá ★★   Like the city and country around it, the W chain's first Colombian hotel is full of vibrant energy, with mostly golden interiors inspired by the legend of El Dorado. The entire reception area feels like Scrooge McDuck's vault, while gold pillows and sinks found their way into the guestrooms. Textiles feature patterns of mountains, forests, and flowers. There's lots of life and color everywhere you look, from the aquamarine mosaic tiles in the bathrooms to the enormous graffiti wall painted by local street artist EKS1 in the bar with its own house DJ. The hotel has become something of a scene since opening in 2014, bringing in neighbors who make use of the fourth-floor spa and dine in Jean-Georges Vongerichten's Market Kitchen.

Carrera 9 No. 115–30. www.wbogota.com. ℂ **1/600-6100.** 168 units. COP$632,000 double; from COP$1,227,000 suite, includes breakfast. Transmilenio: Calle 72. **Amenities:** Restaurant; 2 bars; cafe; indoor pool; spa; concierge; gym; Wi-Fi (US$15 per day).

MODERATE

104 Art Suites ★★   Each room at this funky hotel in the far northern neighborhood of Chicó Navarra was designed by a different artist, leading to a mishmash of styles, ranging from tufted white leather headboards to graffiti. All rooms have terraces or balconies, plus standard amenities that include flatscreen TVs and high-speed Wi-Fi. Some suites add a full kitchen, Jacuzzi, or fireplace. The only downside is the hotel is in a residential area, facing a park, so there's little in terms of shops and restaurants within walking distance.

Carrera 18a no. 104–77. www.104artsuites.com. ✆ **1/744-3890.** 27 units. COP$354,000 double. Transmilenio: Calle 100. **Amenities:** Bar; business center; free Wi-Fi.

B.O.G. ★★ The sparkling metallic interiors of this design hotel in the La Cabrera neighborhood are reminiscent of gold and emeralds, while the granite and stone facade gives it the feel of a mountain in the Andes. Notable Colombian interior designer Nini Andrade Silva continues the natural theme by infusing the rooms with touches of bronze and earthy tones to pair with top-of-the-line electronics. A restaurant from Michelin-starred Spanish chef Ramon Freixa sits on the ground floor, while up on the rooftop is a heated pool and a cocktail bar that brings in a well-heeled crowd.

Carrera 11 no. 86–724. www.boghotel.com. ✆ **1/639-9990.** 55 units. COP$555,000 double, includes buffet breakfast. Transmilenio: Calle 85. **Amenities:** 2 restaurants; bar; pool; gym; spa; free Wi-Fi.

The Belvedere ★ The Hotel Belvedere is well situated close to excellent restaurants and entertainment options, and within walking distance to Parque de la 93. Rooms are standard with minibars, satellite TV, blackout curtains, work tables, and comfortable bathrooms. The hotel is a good deal in comparison to its competition in the same sector. Located 4 blocks from the Transmilenio, the hotel is popular for corporate travelers, but is also well suited for tourists and families. Patrons can relax and dine on the attractive terrace, and the small but tasty restaurant serves both typical Colombian and international fare.

Carrera 17A no. 100–16. www.ghlhoteles.com. ✆ **1/257-7700.** 39 units. COP$190,000 double; COP$225,000 suite, includes breakfast. Transmilenio: 100 (a few blocks away). **Amenities:** Restaurant; bar; free Wi-Fi.

Click Clack ★★ The coolest hotel in Bogotá has a Space Invader–patterned elevator and Earl Grey–scented tissues. This 11-floor, cantilevered design hotel near Parque de la 93 stands out from its peers, with venues like a farm-to-table restaurant and the rooftop Apache burger bar, nightspots that actually bring in non-guests. The rooms mix quality with eccentricities, like floor-to-ceiling windows, an iPad concierge, and balconies with fire pits (in some).

Carrera 11 no. 93–7. www.clickclackhotel.com. ✆ **1/743-0404.** 64 units. From COP$339,000 double; from COP$569,000 suite, includes buffet breakfast. Transmilenio: Calle 85. **Amenities:** 2 restaurants; bar; free Wi-Fi.

Estelar La Fontana ★ Across the street from Unicentro, La Fontana is an elegant hotel in a red brick building popular with businesspeople. Accommodations range from comfortable standard rooms (though the bathrooms are a bit snug) to grandiose "special suites." Prices on rooms and junior suites are cut in half on weekends. La Fontana has a beautiful plant-filled courtyard where free concerts of salsa, tango, Chilean, and Andean music are held on Sundays. If you plan to stay for an extended period of time, the hotel also offers apartments. If you're here over the weekend, be sure not to miss the well-known Cremesse, La Fontana's Sunday artisan fair, where you'll find decently priced jewelry, clothing, and artwork.

Av. 127 no. 15A–10. www.estelarlafontana.com. © **1/615-4400** (1/274-7868 for reservations). 215 hotel units and 97 apartments. COP$315,000 double; from COP$391,000 suite, includes breakfast. Transmilenio: 127. **Amenities:** 2 restaurants; bar; concierge; gym; free Wi-Fi.

INEXPENSIVE

Ibis Museo ★★ Beside the Museo Nacional, this straightforward chain hotel is one of the best value stays in the city. The location—a 2-minute walk to some of La Macarena's top bars and restaurants, plus not far from the center—couldn't be better. The cookie cutter rooms are modern and functional, with dark wood floors and a work desk next to the soundproofed windows. There's a 24-hour restaurant on site.

Transversal 6 no. 27–8. www.ibis.com. © **1/381-4666.** 216 units. COP$158,000 double, includes buffet breakfast. Transmilenio: Calle 26. **Amenities:** Restaurant; bar; free Wi-Fi.

Saint Simon ★ This small, European-style hotel in the heart of the Zona T is a good value-driven choice in northern Bogotá. The hotel's small size allows for personal attention and has many repeat customers, mostly Colombian businesspeople and international solo tourists. All of the cozy rooms have a work area and small but comfortable bathrooms, and some have views of the Zona T and the mountains. Room size and layout vary, so ask to see a room before booking. As an added bonus, there is a small artisan fair in the plaza across from the hotel, where you can buy Colombian-style *mochilas* (backpacks), handicrafts, and clothing.

Carrera 14 no. 81–34. www.hotelsaintsimonbogota.com. © **1/621-8188.** 46 units. COP$152,000 double; COP$184,000 suite, includes buffet breakfast. Transmilenio: Los Héroes or Calle 76. **Amenities:** Restaurant; bar; free Wi-Fi.

WHERE TO EAT

Without exaggerating, Bogotá has tens of thousands of restaurants, so you can rest assured that you'll never be more than a few feet away from a simple or gourmet eatery. Bogotá is experiencing a culinary renaissance of sorts, with international and gourmet restaurants springing up all over the place, though there are still plenty of traditional (and cheap) joints where you can grab an *almojabana* (fried cheese-bread) or an empanada. Most exotic, innovative, and upscale restaurants are found in northern Bogotá, while hole-in-the-wall eateries and set-menu spots are scattered throughout the center and La Candelaria. However, you will also find many atmospheric, bohemian restaurants in La Candelaria. For Bogotá's best restaurants, head to La Zona G, located between calles 69 and 72 and carreras 3 and 6. There are also excellent high-end choices in and around el Parque de la 93, La Zona T, and Usaquén. You can expect to pay COP$30,000 to COP$75,000 per plate at most high-end restaurants, and COP$5,000 to COP$12,000 for set-price menus at budget restaurants.

Other than the restaurants listed below, also plan on making a trip to **Mercado Paloquemao** ★ (www.plazadepaloquemao.com), at Av. 19 and Carrera

BOGOTÁ IN chains

Bogotá is the headquarters of several major restaurant chains, some of the most successful in all of Latin America.

Wok How could a restaurant chain focusing on the cuisines of Japan and southeast Asia be so Colombian? Well, they source their fish from artisanal fishing communities in the Pacific, support responsible farming practices, and have contributed to the sustainable development of many rural companies without increasing their prices dramatically. A model chain, Wok, was founded in 1998 and has more than a dozen locations around the capital, including in the Zona T and near the Museo Nacional. www.wok.com.co.

Crepes & Waffles Perhaps Colombia's most famous restaurant chain, which now has branches around Latin America, Crepes & Waffles was created by a young university couple in the 1980s. It serves up savory crepes and desert waffles and crepes, as well as ice cream. Very admirably, it hires only female heads of households, essentially single mothers, as servers. With more than a dozen locations in Bogotá, the most convenient branches are in La Zona T, Usaquén, Parque de la 93, and Unicentro. www.crepesywaffles.com.co.

Juan Valdez Café If there was one brand name synonymous with Colombia, it would be Juan Valdez, a fictional character that represents the National Federation of Coffee Growers of Colombia. While they've been exporting coffee under the name since 1958, the first Juan Valdez Café, Colombia's answer to Starbuck's, opened in El Dorado airport in 2002. There are now branches all over Bogotá, all over Colombia, and in international destinations, including New York and Miami. www.juanvaldezcafe.com.

25, to taste native fruits like curuba and guanabana, and snack on crispy *lechón* (fried pork) or roasted big-butt Santander ants at the popular cluster of traditional food stalls. It's open Monday to Saturday from 4:30am to 4:30pm and Sunday 5am to 2:30pm. It's best to come early in the morning to see the most activity. As always in any busy marketplace, keep an eye on your belongings.

El Centro & La Candelaria

MODERATE

Casa Vieja ★ COLOMBIAN Decorated with colonial paintings and antiques, Casa Vieja screams tradition. The original La Candelaria location opened in 1964—there are now several others around town—and has that somewhat stuffy, old-school touristy feel. Yet they still do straightforward classic dishes the way they should be done. Their *ajiaco*, a chicken and potato stew, is their signature, though you'll find various regional plates like *sancocho de gallina* (hen stew) and fried *mojarra* with coconut rice.

Av. Jimenéz no. 3–57. www.casavieja.com.co. ✆ **1/334-8908.** Reservations recommended. Main courses COP$28,000–COP$44,000. Mon–Sat noon–5pm; Sun noon–6pm.

INEXPENSIVE

La Escuela Restaurante & Panadería ★ COLOMBIAN In a beautifully restored colonial building that houses a school designed to preserve Colombian cultural heritage, this student-run restaurant and bakery is one of the best breakfast or lunch picks near Plaza Bolívar. The bakery specializes in typical breads like *pan de bono* and French pastries, and even roasts its own fair-trade coffee. The restaurant lists dozens of exotic fruit juices to pair with dishes like *chuleta valluna*, a pork dish from the Valle de Cauca, and *mojarra frita*, a Magdalena River–style fried fish. In both spots, the furniture and decorations were designed by the carpentry program located in the same building.

Calle 9 no. 8–61. www.escuelataller.org. ✆ **1/289-0951.** Main courses COP$12,000–COP$20,000. Mon–Fri noon–4pm (restaurant); Mon–Fri 7am–5pm (bakery).

La Puerta Falsa ★ COLOMBIAN It may be unassuming, but La Puerta Falsa is as authentic as it gets in Bogotá. The quaint two-story eatery is housed in a 400-year-old building and is the best place to enjoy an old-fashioned Santa Fe tamale. Other popular choices are *salchichas* (sausages), eggs with bread, *agua panela* with *queso fresco*, and an assortment of typical Colombian pastries and desserts. Bogotá's oldest functioning restaurant, the family business has been passed down from generation to generation since 1816. Its location, between La Candelaria and Plaza Bolívar, makes it a convenient breakfast or lunch choice. Credit cards not accepted.

Calle 11 no. 6–50. No phone. Reservations not accepted. Main courses COP$2,500–COP$4,000. Mon–Sat 7am–11pm.

La Macarena
EXPENSIVE

Leo Cocina y Cava ★★★ CONTEMPORARY When Chef Leonor Espinosa, nicknamed Leo, opened this fine-dining restaurant in 2007, Colombian food was forever changed. Her impeccable research into the food of the country's isolated indigenous and Afro-Colombian cultures put her in touch with ingredients that no other chef in Bogotá was using, let alone in a fine-dining setting. Some of her classics include seared tuna with a crust of *hormigas culonas*, the big-bottomed ants from Santander, and a smoked rabbit *carimañola*. The wine pairing is arranged by Espinosa's daughter, the sommelier, though more interesting are their ancestral beverages, made from wild cane spirits and flavored with herbs and vines. Leo is the most awarded restaurant in Colombia, as it is listed on the prestigious Latin America's 50 Best Restaurants list, and her development foundation was nominated for the Nobel-like Basque Culinary World Prize in 2016.

Calle 27B no. 6–75, Pasaje Santa Cruz de Mompox. www.restauranteleo.com. ✆ **1/316-3526.** Reservations recommended. Main courses COP$30,000–COP$80,000. Mon–Sat noon–3:30pm and 7–11pm; Sun noon–5pm. Closed holidays.

MODERATE

Donostia ★★ FARM-TO-TABLE/TAPAS This farm-to-table restaurant from Chef Tomás Rueda serves soulful small plates and specials that are marked on a chalkboard above the bar. Everything is perfectly executed, like pork ribs with a *camu camu* BBQ sauce and grilled octopus with potatoes, while the restaurant's brick walls, beamed ceilings, and leather booths make it one of La Macarena's most elegant spaces.

Calle 29 no. 5–84. www.elorigendelacomida.co. ✆ **1/287-3943.** Main courses COP$24,000–COP$58,000. Tues–Sat noon–4pm and 7–11pm; Mon–Sun noon–4pm.

El Panóptico ★★ COLOMBIAN   From Eduardo Martinez, the agronomist chef of cult restaurant Mini-mal (who knows more about what's edible in Colombia than anyone else), El Panóptico is set in the brick-walled building of the same name, which happens to house the Museo Nacional. It's a laidback, light-filled space, offering one of the most interesting menus with some of the hardest-to-find ingredients in the city. Recipes come from grandmothers in rural villages and from indigenous Amazonian groups. You might find chicken braised in *ají negro*, a fermented yuca broth, or *guatilla* (chayote) thinly sliced as carpaccio. The juice selection is one of the best in the city.

Carrera 7 no. 28–66. ✆ **1/342-2170.** Main courses COP$16,000–COP$35,000. Mon–Sat noon–4pm.

Misia ★★ CARRIBBEAN   This laidback spot from celebrity chef Leonor Espinosa focuses on the traditional restaurants and street food from around the country, particularly Colombia's Caribbean coast. The lighter breakfast menu is offered all day, with eggs, house-made sausages, and fresh fruit juices, while the rest of the day includes *arepas* and fried snacks, *posta negra* (coastal black beef), and various rice dishes. The restaurant's updated *comedor* design mimics the theme of the menu, with painted tile floors and old wooden crates turned into lampshades. A second location in the Zona G at Carrera 7 no. 67–39.

Transversal 6 no. 27–50. www.restaurantemisia.com. ✆ **1/321-3940.** Reservations recommended. Main courses COP$20,000–COP$45,000. Tues–Sat 7am–10pm; Sun 9am–4pm.

Tábula ★ MEDITERRANEAN   A few blocks from his restaurant **Donostia** ★★ (see p. 57), Tomás Rueda's family-style restaurant serves rustic, Mediterranean-influenced food with Colombian ingredients. Most of the dishes are cooked over a wood fire, things like osso buco or tiger shrimp and chorizo stew steamed inside a bijao leaf. It's a great place for coming with a group, lingering for a few hours and continually adding to the order.

Calle 29 no. 5–90. www.elorigendelacomida.co. ✆ **1/287-7228.** Reservations recommended. Main courses COP$24,000–COP$58,000. Mon–Wed noon–4pm; Thurs–Sat noon–4pm and 7–11pm; Sun noon–4pm.

Chapinero & the North
EXPENSIVE

Criterion ★ FRENCH   Brothers Jorge and Mark Rausch helped turn the Zona G into a dining destination when, in 2003, they opened this classic French restaurant with wood floors, white walls, and purple banquettes. As the years have gone by, they have moved further away from France and closer to Colombia, adding local ingredients whenever possible. Most commendable is their work with lionfish, an invasive Caribbean reef killer that also tastes great with *lulo* and *tomate de* árbol. The wine cellar is one of the deepest in town, and their Sunday brunch is memorable.

Calle 69a no. 5–75. www.criterion.com.co. ✆ **1/310-1377.** Reservations recommended. Main courses COP$30,000–COP$80,000. Mon–Sat noon–4pm and 7–11pm; Sun 9am–5pm.

El Cielo ★★ AVANT GARDE While celebrity chef Juan Manuel Barrientos's original El Cielo location is in Medellín, the Bogotá location is the one that's listed on the Latin America's 50 Best Restaurants list. The two tasting menus, using avant-garde techniques like a bed of mist on the table to resemble the cloud forest, are similar in both locations, though the larger Bogotá location with a vertical garden and private dining rooms is considerably more elegant.

Calle 70 no. 4–47. www.elcielorestaurant.com. ✆ **1/703-5585.** Reservations recommended. Tasting menu COP$125,000–COP$170,000. Mon–Thurs noon–3pm and 7–10pm; Fri–Sat noon–10pm; Sun noon–3pm.

Harry's ★ PARRILLA/STEAK In 2005, brothers and chefs Jorge and Harry Sasson debuted this popular steakhouse in the heart of the Zona G, and it's been a hit ever since. With its extensive wine list and posh ambience, Harry's has become one of the hippest places in Bogotá to grab lunch, dinner, or an after-work cocktail. The steaks are excellent, as is the service, and the glass ceiling and windows let in plenty of natural light, creating an attractive, pleasant dining space. Note that diners are allowed to bring their own wine and liquor, which can be stored in upstairs lockers and consumed on a subsequent visit. The restaurant will accept dollars if you're hard up for Colombian pesos.

Calle 70 no. 5–27. www.harrysasson.com. ✆ **1/321-3940.** Reservations recommended. Main courses COP$26,000–COP$80,000. Mon–Sat noon–midnight; Sun noon–5pm.

Villanos en Bermudas ★★★ CONTEMPORARY Two chefs with experience at some of Latin America's best restaurants, Mexican Sergio Meza and Argentine Nicolás Lopez, who met while working in Chile, have built what is probably Colombia's most ambitious restaurant. Translating to "Villains in Bermuda shorts," the restaurant, which opened in mid-2016, is set on three floors of a cool, restored house in Chapinero Alto with exposed bricks painted white, wood floors, and marble countertops. They work with small regional producers, creating sophisticated menus only from what is in season and available. If they only have three portions of one ingredient, only one table that ordered the tasting menu will get it. On the second floor is an a la carte menu and cocktail bar where you can come without reservations.

Calle 56 no. 5–21. ✆ **1/211-1259.** Reservations recommended. Main courses COP$26,000–COP$90,000. Mon–Sat 5pm–midnight.

MODERATE

Andrés D.C. ★★ PARRILLA/STEAK Some say that this urban location (and the nearby food court) of the whimsical Chía steakhouse (see p. 67) watered down the brand when it opened in 2010, though others are just happy that they can get a taste of it without leaving the city limits. Even if you prefer the Chía location, this raucous four-floor restaurant and bar still has much to offer. The food is more or less the same, it's reliably filled with people having a good time even on off nights, and the roving troubadours and dancing waitresses always make you smile.

Calle 82 no. 12–21, Centro Comercial El Retiro. www.andrescarnederes.com. ✆ **1/863-7880.** Main courses COP$36,000–COP$70,000. Daily noon–3am.

Astrid y Gastón Bogotá ★ PERUVIAN   This branch of Peruvian mega-chef Gastón Acurio's flagship Lima restaurant introduced true contemporary Peruvian food to Bogotá when it opened in 2005. Since then, dozens of other Peruvian restaurants in the city have opened, yet this refined brick building with white tablecloths and wood floors has maintained its level of service and its menu of updated Peruvian classics. The lounge-y bar area is a good spot for pisco sours and snacking on *cancha serrana* (toasted corn kernels).

Carrera 7 no. 67–64. www.astridygastonbogota.com. © 1/211-1400. Reservations recommended. Main courses COP$22,000–COP$65,000. Mon–Sat noon–3pm and 7–11pm.

Club Colombia ★ COLOMBIAN   In a sprawling, ivy-covered house in El Retiro, Club Colombia has been attracting well-heeled Bogatanos since opening in 2005. The restaurant was founded by noted chefs Harry Sasson and Leo Katz, who wanted to create a menu of traditional Colombian dishes from every part of the country, which they serve in a clubby, convivial setting where buckets of chilled champagne don't seem out of place with plates of tamales and empanadas. Though you'll find better preparations of the dishes from mom-and-pop places around town, you're here for the atmosphere more than anything.

Calle 82 no. 9–11. www.harrysasson.com. © 1/316-3530. Main courses COP$16,000–COP$65,000. Mon–Fri 7am–midnight; Sat–Sun 8am–midnight.

El Gordo ★ BURGERS   Mimicking a Brooklyn-style bistro with a tin ceiling and exposed brick walls, plus a long, lively bar to showcase their craft-beer list and original cocktails, El Gordo is a great break after weeks of typical Colombian cuisine. The menu consists of updated American comfort food like pork belly tater tots and bacon-wrapped dates. Their hefty burgers are the reason most come here.

Carrera 4a no. 66–84. www.gordobar.com. © 1/345-5769. Main courses COP$21,000–COP$44,000. Daily noon–11:30pm.

La Despensa de Rafa ★★ PERUVIAN   From acclaimed Peruvian chef Rafael Osterling, this laidback offshoot of his more sophisticated restaurant Rafael sits in a buzzy corner of Quinta Camacho. Start your meal on the patio with a pisco sour infused with *lulo*, then move on to typical Peruvian appetizers like *causa*, a potato casserole topped with shrimp and octopus, or bowls of ceviche. Mains dabble in Asia and the Mediterranean, like the house-made pastas and an Indian curry of the day.

Calle 70 no. 4–63. www.rafaelosterling.pe/en/la-despensa.html. © 1/321-3940. Main courses COP$22,000–COP$64,000. Mon–Sat noon–midnight.

La Fama ★ BBQ   When the owners of La Fama decided to open an American-style BBQ joint in Bogotá, they brought in a couple of guys from cult butcher shop the Meat Hook in Brooklyn to help them set it up. Aside from teaching them to make brisket, burnt ends, and pulled pork, all sold by weight, they figured out how to BBQ the hump of the tropical Zebu cow, called the *morillo*, which they cure with adobo and put in the smoker for 18 hours. Pair it with sides like coleslaw or barbecued beans, then chase it with their stash of whiskeys and craft beer. If you let them know a couple of days in advance and have a group of six to ten people, they'll even BBQ you an entire suckling pig.

Calle 65 no. 4. www.lafama.com.co. ☎ **1/644-7716.** Main courses COP$16,000–COP$44,000. Mon–Wed noon–10pm; Thurs–Sat noon–11pm; Sun noon–5pm.

Mini-mal ★★★ COLOMBIAN   Mini-mal began more as an experiment in social development than as a restaurant. Chef Eduardo Martinez, an agronomist by trade who was working on the Pacific Coast, saw Mini-mal as an opportunity to help support the region's artisanal fishermen, mollusk collectors, and artisanal farmers. Since opening in 2001 in a quirky Chapinero Alto house, he hasn't looked back and has shifted his attention toward the Amazon and other remote regions of the country, helping to spread awareness about Colombian biodiversity. His approach was years ahead of its time, and the unpretentious fare continues to impress. Inside the restaurant is a small shop selling handicrafts and food products from the communities Martinez works with.

Carrera 4a 70 no. 57–52. www.mini-mal.org. ☎ **1/633-7934.** Main courses COP$11,000–COP$39,000. Mon–Sat noon–midnight; Sun noon–5pm.

Salvo Patria ★★ BISTRO/CAFE   Part neighborhood bistro, part serious coffee bar, Salvo Patria is where locals head for a lunchtime pint of local craft beer and a pastrami sandwich, or to meet their neighbors for an Old Fashioned and rabbit ragú in the evenings. They take sourcing seriously, with origin coffees, line-caught fish, organic vegetables, free-range chicken, and house-aged meats. It's soulful food at reasonable prices with a modest yet attractive vibe in a corner brick building with a small patio.

Calle 54a no. 4–13. www.salvopatria.com. ☎ **1/702-6367.** Main courses COP$18,000–COP$40,000. Mon–Sat noon–midnight; Sun noon–5pm.

INEXPENSIVE

Central Cevicheria ★ SEAFOOD   The interior and patio of Central Cevicheria are decorated like a Caribbean house with colorful wood-panel walls and lots of plants, giving you a sense that you're not at 2,600 meters above sea level. As the name suggests, *ceviches* (raw fish and seafood marinated in citrus) are the specialty. There are more than a dozen varieties, divided into spicy and non-spicy, as well as tartars and *tiraditos* (Japanese-Peruvian style). More straightforward grilled and fried options are also available.

Carrera 13 no. 85–14. www.centralcevicheria.com. ☎ **1/644-7766.** Main courses COP$18,000–COP$28,000. Mon–Sat 11am–1am; Sun 11am–9pm.

Grazia ★ PASTRIES   The French and American couple who own Grazia met while working with renowned Chef Daniel Boulud in New York City, then moved to Bogotá together to open their dream patisserie. The three-floor atelier and restaurant, with a pleasant patio and vertical garden, serves both salty and sweet, with particularly good breakfasts and brunches. Try their Café Liégeois éclair, which adds Colombian coffee and tonka bean to the French classic.

Calle 70 no. 5–27. www.maisongrazia.com. ☎ **1/321-3940.** Main courses COP$10,000–COP$35,000. Mon–Sat noon–midnight; Sun noon–5pm. Closed holidays.

Julia ★ PIZZA   While there are plenty of pizza delivery chains and walk up by-the-slice windows around Bogotá, Julia is where to come for that authentic Naples-style pie with perfect leoparding (a geeky pizza term for the spotted burnt crusts) that you can only get from a wood burning oven. The classic Italian pizzas—like quattro formaggi, margherita and turtufi—are paired with typical antipasti like eggplant parmigiana and plates of prosciutto. Additional locations are located in Usaquén and the Zona G.

Carrera 5 no. 69a–19. www.juliapizzeria.com. ✆ **1/348-2835.** Main courses COP$13,000–COP$26,000. Daily noon–10pm.

Las Margaritas ★ COLOMBIAN   At more than a century old, Las Margaritas has got to be doing something right. There's nothing pretentious or fancy about Las Margaritas, but it has a rustic charm that keeps customers coming back. In the historic Chapinero neighborhood, Las Margaritas offers more than a dining experience; it also gives guests a glimpse of Bogotá and Chapinero history and culture, and friendly and bilingual owner and chef Julio Rios will be happy to tell you the restaurant's history. Start with a serving of empanadas with lemon and spicy *aji* (pepper), popularly considered the best empanadas in Bogotá (they account for 40% of the restaurant's earnings). Continue with *lengua en salsa* (tongue in sauce) served with salad, rice, and potatoes. Or try the roast beef or the *ajiaco*, a typical Bogotá chicken, corn, potato, and avocado soup. For dessert, ask for the *postre de natas*, a mouth-watering and artery-clogging pudding of sorts.

Calle 62 no. 7–77. ✆ **1/249-9468** or 1/217-0781. Main courses COP$14,000–COP$24,000. Sat–Sun noon–4pm; Tues–Fri 8am–6pm.

Rey Guerrero Pescaderia Gourmet ★★ SEAFOOD   Despite this intimate, colorful restaurant decorated with Afro-Colombian murals being located in Bogotá, Cali-born chef Rey Guerrero has become Colombia's ambassador to the cuisine of the Pacific Coast. The enigmatic Guerrero has spent years researching the traditional dishes of the region, and the menu is extensive. There are several combinations of rice and seafood, like the *arroz tumabacatre* with shrimp and shellfish. There is also a ceviche with *piangua*, the region's delicious black clam, a great fish burger, and several excellent seafood stews. Everything is perfectly executed, the ingredients are of impeccable quality, and the prices are reasonable.

Calle 77 no. 14–20. www.reyguerrero.co. ✆ **1/321-3940.** Main courses COP$14,000–COP$30,000. Mon–Sat noon–11pm.

SHOPPING

Shopping options in Bogotá are plentiful and varied. In the city center, look for bargains and handicrafts. In the north, you'll find upscale shopping malls and boutiques. Colombia is well known for its shoes, purses, emeralds, and gold. Good deals can be found on these items, but save your bargaining for El Centro; prices are fixed in more upscale northern Bogotá.

UN TINTO (Y UN BISCOCHO), por favor

Colombia is one of the world's largest exporters of coffee, and its capital city makes New York's cafe scene look meager. Bogotanos love to take a break from their work day to enjoy a good cup of steaming coffee or hot chocolate, sometimes with *queso fresco* or an *almojabana* (fried cheese-bread).

For one-of-a-kind cafes, head to La Candelaria, where the large student population drives the thriving cafe scene. **Café del Sol**, Calle 14 no. 3–60 ((*C*) **315/ 335-8576**; daily 8am–8:30pm), has a laidback, collegial atmosphere and plays mostly chill-out '60s and '70s Spanish music. Enjoy reading the many patron-written poems tacked on the wall while sipping a decent cup of cappuccino or tinto. For a truly unique experience, head to **Café de La Estación** ★, Calle 14 no. 5–14 (www.estacioncafecolombia.com; (*C*) **1/562-4080**; Mon–Fri 7am–10pm, Sat 9am–8pm), a 120-year-old train car where everything but the wood floor is original. The wooden green windowpane, plaid curtain fringes, and many black-and-white pictures of turn-of-the-century Bogotá and Cartagena make you'll feel as if you've stepped back in time. Café de La Estación is popular with businesspeople looking for an afternoon snack. Try the Chantilly hot chocolate or one of the delicious cheese platters while listening to tangos and old-time Colombian music.

More progressive cafes and roasters that source directly from the farms and use pour-over methods are opening all over Bogotá. In the far north in Usaquén, there's **Catación Pública** ★★, Calle 120a no. 3a–47 (www.catacionpublica.co; (*C*) **1/702-4943**; daily 9am–7pm), has one of the most extensive selections of single origin coffees, including green coffees from 22 different provinces. **Azahar** ★★, in a repurposed shipping container at Carrera 14 no. 93a–48 (www.azahar coffee.com; (*C*) **1/703-4799**; Mon–Sat 7am–8pm and Sun 1pm–8pm) usually has three or four single origin coffees at a time, brewed in all of the hipster favorite equipment like a Chemex, Siphon, or Hario V60. They hold weekly public cuppings on Saturdays at 10am.

Inside the Hilton hotel, **Devoción** ★, Carrera 7 no. 72–41 (www.devocion.com; (*C*) **1/600-6100**; daily 7am–9pm), resembles an 1890s New York pharmacy, but it serves 17 different varietals of Colombian coffee that they roast themselves and brew with all of the geekiest toys. They also have a cafe in Williamsburg, Brooklyn. **Salvo Patria**, Calle 54a no. 4–13 (www.salvopatria.com; (*C*) **1/702-6367**; Mon–Sat noon–11pm), which has now grown into a restaurant too, is owned by Juan Ortiz, who spent 8 years in Australia and wanted to recreate the Melbourne-style coffee bar in Bogotá.

Antiques & Jewelry

A couple of good antiques stores are **Anticuarios Gilberto F. Hernández**, Calle 79B no. 7–48 ((*C*) **1/249-0041**), in the Zona T neighborhood, and **Almacén de Antigüedades Leonardo F**, at Carrera 4 no. 12–34 ((*C*) **1/334-8312**), in Candelaria. There are also several antique shops in **Usaquén**.

Most shops selling emeralds are located around Carrera 6 between calles 12 and 13, the Centro Internacional.

Art Galleries

Bogotá has one of the great art scenes in Latin America, with galleries clustered in different neighborhoods all over town.

Meant to be the parking lot for the Muse do Arte del Banco de la República, however, it turned into **El Parquedero** (www.banrepcultural.org/el-parqueadero) at Calle 11 no. 4–21, and became a unique cultural venue of its own, holding frequent exhibitions.

For contemporary work from big names and promising rising artists, there's **Galería El Museo** (www.galeriaelmuseo.com), Calle 81 no. 11–41, and **La Cometa** (www.galerialacometa.com), Carrera 10 no. 94A–25. The three-level **Cero Galería**, Calle 80 no. 12–55, is home to large-format photography and paintings. In La Macarena, there's **Alonso Garcés Galería** (www.alonsogarces galeria.com), Carrera 5 no. 26B–92, which is the reincarnation of an avant-garde gallery that launched in the 1970s and maintains a loyal following. It has eight exhibitions each year focusing on painting, sculpture, and video, as well as a gallery store. **Galería Beta** (www.galeriabeta.com), Calle 75a no. 20c–52 in San Felipe, is more experimental and attracts a young crowd. **Dibs by Culture Shock**, at Carrera 3 #11–24, focuses on graffiti and street art, helping bring in edgy, young urban art into the limelight. There's also a design store on site.

Fashion

Colombian fashion icon (and Cartagena hotel owner) **Silvia Tcherassi's** Bogotá store, at Carrera 12 no. 84–17, is where to come for unique runway style dresses. **Studio F** (www.studiof.com.co), Calle 26 no. 62–47, sells sleek and silky womens-wear. **Amelia Toro** (www.ameliatoro.com), who now has stores in North America, sells her sophisticated seasonal collections from her store at Av. 82 no. 12–10.

If you happen to be here in March, you can attend events at Bogotá Fashion Week (www.bogotafashionweek.com.co), which showcases the city's and the country's top designers.

Handicrafts & Textiles

For handicrafts, try Carrera 15, between calles 74 and 77, the **Centro Internacional** (International Center), the **Centro Histórico** (Historic Center) and **La Plaza de los Artesanos**, located on Calle 63 at Carrera 50. Many handicrafts shops are found around La Candelaria and El Centro, though they're dominated by cheap, mass-produced souvenirs. For something of better quality, **Artesanías de Colombia** (www.artesaniasdecolombia.com.co) has several locations throughout Bogotá, including at Carrera 11 no. 84–12 (© **1/218-0672**). Decent flea markets are held in **Plaza Santander** in the city center (daily 9am–6pm at Calle 24 and Carrera 7) and in **Usaquén**, on Saturday and Sunday, in the parking lot at Carrera 5 and Calle 119. My favorite spot for handicrafts is **Mambe** ★, at Carrera 5 no. 117–25 (© **1/629-8880**), which sources fair-trade handicrafts from rural and indigenous communities around Colombia. Although the prices are a bit higher than at stores in the city center, no one will hassle you, and goods are of more authentic and decent quality.

Leather Goods

For discount deals, head to the Restrepo neighborhood. Quality leather goods can also be found in upscale shopping centers. Good leather stores include

Mario Hernández, which has several locations, including at **Unicentro** (© **1/ 213-0165**) and Carrera 68D no. 13–74 (© **1/292-6266**). Another good option is Julia Rodríguez, at Calle 81 no. 9–25 (© **1/249-5229**).

Markets & Malls

The main shopping areas are in Usaquén, **La Zona Rosa**, Carrera 15, Avenida de Chile, Carrera 13, Calle 53, and the Chapinero neighborhood. Some popular shopping centers are the American-style **Atlantis Plaza**, Calle 81 no. 13–05; the luxury-oriented **Centro Commercial Andino**, Carrera 11 no. 83–71; the 312 shops of **Unicentro**, Av. 15 no. 123–30; the huge and modern **Gran Estación**, Calle 26 no. 62–47; and **Hacienda Santa Bárabara**, Carrera 7 no. 115–60, which was once the property of a wealthy Bogotá family. The latter is a unique shopping center that has both a modern and colonial part built around a beautiful courtyard. Inside, you'll find high-quality boutiques and jewelry stores.

For budget shopping, try **San Andresito**, at Carrera 38 and Calle 12, where you can find more or less anything you're looking for. The shopping centers and stores around **San Victorino Square**, Carrera 10 and Calle 10, in the center of the city are also very cheap, with a great variety of clothing and handicrafts. However, the area can be a bit seedy, so try not to make your tourist status too obvious. *Tip:* Bargain hard around San Victorino, especially if it's obvious that you're not Colombian; otherwise you'll end up paying far too much.

ENTERTAINMENT & NIGHTLIFE

Bars & Pubs

Even though Bogotanos aren't known for their dancing abilities, they do enjoy an enviable nightlife. An active bar and club scene thrives in Usaquén, La Candelaria, La Zona Rosa, and Parque de la 93. Most bars and clubs get going around 11pm and close around 3am. In large clubs, you'll be expected to buy a bottle of liquor if you want to sit at a table; if you just want a shot or two, sit at the bar. Bogotanos dress up to go out, so make sure to look your best.

Bogotá's cocktail culture has progressed considerably in recent years. **The Apache Bar** on the roof of the Click Clack Hotel, Carrera 11 no. 93–77, attracts well-to-do crowds for the burgers, views, and stiff drinks. For gin, **Ocus**, Calle 69a no. 6–17, has several dozen types that are served alongside an eclectic menu. In Usaquén, **Huerta**, Carrera 7 Bis. no. 124–36, has an on-site garden with hundreds of herbs and botanicals that they use in their cocktails, which include tiki drinks and punches. **Black Bear**, at Carrera 11a no. 89–06, has some of the most professional mixologists in town serving original drinks and Colombian takes on classics like the Moscow Mule and Old Fashioned.

The Bogotá Beer Company is popular with the post-university yuppie crowd. It plays '80s and '90s rock beats and serves several varieties of beer produced in a nearby Bogotá beer distillery. All locations are popular with Bogotanos, but some of my favorites are on Carrera 12 no. 83–33 (© **1/603-071**), Carrera 11A no. 93–94 (© **1/621-9914**), Av. 19 no. 120–76 (© **1/215-5150**),

Carrera 6 no. 119–24 (© **1/620-8454**), Calle 85 no. 13–06 (© **1/256-6950**), and the Usaquén location.

The always-popular **Irish Pub** in La Zona T caters to a diverse crowd of Bogotanos and foreigners. One of the few places you'll find quite a few foreigners, the mojitos are excellent and the atmosphere is festive. This typical pub fills up early, so be sure to show up early if you want to get a much-coveted outside table. (Don't worry, there are heaters to warm you up on cold nights.)

If you want local booze hounds to take you around to their favorite spots, join a tour with **Bar Crawl Bogotá** (www.barcrawlbogota.com; COP$72,000 per person), which visits four bars in a night and includes VIP access and free shots.

Live Music Clubs

Owned by Guillermo Vives, the older brother of singer Carlos Vives, the restaurant and dancehall **Gaira Café** (www.gairacafe.co), Carrera 13 no. 96–11, has frequent cumbia and vallenato shows, as well as other lively performances of regional Colombian music.

Bolón de Verde, 1A no. 12b–20, at Plazoleta del Chorro de Quevedo in La Candelaria, has live jazz and blues, as does nearby **El Gato Gris**, Carrera 1A no. 12b–12.

Dance Clubs

Andrés Carne De Res ★★★ in Chía (see below), is considered the king of Bogotá nightlife by many. The kitschy steakhouse has expanded to cover an area of nearly three square miles and attracts thousands of people at a time. The owner opened another Andrés in La Zona T (see p. 59) that is divided into three floors (Heaven, Purgatory, and Hell), but a trip to the original is still definitely worth a visit—it's one of the most iconic nightlife experiences in Colombia.

In La Macarena, **El Bembe ★** (Calle 27B no 6–73) is a lively salsa bar that stays open late. Hipsters gravitate to **Armando Records**, at Calle 85 no. 14–46, which blasts electronic and rock music on multiple levels. At Parque de la 93, **Galeria Café Libro**, Carrera 11A–93–42 (www.galeriacafelibro. com.co; © **1/218-3435**), is one of the better salsa places in Bogotá and fills up Thursday to Saturday. They only play salsa here, so make sure you've polished up your moves. This rumbero caters to a 25-and-above crowd. Expect to be drenched in sweat upon leaving after a night of intense salsa dancing.

Punto G, at Calle 94 no. 11–46 (© **1/616-7046**), is another popular crossover club. It recently underwent a major renovation and is popular with the over-30 crowd. There's live music Wednesday through Saturday (featuring reggae, rock en español, salsa, and traditional Colombian beats), as well as a decent food selection. A night of partying at Punto G will also cost you, though.

Theater & the Performing Arts

Bogotá's premier performing arts venue is the grand **Teatro Colón**, Calle 10 no. 5–32 (www.teatrocolon.gov.co; © **1/284-7420**; Transmilenio: Museo del Oro), in La Candelaria. The theater seats nearly 1,000 spread out over five levels and

BOGOTÁ | Entertainment & Nightlife

hosts the most important concerts, plays, ballets, and operas in the city, if not the entire country. For tickets, call © **1/341-0475** or visit the website. Also in La Candelaria, **Centro Cultural Gabriel García Márquez**, Calle 11 no. 5–60 (www.fce.com.co), the oversized brick cultural complex designed by legendary Colombian architect Rogelio Salmona and named after Colombia's most famous author, occasionally has small performances like concerts and poetry readings.

Gay & Lesbian

Bogotá has a vibrant LGBT scene, with nightspots scattered around town. With 13 different adjoining bars and clubs, multilevel **Theatron** (www.portal theatron.co), Calle 58 no. 10–18, claims to be the largest disco in Latin America. Each space has a theme, like a German beer garden/rock club, a Mexican cantina, and a gothic cathedral, among others. With locations in Chapinero (Calle 62 no. 7–13) and the Zona Rosa (Carrera 14 no. 83–37), restaurant and bar **Estación** (www.estacioncafecolombia.com), open since 2003, has become one of the most popular gay hangouts in Bogotá. There are frequent theme nights and drink specials. The Chapinero location also has an attached terrace bar. Nightclub and bar **El Mozo** (www.elmozoclub.com), Calle 85 no. 12–21, is big and often crowded and sweaty, with DJs pumping house music until 3am.

Cinema

While you can find modern multiplexes all over town from **Cinemark** (www. cinemark.com.co) and **Cine Colombia** (www.cinecolombia.com/bogota), independent movies and most small Latin American productions are seen at **Cine Tonalá**, Carrera 6A no 35–27 (www.cinetonala.co).

SIDE TRIPS FROM BOGOTÁ

Chía ★

23km (14 miles) N of Bogotá

Chances are if you are coming to Chía, you are going to Andrés Carne de Rés, the enormous steakhouse—seriously big, like a small village—that has been continually expanding and filling up with kitsch since 1982. If you are just passing through, as many do on their way to Zipaquirá, you'll find a quiet rural town with a few good country-style restaurants that is slowly getting morphed into Bogotá's urban sprawl.

GETTING THERE

It's absolutely easiest to get to Chía and back by a 45-minute taxi ride, particularly late at night when they are lined up outside Andrés Carne de Rés until the sun rises. They cost anywhere from COP$55,000 to COP$90,000, depending on your negotiating skills and how late you are. Uber is also an option. Several La Candelaria hostels also set up roundtrip party bus transfers there on the weekends.

WHERE TO EAT

Andrés Carne de Rés ★★★ PARRILLA/STEAK   Owner and principal dreamer Andres Jaramillo has covered every inch of the nearly three-square-mile steakhouse with antiques and curios, one on top of the other, and so strung about with hanging lights that you have no idea what is really underneath.

Oh, they have food too. Nineteen pages of it, with countless cuts of Argentine and Uruguayan meat, *arepas*, and *ceviches*, which are cooked at a dozen or so open kitchens that fuse into the dance floors and dining rooms. There are hundreds of employees here, either working the kitchen, as waiters, or as performance artists singing songs, dressed as clowns, or passing out pageant sashes. As the night goes on and more bottles of *aguardiente* are brought to the table, the place becomes more and more debaucherous, with every corner turning into a dance floor. Even after the restaurant closes at 3am, there are outdoor stalls selling bone broth and sandwiches. For those who don't want to make the trip to Chía, a Bogotá location opened in 2010.

Calle 3 no. 11a–56. www.andrescarnederes.com. ✆ **1/863-7880.** Main courses COP$36,000–COP$70,000. Thurs–Sat 11am–3am; Sun 11am–midnight.

4 | Zipaquirá ★

48km (30 miles) N of Bogotá

Zipaquirá was home to a large Muisca population before being settled by the Spaniard Don Luis Henríquez in 1600. Often called Zipa, the rural town with a well-preserved colonial core surrounding a large cobblestone plaza makes for a popular day trip from the capital, particularly for its signature attraction, the Catedral de Sal, an underground church built in a 500-year-old salt mine. While it has a population of about 110,000, the most of any city in the *sabana* (savannah) surrounding Bogotá, it still feels quite compact and easy to get around, because most places of interest are in a relatively small area. If you're not going on to Villa de Leyva, staying in one of Zipa's small hotels for the night gives you a taste of life in a rural colonial town in the Andes, with none of the transportation hassles.

Semana Santa (Holy Week) festivities are particularly lively in Zipa, with passionate processions that see colonial relics marched through the streets of town, ending at the Salt Cathedral. It's also worth noting that Colombian writer Gabriel García Márquez lived here briefly and graduated from high school here in 1946.

GETTING THERE

BY BUS From Bogotá's Portal del Norte Transmilenio station, look for the buses marked Zipa, which depart about every 10 to 15 minutes and take 45 minutes to an hour, depending on traffic.

BY TRAIN The historic tourist locomotive known as the Tren de la Sabana (see p. 48), reaches Zipa in about three hours from Bogotá, then stops for one and a half hours before returning.

EXPLORING ZIPAQUIRÁ

Without question, Zipa's main attraction is on the hill above town, the spectacular **Catedral de Sal ★★★** (www.catedraldesal.gov.co; ✆ **1/852-3010**), open daily from 9:30am to 5pm. Admission is COP$50,000, and includes a guided tour. The massive salt deposits here have been exploited since the time of the Muisca, who traded it with different villages, and later by the Spanish. When Christianity arrived, the miners began hanging religious images on the walls for protection, which soon became a shrine. The first church in the mine was built in 1954, dedicated to Our Lady of Rosary, the patron saint of miners, and could hold 8,000 people. It was still an active mine, until it closed due to safety concerns in 1990. In 1995, a new, three-nave cathedral was built 60m (197 ft.) below the old one. At the entrance to the church are 14 small backlit chapels representing the Stations of the Cross. Masses occur on Sundays, and occasionally concerts are held here too. The entrance to the mine is on the hill above town, a short taxi ride from the center or a 20-minute walk.

The **Plaza de los Comuneros**, Zipa's large cobblestone plaza, is fringed with palm trees and a cathedral that dates to 1805. With the clay-tile roofs of the whitewashed houses and green hills off in the distance, it's a pleasant place for an afternoon stroll.

WHERE TO STAY & EAT

While most visitors to Zipa come for the day, it's an attractive enough town to stay the night. The 34-room **Hotel Camino de la Sal** ★ (www.hotelcamino delasal.com; ✆ **1/851-6159**; Carrera 4 no. 5–03; doubles from COP$120,000) is a modern hotel in the center. There's also the 23-room **Hotel Cacique Real de Zipaquirá** (www.hotelcaciquereal.com; ✆ **311/532-1251**; Carrera 6 no. 2–36; doubles from COP$107,000) in a two-level building with clay-tile roofs and a colonial courtyard. For dining, there are several good rustic restaurants that slow cook meat over open fire pits on the road to the Salt Cathedral, as well as numerous cafes and restaurants with typical foods in the historic center.

Laguna de Guatavita

57km (35 miles) NE of Bogotá

This 20-hectare crater lake, sacred to the Muisca people, is best known as the source of the myth of El Dorado. As the legend goes, when a Muisca *cacique* (chief) died, a nephew would be chosen to replace him. In that ceremony, the nephew would strip naked and be covered with mud and gold dust, then would be rowed out to the middle of the lake where gold and emeralds would be tossed in as a tribute. The lake was actually drained multiple times by the Spanish, who found very little of the treasure they had hoped to find. Cracks at the bottom are still evident. In 1856, a golden raft with the cacique on it, supposedly depicting the ritual, was found in a cave near Bogotá. Known as the Muisca Raft, it is perhaps the most important piece in the collection at the Museo del Oro, not to mention one of the most famous gold relics on earth. While direct access to the lake has been cut off, a trail around the crater gives a nice view. There is a COP$15,000 admission. There is a small restaurant on the way to the lagoon, as well as a snack kiosk at the entrance.

Although coming to Guatavita with your own transportation is possible, most tourists come on a day tour from Bogotá. **Via Colombia** (www.viacolombia. com), has private, 8-hour tours that include a visit to the Catedral de Sal in Zipaquirá (see p. 68), transportation, and lunch for COP$207,000 per person.

THE NORTHERN ANDES

by Nicholas Gill

I n the Colombian heartland, one of the first regions settled by the Spanish, the departments of Boyacá and Santander stretch out north from Bogotá in dramatic fashion. Lush green hills dotted with farmland suddenly turn into soaring snowcapped mountains, whose glacial melt feed whitewater rivers that have carved their way deep into the earth. The jagged terrain attracts countless adventure sport enthusiasts, who come here by the busload to raft, climb, and paraglide. When it is time to relax, cutesy colonial villages with their cobblestone streets and clay-tile roofs make for a nice break from the sweltering heat of the coast. Colombia's northern Andes were the birthplace of Colombian independence, as Simón Bolívar's ragtag army won decisive victories against the Spanish. You won't find beaches or ruins or jungles here, nor is there one main attraction to speak of. Yet, this is where Colombians come to get away from the big cities, to breath in the fresh country air and yes, even drink the local wine.

Before the arrival of the Spanish, this region was home to the Muisca and Guane, cultures whose gold collections inspired the myth of El Dorado, leading to a continent-wide conquest that would change the Americas forever. Later on, nationalists in the town of Socorro first stood up to Spanish rule, starting a movement for independence that lasted until the great liberator Simón Bolívar's army won the battles at Pantano de Vargas and Puente de Boyacá.

This region is paradise for the adrenaline seeker; many pro athletes come from around the region, not to mention the entire world, to experience the rush. In **San Gil** you can start your own X Games, taking part in almost every extreme sport imaginable. You can race downhill on mountain bikes, raft Class V rapids, and rappel down a gorge all in one day, then go horseback riding and bungee jumping the next. After you've ridden the teleférico down to the base and to the opposite rim at the remarkable **Chicamocha Canyon**, you can then paraglide over it, for one of the most breathtaking views you could ever imagine. With some of Colombia's highest mountains and

The Northern Andes

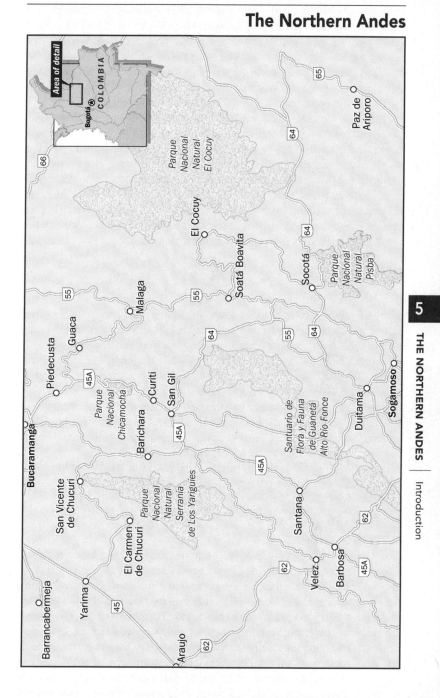

greatest shifts in altitude, the Northern Andes offer highly sought after hikes, like the 7-day circuit in **Parque Nacional Natural Cocuy** (if it ever reopens).

Colonial villages in this region seem like time capsules. Whitewashed houses with clay tile roofs line cobblestone streets where 500-year-old cathedrals and convents hover in the background. Towns like **Villa de Leyva** and **Barichara** have their colonial core almost entirely intact, yet unlike cities like Cartagena and Popayán, few foreign visitors know they exist.

Traditional Colombian cuisine is alive and well in this region. Ingredients like goat, guava, pork, beef, corn, and potatoes find their way into many dishes. Every town seems to specialize in a specific recipe. In **Sutamarchán** it's the skinny chorizos called *longaniza*. In Barichara it is *carne oreada*, a sun-dried cut of beef. In **Bucaramanga** it is *mute*, a hearty stew made from pork cheek and ribs, beef, corn, and potatoes. The big-bottomed *hormigas culonas* ants are a delicacy throughout the region, a tradition introduced by the Guane. They are usually roasted or fried and have a smoky, almost nutty flavor. You'll see them in markets around the region.

VILLA DE LEYVA ★★

162km (100 miles) NE of Bogotá

The perfectly preserved colonial town of Villa de Leyva (pop. 16,500) was named a national heritage site by the Colombian government in 1954, and ever since, it has become a popular weekend hangout for Bogotanos looking for a break from hectic city life. The town was founded in 1572 as a retreat for Spanish clerics and viceroys. Today the cobblestone streets, Spanish-style villas, and small-town pace give the town a charming, lost-in-time feel. Villa de Leyva and the surrounding countryside are among the safest places in Colombia to wander off the beaten track and do a bit of exploring—and with multiple waterfalls, a nearby desert, adventure-sport opportunities, and even a couple of vineyards, there's plenty of exploring to do.

Even though the Villa de Leyva's main sights can easily be explored in 1 day, most visitors end up staying at least 2 to 3 days, drawn in by the town's irresistible charm.

Essentials
GETTING THERE
Los Libertadores (© **1/423-3600**) offers two direct daily **buses** from the Bogotá bus station to Villa de Leyva, at 4:30am and 2:20pm. Trip time is about 4 hours. Several other bus companies also offer direct routes, especially on weekends and holidays, but they often stop for passengers along the way, making for a long ride. If you can't make one of these two routes, take one of the buses to Tunja, which depart every 5 minutes or so, and from Tunja you can catch a 45-minute **colectivo** to Villa de Leyva. (At the Tunja station, head upstairs, and then outside and board any of the large vans labeled VILLA DE LEYVA.) All buses and colectivos will drop you off 3 blocks from the main plaza in Villa de Leyva, walking distance from most hotels. If you have a lot

of luggage, you may want to consider taking a short taxi ride, especially if you're staying in one of the many farms or inns around town.

VISITOR INFORMATION

The Villa de Leyva tourist office is located right off the main plaza at Carrera 9 no. 13–04 (www.villadeleyva.net; © **8/732-0232**) and is open daily from 8am to 5pm. If you plan to be in town for at least a couple of days, you might want to invest in the English/French Villa de Leyva Tourist Guide, available for COP$12,000 at the tourist office and in some hotels.

TOUR OPERATORS

In addition to the sights listed below, walking tours and day trips into the Boyacá countryside are available with numerous tour companies. **Colombian Highlands**, Carrera 10 no. 21, Finca Renacer (www.colombianhighlands.com; © **8/732-1862**), is run by bilingual biologist Oscar Gilede and offers many eco- and adventure tours that can be done by car or horse, including hiking trips along Musica and Guane trails and trips to the Sierra Nevada de Cocuy. He also runs the clean Hostal Renacer (p. 75), a pleasant hostel where the office is located. Cycling agency **Ciclo Trip** (www.ciclotrip.com; ©**320/899-4442**), Carrera 9 no. 14–101, offers mountain-bike cross-country tours in the countryside outside of Villa de Leyva, including to waterfalls and wineries. They use Trek MTB bikes, which they also rent.

If you're looking for horseback-riding opportunities, contact **Hacienda Flamingo** (© **8/732-0538**; ask for Rafael Orejuela or Patricia Delgado). They rent out horses by the hour or day. Your hotel should also be able to provide you with information regarding horse tours, which usually run about COP$30,000 per hour.

At the bus terminal, taxis run tours to attractions outside of town, like El Fósil and Ráquira. Most roundtrips are around COP$150,000, but be prepared to negotiate.

Exploring Villa de Leyva

Villa de Leyva's main attraction is its large cobblestone square, the **Plaza Mayor ★★★**, one of the largest town plazas in all of the Americas. Anchored by just a small Mudejar fountain at its center, it is surrounded by beautifully preserved colonial buildings and the **Iglesia Parroquial De Villa de Leyva**, which was constructed in 1604 and where independence hero Antonio Nariño lived from 1823 to 1846.

Casa Museo de Antonio Nariño ★ MUSEUM   Here you'll find documents and items belonging to Antonio Nariño, who is known for helping to inspire Colombian independence—he even translated Thomas Paine's *The Rights of Man* into Spanish. The house was built in 1600, and the independence hero spent a few years here prior to his death.
Carrera 9 no. 10–21. © **8/732-0342.** COP$3,000. Thurs–Tues 8am–noon and 2–6pm.

Museo del Carmen ★ MUSEUM   One of the country's best collections of religious art (17th–20th c.) is here in this former convent. Inside are original paintings from Vásquez Ceballos, plus altarpieces and various other religious objects.
Plazoleta del Carmen. © **8/732-0214.** Admission COP$3,000. Sat–Sun and holidays 10:30am–1pm and 2:30–5pm.

Museo del Maestro Luis Alberto Acuña ★ MUSEUM   Located on the Plaza Mayor, this house museum is dedicated to the life and eclectic works of the eponymous artist. If the museum appears closed, simply knock and someone will let you in.

Plaza Mayor. ✆ **8/732-0422.** COP$2,000 adults, COP$1,500 children. Daily 9am to 6pm.

Waterfalls ★ NATURAL ATTRACTION   There are several waterfalls not far from town. Near Santa Sofía, the Paso del Angel, a narrow natural bridge, meanders near the 80m Guatoque waterfall. The 15m Cascada La Periquera, about 10km outside of town on the road to Alto de los Migueles, is accessed through an eco-park, where you can zipline and bungee jump. Admission is COP$5,000.

Where to Stay

Villa de Leyva has about 150 lodging options. Unless you're going to be in town in December, January, or during a holiday weekend, it should be pretty easy to find a hotel room—though since Colombia seems to have more holidays than any other country, it's best to book in advance. It's imperative that you make advance reservations during the Astronomical Festival in early February, Holy Week in March or April, Villa de Leyva's anniversary on June 12, the Gastronomical Fair in July, the National Kite Festival in August, the National Tree Festival in September, or the Festival of Lights in December. Most hotels and posadas here are charming, colonial-style places, so it's hard to make a bad hotel choice.

El Messon de los Virreys ★★   A contemporary vibe runs through this colonial house, which has been outfitted with an indoor pool and hot tubs in its courtyard. Much of the structure of the building remains and antique furnishings can be found throughout, though there are tasteful updates like tile floors and lounge chairs. The airy rooms with wood-beamed ceilings are less polished, though some rooms add private terraces and hot tubs.

Carrera 9 no. 14–51. www.hotelmesondelosvirreyes.com. ✆ **8/732-0252.** 30 units. COP$235,000 doubles, includes breakfast. **Amenities:** Restaurant; bar; indoor pool; hot tub; fitness center; free Wi-Fi.

Hospedería Duruelo ★★   This sprawling Spanish-style residence, a hotel since 1973, is surrounded by beautiful, well-kept gardens and spectacular views of Villa de Leyva and the surrounding countryside. Guest rooms are standard, if not particularly impressive, though a splurge on one of the suites will get you a great view of the orange thatched roofs, unspoiled nature, and impressive mountains of Villa de Leyva. As most hotels in Villa de Leyva are rather small, the addition of convention facilities, a pool, and several restaurants seem almost out of place. The full-service spa is the most complete in the region, containing a Jacuzzi, gym, sauna, Turkish baths, and treatment rooms.

Carrera 3 no. 12–88. www.duruelo.com.co. ✆ **8/732-0222.** 93 units. COP$393,000 doubles; COP$721,000–COP$980,000 suite. **Amenities:** 2 restaurants; bar; outdoor pool; full-service spa; fitness center; chapel; convention center; free Wi-Fi.

Hostería Molino La Mesopotamia ★   The town's former grain mill was built in 1568, 4 years before Villa de Leyva itself was founded, and for the last 50 or so years, it's been a hotel. The hotel is an easy 4-block walk from the main square, and it's one of the most unique stays in the area. The antique furnishings that adorn the guestrooms make it feel as if you are sleeping in history, a feeling that is enhanced by the dampness that sometimes seeps in at night.

Carrera 8 no. 15a–265. www.lamesopotamia.com. © **8/732-0235.** 32 units. COP$220,000 doubles, includes breakfast. **Amenities:** Restaurant; bar; free Wi-Fi.

Hostal Renacer ★   This ecofriendly hostel about 1km from town is run by biologist/environmentalist Oscar Gilede, who also runs tour agency Colombian Highlands, which keeps its office here. It's set in a beautiful, colonial-style farmhouse on a hill with beautiful views of the Villa de Leyva countryside. Both backpacker dorms and double rooms are available.

Carrera 10 no. 21. www.renacerhostel.com. © **8/732-1201.** 9 units. COP$135,000 doubles; COP$40,000 dorm beds. **Amenities:** Restaurant; bar; tour desk; bike rentals; BBQ area; free Wi-Fi.

La Posada de San Antonio ★   Set in three beautiful adjoining colonial houses on Plaza Nariño, this hotel maintains many of the original details, like the wood railings and original brick, to impart an authentic, worn-in feel. The rooms feature replica colonial artwork and antique furnishings that somehow don't feel out of place with the LCD TVs. Suites add extra living space and a fireplace. The maze-like property oozes with character in places like the reading room, with its stone hearth, and the garden-filled courtyards.

Carrera 8 no. 11–80. www.hotellaposadadesanantonio.com. © **8/732-0538.** 32 units. COP$319,000 doubles; COP$409,000 suites, includes breakfast. **Amenities:** Restaurant; bar; game room; art gallery; spa; free Wi-Fi.

Suites Arco Iris ★★   Perched up on a green hillside, this luxury property with a full-service spa is even quieter and more relaxed than town, which is just a few kilometers away. All units are suites and have unique layouts and decorations, including stained-glass windows that act as frames for larger windows that look out on the countryside. Each has a terrace or balcony with a hammock, though upgrades may add extra living space, kitchenettes, and private hot tubs.

2.5km NE of Villa de Leyva. www.suitesarcoiris.com. © **310/873-3121.** 26 units. COP$254,000 doubles, includes breakfast. **Amenities:** Restaurant; bar; full spa; fitness center; free Wi-Fi.

Where to Eat

For a small town, Villa de Leyva has a decent dining selection. Monday through Thursday, hours can be limited and many restaurants close down. When possible, call in advance to check hours.

Centro Gastronomico Casa Quintero ★ ECLECTIC   To the right side of the church on the Plaza Mayor is this colonial mansion that has been retrofitted to house a gourmet food court and several small, upscale restaurants. There's a rustic steakhouse called Mil977 and a Mexican restaurant called La Bonita, not to mention a bar and ice cream stand.

Calle 9 at Carrera 12, Plaza Mayor. Main courses COP$15,000–COP$45,000. Thurs–Tues 10am–11pm.

La Tienda de Teresa ★ COLOMBIAN   Here you can have *arepas* with almost anything you can imagine—cheese, chicken, beans, and even hamburger. It's open early, so it's one of the most popular cheap breakfast options in town. If you're here later in the day, try one of their great desserts, starting at COP$1,000. You can even leave your mark by signing the wall, as many visitors have.

Carrera 10 no. 8–72. © **316/542-0387.** Main courses COP$10,000–COP$20,000. Wed–Mon 9am–7pm.

Mercado Municipal ★★ COLOMBIAN   Mercado Municipal is the closest thing Villa de Leyva has to a hip, Bogotá-style restaurant. Enter into this colonial building that dates to 1740 and the first thing you'll see are black-and-white checkered tile floors and a wood-burning oven, where many of the dishes are cooked. On the wall is a blackboard listing updated comfort foods that focus on seasonal produce—think crispy duck salad, grilled octopus, sweetbreads, and artisan pizzas. Tables surround a central patio. Within the same building are Rosa Cremosa, a gourmet sweet shop, and Bolivár Social Club, a swanky cocktail bar.

Carrera 8 no.12–25. © **8/732-0299.** Main courses COP$15,000–COP$45,000. Wed–Mon 12:30–4pm and 7–10pm.

Rincón del Bachue ★ COLOMBIAN   This divey spot specializes in typical Boyacá dishes including *mazamorra chiquita* (well-cooked corn, often in a milky broth), *cuchuco de trigo con espinosa* (wheat/potato vegetable soup), and *cocido boyacense* (a sort of sampler platter that includes soup, potato, beef or pork, and rice). Rincón del Bachue has its own mini-greenhouse, a ceramics workshop, several dining rooms—including an outdoor eating area—and even offers guest rooms during high season.

Carrera 9 no. 14–9. © **8/732-0884.** Main courses COP$10,000–COP$20,000. Daily 8am–5pm.

Sybarita Caffe ★ CAFE   This hip coffeehouse focuses on geeked-out pour over methods (Chemex, French press, Siphons, etc.) and single-origin

---

pastries IN VILLA DE LEYVA

Villa de Leyva is well known for its charming, popular pastry shops. **La Galleta** ★, Calle 13 no. 7–03 (www.lagalleta.com.co; © 8/732-1213), is famous for its *milojas,* a typical Colombian dessert made with a cookie base, cream, and *arequipe* (dulce de leche). This cozy little coffee/dessert shop hosts jazz and blues musicians and is open from noon to 7pm on Monday to Friday and 9am to 9pm on Saturday, Sunday, and holidays. The newly opened **Tartas y Tortas**, right off the plaza (© 315/330-5032), is open Thursday to Tuesday from 10am to 8pm and makes low-fat, low-sugar desserts, in case you're watching your waistline. This comfortable pastry shop is owned by a friendly couple from Bogotá and specializes in Colombian desserts. Finally, **La Pasteleria Francesa**, Calle 10 no. 6–05 (no phone), owned by Frenchman Patrice Rio, bakes delicious bread and serves up a variety of quiches and European-style pastries, jams, and chocolates, and it is always crowded on weekends.

coffees from Cauca, Huila, Tolima, and Nariño. It's a good place to pick up bags of quality coffees to take home as gifts as well. A few cakes and baked goods are usually on offer.

Carrera 9 no. 11–88. ℂ **315/792-8857.** Baked goods COP$10,000–COP$20,000. Tues–Sun 10am–8pm.

Shopping

If you're in town on the weekend, be sure not to miss the Saturday market, when peasants from Villa de Leyva's rural sector come to town to sell their fruits and vegetables. The market is located 3 blocks from the main plaza, walking southeast toward the Hospedería Duruelo (see p. 74).

In the shops around the Plaza Mayor, look out for handwoven sweaters and *ruanas* (ponchos) made in surrounding villages. At **La Tienda de Feroz** (www.latiendaferoz.com; ℂ **317/435-5202**), Carrera 9 no. 14–101, you'll find unique gifts and designs inspired by Colombian nature, art, and culture.

Side Trips from Villa de Leyva

About 6km west of Villa de Leyva on the road to Santa Sofía, an area known for fossils, is the **Museo El Fósil ★** (www.museoelfosil.org; admission adult/child COP$6000/4000; daily 8am–6pm), which was built around the near-complete skeleton of a bus-size 115-million-year-old baby kronosaurus. It's the most complete specimen of this prehistoric alligator-like reptile. A few other glass cases house smaller fossils excavated in the area, though for the most part the kronosaurus takes up the entire room. Just across the main road, the more sophisticated **Centro de Investigaciones Paleontológicas ★** (ℂ **321/978-9546**; admission COP$8000 adult, COP$4000 child; Tues–Thurs 9am–noon and 2–5pm, Fri–Sun 9am–5pm) has a bigger display of fossils, which include a full plesiosaurus skeleton and saber-tooth tiger.

El Infiernito ★ (ℂ **310/235-6079**; admission COP$6,000; Tues–Sun 9am–noon and 2–5pm), 2km north of El Fósil, is one of the most important Muisca archaeological sites in Colombia. The site is home to more than a hundred stone phalluses standing vertically in two lines 9m from each, which allowed them to identify the planting season by measuring the shadows. When the Spanish discovered the site they found it improper, proclaiming that the Muisca should go to hell, hence the name.

The **Convento del Santo Ecce Homo ★** (admission COP$5,000; Tues–Sun 9am–5pm), 6km beyond Infiernito, is a stone-and-adobe building in various states of repair. It's full-on strange, with wonderful details like the stone floors paved with fossils and an original wooden ceiling with images of pineapples, suns, and moons that were carved to help convert the native population. The complex was built by Dominican fathers in the mid-17th century, though it was taken over by the military a century later and then abandoned. It has since been spruced up, though many of the original artifacts have been removed.

On the road to Ráquira, 14km west of Villa de Leyva, is **Sutamarchán ★**, which is known for its *longaniza*, a regional sausage similar to Portuguese *linguiça*, as well as *rellena* (blood sausage). Nearly the entire town is made up

too much of a good thing
PARQUE NACIONAL COCUY & THE U'WA

The Sierra Nevada del Cocuy is a mountain range containing more than a dozen peaks that reach beyond 5,000 meters in altitude. It's the highest section of the Colombian Andes and is home to some of the best hikes in South America. There are thundering waterfalls, blue mountain lakes, and rapidly disappearing glaciers, not to mention rich biodiversity that includes spectacled bears, pumas, and Andean condors. It's also the ancestral home of the U'wa, who live in constant spiritual communication with the mountains. Unfortunately, the entire 306,000 hectare **Parque Nacional Natural El Cocuy ★★**, including the signature 7-day circuit, has mostly been closed to visitors since late 2013. The combination of too much trash brought in by an increasing number of visitors and not enough supervision was having a terrible impact on the environment, pushing the government to close the park to ecotourism. Some park officials have been pushing for it to reopen, but the U'wa have resisted, insisting that they are the traditional authorities over the terrain. Until some sort of agreement is in place, all entrances to the park have been closed. Be sure to contact the national park offices (www.parques nacionales.gov.co) well in advance before planning any hikes in the park.

of open-air restaurants with these hanging sausages. The best are right in the center of town, around the corner from each other. There's **Robertico ★** (Carrera 2 no 5–135), which is more rustic, and the cleaner **El Fogata ★** (Carrera 5 no. 5–55). Both keep similar hours (daily 8am–8pm). From town you will see signs for several different wineries. The best known is **Viñedo Ain Karin ★★** (www.marquesvl.com), which produces the Marqués de Villa de Leyva label. While Colombia is not a typical wine destination, the area's unique microclimate allows for some production of cabernet sauvignon and sauvignon blanc. Rather than one harvest per year, they're able to have three harvests every 2 years. Tours (COP$10,000) are daily from 10am to 5pm and include a guided walk through the vineyards and facility, plus a tasting.

Another 10km beyond Sutamarchán is **Ráquira ★**, a village that thrives in making ceramics. Right on the main drag you'll see dozens of studios and shops where artisans are hard at work creating colorful bowls, cups, and piggy banks, as well as hammocks, ponchos, and carvings. There's a market on Sunday when you'll likely get the best deals.

Forty-five kilometers west of Villa de Leyva is **Chinquinquira ★**, the home to an image of the Virgin Mary that is credited with a 16th-century miracle. Painted around 1555 by Alonso de Narváez in Tunja, the painting wasn't well taken care of and began to fade. Eventually it was moved to Chiquinquirá and more or less forgotten, until a Sevillan woman named Maria Ramos found it and began praying to it. On December 26, 1586, as she prayed to it, the painting was suddenly restored to its original glory. The legend became famous and countless other miracles are attributed to it. Pope Pius VII even declared the Virgen de Chiquinquirá, nicknamed locally La Chinita, the patroness of Colombia. The chapel built to house the image now attracts pilgrims from all over Colombia.

BARICHARA ★★

321km (200 miles) NE of Bogotá; 120km (75 miles) S of Bucaramanga

Barichara, set on a hot, dry plateau, is sometimes called the most beautiful town in Colombia. The colonial town is paved with oversized reddish clay stones, and its clay-roofed houses are supported by whitewashed adobe walls, making it look as if it hasn't changed in 3 centuries; a reason why so many Colombian films and telenovelas are shot here.

The town, founded in 1741, is a place to come and relax. There isn't much to do but wander through the bohemian streets, stopping in to shops and cafes. It's more upscale than Villa de Leyva, though it sees far fewer tourists. Barichara also makes a good base for partaking in adventure sports in nearby San Gil. Cotrasangil (www.cotrasangil.inf.travel; © **7/724-2942**) has **buses** every 30 minutes between San Gil and Barichara, a 45-minute ride.

What to Do

Barichara's main attraction is its architecture. All of it is contained within a 12-by-12 grid of streets. On the **Parque Principal** is the **Catedral de la Inmaculada Concepción** (daily 5:45am–7pm), a huge, golden-hued 18th-century church with two towers that are illuminated in the night. Inside is a carved wooden ceiling and fluted columns. Also on the plaza is the **Casa de Cultura Emiliano Pradilla Gonzalez** (Wed–Mon 8am–noon and 2–6pm; admission COP$1,000), a colonial house with a small collection of fossils and Guane artifacts.

Several other interesting churches can be seen in town. The most attractive is **Capilla de Santa Barbara**, fronting a small plaza. There's also the **Capilla de Jesús Resucitado**, a partially restored chapel that lost part of its tower after being struck by lightning. Take note of the stone graves in the attached cemetery.

The paper factory **Fundación San Lorenzo** (www.fundacionsanlorenzo. wordpress.com), Carrera 5 no. 2–88; admission COP$2,500) gives tours of the process of making paper from fique, a fiber found in the leaves of a native plant.

The **Camino Real** is a 9km hike to the tiny village of Guane, a path through green pastures and fruit orchards that was once used by the indigenous Guane and later the Spanish. Most of the original stone path remains or has been restored. The walk begins at the rim of a canyon, mostly goes downhill and takes about two hours. Head out early, before the sun gets too hot. Bring water and sunscreen, though you'll be able to buy refreshments from a few fincas along the way. To reach the start of the trail, go to the north end of Calle 4 and look for the sign.

In the quiet town of **Guane**, you'll find a pleasant plaza with a church that dates to 1720, as well as a small archaeological and paleontological museum with Guane artifacts, a few fossils, and religious art. It's technically open daily from 8am to noon and 2 to 6pm, but you might need to ask around at the church for the caretaker. You can find buses back to Barichara around the plaza for COP$5,000.

Where to Stay & Eat

Casa Oniri Hotel Boutique ★ The owners of Casa Oniri have brought a colonial house into the 21st century to make a chic hotel. The standard rooms are smallish, with beamed ceilings painted white and little natural light, while suites add some much needed space. The bathrooms are clean and modern, with wood accents and stone floors. An old courtyard now forms the pool area.

Calle 6 no. 7–55. www.casaoniri.com. ⓒ **7/726-7138.** 12 units. COP$220,000 double; COP$500,000 suites, includes breakfast. **Amenities:** Restaurant; bar; outdoor pool; massage facilities; free Wi-Fi.

Color de Hormiga Reserva Natural ★

This finca is set on a 29-hectare private reserve on the outskirts of town off the Camino Real. The owner, a former chef, breeds *hormigas culonas*, the big-butted ants that are famously used in the region's cuisine. Rooms are simple yet cute, with wood floors and whitewashed walls. Countless terraces and patios make for good spots to sit with a book or binoculars (to search for hummingbirds). They also own a small hostel in the center of town with similar prices, which is also recommended.

Vereda San José, 1.5km from town. www.colordehormiga.com. ⓒ **7/726-7156.** 4 units COP$220,000 double; COP$500,000 suites, includes breakfast. **Amenities:** Restaurant; shared kitchen; patios; free Wi-Fi.

El Compa ★ COLOMBIAN

You'll find all sorts of restaurants in Barichara, from Italian to vegetarian to burgers, yet it can be hard finding a great local joint. That's where El Compa steps in. Expect a homey place serving straightforward regional recipes like *pescado frito* (fried fish), *carne oreada* (sun-dried beef), and *cabrito* (goat).

Calle 5 no. 4–48. No phone. Main courses COP$15,000–COP$30,000. Daily 8am–6pm.

Filomena ★ COLOMBIAN

In the courtyard of a quirky, colorful colonial house, this gourmet sandwich shop is one of my go-to spots in Barichara. It has a fun, friendly atmosphere with a small bar. The grilled sandwiches, served with chips and fries, are always on point.

Carrera 9 5 no. 6–34. ⓒ **315/455-9820.** Sandwiches COP$10,000–COP$20,000. Tues–Fri 6–10pm, Sat–Sun 1–10pm.

Tinto Hostel ★

Three blocks from the Parque Principal, Tinto Hostel attracts both backpackers and budget travelers, but don't expect a dive. This multi-level home is full of character and decorated with antique furnishings and artistic touches. The individually decorated rooms all feature vaulted ceilings and clay tile floors.

Carrera 4 no. 5–39. www.tintohostel.com. ⓒ **310/280-0218.** 6 units. COP$125,000 double; COP$40,000 dorm beds, includes breakfast. **Amenities:** Shared kitchen; tour desk; free Wi-Fi.

SAN GIL ★

95km (60 miles) from Bucaramanga

This quaint, 300-year-old town is charming enough, but there was little reason to come here until a couple of decades ago, when adventure sport enthusiasts began descending upon the mountain hamlet. Today San Gil is the adventure sport capital of Colombia, and many adrenaline focused travelers plan their entire trips to Colombia around what they can do here. Rafting, kayaking, hiking, paragliding, mountain biking, caving, rappelling, paragliding, and many other dangerous (yet for some reason appealing) activities can easily be arranged through the many operators that call San Gil their base.

The town itself has little going on other than **Parque El Gallineral** (daily 8am–6pm; admission COP$6,000), a 4-hectare park on an island in the Río Fonce, where thousands of trees drip with Spanish moss. There are a few short trails, a pool, and some small cafes.

Essentials

On the highway between Bogotá (6 hr.) and Bucaramanga (2½ hr.), frequent **buses** reach San Gil from most major cities on the Caribbean coast and central Andes. The Terminal Principal is located 3km west of town (a COP$4,000 taxi ride). Buses for Parque Nacional Chicamocha depart every 20 minutes or so during the day and take about an hour.

For tourist information, your best bet is with one of the agencies, though keep in mind they'll likely be trying to sell you something. There are several ATMs in town, as well as a tourist police station at Carrera 11 at Calle 7.

Outdoor Activities

BIKING Following whitewater rafting, mountain biking on the hot, dry, jagged terrain is San Gil's favorite sport. The Suarez and Chicamocha canyons offer spectacular downhill rides, passing waterfalls and remote farming villages. The Suarez Canyon ride passes through Yariguíes National Park and Barichara, while the Chicamocha ride ends in a natural spring.

Colombian Bike Junkies (www.colombianbikejunkies.com; ✆ 316/327-6101), Calle 12N no. 12–35, offers day rides for COP$250,000 on either route, as well as multi-day, multi-sport tours that add rafting, hiking, and rappelling.

BUNGEE JUMPING A 70m-high bungee jump has been set up over the Rio Fonce, 2km from San Gil on the road to Charalá. It's open daily 9am to 5pm and operated by Colombia Bungee Jumping (www.bungee.co; ✆ **300/770-9700**; COP$70,000 per jump).

CAVING Outside of San Gil, several extensive cave networks can be found. The most famous is the Cueva del Indio, where 1.6km hikes through the galleries end with a 4m jump into a natural pool. Colombia Rafting (see p. 82) offers 2-hour excursions into the cave, as well as to the Yeso and Vaca caves near Curiti.

PARAGLIDING There's no more spectacular view of the Chicamocha canyon or surrounding countryside than from the air. Thirty-minute tandem paragliding trips are offered by **Parapente Chicamocha** (www.parapente chicamocha.com; ✆ **318/745-9955**), Carrera 7 no. 7–33.

RAFTING/KAYAKING If you had to narrow down San Gil to a single sport (which would be silly), it would whitewater rafting. You can take on three different rivers, each resulting in a completely different experience. The Rio Fonce is the original and most popular river rafted in the region. It's family friendly and suitable for beginners. The 10km trip, lasting about 1½ hours, features Class I–III rapids. The Rio Chicamocha is for more experienced rafters, with Class II–IV rapids and dramatic canyon scenery. Most rafting trips on the Chicamocha last just a few hours, though some operators can set up longer, multi-day segments with camping or hotels in small towns along the route. The most intense whitewater near San Gil is found on the Rio Suarez, which has Class IV–V rapids. Depending on the operator, prices range from about COP$40,000 per person for a short excursion on the Rio Fonce to COP$130,000 for the Rio Suarez. Trips include transportation and lunch.

Colombia Rafting Expeditions (www.colombiarafting.com; ☏ **311/291-2870**), Calle 12 no. 8–32, is the preferred rafting agency and has been operating rafting, kayaking, and hydro-speed tours in the region for years.

Where to Stay

Most of the hotels in San Gil's center are hostels, though most do have private rooms as well as dorm beds. There are more upscale properties on the outskirts of town, though many non-budget travelers prefer to stay in Barichara, which has an all-around better atmosphere and is still close enough to San Gil to partake in activities.

Hotel Boutique Wassiki Campestre ★ This all-suite countryside lodge, just a few kilometers out of town, is one of the better value properties in San Gil. The rustic-chic rooms, all with balconies or patios strung with hammocks, feature wood-beamed ceilings and clay tile floors. There's an outdoor pool with nice views of green farmland, plus a full-service restaurant. A variety of adventure sport tours can be booked at reception.

Vía San Gil-Bogotá Km 3, Pinchote. www.hotelwassiki.com. ☏ **320/323-1322.** 15 units. COP$195,000 suites, includes breakfast. **Amenities:** Restaurant; bar; tours; outdoor pool; hot tub; free Wi-Fi.

Sam's VIP Hostel ★ From the same owner as **Sam's Gastropub ★** (see below), this laidback hostel with a mix of private rooms and dorm beds is one of the most consistent accommodations in San Gil's center. Like a hostel, it's a very communal place, with travelers hanging out at the bar. But unlike a hostel, it has extras like a rooftop pool and sauna.

Carrera 10 no. 12–33. www.samshostel.com. ☏ **310/249-7400.** 8 units. COP$85,000 double w/shared bathroom; COP$110,000 double w/private bathroom; COP$32,000 dorm bed, includes breakfast. **Amenities:** Bar; tours; outdoor pool; sauna, guest kitchen; free Wi-Fi.

Where to Eat

San Gil is a good place to sample regional Santander specialties like *hormigas culonas* (big-butted ants), *changua* (milk soup with egg), *arepa Santandereana* (arepas with bits of pork), and *carne oreada* (sundried beef). Check the food stalls at the Plaza de Mercado, at Carrera 11, where you will find tasty food stalls serving *arepas*, tamales, and various local snacks.

El Zaguán ★ COLOMBIAN   Near the market, this no-frills spot makes the best arepas and empanadas in town, stuffed with ingredients like chicken, sausage, chorizo, or avocado. They have been open for more than three decades.
Calle 13 no. 10–35. ✆ **310/724-2173.** Main courses COP$8,000–COP$20,000. Daily 9am–1pm.

Gringo Mike's ★ INTERNATIONAL   A gringo from Seattle named Mike has created what might possibly be the most popular restaurant in San Gil. Inside the colonial house is a menu of U.S. West Coast–style food, primarily gourmet burritos, sandwiches, burgers with breads and tortillas from their in-house bakery. There are also cheese fries, seriously awesome sticky buns, and milkshakes.
Calle 12 no. 8–35. www.gringomikes.net. ✆ **7/724-1695.** Main courses COP$16,000–COP$30,000. Daily 3–10pm.

Sam's Gastropub ★ STEAKHOUSE   From the owner of Sam's VIP hostel, this meat-centric restaurant is set in a colonial courtyard decorated with knick-knacks. Steaks are the specialty and come with a choice of sauce like mustard, mushroom, or even one made from the fat-bottomed Santander ants. There are also burgers, BBQ ribs, and a short list of Colombian microbrews.
Calle 12 no. 8–71. www.samshostel.com/our-restaurant. ✆ **310/249-7400.** Main courses COP$22,000–COP$35,000. Daily 7:30am–10pm.

Side Trips from San Gil

Parque Ecólogico Juan Curi ★   About 40 minutes from San Gil on the road to Charalá is this small eco-park, home to the stunning 180m-high Juan Curi waterfall, which has a natural pool at its base. Tour operators in town can set up rappelling off the rock face beside it. There is a small restaurant within the park.
22km from San Gil on the road to Charalá. www.lascascadasdejuancuri.com. ✆ **311/489-3272.** Admission COP$4,000.

Parque Nacional Chicamocha ★★ NATIONAL PARK   Open since 2006, this one-of-a-kind national park on the edge of the canyon of the Río Chicamocha is home to countless attractions. Some of them are spectacular; some of them are unnecessary. First, the spectacular: The mirador and its dramatic view of the canyon below are only topped by the 6.3km *teleférico* (cable car) that runs to the base of the canyon and up to the top of the opposing rim. You can also go paragliding here over the canyon (COP$180,000 per 20–30 min.), though you'll find better prices from agencies in San Gil. Much of the rest of the park attractions can be skipped: the waterpark, ostrich farm, 4D theater, and dune-buggy rides. There are several restaurants on site.
Km54 Via Bucaramanga–San Gil. www.parquenacionaldelchicamocha.com. COP$17,000 adult, COP$11,000 child. Wed–Fri 10am–6pm, Sat–Sun 9am–6pm.

BUCARAMANGA ★

Founded in 1622, Bucaramanga has ballooned to become one of the largest cities in Colombia, with a metro population of more than 1.2 million people. Nicknamed Buca, the capital of the department of Santander is set on a plateau surrounded by the peaks of the Cordillera Oriental. The energy sector and footwear industry provide a growing number of jobs here, giving Buca a thriving middle class and quite a few uninteresting skyscrapers. There are many malls, comfortable hotels, and great nightlife, makings the city nice enough to stay for a day or two before setting off to San Gil or Barichara, as most do.

Essentials

GETTING THERE

BY PLANE   Palonegro International airport sits on a hill 30km west of the city center. **Avianca** (www.avianca.com) has flights to most large cities in Colombia, while **LATAM** (www.latam.com), **Aero Mexico** (www.aeromexico.com), and **Copa Airlines** (www.copaair.com) connect to regional destinations like Panama City and Mexico City. Taxis to the center from the airport run about COP$40,000.

BY BUS   The **Terminal de Transportes** (www.terminalbucaramanga.com) is in the southwest corner of the city. Most long-distance routes are run by **Copetran** (www.copetran.com.co), which has direct service to Bogotá (10 hr.), Cartagena (13 hr.), and Santa Marta (11 hr.). Smaller companies have frequent service to regional destinations like San Gil (1½ hr.) and Barichara (3 hr.).

What to Do

Museo Casa de Bolívar ★ MUSEUM   This is more like Simón Bolívar's timeshare than his actual house, as he only stayed in this colonial mansion for about 70 days in 1828. On display are an interesting collection of documents from Bolívar's time, as well as artifacts from the Thousand Days' War and from Guane culture. Calle 37 no. 12–15. COP$2,500. Mon–Fri 8am–noon and 2–6pm, Sat 8am–noon.

On the **Ruitoque Mesa** overlooking the city, conditions are good for paragliding year round. **Colombia Paragliding** (Via Mesa Ruitoque Km 2; www.colombiaparagliding.com; © **312/432-6266**) offers tandem rides from COP$60,000, as well as 10-day learn-to-fly courses and instructor training. They'll also set up flights in Chicmocha and launch spots farther afield.

Where to Stay & Eat

The **Mercado Central**, Calle 34 at Carrera 16, is surprisingly clean and well organized, almost like a European market. You'll find hundreds of different varieties of native fruits on display. Up on the fourth floor is a food court with inexpensive set meals and regional delicacies.

Mercagen ★★ STEAKHOUSE   One of the best all-around steakhouses in Colombia, Mercagen has few gimmicks, just good cuts of beef grilled to order. *Lomo fino* is the prize cut, though there are also regional cuts like the sundried oreada and *morilla*, the hump of the Cebu cow. Goat, fish, and burgers are also on the menu. The first location opened in 1999, and there are now more than a dozen branches in the area, including most of the shopping centers in town. Carrera 33 no. 42–12. www.mercaganparrilla.com. © **7/632-4949.** Steaks COP$25,000– COP$45,000. Daily 11:30am–11pm.

Mia Nonna ★ ITALIAN   There are dozens of Italian restaurants in Bucaramanga, but Mia Nonna stands above the pack. It's more chic than the typical Bucaramanga restaurant, with exposed bricks, subway tiles, and hanging Edison lightbulbs. The menu goes beyond classics, with a long list of thin crust pizzas and house made pastas, as well as grilled octopus. The wine list is above average for the city, though cocktails are the real libation here. Carrera 35 no. 52–97. www.mianonna.co. © **318/344-1824.** Steaks COP$22,000– COP$42,000. Daily noon–1am.

Tamarindo Hotel ★   In lively Cabecera, this small design hotel is Bucaramanga's most original property. The individually decorated rooms are quirky and colorful, with inspiring quotes painted on the walls and mosaic-tile bathrooms. A second-level terrace opens onto the interior courtyard. Less than the price of the midrange chains, it's an excellent value. Carrera 34 no. 46–104. www.hoteltamarindobucaramanga.com. © **7/643-6502.** 7 units. COP$200,000 double, includes breakfast. **Amenities:** Restaurant; free Wi-Fi.

Tryp by Wyndham Bucaramanga ★   Set in a contemporary brick building in the commercial heart of the city, Tryp's Bucaramanga property, with its industrial-chic gastro bar and reclaimed-wood tables feels more like a boutique hotel than an international chain. The stylish rooms, most with balconies, have wood floors and are painted in bright shades of yellow and purple. Carrera 38 no. 48–66. www.hoteltrypbucaramanga.com. © **7/643-3030.** 67 units. COP$280,000 double, includes breakfast. **Amenities:** Restaurant; bar; free Wi-Fi.

Side Trips from Bucaramanga

Though it's just 9km from Bucaramanga, the tiny town of **San Juan de Girón ★** on the banks of the Río de Oro seems like another country. While Bucaramanga is big and brash, this laidback bohemian village, which dates to 1631, is full of stone bridges, whitewashed houses, and cobblestone streets. Until the 19th century, it was actually bigger and more important than Bucaramanga. Today there are several colonial churches and plazas, including the Catedral del Señor de los Milagros on the Parque Principal, which dates to the mid-1600s.

Nightlife

Bucramanga has one of Colombia's great nightlife scenes, rivaling larger cities like Bogotá and Medellín. For craft beer, there's the pub and sports bar **Birreria 1516**, Carrera 36 no. 43–42, which stays open until 3am on the weekends. There are around 30 types of beer, both on draught and in bottles available. **Saxo** (www.saxopub.com), Carrera 27 no. 42–53, an Irish pub, is also a popular drinking spot. **Vintrash**, Calle 49 no. 35A–33, is a popular dance bar with top DJs spinning house, electronic, and alternative tunes to a crowd of hipsters.

CARTAGENA & THE CARIBBEAN COAST

by Caroline Lascom

I t's hard not to fall for Cartagena. Colombia's Caribbean jewel stuns in an instant and will keep you mesmerized for a lifetime. The most beautifully preserved colonial city in the Americas, Cartagena is where pre-Columbian legends, colonial majesty, and tropical sensuality create a romantic dreamscape that rarely lapses into cliché. Over the course of 400 epic years, conquistadors, liberators, pirates, priests, and ghosts have all left an imprint on the ravishing and sultry city that stirred Gabriel García Márquez to Nobel Prize–winning fame and fortune.

Along Cartagena's old town streets, magical realism seems to imbue every moment. There are the taut, sinewy vendors who haul carts improbably stacked with exotic fruits along streets where pastel-hued colonial homes are draped with psychedelic bougainvillea. There's the clip clop of horses' hooves on the cobblestones below your window as you drift off to sleep, and there are sunset strolls along the 17th-century city's walls, as pelicans soar overhead.

For all her tourist cachet, Cartagena is a city that remains remarkably true to herself, a place where high style and real life—with all the grit and chaos that goes with it—coalesce.

Behind magnificently carved wooden doors with gargantuan doorknobs, grandiose mansions with lush arcaded patios have been converted into gorgeous boutique hotels. The sounds of salsa drift around every corner, but as night falls Afro-Caribbean drumbeats erupt in the city's squares. There are dazzling gold artifacts that escaped Spanish plunder, gilded churches, haute cuisine, and contemporary art galleries that would not be out of place in New York's Nolita. But there are also edgy murals emblazed on crumbling buildings, earthy street food sold off the back of a cart, and sinister vultures that stare down from red-tiled rooftops. Just when you think that Cartagena may be almost too perfect, there's a gratifying hint or reminder that she is a city all too real.

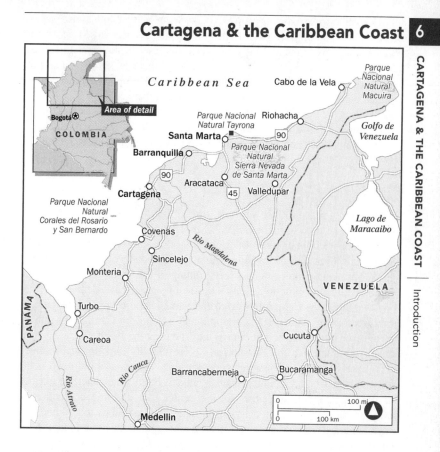

Caribbean Sea

Cabo de la Vela

Parque Nacional Natural Macuira

Bogotá

Area of detail

COLOMBIA

Parque Nacional Natural Tayrona

Santa Marta

Barranquilla

Riohacha

90

Golfo de Venezuela

Parque Nacional Natural Sierra Nevada de Santa Marta

Aracataca

45

Valledupar

Cartagena

90

Parque Nacional Natural Corales del Rosario y San Bernardo

Covenas

Rio Magdalena

Sincelejo

Lago de Maracaibo

Monteria

VENEZUELA

PANAMA

Turbo

Careoa

Cucuta

Rio Cauca

Barrancabermeja

Bucaramanga

Rio Atrato

Medellin

0   100 mi
0   100 km

While Cartagena has (quite rightly) always stolen the limelight, travelers are now beginning to explore regions that remained off limits to travel for decades due to right wing paramilitary and guerrilla violence. From the ethereal landscapes of the remote La Guajira Peninsula to the wild beaches and foreboding jungles of the Darién Gap, **Colombia's Caribbean coastline** is an embarrassment of riches. On the western Caribbean, the breathtaking islands of San Bernardo satisfy even the most seasoned traveler's Caribbean island fantasies. Farther west, the end of the road before the Panamanian border, the Afro-Caribbean towns of Sapzurro and Capurganá summon wild-at-heart travelers looking to get off the beaten path and immerse themselves in nature.

Santa Marta, the oldest colonial city in the Americas, is in the throes of a renaissance and makes a lively base to explore the heart-stopping landscapes of **Tayrona National Park**. Where jungle-draped mountains plunge into crystalline Caribbean waters, Tayrona is one of the most captivating landscapes on the continent. The arduous 5-day hike to Ciudad Pérdida, or the "Lost City"—touted as an archaeological site to rival Machu Picchu—leads to a series of evocative ruins encroached by dense jungle that will leave you utterly spellbound. In the Sierra Nevada de Santa Marta Mountains, you can breathe crisp mountain air and feel the holistic vibe of charming Minca, where coffee plantations carpet lush hills and waterfalls cascade into crystalline rivers surrounded by butterflies and birdlife. The Magdalena River oozes like time itself through the UNESCO-protected streets of **Mompox**, a 16th-century colonial gem where mule carts are more common than cars.

Straddling the boarder with Venezuela, **La Guajira**—the ancestral home of the Wayúu people—are Colombia's badlands. Within this ethereal landscape, massive sand dunes and beaches cast in every conceivable shade of gold and brown drop into a brilliant blue ocean.

CARTAGENA ★★★

Cartagena is a place to lose yourself, to give into the timeless magic of the moment. Certainly, within the UNESCO-protected city walls there are a clutch of captivating landmarks and fine museums that should not be missed, but Cartagena's allure lies in strolling without an agenda through the old town's irresistibly photogenic colonial streets; dining in one of its stylish, romantic restaurants; and reveling in the city's music, art, and theatrical street life.

Within the walls, **Centro Histórico** and **San Diego** form the colonial neighborhoods that are almost 100% restored and account for Cartagena's pulling power (even during the height of civil unrest during the 1990s, Cartagena was considered a safe haven). At sunrise, before the city stirs and cabs careen down streets barely wide enough for a fat goat, Cartagena's old town is the closest it gets to a 16th-century Spanish fantasy. Pretty much unchanged since the time of Don Quixote, the historic center is a dazzling confection of 400-year-old plazas, ornate palaces, churches, and mansions in a rainbow of colors. Just a 10-minute walk east, the up-and-coming neighborhood of **Getsemaní**, a district that once bristled with a lurid edginess, is now Cartagena's most dynamic quarter with crumbling colonial buildings recast as cool galleries, boutique hotels, and hip restaurants. This is where one of the city's most storied dance halls, Café Havana, is located.

While no one should come to Cartagena for a beach holiday, the most popular stretch of sand (within the city) for tourists and locals is **Bocagrande**, a curling slip of a peninsula that is comparable to Panama City. Just a short cab ride from the old town, this once-elite enclave has fallen out of favor over the last few years as Colombia's trendsetters have begun to turn their attention to the old town. Monolithic condo buildings, apartments, and hotels (in various states of health) stand sentinel along a brown sand beach where fisherman haul their catch and kids play soccer—it's fun, but it's a far cry from Caribbean bliss. For that, you'll need to take a 45-minute boat ride to the **Rosario Islands**, a gorgeous archipelago of white sands and translucent waters cast in impossible shades of blue.

The exclusive neighborhood of **Manga**, a 15-minute taxi ride from the old town, is home to Cartagena's yacht club and the departure point for many boats and yachts heading to the Rosario Islands and Islas San Bernardo.

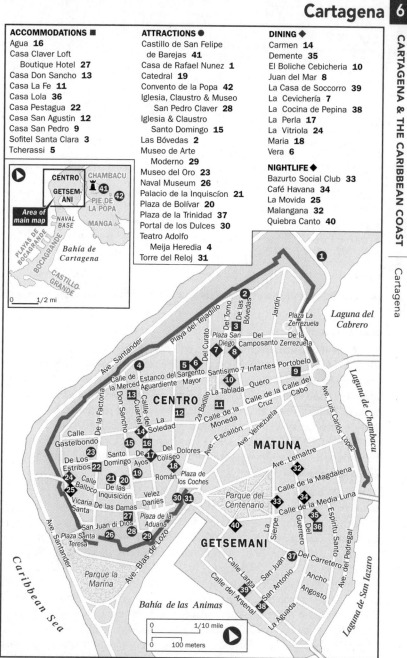

ACCOMMODATIONS ■
Agua **16**
Casa Claver Loft
  Boutique Hotel **27**
Casa Don Sancho **13**
Casa La Fe **11**
Casa Lola **36**
Casa Pestagua **22**
Casa San Agustin **12**
Casa San Pedro **9**
Sofitel Santa Clara **3**
Tcherassi **5**

ATTRACTIONS ●
Castillo de San Felipe
  de Barejas **41**
Casa de Rafael Nunez **1**
Catedral **19**
Convento de la Popa **42**
Iglesia, Claustro & Museo
  San Pedro Claver **28**
Iglesia & Claustro
  Santo Domingo **15**
Las Bóvedas **2**
Museo de Arte
  Moderno **29**
Museo del Oro **23**
Naval Museum **26**
Palacio de la Inquisición **21**
Plaza de Bolívar **20**
Plaza de la Trinidad **37**
Portal de los Dulces **30**
Teatro Adolfo
  Meija Heredia **4**
Torre del Reloj **31**

DINING ◆
Carmen **14**
Demente **35**
El Boliche Cebicheria **10**
Juan del Mar **8**
La Casa de Soccorro **39**
La Cevichería **7**
La Cocina de Pepina **38**
La Perla **17**
La Vitriola **24**
Maria **18**
Vera **6**

NIGHTLIFE ◆
Bazurto Social Club **33**
Café Havana **34**
La Movida **25**
Malangana **32**
Quiebra Canto **40**

RUMBA chiva

Because several of the city's main sites are spread out from the old town, you may want to take a *chiva* or carriage tour to get the most out of your time. For a uniquely Colombian experience and to get the lay of the land, try the colorful *chiva* (traditional bus) city tours, which depart at 1:30pm from Barrio Laguito neighborhood (around COP$7,000 by taxi from the walled city). The 4-hour tour costs COP$50,000, which is a good deal, because it includes admission to the Castillo de San Felipe de Barejas and Convento de la Popa. If you are not intent on partying too much at ground level, the nighttime chivas (COP$45,000, pick up from Barrio Laguito at 8pm) provide a memorable oversight of Cartagena at night. In addition, you'll get an unlimited amount of national liquor (*aguardiente*, local rum, and other fire waters), a taste of typical Cartagena fried treats (yuca, plantain, *arepa*), a live band onboard, and a demonstration of traditional Colombian folkloric dances. You'll be dropped off at a beachside nightclub around 10:30pm, where you can choose to stay or go back to your hotel at around midnight. Sure it's hot and it's cheesy, but it's a riot, and you're guaranteed to make new friends.

Your hotel will be able to provide (and even book) *chiva* and carriage tours, or you can inquire at the tourism office (see below). If you decide to opt for a more romantic horse-drawn carriage tour, that should cost around COP$75,000 (per hour) depending on the length of your trip and how well you can negotiate.

Essentials

VISITOR INFORMATION   Cartagena's main tourist offices are located in La Plaza de La Aduana (Casa del Marqués del Premio Real; www.cartagenadeindias. travel; ✆ **5/660-1583**; Open Mon, Wed, Thurs–Sat 8am–7pm, Tues 8am–12pm, 2pm–4pm, Sun 9am–5pm), east of the Torre de Reloj, and at Rafael Núñez International Airport. Both offices are efficient, helpful, and provide maps and information (in Spanish and English). Small tourist information kiosks are located at Plaza San Pedro Claver, Plaza de los Coches, and Centro de Convenciones de Cartagena (Open Mon–Sat 9am–1pm and 4–8pm, and Sun 9am–5pm).

WHEN TO GO   While Cartagena is a year-round destination, the optimum time is December to late April, when daily temperatures range from upper 70s to the high 80s, and breezes provide respite from the intense humidity. Hotel reservations within the walled city are always advised, but essential during Christmas, Easter, and **New Year's Eve**, when hotel rooms sell out up to 6 months in advance. With fireworks, outdoor concerts, block parties, and salsa dancing on the city's 16th-century walls, New Year's Eve in Cartagena is simply unforgettable. The party just keeps on going. The first weekend after New Year's Day, the **Storyland Festival**—the biggest electronic dance music festival in Latin America—takes place at various venues across the city and draws big-name DJs, including David Guetta, Sasha, and Tiësto.

Most of the city's most illustrious cultural events occur from January to March. The **Hay Festival** (www.hayfestival.com), pronounced "*ai*" in Spanish, is held in late January, with readings, lectures, educational programs, and seminars, held at the gorgeous Teatro Heredia (**El Teatro de Adolfo Mejia Heredia ★**, see

p. 95); previous attendees have included writers Hanif Kureishi, Lionel Shriver, and Gonçalo Tavares. In late February/early March, Cartagena hosts the **Festival International de Cine de Cartagena de Indias** (www.ficcifestival.com), one of the oldest film festivals in Latin America, which presents an eclectic series of Latin American short and feature length movies and documentaries that spotlight an intriguing mix of the up-and-coming Colombian movie industry talent.

Getting There

BY PLANE   Cartagena's Rafael Núñez Airport (airport code CTG; www. sacsa.com.co; ✆ **5/666-6610**) is located 3km (about 2 miles) from the historic old town. Apart from lengthy immigration lines (which you bypass if have young children in tow), the clean, efficient airport is (generally) a smooth and pleasant experience. Cartagena is serviced by several North American carriers (see "Planning," chapter 12), as well as national carriers **Avianca** (www.avianca. com) from New York (Wed, Fri, Sun) and Miami (daily) as well as Panamanian carrier **Copa** (www.copaair.com), via Panama City (code share with United; one of the best deals around for redeeming miles). Within Colombia, Avianca and **LATAM Colombia** (www.latam.com) offer frequent daily flights from Bogotá, Cali, Medellín, and Barranquilla. Low cost local airline **Viva Colombia** (www.vivacolombia.co) offers fares (less than COP$80,000, one way) from Cartagena to Medellín, Bogotá, Cali, and Pereira.

The short 10-minute taxi ride from the airport to the old town will set you back around COP$13,000 (more at night); to Getsemaní around COP$18,000. You buy your ticket from the official taxi kiosks just outside the baggage claim area, but pay your driver directly. While a de facto set-fare system is employed and rarely abused in Cartagena, it's always sound policy to confirm the rate before you get in the cab.

BY BUS   Buses depart from the main airport terminal every 15 minutes for the old town and cost COP$2,000. Long-distance buses arrive at the Terminal de Buses, on the eastern end of the city; you're better off taking a taxi to your hotel (around COP$22,000). While taking a bus to travel the Atlantic coast can be cost- and time-effective, a bus trip from Medellín will run around 13 hours (from COP$85,000), 19 hours from Cali (COP$90,000), and 21 hours from Bogotá (COP$97,000). **Brasilia** (www.expresobrasilia.com/en) and **Copertran** (www.copetran.com.co) provide good service and comfort, and, if you can navigate in Spanish, you can buy tickets online.

With drug gang activity along Colombia's borders with Venezuela and Ecuador, it is not advised to enter Colombia overland by bus or by car. Flying is much more secure, quicker, more comfortable and, with increasing low-cost airline options in play, much more time/cost efficient. If you are determined to travel by bus, always travel during the day and keep yourself updated and informed on Colombia's political situation domestically, and with its less than bosom buddy neighbors. You'll probably have to transfer buses at the border.

BY CRUISE SHIP/YACHT   Cartagena has become the latest Caribbean hotspot for cruise liners; the number of cruise-ship passengers jumped from some 42,000 in 2006 to more than 300,000 in 2014. When the trade winds relent (July–Nov), private yacht owners and sailing companies offer trips from the San Blas Islands in Panama to Cartagena, starting at US$400 each way. Trips normally include 3 days sailing around the San Blas Islands and 2 days sailing in open seas to/from Cartagena (seasonal). **San Blas Adventures** (www.sanblasadventures.com) comes highly recommended for sailing trips from Carti (Panama) to Sapzurro (Colombia). See p. 151.

Getting Around

BY FOOT   Traveler attention is rightly focused on the historic old town, which packs its main sights into a small, walkable area; and the hip and happening district of Getsemaní, a 10-minute walk away. Strolling through the old town is the best way to appreciate Cartagena's charms. To walk from Plaza de Santa Teresa east to Plaza de las Bóvedas in the San Diego district will take around 20 to 25 minutes.

BY TAXI   If the heat becomes intolerable, hailing a yellow cab is very safe and relatively easy, apart from during peak holiday periods. For short trips within the old town, a set fare of COP$6,000 applies (always confirm the rate with the driver when you get in). A ride from the old town to Getsemaní or Bocagrande will set you back around COP$8,000 to COP$10,000.

BY BUS   Buses from the old town to Bocagrande ply Avenida Santander; you shouldn't have to wait more than 10 minutes during peak hours (COP$1,700). Metrocar buses (signed TERMINAL) run along Avenida Carlos López to the bus terminal (12km/7½ miles) every 30 minutes (COP$2,500; 45 min.–1 hr.).

[FastFACTS] CARTAGENA

ATMs/Banks   As soon as you land, the best bet is to take out local Colombian pesos from the ATMs (*cajero automático*) located in the baggage claim area of Rafael Núñez Airport: BBVA and Banco Santander. In the old town, on Plaza de Aduana, Bancolombia and BBVA banks have 24-hour ATMs. There's a Citibank ATM (Centro Edificio Citibank) on Calle Venezuela (Barrio San Diego). You will lose heavily if you change dollars into Colombian pesos in hotels and at *cambios*; always try to use ATMs.

Business Hours   Banks are open 8am to noon and 2 to 4pm. Stores in the old town tend to be open from 10am until 8 or 9pm.

Dentist   Urgencias Odontologicas (24 hr.), Carrera 18 no. 25–150. ℂ **5/ 660-4211**.

Doctors & Hospitals   Hospital Bocagrande, Calle 5/Carrera 6, Castillogrande (ℂ **5/665-4380**). Hospital Naval, Carrera. 2 no. 14–10, Bocagrande (ℂ **5-655-5759**).

Emergencies   For police and medical emergencies dial **123**.

Internet Access   Wi-Fi is ubiquitous in Cartagena, and most hotels/hostels provide free connections.

Mail & Postage   Deprisa, Avenida Venezuela (Centro Edificio Citibank, local B1; ℂ **5/664-7822**). A stamp to the US will cost around COP$3,500.

Safety   Generally speaking, Cartagena's main tourist areas are well policed and considered very safe for travelers. But you still need to be mindful of pickpockets and armed robbers, especially at night and in more out of the way spots, including La Popa; a number of robberies have been reported on the road up to the convent. Vendors can be persistent but a strong and simple "*No, gracias,*" usually suffices.

The Historic Old Town

No matter how hard you resist, colonial Cartagena will make a romantic of even the most hard of hearts. A UNESCO World Heritage Site since 1987, Cartagena's old town is an almost perfectly preserved walled city. With searing temperatures year round, it's easy to fall into the city's timeless rituals and rhythms. Sit in a rocking chair with a refreshing mojito and fix your gaze upon gracefully aging colonial palaces, imperious churches, and sumptuous mansions that nudge up against colonial rainbow-hued buildings where an efflorescence of exotic flowers erupt from wooden balconies.

The old town's center of gravity is Plaza Bolívar, an elegant plaza framed with beautifully restored colonial palaces, now home to two of the city's cultural highlights: The **Museo del Oro** and the **Palacio de la Inquisición** speak of conquest, plunder, piracy, and the Spaniards' insatiable lust for blood and gold. With its lively cafes and bars, street vendors, and resplendent *palenquera* women selling artful displays of fruit, **Plaza de Santo Domingo** is one of the city's most animated and historic plazas. It's also the setting for one of the finest and oldest churches in Latin America: Cartagena's monumental cathedral, the **Iglesia de Santo Domingo**. Still within the walls, the neighborhood of San Diego is where you'll find timeless Cartagena, a living, working, yet truly magical part of the city where locals by far outnumber tourists and where the magical realism of Márquez lingers on every corner. Just outside the historic center, the Getsemaní neighborhood is where Cartagena's gorgeous colonial architecture, creative verve, and raw street life coalesce to produce Cartagena's most authentic and spirited enclave.

TOP ATTRACTIONS

Las Murallas ★ HISTORIC SITE   Cartagena's monumental walls aren't just a photogenic relic; they represent a formidable feat of military architecture that is, arguably, without peer in Latin America. Extending for 4km (2½ miles), the walls are the main reason that Cartagena de Indias established itself as the Spanish empire's most important citadel. Construction began in the late 16th century after a series of pirate attacks, including a particularly zealous raid in 1585 by Sir Francis Drake, whose more common name in Latin America "El Draque," generally uttered with a slur. By the early 1700s, Cartagena was impregnable: In 1741 it held off 186 British warships, the largest fleet ever assembled before World War II. A walk along the walls at sunset—when breezes provide relief from the suffocating temperatures—is something of a rite of passage for visitors to Cartagena. The most stirring sections of the walls run parallel to sea, where lovers kiss and children play in the shaded embrasures where Spanish cannons once aimed at enemy battalions.

There are three *baluartes* (bulwarks or ramparts). At the northern limit, the Baluartes de San Lucas y de Santa Catalina are known as Las Tenazas (due to their pincer-like formation). Here, you can gain insight into the construction of the city walls at the **Museo de las Fortificaciones** (Baluarte de Santa Catalina; ✆ **5/656-0591**; 8am–6pm daily; COP$7,000). At the southwest corner of the Centro Histórico, the impressive Baluarte Santo Domingo courts most tourist attention thanks to **Café del Mar** (© **5/664-2945**; 5pm–2am daily), a popular spot for a sunset cocktail. Facing the sea at the southern fringes, next to Plaza Santa Teresa, are the Baluartes de San Ignacio and San Francisco Javier, where there is another lively bar with an outside terrace.

The city's poster child, Cartagena's historic **Torre del Reloj** ★ clock tower was built as the main gateway to the city in 1601 following the construction of *las murallas* (city walls). A paradigm for military architecture, the tower's baroque doorway features three arches carved from coral stone. Originally named *Boca del Puente* (Mouth of the Bridge), the clock tower linked the Old City to Getsemaní via a drawbridge over a moat. The tower's weapons room and chapel were replaced with a United States pendulum clock in 1874, followed by a Swiss clock (which you see today) in 1937. Behind the tower, **Plaza de los Coches** has assumed a myriad of names and vocations over the centuries. Having transcended its inauspicious beginnings as the city's slave market to adopt a more prosaic role as a parking lot, today the lively square is tourism ground zero. Hawkers, performers, and a flurry of tour groups orbit the square's centerpiece bronze statue of Pedro de Heredia, the city's founder, immortalized by Spanish artist Juan de Ávolas in 1963. Across the square, **Portal de Los Dulces** is a colorful arcaded walkway where you can buy traditional Colombian and Cartagenian candy.

Casa de Rafael Núñez ★ HISTORIC SITE

This gorgeous colonial mansion was the home of former president and poet Rafael Núñez, who was the driving force behind *La Regeneración* movement of 1884 and the seminal 1886 constitution (Colombia is currently on its ninth iteration), which transformed a messy federal government structure into a centralized system with increased presidential powers. Immaculately restored and now functioning as a well-conceived museum, guided tours of the home take in the understated rooms decorated in period style, including a delightful patio dining room and rustic kitchen. Throughout the home, mementoes, documents, artifacts, memorabilia, antiques (including Núñez's lavish desk), and pictures of his time in Panama and his funeral evoke the esteemed president's life.

Calle Real del Cabrero no. 41–89. © **5/660-9058.** Free. Tues–Fri 9am–5pm, Sat and Sun 10am–4pm.

Catedral Basílica de Santa Catalina de Alejandria ★ HISTORIC SITE

Cartagena's magnificent Cathedral exerts an uplifting spiritual presence. Built in 1575, it was destroyed by irksome English pirate Francis Drake, who unleashed his canons upon the city in 1586. Rebuilt as a classic citadel structure, the cathedral's second iteration was completed in 1612. The first archbishop of Cartagena left his imprint in the early 20th century when he embellished the facade with stucco and placed a large dome atop the tower. The church's original exterior limestone form still prevails, along with the original baroque 18th-century gilded altar and retable, and a lavish Carrera marble pulpit.

Callejón Santos de Piedra no. 34–55. Free (audio tour COP$12,000). Mass: Mon–Sat 10am–12pm; Sun 8am, 12pm, and 7pm (open during Mass only).

El Teatro de Adolfo Mejia Heredia ★ HISTORIC SITE   On Plaza de La Merced, the pastel-hued Teatro Adolfo Mejia, known affectionately as Teatro Heredia (after the city's founder), was built to commemorate the first centenary of the Colombian Republic in 1911. Renowned architect Luis Felipe Jaspe transformed the former 17th-century Merced Church (which had fallen on hard times) into a center of arts and culture based on Havana's Teatro Tacon, to showcase Cartagena's cultural élan. One of Cartagena's architectural highlights, the theater's interior is lavish and graceful in equal measure. The glorious marble staircase was shipped in from Italy in 1988. There are ornate gold-plated fittings, seat dividers fashioned from cedar wood, and a striking figure of the beautiful India Catalina (Pedro Heredia's intermediary and translator; Colombia's answer to Sacajawea). The theater's crowning jewel is the glorious ceiling fresco, *El Triunfo de las Musas* (painted by renowned local artist Enrique Grau), which depicts the dance of the nine muses of the arts. As well as hosting the Hay Festival in January, the theater offers a diverse schedule of classical music concerts, films, literary gatherings, and theatre productions.

Plaza de la Merced no. 38–101. ✆ **5/664-6023.** Tours are offered (no impromptu visits) but hours vary according to events and performances; COP$10,000.

Iglesia/Claustro/Museo San Pedro Claver ★ HISTORIC SITE   It's the compelling backstory to this majestic three-story convent located on Plaza de San Pedro that makes for a thought-provoking visit. Built by the Jesuits in 1603 as the Iglesia de San Ignacio de Loyola, it was later dedicated to San Pedro Claver Corberó (1580–1654). One of the more interesting protagonists when it comes to Spanish colonial religious history, Corberó was a Spanish-born clergyman and descendent of a noble Spanish family who arrived in Cartagena in 1610, when the city formed the epicenter of the slave trade in the New World. Distressed by the treatment of Africans, the freshman priest dedicated his life to caring for the thousands of black slaves brought from Africa to fortify the city. The first individual to be canonized in the new world (in 1888), San Pedro Claver enacted what was then termed "Equal Human Rights," the momentous first steps toward the abolition of slavery in Colombia and the New World.

In contrast to the church's corpulent stone facade, the interior is embellished with intricate stained glass and a marble altar where a glass coffin preserves the remains of the revered Claver (with his bones on show); you can also visit Claver's quarters. An important pilgrimage site for the faithful, much of the convent now functions as a museum with a small collection of pre-Columbian ceramics, colonial artifacts, sculptures, and religious art. The whimsical wrought-iron sculptures that front the church on Plaza de San Pedro are by contemporary Colombian artist Eduardo Carmona, and are part of the Museo de Arte Moderno's collection (see p. 96).

Plaza de San Pedro Claver no. 30–01. www.sanpedroclaver.co. ✆ **5/664-4991.** COP$11,000 adults, COP$7,000 children. Museum: 8am–5pm. Convent: Mon–Fri 8am–5:30pm, Sat–Sun 8am–4:30pm. Church, Mass: Mon–Sat 6:45am and 6pm, Sunday, 7am, 10am, noon, 6pm (free for Mass attendees).

Iglesia/Claustro Santo Domingo ★★ HISTORIC SITE   If you only plan to visit one church in Cartagena, make it this one. Located on one of the city's most vibrant plazas, spilling over with cafes and vendors, the Church of Santo Domingo is the oldest church in Cartagena (built in the 1570s) and one of the finest in Latin America (the competition is fierce). The church is famous for its baroque, marble altar replete with an image of the Virgin with a gold-and-emerald encrusted crown and a 19th-century wooden image of Christ. As legend would have it, if anyone should have the audacity to try to remove the Christ from the church, it would grow too large to fit through the door—a magical realist move that is straight from the pen of Gabo. There's a dash of the surreal in the church's lopsided bell tower and the 19th-century tombstones that comprise the two aisles. The addition of buttresses (*estribos*) to shore up the structure and maintain the colossal roof gave rise to the Callejón de los Estribos.

Plaza de Santo Domingo. © **5/655-1916.** COP$10,000; free during Mass: Mon 7am, 11am and 5pm, Tues–Sun 11am and 5pm.

Las Bóvedas ★ ATTRACTION   In the old town's quieter San Diego district, Calle de las Bóvedas leads to a series of military dungeons used during the War for Independence. With impressive 15-meter-thick walls, the jail, vaults, and ammunition storerooms were constructed between 1792 and 1796. While the setting is certainly evocative, most of the crafts, or *artesanías*, are aimed at the cruise ship market and tour groups, and what you'll find here is of dubious quality and overpriced.

Open daily 9am–6pm.

Museo de Arte Moderno ★ MUSEUM   Evocatively housed in the old Customs House, just off Plaza de San Pedro Claver, this small modern art museum, founded in 1959, provides a worthy introduction to Colombia's most important 20th-century artists. On the ground floor, permanent exhibits showcase seminal works by native sons Alejandro Obregón (1920–1992), Eduardo Carmona, and Enrique Grau. One of the museum's highlights, Grau's surrealistic *Triptico de Cartagena de Indias* (1998) evokes two quintessential Colombian characters who also happened to be his relatives: an uncle who parachuted into bullfighting rings, and a beauty queen aunt. There are also several of Grau's signature voluptuous nudes, including *Desnudo Feminino* (1971). Grau's representation of Afro-Colombian and Indian figures came to define contemporary art in Colombia and redefined Colombian art's status on the international market; Western interest in Colombian art has skyrocketed over the last decade. Along with Fernando Botero and Alejandro Obregón, Enrique Grau belongs to the triumvirate of Colombia's most celebrated and beloved artists. In many ways, Alejandro Obregón's vivid landscapes, exotic wildlife, and passionate depiction of women and family distill the essence of all that is Cartagena. Obregón's self-portrait *Dedalo* (1995) is mesmerizing and confounding in equal measure.

Calle 30 N. 4–08, Plaza de San Pedro Claver. www.mamcartagena.org. © **5/664-5815.** COP$8,000 adults, COP$3,000 children, free on Wed. Mon–Fri 9am–12pm, 3–7pm; Sat 10am–1pm, Sun 4pm–9pm.

Museo del Oro ★★ MUSEUM   On the east side of Plaza Bolívar, located inside a gorgeous colonial mansion, the Gold Museum presents an exquisite collection of ceramic, metalwork, and pre-Columbian gold jewelry created by the indigenous Zenú people; inhabitants of the region from 200 B.C. to about 1600 A.D. The Zenú were master artisans and, for their people, gold was imbued with immense spiritual value. The Zenú's ritual of burying their dead along with their gold possessions beneath trees strewn with a kind of pre-Columbian wind chime made life easy on the Spanish. The brutal, and more economically minded, conquistadors simply followed the sound of the bells and proceeded to plunder Zenú's ancestral tombs. Within a series of artfully conceived, illuminated cases, an astounding delicacy of form, sublime craftsmanship, and mystical themes marry to provide compelling viewing. There are whimsical animals, funerary urns, dazzling gold pendants, men metamorphosing into mythic creatures, and ornate filigree brooches.

Carrera 4 N. 33–26, Plaza de Bolívar. ☏ **5/660-0778.** Free. Tues–Sat 10am–1pm, 2pm–5pm; Sun and holidays 10am–4pm.

Naval Museum ★ MUSEUM   Although it can be quite fusty for laymen, the Naval Museum will enthrall military historians. Constructed in the early 1600s, the original colonial wing housed the first Jesuit school in the Americas. The Republican (or Eastern) wing was added some 300 years later to house the Navy. The museum does a fine job (if you speak Spanish) of explaining Cartagena's strategic importance as a port, as well as lingering over the exploits of Britain's nefarious pirates. Along with an exhaustive display of antique naval instruments, maps, and dioramas, a series of intricate exhibits featuring miniature ships depict Cartagena's most significant battles and invasions, as well as the engineering techniques used in the construction of Cartagena walls, bastions, and fortresses. For kids, there's a hugely popular interactive submarine. Try to visit early morning; the museum has no air-conditioning.

Calle 31 no. 3–62, Calle San Juán de Dios. www.museonavaldelcaribe.com. ☏ **5/664-2440** or 5/664-9672. Admission COP$8,000 adults, COP$6,000, children. Daily 10am–5:30pm.

Palacio de La Inquisición ★ MUSEUM   Across Plaza Bolívar from the Gold Museum, the Palacio de la Inquisición tells yet another side of the conquistadors' blood lust. From the early 17th century through independence, Cartagena was a stronghold of the Inquisition. This archetypal late-colonial palace is now home to a history museum that highlights the gruesome methods used by the Spanish church to convince alleged heretics to see the light; for the Spanish, witchcraft and blasphemy topped the list of the most odious crimes, and the condemned would face a public *auto-de-fé* (execution). Behind the palace's magnificent baroque facade, emblazoned with the Spanish coat of arms, the first floor displays a series of artifacts related (often tenuously) to the methods employed by the Tribunal del Santo Oficio (Holy Office) in their mission to save around 900 souls from evil. There are historical dioramas, artifacts related to witchcraft, and the Virgin of Candelaria (Cartagena's patron saint and force against evil), evocative paintings by contemporary Colombians and, attracting most interest, a collection of torture devices including the rack and the Spanish tickler. On the side of the building, look out for a small window with a cross above it; this was the place where alleged heretics would be denounced by their neighbors.

Calle 34, N. 3–11, Plaza de Bolívar. www.muhca.gov.co. © **902/963-3050.** Adults COP$15,000 adults, children COP$9,000. Mon–Sat, 9am–6pm, Sun and holidays 10am–4pm.

Plaza de Bolívar ★★ HISTORIC SITE   Surrounded by beautiful, historic buildings, Plaza de Bolívar is the heart and soul of Cartagena's old town. The city's emblematic Palenque women dressed in bright dresses purvey artful arrangements of the Caribbean's bounty of exotic fruits. In the shade of palm trees, couples swoon, old men play chess, shoeshine merchants tout for business, and tour groups convene beneath the iconic statue of South American liberator Simón Bolívar. In the evening, as the heat subsides, you can feel the quickening pulse of the city right here as drums beat and impassioned dancers demonstrate that quintessential South American fusion of music and life.

Intersection of Calle de la Inquisición and Calle Santos de Piedra.

Plaza de San Diego ★★★ HISTORIC SITE   The epicenter for the San Diego neighborhood, this lovely square retains an authentic vibe and remains somehow immune to the heavy tourist traffic. The setting for the legendary hotel **Santa Clara** ★★★ (see p. 104), the 16th-century convent that provided the inspiration for Márquez's novel *Of Love and Other Demons*, Plaza de San Diego and the quiet streets that surround it fulfill the dream of Cartagena for many travelers. There's a pulsating energy and creative zeal courtesy of the students at the **Escuela de Bellas Artes** (another converted convent) on the east side of the square; on any given night you can drop in and watch a performance, rehearsal, or impromptu celebration. If you stroll south, east, or several blocks west of the square, you can escape the hustle and bustle of the old town's main arteries.

Getsemaní

Over the last few years, Getsemaní has cast off its nefarious image as the city's seedy underbelly, a no-go area rife with drugs and prostitution, and embraced a dynamic cult of restoration and revitalization that has yet to morph into cookie-cutter territory. Known as the "people's quarter," Getsemaní has always played a starring role in Colombia's turbulent history. In 1811, Pedro Romero, leader of the radical group known as the Getsemaní Lancers, organized a revolt in front of the neighborhood's church. Armed with guns and daggers, the Lancers laid siege to the Governor's Palace, compelling the Royal Junta to proclaim independence from Spain.

The "culture quarter" where poets, artists, dancers, and photographers flee the exorbitant rents of the old town, Getsemaní has rewritten its narrative. The neighborhood's independent spirit finds expression in the jumble of hip new bars, innovative restaurants, dance clubs, and boutique hotels carved from candy-colored colonial homes. With a palpable edge (at night) and lacking the architectural prowess of the Centro Histórico, the cruise ship crowds don't come here (just yet). But the backpackers do, along with adventurous-minded travelers looking to get under the skin of this magical city.

Vibrant street art has become a way of trumpeting the democratic spirit and talent of local residents. Along **Calle San Juan** and **Calle de la Sierpe**, crumbling 18th-century buildings are emblazoned with museum-worthy paintings, murals, and graffiti by emerging and legendary street artists such as Bogotá-based Lik Mi and Yurika as well as London-based artist Fin DAC, known for his signature "stencil women." Calle de la Sierpe was the site of 2010's *Pedro Romero Vive Aqui* (Pedro Romero Lives Here) street art project, and much of the street's storied works date from that watershed moment, with new vibrant pieces added continuously. Faithful to the *costeño* experience, most of Getsemaní's street art celebrates Colombia's Caribbean landscape, exotic wildlife, and protagonists, including the emblematic *palenquera* women, but you will also come across works underscored with a sociopolitical or historic theme.

Plaza de Trinidad is Getsemaní's beating heart, where young and old convene on benches beneath the humble facade of a 17th-century marigold church to gossip, muse, flirt, play chess or dominoes, and put the world to rights over *arepas* and *choclo* (grilled corn). Under gangly palm trees, before the triumphant gaze of priest-hero Pedro Romero (immortalized in a series of bronze sculptures), kids play soccer, women serve potent mojitos from the back of a cart, and hips begin to swing as the sound of champeta music emanates from the myriad cafes and bars that line the square.

If you visit on Sundays, Colombia's passion for baseball (the nation's second-favorite sport) finds expression. **Avenida del Pedregal** is closed to traffic and transformed into a pseudo baseball diamond.

Certainly, for better and for worse, gentrification is afoot in Getsemaní. In 2017, Four Seasons and Viceroy will open new hotels in Getsemaní and thrust the neighborhood and, indeed, Cartagena's traveler demographic into an entirely new luxury bracket.

To get there: A taxi from the old town to Getsemaní will cost around COP$8,000. It takes around 10 min. to stroll from the Torre del Reloj; walking is not advised late at night.

Other Tourist Sights

Bazurto Market ★★ MARKET   Not a place for sensitive souls, the Bazurto market is a psychedelic maelstrom that is guaranteed to bombard your senses. A far cry from the old town's manicured, colonial grandeur, it's a fascinating excursion into Cartagena's unsanitized local rituals. Dirty, seedy, cacophonous, and sometimes shocking in a visceral kind of way, locals flock here to buy everything from knock-off brand clothing to super-fresh fish, ripe to burst produce, and even traditional crafts. Amid butchers wielding their cleavers with abandon, crates are loaded with exotic fruits you won't see in the supermarket, and gory pigs' heads are stacked on tables. You might see Cartagena's star chefs plan their evening menus as they survey 25-pound tuna fish and live lobsters displayed on makeshift tables; what generally ends up on Cartagena's top restaurant menus is sourced here. If you venture here, be sure to be extremely mindful of petty thieves and pickpockets.

Avenida Pedro Heredia. Daily 5am–4pm. To get here, a taxi from the old town will cost around COP$8,000.

Castillo de San Felipe ★★ HISTORIC SITE   Built with coral mined from the region's reefs, the imposing Castillo de San Felipe de Barajas is considered the greatest fortress constructed by the Spaniards in the New World. Built in several phases, beginning in 1656, atop the 40-meter-high San Lázaro hill, the Castillo de San Felipe ranks as one of the great military wonders of the world. It was Sir Francis Drake's attack of 1586—the British pirate pillaged the town for some 50 days—that focused the attention of the Spanish Crown, which then embarked on an unprecedented mission to bolster the city's defenses. After the fort was enlarged in 1762, Cartagena became impregnable. The most important port (and the most heavily fortified city in the New World), Cartagena was the nexus for the Spanish flotillas that transported gold and silver via Havana to Spain. The castle's labyrinthine, rather ghoulish, tunnels are open for self-guided audio tours (available in English) which relate the castle's seminal architectural accomplishments; famed engineer Antonio de Arévalo designed the tunnels such that any noise would carry for the entire length of the tunnels to alert the Spanish to enemy advances.

Avenida Arévalo, Pie del Cerro. ℂ **5/656-6803.** COP$17,000, audio tour COP$10,000, free last Sun of month btw. Feb and Nov. Daily 8am–6pm.

Convento de la Popa ★★ HISTORIC SITE   Mention La Popa to any Cartagenero and he will invariably turn dreamy eyed. Visible for miles around on Cartagena's highest hill (150m high), the Convento de Nuestra Señora de la Candelaria (as it is officially known) was founded in 1608 by an Augustinian monk who, delirious from fasting, had a vision/hallucination that the Virgin Mary ordered him to build a monastery on Cartagena's highest point. As legend has it, Father de la Cruz destroyed the temple the Indians had built to honor their idol (a golden goat called Burizago) which the monk tossed down what is referred to as the Goat's Precipe (Salto del Cabron). Devout Colombians flock to La Popa to view a compelling image of the beloved La Virgin de la Candelaria, the patroness of the city, in the convent's chapel. For nonbelievers, the gorgeous cloister and courtyard awash with shocking-pink bougainvillea, and the superb panoramic views of the city below, are worth the visit alone. The main road snakes up to the convent (no public transportation) and while there are paths (it takes around 25 min. to ascend), it's advisable to take a taxi (pickpockets and armed robberies have been reported). Expect to pay around COP$45,000 for the round-trip journey; always negotiate.

Cerro de la Popa. ℂ **5/666–2331.** COP$9,000 adults, COP$6,000 children. Daily 8am–6pm; June and Sept daily 10am–4pm; July–Aug daily 9am–5pm.

Excursions
LAS ISLAS DEL ROSARIO ★★

No one visits Cartagena for its beaches. For a day excursion, the Rosario Islands National Park, 45km (28 miles) away from the city, satisfies most visitors' Caribbean island fantasy. This photogenic constellation of 30 islands features coral reefs, crystalline waters in every shade imaginable of blue and green, rocky coves, and swathes of white-sand beaches. Now, rather controversially, developers keen on building lavish second homes and eco-chic hotels have commandeered many of the islands. Isla Grande is the largest of the Rosario Islands, where you will find most accommodation options and some of the best snorkeling. The smaller **Isla San Martín de Pajarales** (no beach) features on most tours for its small **Oceanarium** (www.oceanariocolombia.com; ℂ 316/830-7888; Tues–Sun 10am–3pm; COP$25,000) which, while certainly not to everyone's taste, is a big hit with Colombian holidaymakers and kids. The Oceanarium has shark feedings, sea turtles, sting rays, and a dolphin show in a lagoon; if it's not your thing, many tours offer a snorkeling option instead (always check before you book). After visiting the aquarium, most boats will head to **Isla de Barú** (for around 3 hr.) for a traditional Caribbean lunch of grilled fish, coconut rice, and fried plantains. You can relax, swim, sunbathe, or explore the island (there's not a great deal to see) before heading back late afternoon to Cartagena. Prices from COP$160,000 include transportation and lunch. The boat trip (which can be choppy on the way back) takes around 45 minutes departing from La Bodeguita pier in the Muelle Turístico or from the marina at La Manga (15 min. by taxi from Centro Histórico, from COP$12,000). Most hotels can arrange tours for you (prices and standards don't vary greatly from operator to operator).

PLAYA BLANCA ★

Another of Cartagena's most popular day trips is to the white-sand beach of Playa Blanca on Isla Barú, the only accessible beach on the island. Certainly, the beach is gorgeous, with fine white sand and crystalline blue, warm waters backed by lush vegetation. Sadly, the tourist onslaught has tarnished the beach's natural beauty. Ramshackle thatched cabins line the beach, and throngs of hippies, tourists, backpackers, and Colombian holidaymakers throw down their towels and tie-dye sarongs in front of the makeshift bars and restaurants where pumping salsa and reggaeton competes for the airwaves and vendors are undeterred by *no gracias*. Still, it's a pleasant boat trip from Cartagena, with most tours heading through the Strait of Bocachica, where you can marvel at three impressive 18th-century fortifications built by the Spaniards: Fuerte de San Fernando, Batería de San José, and Batería de Ángel. Most tour boats will make a stop at the **Oceanarium** (see above) before stopping for lunch at Playa Blanca.

Tip: The best way to visit the Rosario Islands and Playa Blanca is to spend up and customize your trip through **Boats 4 You** (www.boats4u.co/en; ℂ 304/459-4905), which offers day-long private charters. Another option is to stay at one of the more upscale hotels on the islands, which will arrange boat transfers and tour packages as part of an overnight stay. Don't expect the kind of swanky luxury resorts that you will find on other Caribbean islands, but rather comfortable rustic-chic rooms, tranquility (when the tour groups have all departed), and plenty of amenities to make for a very relaxing and enjoyable overnight stay. The most upscale option is **Agua Azul Beach Resort** (www.aguazul beachresort.com; ℂ 320/680-2134; rates from COP$1,250,000), on Isla Barú, a whitewashed plantation-style house with colorful, design-conscious rooms (with air-conditioning), an inviting pool, and a very good seafood restaurant.

VOLCÁN DE LODO EL TOTUMO ★

This 50-foot-tall, 15-foot-diameter mud volcano, just 45 minutes by bus/taxi from Cartagena, has become a rather curious tourist spectacle. According to local lore, the once-active volcano, El Totumo, puffed and sizzled until a savvy priest doused the tempestuous crater with holy water and transformed it into a more innocuous mud bath, supposedly with therapeutic qualities. A sign at the base of the cone reveals the mud's skin-enhancing elements, including magnesium, calcium, and aluminum. The routine involves climbing a series of steps to the top of the crater, then climbing into the thick pool of goo to wallow (it's actually more of a floating Dead Sea kind of sensation). You'll be slathered and massaged in rudimentary fashion by entrepreneurial locals (many will attempt to dip your head back into the mud in a curious baptism kind of ritual), have your picture taken, and then clean yourself off in a nearby lagoon. On the weekend, the volcano/mud-bath crowd reaches critical mass. Volcán de Lodo el Totumo is best experienced as part of a day tour, which can be easily arranged through hotels and agencies in town; around COP$50,000 including transport, lunch, and entry fee: $5,000. Tourists are expected to tip their masseurs around COP$4,000.

Via al Volcán de Totumo, Santa Catalina (on the road to Barranquilla).

Where to Stay

Agua ★★   Behind a magnificent wooden doorway, this 17th-century white-washed colonial mansion is a sophisticated labyrinth of tasteful rooms, intimate sitting areas, and outdoor spaces that triumph the art of relaxation. Beautifully appointed rooms are scattered with Colombian artworks (including an original Botero), artifacts, and books from convivial owners Sergio and Gustavo's personal collection. The overall look is sleek and modern, with an artful balance of elegant dark-wooden furnishings, crisp white linens, and flowing drapes. Rooms are not huge, so for families with children it's worth upgrading to the two-bedroom/bathroom suites. The small rooftop terrace has a pool where you can take a cooling dip while taking in the views of the cathedral tower.

Calle 35 no. 4–29. www.hotelagua.com.co. ℂ **5/664-9510.** 11 units. Doubles from COP$782,754, suites from COP$1,797,435. **Amenities:** Restaurant/bar; outdoor pool; spa; hot tub; free Wi-Fi.

Casa Claver Loft Boutique Hotel ★   An intimate, friendly, and great-value hotel with a terrific location and excellent amenities—including kitchenettes and dining rooms—Casa Claver is one of the best options in the walled city for families or longer-stay guests. The sleek, light-filled rooms—many overlooking the leafy courtyard swimming pool—may lack the period detailing that prevail in Casa Claver's old town peers, but each impeccable space delivers high levels of comfort and functionality. There are inspired town and cathedral views from the rooftop terrace with a heated swimming pool.

Calle de los Damas no. 3–134. www.casaclaver.com. ℂ **5/664-9953.** 7 units. Doubles from COP$347,891, includes breakfast. **Amenities:** 2 outdoor pools; sauna, free Wi-Fi.

Casa Don Sancho ★★ In a lovely part of town, close to Teatro de Heredia, an aristocratic aura and artistic sensibility prevails at Casa Don Sancho, named after the governor who resided here during the 17th century. The six bright rooms in soothing neutral tones balance rustic period charm with ornate decorative flourishes and modern amenities. The marble bathrooms marry style with functionality; L'Occitane bath products are a nice touch. You can browse the books and music in the drawing room, relax on the terrace, or take a dip in the inviting courtyard swimming pool. Made-to-order breakfasts are served in the contemporary dining room, plucked straight from the pages of an interior design magazine, with a black-and-white tiled floor, white sofa, centerpiece pillar-candle chandelier, and overtures to design symmetry.

Calle Don Sancho no. 36–126. www.casadonsancho.com. ℭ **5/668-6622.** 6 units. Doubles from COP$724,772, includes breakfast. **Amenities:** Outdoor pool; hot tub; restaurant; bar; free Wi-Fi.

Casa La Fe ★ If your decorative tastes sway more toward the Republican epoch than the colonial, then Casa La Fe (part of the Kali boutique hotel brand) provides a fine riff on the period's Belle Epoque. Tiled stairways and floors, stately wooden furniture, brass lamps, gilded picture frames, and bold red arabesques swirled across crisp white linens add style and substance to this faithfully restored 19th-century building. Standard rooms are grouped around the interior courtyard, while rooms with balconies overlook Plaza Fernandez de Madrid. The pomp and sobriety of the living spaces—think niches with winged cupids and religious iconography—give way to a vibrant interior courtyard (where breakfast is served daily) with its untamed foliage, and a rooftop terrace painted in broad strokes of primary colors that add energy to the terrace with plunge pool.

Calle de Badillo no. 36–125. www.kalihotels.com. ℭ **5/664-0306.** 14 units. Doubles from COP$433,000, includes breakfast. **Amenities:** Plunge pool; bar; free Wi-Fi.

Casa Lola ★ There's nothing formulaic about this edgy, eclectic hotel at the heart of Getsemaní's thriving cultural scene. Zen water features, vibrant foliage, flamboyant textiles, striking artworks, and finds from the well-traveled owner's personal collection decorate every nook and cranny of this 17th-century colonial mansion. Individually conceived rooms with exposed-stone walls feature an elegant mismatch of colonial antiques, ethnic rugs, and modern design statements (all the art and objects in the hotel are available for purchase). There are stunning views over the ramparts from Casa Lola's rooftop, complete with a small pool.

Calle de Guerrero no. 20–108. www.casalola.com.co. ℭ **5/664-1845.** 14 units. Doubles from COP$390,000, includes breakfast. **Amenities:** 2 (small) outdoor pools; bar; free Wi-Fi.

Casa Pestagua ★★ This gorgeous boutique hotel, which occupies a magnificent 18th-century palace, marries colonial charm and modern élan with aplomb. Spacious rooms—some of the largest rooms in the walled city—ooze colonial splendor, with antiques, gilded mirrors, polished wooden floors, hand-woven rugs, beamed ceilings, and oversize bathrooms flush with marble floors and bronze faucets. With a rooftop hot tub, luxurious spa, and inviting courtyard pool surrounded by exotic foliage, the Pestagua provides a romantic haven in a primo location at the heart of the old town.

Calle de Santo Domingo. www.hotelboutiquecasapestagua.com. © **5/664-9510.** 11 units. Doubles from COP$782,754, suites from COP$1,797,436. **Amenities:** Outdoor pool; spa; hot tub; bar; restaurant; free Wi-Fi.

Casa San Augustin ★★★ Despite growing competition, the 30-room Casa San Augustin, which opened in 2012, is Cartagena's most desirable small hotel. Three 17th-century colonial mansions combine to form an exquisite and intimate space with a soothing Andalusian theme. Romantic white-on-white rooms with canopied beds, furnishings crafted from exotic hardwoods, beamed ceilings, and mosaic-tiled bathrooms are spacious and feature all the amenities and flawless service that you would expect of a five-star hotel. Premium rooms have a private plunge pool. A historical aura permeates the hotel's art-filled public spaces adorned with original frescoes. From heavenly massages to delectable breakfasts, refreshing dips in the L-shaped pool, and fine cocktails at the chic Alma restaurant—one of the city's finest—Casa San Augustin is a haven of impeccable taste and understated luxury. If money is no object, the huge Virrey Suite (US$1,050) has separate living and dining areas, two large balconies with lovely rooftop views, and an outdoor plunge pool.

Calle de la Universidad no. 36–44. www.hotelcasasanagustin.com. © **5/660-1432.** 30 units. Doubles from COP$956,700, suites from COP$1,163,064, includes breakfast. **Amenities:** Restaurant; outdoor pool; spa; free Wi-Fi.

Casa San Pedro ★★ Casa San Pedro feels rather like staying in the home of your rich aristocratic uncle. Pleasantly tucked away in the old town's quieter San Diego district town, this Andalusian-style mansion is one of Cartagena's most evocative hotels. Behind the colossal Roman Doric door, a wrought-iron gate leads to a central courtyard where plants are woven amid magnificent Romanesque archways that enclose a mosaic-tiled swimming pool. Each of the eight grand rooms ooze colonial grandeur with period furnishings, eclectic antiques, and rich fabrics of deep burgundy, indigo, or gold. The small rooftop terrace with a hot tub has views of Castillo de San Felipe de Barajas. What really distinguishes Casa San Pedro (at this price point) is the warm service and thoughtful touches: welcome drinks, a complementary foot massage in the basement spa, and an elaborate breakfast served in the courtyard or beneath chandeliers of the regal salon.

Calle San Pedro Mártir no. 10–85. www.sanpedrohotelspa.com.co. © **5/664-5800.** 8 units. Doubles from COP$376,882, suites COP$695,781, includes breakfast. **Amenities:** Outdoor pool; hot tub; bar; spa; free Wi-Fi.

Sofitel Santa Clara ★★★ There's magic in the air at this gorgeous, faithfully restored Clarissa convent (built in 1621), which combines the soul, mystery, and colonial charm of Cartagena with the luxury, amenities, and flawless service that you would expect of a luxury resort hotel. A lush courtyard complete with a Botero sculpture, an inviting heated pool (in the former orchard), a heavenly spa, and an elegant restaurant, the Sofitel excels when it comes to sybaritic pleasures. Standard rooms are bright, crisp, and equipped with Nespresso machines, Bose stereos, and iPod docks. Most have balconies that overlook the pool, but you will have to splash out on a suite to revel in the character, space, and colonial features of one of Cartagena's top boutique hotels. A skeleton uncovered from the crypt—now home to the atmospheric bar, El Coro—inspired Márquez's magical realist tale, *Of Love and Other Demons*. If you are traveling with children, this is by far the best upscale choice.

Calle del Torno no. 39–29. www.sofitel.com. © **5/650-4700.** 148 units. Doubles rooms from COP$927,000, suites COP$2,235,893. **Amenities:** 2 restaurants; 2 bars; pool; free Wi-Fi.

Tcherassi Hotel & Spa ★★ Owned by Colombian fashion designer Silvia Tcherassi, this super-stylish boutique hotel carved from a 250-year-old mansion is a perfect expression of the owner's creative spirit. Behind a monumental studded doorway, contemporary black-and-white portraits, flamboyant furnishings, colonial architecture, and Colombian artifacts coalesce to striking effect. The serene courtyard/reception area—with its centerpiece swimming pool (more decorative than recreational), framed by a shimmering glass waterfall and lush vertical garden—provides the setting for acclaimed Italian restaurant Vera. Light-flooded, sensual rooms feature original exposed brickwork, polished wooden floors, and soaring ceilings. The rooftop terrace with a hot tub has enchanting views of the walled city. There's a fabulous spa, and a cocktail at Aquabar forms a perfect early evening ritual. Service is discreet and poised.

Calle del Sargento Mayor no. 6–21. www.tcherassihotels.com. © **5/664-4454.** 7 units. Doubles from COP$724,247, includes breakfast. **Amenities:** Restaurant/bar; outdoor pool; hot tub; spa; free Wi-Fi.

Where to Eat

In recent years, much ink has been spilled over Cartagena's culinary cachet. With peace and prosperity, a thriving tourist industry and a dynamic restaurant scene have lured young Colombian chefs fresh from Michelin-starred restaurants overseas back home to open their own gastronomic temples. From sophisticated Caribbean tasting menus that showcase meticulously curated produce to innovative takes on French, Italian, and Spanish cuisine, Cartagena's restaurant scene is a constantly evolving journey. And few cities provide such a magical setting. Colonial mansions ooze timeless splendor, hip rooftops buzz with a mix of stylish locals and travelers who sip tropical cocktails and graze on ceviche iterations that would hold their own in Lima. Ebullient squares, such as Plaza de Trinidad in Getsemaní, offer tantalizing takes on that quintessential Colombian staple: *arepas* (corn cakes with infinite filling choices), prepared on the back of a wagon and savored on a park bench as Colombian life unfolds.

Carmen ★★★ MEDITERRANEAN Set in a lovely colonial mansion—within the delightful Ananda hotel—with a poised but unpretentious vibe, Carmen has raised the bar on Cartagena's gourmet dining scene. California transplant Chef Rob Pevitts delivers a seafood menu exquisitely conjured from fresh local ingredients as well as rare Amazonian produce, including the *cupuaçu* (a relative of cacao but with a fruity aroma). Gastro-molecular techniques are expertly deployed without the pomp and go-home-hungry complex common to the genre. There are no duffs on the menu. For a fine preamble, start with the *cebiche lamindo* (fish infused with fermented coconut and served with the theatrical enhancement of "coconut smoke"). The fish of the day (wrapped in a green plantain crust and served with coconut rice risotto, and drizzled with a rum raisin purée) is heavenly, or there's an outrageously good pineapple and cachaça–encrusted red snapper bathed in a curry sauce and dressed with creamy yam, tempura banana, and a lychee chimichurri. Desserts display the same exoticism, attention to detail, and stunning presentation. Guests can dine in the romantic courtyard, on the roof terrace with gorgeous views, or in the modern dining room.

Calle del Cuartel no. 36–77. www.carmencartagena.com. © **5/660-6795.** Reservations required well in advance. Main courses COP$24,000–COP$52,000. Daily, noon–3pm, 7–10pm.

Demente ★★ MEDITTERANEAN When a place is this cool and the people this nice, it's hard not to become an instant acolyte. For all its hip design, Nicolas Wiesner's space remains grounded in the neighborhood spirit of Getsemaní. The exterior is unreconstructed, there's a retractable roof that connects Demente to the verve of Plaza de la Trinidad, and rocking chairs on the sidewalk outside pay homage to every Cartagenero's favorite pastime. Inside, bare stone walls are juxtaposed with slick aluminum rocking chairs, and the Cuban theme runs riot with a fantastic rum and cigar cellar. While this is a place to linger late at night over well-executed cocktails or craft beers, the tasty menu is a fine dinner choice, with a small, rotating menu of Spanish-inspired dishes—think oxtail sliders, tuna tartar, meatballs, and grilled octopus—with a distinctively Colombian spin.

Carrera 10 no. 29. © **5/664-3105.** Main courses COP$16,000–COP$22,000. Daily 6pm–2am.

El Boliche Cebicheria ★★★ SEAFOOD For an extravagant lunch, this intimate restaurant—there are just seven tables—in San Diego serves meticulously curated seafood dishes that speak to the artisanal tendencies and wildly creative flair of Oscar Colmenares, a chef of outstanding pedigree. Colmenares is an alum of the multi-Michelin-starred Martín Berasategui restaurant in Spain and Astrid & Gaston in Bogotá. Super-fresh octopus, squid, shrimp, snapper, and conch are marinated in tamarind, coconut milk, or *suero costeño* (a kind of cream cheese) to produce an inimitable repertoire of ceviche that strike either a purist, exotic, or decadent note. More robust, but equally delectable, counterpoints include the crab empanadas, grilled octopus, and grilled catch of the day with coconut rice.

Calle Cochera del Hobo no. 38–17. © **5/660-0074.** Reservations recommended. Main courses COP$26,000–COP$42,0000. Mon–Sat noon–3pm, 6:30–11pm.

Juan del Mar ★★ SEAFOOD   With outside tables that spill onto lovely Plaza de San Diego, there's an infectious energy at the very popular Juan del Mar. With the buzz from the semi-exposed kitchen, live music, and a gregarious international crowd, Juan del Mar is more about the experience than epicurean excellence. Certainly, the creative menu caters to most tastes with Peruvian, Caribbean, and Asian-inflected dishes that are satisfying, fresh, and flavorful; but neither the cuisine nor the cocktails reach the finesse and complexity of Cartagena's gastronomic enclaves such as Carmen (see above). Signature dishes have a heavy fish-and-seafood slant with a tasty *cebiche estilo Caribe* (smoked shrimp in a tomato-based broth), *tiraditos Nikkei* (sashimi tuna), and imaginative renditions of *pescado del dia* including seared tuna steak flambéed in Grand Marnier then drizzled with an orange and passion fruit reduction.

Plaza de San Diego no. 8–21. www.juandelmar.com. ✆ **5/664-2782.** Main courses COP$24,000–COP$51,000. Daily noon–3pm, 7pm–1am.

La Casa de Socorro ★★ COLOMBIAN   With an unpretentious vibe and easygoing charms, it's tempting to underestimate this Getsemaní gem's culinary pedigree. An homage to Cartagena's Caribbean roots, fresh, simple seafood and hearty meat dishes combine with more adventurous, exotic fare including *picada de Tortuga* (stewed turtle) and turtle soup. Of the greatest hits that have made the *Casa* a locals' favorite, try the *cazuela de marisco*, a succulent seafood stew baked with cheese. With a diverse clientele as colorful as the decor, an infectious energy prevails in the breezy open-air dining room. This is good, honest cooking that won't break the bank.

Calle Larga no. 8B–12. ✆ **5/664-4658.** Main courses COP$16,000–COP$42,000. Daily 11am–midnight.

La Cevichería ★★ SEAFOOD   This petite locale, with outdoor seating just off lovely Plaza de San Diego, was put on the culinary map by Anthony Bourdain. Regardless of its celebrity status, what's not to love? There's the whimsical nautical decor interspersed with Cuban iconography, the laidback staff, and the super-fresh ceviche that headlines the menu. Order from the hot and cold menu sections for a bespoke feast. Peruvian-style shrimp, octopus, or lobster ceviche marinated in lemon and orange is the purist's choice, or there's a Mexican-style rendition with shrimp, diced avocado, tomato, and sour cream. Grilled and fried fish and seafood specialties include hearty paella, piquant grilled shrimp, and a perfectly executed *pescado del dia* topped with mouth-popping cherry tomatoes and drizzled with a basil/mint pesto. La Cevichería is one of those places that you will want to keep going back to.

Calle Stuart no. 714. www.lacevicheriacartagena.com. ✆ **5/660-1492.** Reservations recommended. Main courses COP$24,000–COP$47,000. Daily noon–3pm, 7pm–10pm.

La Cocina de Pepina ★★★ COLOMBIAN   This treasure trove of soulful cooking in the heart of Getsemaní is the kind of place where you feel like (or yearn to be) a regular. One of Colombia's most cherished chefs, María Josefina Yances (aka Pepina) devoted herself to creating Colombian and

Caribbean specialties faithful to century-old recipes and techniques. While the baton may have passed to her nephew, Cocina de Pepina is still the real deal with the same vibrant ambience, unpretentious attitude, and superb signature dishes that garnered the loyalty of Gabriel García Márquez. Don't miss Pepina's signature *mote de quesa* (soup made from local cheese) or legendary stuffed peppers. Other menu highlights include shrimp ceviche, seafood stew, and *fiambre de res* (a Colombian version of corned beef).

Callejón Vargas no. 9A–06. ✆ **5/664-2944.** Main courses COP$19,000–COP$32,000. Daily noon–3:30pm, Tues–Sat 7–9:30pm.

La Perla ★★ SOUTH AMERICAN   Nods to Peru are a dime a dozen on Cartagena's restaurant menus, but with Lima transplant Chef Carlos Accinelli at the helm, the Peruvian dishes at the rustic-chic La Perla (a 5-min. walk from Plaza Bolívar) are among the city's most interesting preparations. The raw appetizers steal all the glory, so a share-and-sample approach works well here. Highlights including tuna *tiraditos* cured in yellow chile and ginger. If you have more carnivorous inclinations, this is one of the best places to satisfy the itch with a hearty suckling pig or a tender Steak La Perla. Owner Roberto Carrascal is one of the city's renowned mixologists, so it's no surprise that his finely curated cocktail list is worth lingering over. Latin American classics are tweaked with aplomb; try the Pisco Sour Maracuya or Mojito Mango Biche.

Calle de Ayos no. 4–42. ✆ **5/664-2157.** Reservations recommended. Main courses COP$26,000–COP$54,000. Mon–Sat noon–3pm, daily 7–11pm.

La Vitrola ★★ MEDITERRANEAN   A beloved institution for locals and a rite of passage for many visitors, La Vitrola exudes an air of Old Havana gloriously brought into the present with whirling ceiling fans, a tiled floor dotted with potted palms, and debonair waiters in starched white uniforms. This is the place where local politicians, writers, and artists meet and muse over aged rum and Caribbean classics such as grilled *langostinos* or tuna steak with shaved mango and avocado, or traditional Cuban *ropa vieja*, all the while toe-tapping to an exhilarating soundtrack courtesy of the six-man Cuban band. Certainly, there is an old school formality here that may not be to everyone's taste; shorts, flip-flops, and kids under 15 are politely shunned. The ambience and people-watching arguably trumps the quality of the food, which, in resting hard on its laurels, has lost much of its cachet to Cartagena's newer and more innovative culinary haunts.

Calle Baloco no. 2–01. ✆ **5/660-0711.** Reservations recommended. Main courses COP$27,000–COP$56,000. Daily noon–3pm, 7–10pm.

Maria ★★ SEAFOOD   Alejandro Ramirez honed his skills in London with Gordon Ramsay before he came home to Cartagena to open Maria. The striking room—with soaring ceilings, white wicker chairs, and striped banquettes beneath whimsical "pineapple" chandeliers and jungle-themed tapestries—provides the backdrop for a refined dining experience. The balanced meat and fish selection infuses traditional Caribbean flavors with an Asian slant. Highlights include a jalapeño-infused salmon appetizer, risotto with shrimp and chorizo, salmon bathed in coconut milk curry, and pork chops in a sweet-and-tangy hoisin sauce. Round off with a simple, light dessert of strawberries topped with vanilla and swirled with a balsamic reduction.

Calle del Colegio no. 6A. www.mariacartagena.com. ℂ **5/660-5380.** Reservations recommended. Main courses COP$26,000–COP$48,000. Sun–Fri noon–3pm, daily 6:30–11pm.

Vera ★★ ITALIAN   Within the confines of the super-chic Tcharassi Hotel, Vera's white-on-white decor and flamboyant style set the tone for a sublime dining experience. Vera's lauded Chef Daniel Castaño crafts a coastal Italian menu which, rather than being loaded with adjectives, allows the distinct flavors of each ingredient to do the talking. Antipasti, carpaccio, salumi, and formaggio form a tantalizing prelude to the menu's star dishes: *risotto alla pescatore* (seafood risotto), *fettuccini maiale* (pork belly), a silky beef fillet with cherry and rosemary, and lamb with pumpkin and dates. Traditional Italian desserts are given a tropical spin with a refreshing limoncello sorbet with pepperoncino and honey, and a creamy panna cotta with wild berries.

Calle del Sargento Mayor no. 6–21. www.tcherassihotels.com. ℂ **5/664-4445.** Main courses COP$22,000–COP$45,000. Daily 11am–11pm.

Shopping

There's a style surge rippling through every street of the old city. With dazzling emeralds, contemporary art, colonial antiques, catwalk-worthy fashions, and stunning designer homewares, exploring the shops and boutiques of the Centro Histórico can fast become a passion and a compulsion. You can literally devote days and days just to the fine art of conspicuous consumption. And, while it's a hardly a bargain by Colombian standards, prices fare well compared to Europe and the U.S.

Abaco ★★ CAFE/BOOKSTORE   Cartagena's literary set find expression at Abaco, a wonderful bookshop/cafe that forms a community hub for the city's intelligentsia. The inventory covers a wide sweep of fiction, photography, art and architecture, with a strong slant toward Latin American and Colombian writers. There's plenty of material with a Cartagena theme, and of course, English-language editions of Gabriel García Márquez's prodigious bibliography. As well as a star-studded lineup of events during the Hay Festival in January, there are readings and literary gatherings each Wednesday evening. Calle de la Iglesia no. 3–36. www.abacolibros.com. ℂ **5/664-8338.**

Anticuario El Arcon ★★ ANTIQUES   If you are serious about antiques, this is the place to head. El Arcon is treasure trove of colonial and Republic-era antiques with an eclectic cache of furniture, religious statues, weapons, and off-beat decorative artifacts along with wooden doors, ceremonial plates, silverware, first-edition books, paintings, candelabras, lanterns, chandeliers, sconces, and Cartagena's signature gargantuan door knobs. Calle del campo Santo no. 9–46. www.arconanticuario.com. ℂ **5/664-1197.**

Bettina Spitz ★★ CLOTHING   Bettina Spitz's vibrant collection embodies Colombia's fashion design ethos. Lightweight, artisan fabrics, ablaze with color, are embroidered with distinctive Caribbean imagery and inspired by the Colombian landscape, wildlife, and indigenous culture. Every piece is ultra-fresh, feminine, and timeless. The beachwear collection has drawn plenty of press attention for its classic one-pieces, flattering bikinis, and eye-catching accessories including stylish hats and unique beach bags. Calle La Mantilla no. 3–37. www.bettinaspitz.com. ⓒ **5/664-1516.**

Casa Chiqui ★★ DESIGN/JEWELRY   Casa Chiqui represents the high-water mark of Cartagena's sophisticated design store culture. Legendary Cartagena hostess and arbiter of style Chiqui de Echavarría channels Moroccan, Asian, Indonesian, and Colombian artifacts and objects of desire at this vibrant emporium. The international style set flock here for inspiration for their colonial home conversion or boutique hotel restoration. The kaleidoscopic cornucopia includes rugs woven with cashmere, vibrant Mexican ceramics, exotic lanterns, day beds fashioned from exotic woods, and religious relics and iconography. Calle de la Universidad no. 36–127. www.casachiqui.com. ⓒ **5/668-5429.**

Ego ★★ CLOTHING   Guayaberas are to the Caribbean coast of Colombia what baseball caps are to the U.S. The region's signature linen pleated shirts are custom made by master tailor Edgar (Ego) Gómez Estévez. Since the 1970s, the globally esteemed tailor has been dressing royals, celebrities, pop stars, and politicians with his clean, simple, and airy designs produced from all-natural fabrics. At Ego's workshop, you can browse Estévez's famed guayabera designs (Bill Clinton and Bill Gates broadened their sartorial horizons here) as well as exquisite contemporary blazers and jackets. Calle de Portobello de la Iglesia no. 10–92. ⓒ **5/668-6016.**

Love Me Wappa CLOTHING   Colombians, like Brazilians, like to put a lot of thought into their beachwear. The store's name, a play on *guapa* (beautiful girl, which sounds a lot like *Wappa* with a *costeño* twang), tells it all. Sexy bikinis and elegant one-pieces in a myriad of flattering styles and prints are aimed at either accentuating curves or streamlining them, depending on your proclivity. The added bonus is that all the designers here are Colombian. Calle del Porvenir no. 35–15. ⓒ **313/877-6259.**

Lucy Jewelry ★★★ JEWELRY   The revered national stone, Colombian emeralds rank among the world's finest. They find the perfect stage here at Lucy Jewelry, in a radiant 17th-century mansion. Lucy's is hands-down the best place to acquire a quality emerald at a competitive price. For more than 40 years, jeweler Lucy Sanchez has been passionately curating emeralds renowned for their superlative sparkle and cut and seemingly infinite qualities and tones. Along with custom jewelry, you can browse elegant rings, bracelets, and delicate necklaces; many emeralds are set in stunning ornate filigree fashioned by Mompox's (see p. 155) revered silversmiths and goldsmiths. Calle Santo Domingo no. 3–19. www.lucyjewelrycartagena.com. ⓒ **5/664-4255.**

NH Galeria ★★★ ART   An outpost of the Nora Haime gallery in New York, this beautiful gallery redefined Cartagena's contemporary art scene when it opened in 2011. Exhibitions feature emerging and established Colombian and international artists in a variety of media. There's surrealism and pop art from Barranquilla's Alvaro Barrios; abstract oils from Canadian Julie Hendrick; dazzling genre-defying works from Bogotá's Olga de Amoral; sculptures from Greek artist Sophia Vari; and thought-provoking works by Colombian artist Ruby Rumié, whose projects resonate with political and psychological consciousness. If you want to invest in a piece of Colombian art, this is the place. Playa de la Artilleria no. 33–36. www.nhgaleria.com. ⓒ **5/664-0561.**

Cartagena After Dark

Bazurto Social Club ★★★   Named after Cartagena's boisterous central market, this kaleidoscopic club strewn with flags and whimsical artwork pays homage to all things Colombian, with a particular nod to Cartagena's Afro-Caribbean heritage, cultural giants including Márquez and Colombia's king of salsa, Joe Arroyo. As well as the standard-issue salsa, you'll get a broader Latin musical range here, with live champeta, cumbia, and reggae Thursday to Saturday. Although the music doesn't start until around 10pm, you can arrive between 7pm and 8pm for happy hour—try the Machacao, a fruity house cocktail laced with rum and honey—and you can even take a dance class. This is one of Cartagena's most authentic spots. Carrera 9 no. 30–42. www.bazurtosocialclub.com. ⓒ **5/664-2157.** Cover COP$10,000. Thurs–Sat 7pm–3am.

Café Havana ★★★   This iconic Cuban bar/dance hall has all the components that you dream of in a night spot. Along the walls, evocative black-and-white images of Cuba's musical legends set the tone for exhilarating, soul-stirring salsa music or Son Cubano from world-class musicians. Over free-flowing mojitos, daiquiris, and Cuba libres, locals and visitors passionately inhabit the moment at the inviting horseshoe bar before taking to the dance floor; once the band starts around 11pm, every bit of real estate is given over to Cuban dance in all its sultry, wild, and creative forms. Although Café Havana is well established on the tourist trail (in 2012, then Secretary of State Hillary Clinton hosted a bash for visiting dignitaries during the World Summit), the place somehow retains its incredible energy and authenticity and should not be missed. Intersection of Calle Media Luna and Calle del Guerrero. www.cafehavanacartagena.com. ⓒ **314/556-3905.** Cover COP$10,000. Wed–Sat 8:30pm–4am, Sun–Tues 5pm–2am.

La Movida ★   While it may not have the counterculture vibe associated with Madrid's La Movida, the clientele at this fashionable namesake dance club certainly share the movement's pursuit of hedonistic pleasures. The decor is slick, the vibe showy, and the playlist jumps from local pop hits to Latin to international to EDM in two separate spaces. The beer and spirits come with the kind of sticker shock that adds to its exclusive aura. But if it's Monday night at midnight (when much of the city is closed) and you want to dance or people watch, this might be your only option. While the claustrophobic, very hot space may not be the best place to appreciate it, the food here is pretty good; standouts on the well-conceived tapas menu include grilled octopus salad and tuna tartar. Calle 33 no. 2–14. ⓒ **5/660-6126.** Bypass the strict door policy and ask your hotel concierge to call ahead to reserve a table. Cover price varies, around COP$20,000. Daily 7pm–3am.

Malangana ★★ Arguably the most fashionable terrace in hip Getsemaní, Malangana is popular with a younger crowd that comes here to sip fruity renditions of classic cocktails on the lovely mosaic rooftop. The creative lair of designer duo Diana and Maria Carolina Herrera Ordosgoitia, Malangana's three social spaces each provide a different mood. Malangana has earned cachet as the place where the after-hours crowd gathers; Marisa Tomei, Clive Owen, and Gael García Bernal have all been spotted on the rooftop. If you are in town the first week in December, don't miss Malangana's annual street party. And, from 6 to 8pm, you can sample two for one cocktails along with a light menu that conjures tasty iterations of Colombian classics. Calle Tripita y Media 31–55. ✆ **5/660-1360.** Main courses from COP$22,000. Mon–Thurs 3:30pm–2:30am, Fri–Sat 3:30pm–1:30am.

Quiebra Canto ★★ This small Getsemaní bar/club, just 5 minutes from the Puerto de Reloj, is the real deal. There's a raw vibe to the second-floor nightclub, with its original tile floors and evocative jazz posters strewn across the walls. When there's live music on Fridays and Saturdays, everyone comes here just to dance, but you'll need to buy a half bottle of rum at least (COP$37,688, which is around US$13) if you want to score a table; however, there's no cover charge to get in. On quieter nights, the balcony is a great place to watch the street life unfold below. On the third floor, there are often screenings of independent Latin American movies. Calle 24, Media Luna 8B no. 25–100. www.quiebracanto.com. ✆ **5/664-1372.** No cover. Tues–Sun 7pm–4am.

BARRANQUILLA ★

A gritty, modern city with a major port overlooking the Magdalena River, Barranquilla is not the kind of place that courts or warrants tourist attention. The main reasons travelers wind up here are either for onward travel connections or to attend the spectacular Carnaval de Barranquilla celebration (it was even given a UNESCO nod) in February/March, which is second only to Rio in both its size and unbridled revelry. For the rest of the year, Barranquilla keeps its head down, works hard, and doesn't too defer too much from its status as an industrial, no-nonsense (and often seedy) town.

Still, for a 24-hour visit, Barranquilla offers interesting sights and attractions and expansive parks to pass the time. With an invigorated economy, signs of a much-needed rejuvenation are afoot within the city's historic kernel. Certainly there's no shortage of historical and popular culture touchstones to muse over. Barranquilla proved fertile territory for intellectuals, artists, and philosophers who converged here to form the "Group of Barranquilla" in the mid-20th century, spearheaded by Gabriel García Márquez and **Álvaro Cepeda Samudio.** And no one forgets Barranquilla's pride and joy, pop icon (and philanthropist) Shakira, cherished throughout Colombia, who was born here in 1977.

Getting There

BY PLANE   Barranquilla's airport, Aeropuerto Internacional Ernesto Cortissoz (www.aeropuertobaq.com; airport code BAQ; ✆ 5/316-0900) is located 11km (7 miles) south of the city. This used to be Colombia's largest airport, and it remains extremely well connected to the rest of the country. There are direct international flights from Miami with **American Airlines** (www.aa.com) and **Avianca** (www.avianca.com) which also boasts the most extensive network with non-stop flights to Colombia's major cities. Low cost airline **Viva Colombia** (www.vivacolombia.org), launched in 2012, flies to Medellín and Bogotá (which can cost as little as COP$153,000 [US$50] each way if you book a couple of months in advance), and **Copa** (www.copaair.com) provides direct flights to Panama City and San Andrés Island. **LATAM Colombia** (www.latam.com) flies to Bogotá. A taxi from the airport to downtown Barranquilla will cost around COP$25,000.

BY BUS   Buses arrive to the Terminal Metropolitana de Transportes on the south side of the city (around COP$22,000 by taxi). Ticket prices vary according to each company, route, and class. There are buses every 30 minutes from Barranquilla to Cartagena (2 hr., from COP$15,000), hourly buses to Medellín (14 hr., COP$65,000) and at least hourly to Bogotá (17 hr., from COP$75,000). Efficient and comfortable door-to-door services operate between Cartagena and Barranquilla with **BerlinasTur** (www.berlinastur.com/Servicio_Especial) or **MarSol** (www.transportesmarsol.net/wp/servicios) and cost between COP$17,000 to COP$22,000.

Getting Around

BY TAXI   Barranquilla is not the kind of place you will want to stroll. Taxis are readily available and easy to hail, but they are not metered, so make sure you establish a price first. Minimum fare is COP$5,000; within the city and old town you should never pay more than COP$11,000. To travel beyond the city limits to the beaches of Salgar, expect to pay COP$15,000 to COP$20,000. Whenever possible, call a radio taxi (*taxis de confianza* or *taxis registrados*), which can be used in tandem with the terrific **Tappsi** app, a highly successful Colombian start-up company and Uber-like travel application, which includes security features (driver's license provided, links to e-mail your taxi details to a friend, etc.), and is compatible with Android and iOS devices.

BY BUS   While taxis are the most time/cost efficient means of exploring the area, Barranquilla's bus system (colorful, retrofitted school buses) is an extremely cheap means of getting from A to B—if you have time and can tolerate standing up with no air-conditioning. The bus route is usually written on a small placard on the front window of the bus. You can wave down buses pretty much anywhere, and you can alight the bus at any point, within reason. A journey around town will cost around COP$1,500 to COP$1,600. If you are traveling to small towns outside Barranquilla, such as the beaches of Puerto Colombia, Santo Tomás, or Malambo, it will cost anywhere from COP$2,000 to COP$4,000. *Busetas* operate according to the same principal, they are just smaller and a lot more cramped. The best mode of bus transportation is the government-run rapid transit system or **Transmetro** (www.transmetro.gov. co) service, which has three central lines or *rutas troncoles* that connect to a network of 25 different routes or *rutas alimentadoras*. You'll need to buy a Transmetro card at any of the stops on the main routes. A single trip costs COP$1,800; transfers to a feeder line are free, within 1 hour.

Top Tourist Attractions

Barranquilla's action centers on **Paseo Bolívar ★**, the city's commercial nexus, which funnels south to **Parque Simón Bolívar ★**, with its bold equestrian statue of South America's great liberator. Flanked by Republican buildings in varying states of health, Paseo Bolívar is the quintessential Latin American boulevard, a vortex of cacophonous market stalls, newsstands, and second-hand bookstalls. It's not pretty, but there's never a dull moment. Just south, the imposing neo-Gothic **Iglesia San Nicolás ★**, fronted by a statue of Christopher Columbus, dominates its newly restored namesake square. The Church of Saint Nicholas used to be the main cathedral before the honor was passed to the modern **Catedral Metropolitana ★**, opposite Parque la Paz. A short stroll farther south, the anachronistically named **Museo Romántico ★** (Carrera 54 no. 59–199; ℂ **5/344-4591**; Mon–Fri 9:30–11:30am, 2:30–5pm; COP$5,000 adults, COP$3,000 children) doesn't triumph the Latin art of romance, but rather functions as a small history museum. Worth stopping in for an hour or two, there are interesting exhibits on Carnaval, including the costume worn by the first Carnaval Queen in 1918, an exhibit on the history of radio in Colombia, letters written by Simón Bolívar, and a typewriter that belonged to Gabriel García Márquez.

Far and away the city's cultural highlight is the **Museo del Caribe ★★★** (Calle 36 no. 46–66; www.culturacaribe.org; ℂ **5/372-0581**; Tues–Thurs 8am–5pm, Fri 8am–6pm, Sat and Sun 9am–6pm; COP$13,000) which triumphs the history, anthropology, environment, and popular culture of Colombia's *costeño* (Caribbean) region. Spread over seven floors, a broad sweep of engaging multimedia exhibits cover the region's indigenous tribes, the arrival of immigrants from Africa and the Middle East, culinary history and tradition, and ecosystems and wildlife. There's a whole room devoted to Márquez, which examines the inspiration behind Gabo's magical realist tales, and a floor dedicated to Barranquilla's famed carnival with an instrument showcase, an audiovisual romp that highlights carnival's glorious history, and displays that evoke the evolution of music and dance across the Caribbean. There are plenty of interactive activities for kids, as well as a children's library and a small butterfly garden.

Another worthy cultural attraction that keeps with the carnival theme, the **Casa de Carnaval ★★** (Carrera 54 no. 49B–39; ℂ **5/370-5437**; Mon–Sat 9am–5pm; COP$5,000) is housed in an evocative colonial mansion. A multisensory homage to all things Carnaval, there are vibrant displays of costumes (which you can try on; yes, kids love this place) from each of the distinct Carnaval dance troupes (congo, Garabato, Cumbia, Marimondas, etc.), instruments, and a cursory examination of the cultural roots, symbolism, and popular culture expressions attached to Colombia's biggest fiesta. There are exhibits on the often-baffling musical genres—everything from son to cumbia and mapalé—heard not only at Carnaval but blasting from every car, bar, and home stereo all year round.

In front of the **Estadio Metropolitano Roberto Meléndez** (Corner of Av. Circunvalar, Murillo Toro), home of local soccer team Junior, Colombian tourists come in droves to wield their selfie sticks beside the 16-foot-tall, 6-ton steel **statue ★** of Grammy award–winner Shakira, emblazoned with the words, "When you look at me, think that you too can accomplish what you want."

Where to Stay

Most of Barranquilla's best accommodation choices are located about 4km (2½ miles) north of the city in El Prado district. Be sure to book at least 2 or 3 months ahead of time for Carnaval.

Hotel El Prado ★   While it may not live up to its glorious 1930s heyday, the Prado is still Barranquilla's best hotel, with an array of crowd-pleasing amenities. The beautiful neoclassical building features striking arcades with a black-and-white tiled floor and encloses a terrific pool (the main draw) surrounded by palm trees. Some of the traditional rooms are drab, and bathrooms could do with an update, but they are clean, well-equipped, and spacious. Although it's a stretch to call El Prado luxurious, it's a relaxing place to unwind before or after a flight with a couple of decent restaurant/bar options, a small gym, and a well-priced spa.

Carretera 54 no. 70–10. www.hotelelpradosa.com. ✆ **5/369-7777.** 200 units. Doubles COP$236,000, includes breakfast. **Amenities:** Restaurant/bar; spa; pool; free Wi-Fi.

Meeting Point Hostel ★   This laidback hostel in a peaceful part of town operates as Barranquilla's international travelers' hangout. Clean, fresh dorms with shared bathrooms all have lockers and air-conditioning, and there's a communal kitchen and patio area with hammocks. The hosts are happy to provide information on sights and activities in the area as well as help you figure out travel connections.

Carrera 61 no. 68–100. www.themeetingpointhostel.com. ✆ **5/318-2599.** 5 units. COP$60,000 (private room) COP$25,000 (dorm.) **Amenities:** Free Wi-Fi.

Washington Plaza Hotel ★★   This is a great-value boutique hotel that checks the boxes for location, functionality, comfort, and customer service. Modern, minimalist rooms are freshly decorated and equipped with flatscreen TVs, rainfall showers, comfortable beds, and reliable Wi-Fi (a novelty in these parts). A lot of thought has gone into the design-conscious public spaces, including a sleek restaurant and bar/terrace, which successfully offset the architect's boxy right angles. Flamboyant furniture, decorative objects, and polished floors are pleasingly juxtaposed with potted plants, flowers and exposed brick.

Carrera 53 no. 79. www.washingtonplaza.co/en. ✆ **5/319-9980.** 51 units. Doubles from COP$170,000. **Amenities:** Restaurant/bar; free Wi-Fi.

CARNAVAL DE BARRANQUILLA: COLOMBIA'S
wildest party

Barranquilla's carnival slogan is *"Quien lo vive es quien lo goza"* (He who lives it, enjoys it), which seems quite an understatement. Mention Barranquilla to any Colombian and they will unabashedly claim the city's Carnaval is the biggest and best in the world. After Rio, it certainly is. Barranquilla's raucous spectacle of flesh, fantasy, and gyrating hips puts to shame the lackluster Carnaval celebrations displayed by the country's biggest cities. Dating back to 1903, when Carnaval celebrations marked the end of the Thousand Days' War (Guerra de Mil Días), **El Carnaval de Barranquilla** (www.carnavaldebarranquilla.org) is more than just a citywide bacchanalian romp. A fabulous expression of the region's cultural heritage, historic events, mythical characters, and indigenous mysticism underscore each impassioned parade, song, and dance.

Carnaval is held the 4 days before Ash Wednesday (late Feb/early Mar), but celebrations begin much earlier. Festivities kick off on the Friday with **La Guacherna**, an outlandish drag show. On Saturday, the main event is **La Batalla de las Flores** (Battle of the Flowers). Fully regaled dancers perform traditional Spanish *paloteo*, African *congo*, and native *mico y micas* as theatrical *comparsas* (troupes) and beauty queens atop floats—decked out with elaborately handcrafted masks, ornaments, and costumes—wave and smile at crowds baking in the bleacher seats (*palcos*) along Calle 40's parade route. On Sunday afternoon, the **Gran Parada de Tradición y Folclor** pays homage to Colombia's folkloric traditions with 245 masqueraded dance troupes that perform intense, choreographed routines to a traditional Caribbean regional soundtrack that fuses African, indigenous, and Spanish influences: cumbia, champeta, vallenato, and poyo. There's no shortage of burlesque, with campy theatrical performances that satirize contemporary political life. In 2003, UNESCO declared Barranquilla's carnival an "Intangible Cultural Heritage" at risk from increased commercialization.

In 2017, Carnaval will run from February 25 to 28, and in 2018, February 10 to 13. If you plan to visit during Carnaval, you will need to book your accommodation well in advance. Be aware that the city swelters at this time of year (all year in fact), and everything grinds to an abrupt halt for 3 days. Consider yourself in for the duration. Bleacher tickets (partly shaded) cost around COP$180,000 (www.vive.tuboleta.com) for 3 days, more if you book through a hotel or agency.

Where to Eat

Cocina33 ★★ COLOMBIAN/SEAFOOD Barranquilla's most upscale restaurant brings poise and a dash of elegance to the city's generally uninspiring dining scene. Eye-catching furnishings, exposed brick, and romantic lighting set the mood for a memorable experience. The menu aims high, with classic Caribbean dishes given a gastronomic spin. Artfully presented menu highlights include silky tuna tartar, Angus beef rib-eye, ceviche with lychee and lobster, fish infused with truffle oil, and salmon glazed with honey in a coconut curry reduction. For Barranquilla, this is an epicurean treat, but you will pay heavily (by Colombian standards) for the experience.

M Restaurant Bar La Cueva ★ COLOMBIAN   Behind the unassuming facade, there's no shortage of story value to this classic Colombian restaurant (with a pretty impressive art collection) which serves well-executed Caribbean seafood dishes and popular Colombian dishes for carnivores. Try the *posta negra*, a steak cooked in a viscous sauce made from Coca-Cola, onion, garlic, Worcestershire sauce, cumin, and brown sugar. There are also plenty of exotic seafood combinations, including crab and queen conch, fresh fish of the day with tropical fruit and coconut milk, and a seafood stew with coconut rice. There's live music on the weekend.

Carrera 43 no. 59–03. www.fundacionlacueva.org. ⓒ **5/340-9813.** Main courses COP$25,000–COP$34,000. Mon–Thurs noon–3pm, 6pm–10pm; Fri–Sat noon–3pm, 6pm–1am.

Varadero ★ CUBAN/SEAFOOD   This popular Cuban-themed restaurant serves an imaginative menu of seafood and fish specialties including fine ceviche, lobster tail in a cream sauce, grilled octopus, Cuban-style steak topped with seafood and melted cheese, and grilled fish with a passion-fruit glaze. The Caribbean-inspired selections tend to be the most successful dishes. With live Cuban music, warm service, excellent mojitos, and plenty of decorative nods to old Havana, Varadero make for an inviting ambience and pleasurable way to spend an evening. It is quite pricey for Barranquilla.

SANTA MARTA ★

Located 98km (61 miles) N of Barranquilla and 200km (124 miles) NE of Cartagena

Santa Marta is one of those cities that slowly works its magic. Beyond the architectural eyesores, crumbling behemoths, and bumper-to-bumper traffic, there lies a historic, dynamic city which promises (and often delivers) moments of majesty. Wearing the mantel of Colombia's oldest city and the second-oldest surviving city in Latin America, there's no shortage of historical touchstones, colonial charm, and iconic monuments to make for an interesting short stay. Much is made of Santa Marta's associations to Simón Bolívar; it was here that the great liberator—a close second to Jesus in Latin America's pantheon of heroes—died of tuberculosis in 1830 (age 47).

Seduced by the vision of infinite gold, Spanish conquistadors established a colony here in 1525. It took less than a century for the Spanish to decimate the Tayrona people, who had inhabited the Sierra Nevada de Santa Marta since 200 B.C., and plunder their gold for the pleasure of the Spanish crown. During the colonial period, Santa Marta yielded its influence to the more dynamic (and impregnable) city of Cartagena. In the 20th century, Santa Marta's once bustling port found a new vocation, running a brisk trade in bananas and coal and, more infamously, as the center of contraband; even today more drugs (primarily cocaine) pass through Santa Marta than any other Colombian port.

Nowadays, Santa Marta's number one industry is tourism, with fun-loving Colombian vacationers flocking to the town's beaches, excellent restaurants, and lively streets where, once the sun goes down, salsa and son drifts around every corner. The city provides the launch pad for the country's most fabled attractions: Parque Nacional Tayrona and Ciudad Pérdida. While Santa Marta doesn't have the cachet, style, or grace of Cartagena, savvy travelers have found fulfillment in coupling the glamor and polish of Cartagena with the grit and authenticity of Santa Marta. Thanks to government initiatives and intrepid businesspeople, the city now boasts a newly restored colonial kernel that centers on Parque de Novios, converted pedestrianized zones, a new boardwalk, and the city's crowning achievement: a dazzling new marina with a healthy quota of bobbing super yachts. While the situation has improved over the last few years, Santa Marta still has a reputation for street crime. Keep your valuables at your hotel and your devices concealed, and don't venture beyond the main tourist areas at night.

Essentials

TOURIST INFORMATION   On the new waterfront, the helpful and enthusiastic Punto de Información Turística (Carrera 1 no. 10A–12; ✆ **5/438-2587**; open Mon–Fri 9am–noon, 2pm–6pm, Sat 9am–1pm) provides helpful information and maps on Santa Marta as well as tours to Tayrona National Park and treks to Ciudad Pérdida.

GETTING THERE

BY PLANE   Aeropuerto Internacional Simón Bolívar is located 16km (10 miles) south of Santa Marta. Domestic airline **Avianca** (www.avianca.com), low-cost airline **Viva Colombia** (vivacolombia.org), and **LATAM Colombia** (www.latam.com) fly to Medellín (90 min.) and Bogotá (90 min.). **Copa** (www.copaair.com) provides direct flights to Panama City and San Andrés Island. A **taxi** from the airport to downtown Santa Marta will set you back between COP$25,000 and COP$28,000. Or you can take a **city bus** (COP$1,400); they run along the main highway outside the main terminal (approximately every 30 min.) to the center of Santa Marta via Rodadero.

BY BUS   Intercity buses arrive to the Terminal de Transportes (Calle 41 no. 31–17; ✆ **5/430-2040**), 5km (3 miles) south of the city. Local buses run from Santa Marta to Cartagena (4 hr., COP$28,000,) to Medellín (15 hr., COP$108,000) to Bogotá (18 hr., COP$110,000). Highly recommended, efficient, and comfortable door-to-door services operate between Cartagena and Santa Marta with **BerlinasTur** (www.berlinastur.com) or **MarSol** (www.transportesmarsol.net/wp/servicios) and cost around COP$45,000.

GETTING AROUND

The main area of interest in Santa Marta, the historic center around Plaza de Novios and Plaza Bolívar, is best negotiated on foot. Buses ply the route along the water from Santa Marta to Rodadero, west of Santa Marta, and cost COP$1,400. Local *colectivo* buses depart from Carrera 5 and the market (Carrera 11) to Taganga cost COP$1,400. A **taxi** to Taganga will cost COP$10,000 to COP$14,000; to Rodadero, COP$8,000.

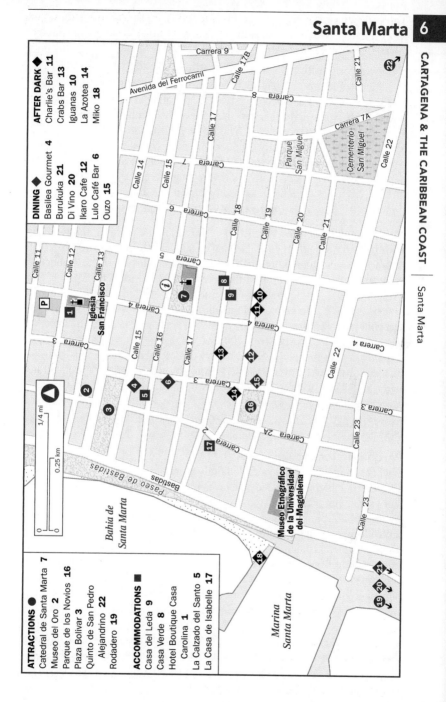

DINING ◆
Basilea Gourmet **4**
Burukuka **21**
Di Vino **20**
Ikaro Cafe **12**
Lulo Café Bar **6**
Ouzo **15**

AFTER DARK ◆
Charlie's Bar **11**
Crabs Bar **13**
Iguanas **10**
La Azotea **14**
Miko **18**

ATTRACTIONS ●
Catedral de Santa Marta **7**
Museo del Oro **2**
Parque de los Novios **16**
Plaza Bolívar **3**
Quinto de San Pedro
  Alejandrino **22**
Rodadero **19**

ACCOMMODATIONS ■
Casa del Leda **9**
Casa Verde **8**
Hotel Boutique Casa
  Carolina **1**
La Calzado del Santo **5**
La Casa de Isabelle **17**

Bahía de
Santa Marta

Marina
Santa Marta

Museo Etnográfico
de la Universidad
del Magdalena

Top Attractions

Catedral ★ HISTORIC SITE   Contender for the oldest cathedral on the continent, Santa Marta's gleaming white cathedral with a magnificent wooden portal was originally built in 1765. A slew of English, French, and Dutch pirate attacks led to constant renovations, which explain the colonial structure's mish mash of architectural styles. Captivating at sunset, the handsome tower, a lofty spire in its clutches, rises above the humble low-slung colonial structures that squat beneath it. The ashes of Rodrigo de Bastidas (1460–1527), the city's 16th-century founder who mapped out most of the northern coast of South America, are on the left as you enter the cathedral. The cathedral also served as Simón Bolívar's first resting place; 12 years after his death in 1842, his ashes were taken to his hometown of Caracas.

Calle 17 and Carrera 4. ℂ **5/421-2434.** Free. Daily 7–10am, 2–6pm.

Museo del Oro ★★ MUSEUM   The stately *Casa de la Aduana* (Customs House) was built in 1531. Now an engaging museum, the Museo del Oro is Santa Marta's cultural highlight, with a stunning display of pre-Columbian gold and ceramics that survived the greed and bloodlust of the Spanish conquest. The ground-floor galleries present (with some information in English) a dazzling collection of pre-Columbian jewelry with exquisite jade, copper, and gold work fashioned by the Tayrona and Nahuange people who inhabited the Magdalena region between 200 and 1600 A.D. On the second floor, an illuminating exhibit elucidates the history of Colombia's indigenous groups—including the Kogi, Arhuaco, and Wiwa—through a series of well-curated artifacts. Be sure to take a look at the wonderful model of Ciudad Pérdida, especially if you intend to visit.

Calle 14 no. 1–37. http://proyectos.banrepcultural.org/museo-del-oro-tairona. ℂ **5/421-0953.** Free. Tues–Sat 9am–5pm, Sun 10am–3pm.

Parque de los Novios ★ LANDMARK   The "Park of the Newlyweds" is where Santa Marta's rejuvenation finds expression. Until just a few ago, this square was a dilapidated, seedy enclave populated by prostitutes, drug dealers, and vagrants of every ilk. After a serious makeover, the park now lives up to its romantic aspirations. Newlyweds pose for pictures in the park's centerpiece **Templete del Parque** (a sort of ornamental, whitewashed gazebo), young couples kiss amid potted flowers under burnished street lamps, and salsa spilling from nearby bars stirs elderly couples to an impromptu salsa performance. Pedestrianized **Calle 19**, which runs east from the square, is punctuated with atmospheric bars, cafes, and restaurants that increasingly cater to a hip crowd with a more gourmet palate. All the while, tantalizing street food still corners the backpacker market as travelers meet and exchange stories over *arepas*. On the south side of the park, the luminous **Palacio de Justicia** is a fine example of 19th-century neoclassicism, with its buffed white bricks standing in dazzling contrast to the park's red-brick tile surface.

Intersection of Calle 19 and 20, Carrera 2 and 3.

Plaza Bolívar ★ LANDMARK   With its shoeshine boys, street vendors, mustachioed men playing board games, and couples making out, Plaza Bolívar (which stands on the same spot where the original Plaza Mayor once stood) is your quintessential Latin American square. On the square's north side stands the stately, mustard-yellow **Alcaldía** (city hall). A statue of a mounted Bolívar is the centerpiece for the leafy western end. The new *malecón* (boardwalk) funnels south from the gritty port area, with its unsightly cranes and container ships, to the slick, flashy marina, where there is also a small beach (but don't think about swimming here).

Calle 14 and 15, btw. Carrera 2B and Carrera 1 (Malecón).

Quinto de San Pedro Alejandrino ★★ MUSEUM   Five kilometers (3 miles) from the center of Santa Marta, this magnificent 17th-century hacienda is where Simón Bolívar spent the last days of his epic life; Bolívar was a guest of the hacienda's Spanish owner, Joaquín de Mier, a passionate acolyte of Bolívar and staunch backer of Latin American independence. The hacienda, which produced rum, honey, and sugarcane, has been transformed into a museum that commemorates El Libertador through a series of Bolívar-themed exhibits within the hacienda and monuments that dot the expansive grounds. The hacienda is worth a visit alone for its evocative rooms preserved in period style, which include a chapel and the room where Bolívar died. Of the monuments that dominate the hacienda's grounds, the Altar de la Patria forms the most striking homage to the legend who liberated six countries from Spanish colonial rule. Commissioned in 1930 to celebrate the centenary of Bolívar's death, the impressive white-marble memorial is composed of three monumental statues that depict Bolívar in different stages of his life. Also within the hacienda's grounds, the 22-hectare Jardín Botánico is a relaxing place to stroll. Adjacent to the hacienda, the eclectic Museo Bolivariano triumphs the work of Latin American artists; don't miss Alejandro Obregón's affecting canvas *Don Simon en San Pedro Alejandrino*, a portrait of a withered Bolívar shortly before his death. There are also nudes by Darío Morales (1944–1988) and Alfredo Guerrero (1936).

Avenida Libertador 14 no. 1–3. www.museobolivariano.org.co/quinta-de-san-pedro-alejandrino. ✆ **5/433-1021.** Free. Daily 9:30am–4:30pm. Take bus from Carrera 1C/waterfront, direction Mamatoco, COP$1,500. A taxi will cost around COP$6,000.

Rodadero ★ BEACH   Developed in the 1940s and a big hit with Colombian holidaymakers, Rodadero is to Santa Marta what Bocagrande is to Cartagena. Thrusting condo buildings flank a ribbon of grey sand fringed with palm trees. Although it's not a picture perfect Caribbean dreamscape by any stretch, it's worth the short 10-minute taxi ride to experience the infectious frivolity of families at play on the beach and to take a dip in the clear water. Eating and drinking here provides a cheap and tasty immersion into Colombian delicacies, with local snacks hawked in abundance along the boardwalk. The constant rhythms of *vallenato* music provide a clear reminder that you are in Colombia's Caribbean region. If you are looking for escapism, launches depart from

Rodadero to the prettier crescent beach of **Playa Blanca** (15-min. boat ride) where you can rent chairs and umbrellas and relax on pristine white sands.

A taxi to Rodadero from the Centro Histórico will cost around COP$8,000. Local buses ply the waterfront and cost COP$1,400.

Where to Stay

Casa del Leda ★★   The original features of a 19th-century mansion have been artfully incorporated into the design of this tasteful new boutique hotel that is emblematic of Santa Marta's flourishing hotel scene. From the spacious rooms to the serene public spaces, the Casa del Leda demonstrates impressive attention to detail. Stylish, sensual rooms are decorated with textured rugs, breezy drapes, four-poster beds, and colorful artworks. Thoughtful amenities include aromatherapy kits and media players, and some rooms have hot tubs. With a prime location; friendly, efficient staff; a lovely roof terrace with views over Santa Marta's colonial area; and two lovely pools, the Casa de Leda is one of the city's most characterful choices. Breakfast is cooked to order to each day.

Calle 18 no. 4–38. www.kalihotels.com. ✆ **5/422-1302.** 10 units. Doubles from COP$236,000, suites COP$365,000, includes breakfast. **Amenities:** 2 pools; free Wi-Fi.

Casa Verde ★   Built in the 1920s, this distinctive Republic building has been recast as a charming boutique hotel with six functional and smart green-on-white rooms that marry natural materials—wooden floors, bamboo doors, rattan chairs, beamed ceilings, and wooden shutters—with contemporary amenities that include flatscreen TVs and air-conditioning. The lush central courtyard encloses a small swimming pool, and indulges everyone's inner sybarite with potted palms, mosaic tiled floors, and Doric columns strewn with hammocks.

Calle 18 no. 4–70. www.casaverdesantamarta.com. ✆ **5/431-4122.** 6 units. Doubles from COP$184,000; suites (with kitchenettes) from COP$270,000, includes breakfast. **Amenities:** Pool; free Wi-Fi.

Hotel Boutique Casa Carolina ★★   An oasis in the heart of the old town, this English/Colombian-owned gem of a hotel is stylish, welcoming, and comfortable. Slick rooms are clean and bright with white tiled floors, exposed brick, and large contemporary bathrooms with granite-tiled showers and design-centric faucets and sinks. Well-conceived amenities include iPad docking stations and flatscreen TVs. Larger, flashier suites have big terraces with sunbeds and Jacuzzis, and there's a small, fully equipped apartment that is a great choice for families. The inviting public spaces include a lovely inner courtyard and fantastic rooftop terrace with a small pool and sweeping views of the city. The hotel's highly praised restaurant, Eli's, serves fresh, innovative Caribbean dishes as well as tapas, sashimi, and fabulous cocktails. Highly recommended.

Calle 12 no. 4–70. www.hotelcasacarolina.com. ✆ **5/423-3354.** 25 units. Doubles COP$250,000, COP350,000 suite, COP450,000 apartment, includes breakfast. **Amenities:** Restaurant; pool; hot tub; free Wi-Fi.

La Calzada del Santo ★   Tucked away in the historic district, this welcoming hotel offers bright, clean rooms in all shapes and sizes (a little too generic for some tastes) with tiled floors, flatscreen TVs, air-conditioning, and occasional design nods to Colombia's artisan heritage. The main draws here are the location (less than a 10-minute walk from Santa Marta's main attractions), the chilled-out traveler vibe, and the gracious hospitality from the staff, who will happily help arrange onward travel and day trips to the area's attractions. There's an outdoor pool and a social rooftop terrace with hammocks.

Calle 16 no. 2–43. ✆ **5/420-4538.** 12 units. Doubles from COP$260,000, COP$340,000 suites. **Amenities:** Pool; free Wi-Fi.

La Casa de Isabelle ★★ Another impressive Kali boutique hotel, the fabulous La Casa de Isabelle is an 8-minute walk from Santa Marta's new marina. Behind a bold indigo and violet painted facade, the thoughtfully converted colonial mansion fuses tradition and modernity with aplomb. Cheerful, spacious rooms feature contemporary styling with a distinctly Colombian sensitivity—think salvaged furniture, handcrafted textiles, and indigenous artifacts—while state-of-the-art amenities include a complementary Apple TV and iPad. An aura of relaxation permeates every alcove, stairway, and terrace of the hotel, with Mudéjar-style mosaic tiles, exuberant vertical gardens, arabesques of wrought iron, and thoughtfully conceived ambient lighting. And, to soothe the soul, the onsite spa offers a myriad of restorative treatments.

Carrera 2 no. 19–20. www.kalihotels.com. ✆ **5/431-2082.** 10 units. Doubles from COP$244,000, suites from COP$378,000, includes breakfast. **Amenities:** Pool; spa; free Wi-Fi.

Where to Eat

Basilea Gourmet ★ FRENCH This intimate French/Mediterranean inspired restaurant close to Parque de los Novios offers classic French dishes with a Caribbean spin, including French onion soup, salmon carpaccio, steak frites, grilled snapper in a coconut sauce, and citrus crepe Suzette. They're paired with a thoughtfully conceived wine list. Formal white tablecloths, buffed silverware, wooden furniture, and subdued lighting yield to a relaxed tropical aura with local artwork, religious iconography, green painted walls, fresh heliconia flowers, and exposed brick. It is a little overpriced by Santa Marta standards.

Calle 16 no. 2–58. www.basileagourmet.inf.travel. ✆ **5/431-4138.** Main courses COP$26,000–42,000. Mon–Sat noon–3pm, 7pm–midnight.

Burukuka ★★ STEAK/INTERNATIONAL It's hard to beat the location and views at this contemporary restaurant/bar overlooking Rodadero beach. With an ambitious culinary scope that includes lobster tail, BBQ ribs, and a classic selection of pasta, some dishes are certainly more successful than others. Regulars come here to choose their cut of steak, which is simply chargrilled or served with a red wine reduction. The cavernous dining room is smart, with vivacious red walls and slick furniture with exotic wood, bamboo, leather chairs and an exposed-brick open bar. It's worth the trip here for a pre/post-dinner sunset cocktail (potent caipirinhas) on the outdoor terrace with sweeping views of the coast. On weekends, locals flock here for the wild live rumba party.

Carrera 1 at Calle 1. www.burukuka.com. ✆ **5/422-3080.** Main courses COP$26,000–COP$60,000. Daily noon–3am.

Di Vino ★ ITALIAN   A block from the beach in Rodadero, this upscale Italian restaurant/wine bar is a popular choice for its broad menu of Italian classics with a seafood slant. The rustic dining room, with distressed wooden furniture and floor-to-ceiling windows, provides a lively setting for pasta, bruschetta, thin-crust pizza, and fish specialties. Try the signature fettuccini marinara with seafood, or perhaps shrimp-stuffed ravioli, or steak medallions in a red wine sauce; a few Caribbean classics also creep onto the menu, including ceviche and fruity rum-based cocktails. A good wine list, warm (if spotty) service, and thoughtful touches—including free sangria and canapés while you peruse the menu—have made Di Vino a staple for travelers and locals.

Calle 6 no. 1–26. ℂ **5/421-3725.** Main courses COP$22,000–COP$32,000. Daily noon–11pm.

Ikaro Cafe ★★ COFFEE SHOP/LIGHT MEALS   This traveler-oriented coffee shop/roaster with a holistic vibe serves excellent organic coffee produced on their own plantation in the Sierra Nevada de Santa Marta. With lounge seating, plants, a waterfall, soothing tunes, and oriental knickknacks, it's a laid-back spot to hang out and graze on piquant Thai and Asian fusion dishes as well as healthy salads, soups, sandwiches, and pasta, with plenty of vegetarian and vegan options. Breakfast is very popular with terrific homemade bread, granola and pancakes studded with pecans. Proceeds from the Ikaro Cafe are donated to a foundation that supports the local indigenous Kogi Community.

Calle 19 no. 3–60. www.ikarocafe.com. ℂ **57/643-0558.** Main courses COP$15,000–COP$28,000. Mon–Sat 8am–10pm.

Lulo Café Bar ★★ JUICE BAR/CAFE   With a cozy setting, chilled-out ambience, gracious staff, and a diverse clientele, Lulo (named after a type of locally grown passion fruit) is one of those eateries that fast becomes a daily routine if you spend more than a few days in a place. Invigorating and unusual smoothie and juice combinations are Lulo's claim to fame, but the light meals here are also excellent. You can fuel the day with tasty breakfast tortillas, or try one of the delicious *arepas* with "gourmet" toppings including shrimp, avocado, and mango, or grilled octopus with avocado and chile. The fresh and healthy theme extends to an imaginative selection of panini, wraps, ceviche, and salads. At night, the mood winds down with free-flowing creative libations; try the signature *Lulo* cocktail with vodka, passion fruit, and organic honey or the Sol de Hoy, an inspired mix of rum, mango, and basil.

Carrera 3 no. 16–34. www.lulocafebar.com. ℂ **5/423-2725.** Main courses COP$14,000–COP$23,000. Daily 8am–10pm.

Ouzo ★★ MEDITERRANEAN   Santa Marta's top restaurant, just off Parque de Novios, Ouzo has raised the bar on Santa Marta's dining scene. Ouzo serves a balanced menu of Greek and Mediterranean dishes in a convivial, traditional setting with a lovely open-air patio. Chef/owner Mike McMurdo earned his stripes at a Michelin-starred restaurant in New York, and there's no lack of ambition and creative zeal. Start off with tender signature roast octopus (braised for 2 hours) with feta and olives, or share a Greek meze platter as a prelude to tasty entree highlights, including baked chicken orzo, rich lamb ragu served over pappardelle, or Greek paella (with orzo). The fantastic wood-oven pizzas are the talk of the town, with innovative sweet and savory toppings that range from duck confit to creamy eggplant, or the house special: a wild combination of creamy gruyere, summer squash, arugula, serrano jam, and black truffle honey. Don't miss the Corozo cocktail (a Colombian version of a French 75). You'll definitely pay Cartagena prices here, but it's worth it.

Carrera 3 no. 19–29. www.ouzosantamarta.com. © **5/423-0658.** Main courses COP$23,000–COP$38,000. Mon–Thurs noon–10:30pm, Fri and Sat noon–11pm.

Santa Marta After Dark

Most of Santa Marta's nightlife pivots around the newly restored Parque de los Novios and pedestrianized Calle 19. With friendly staff, great drinks, loud music, and a fun atmosphere, **Charlie's Bar** (Calle 19 no. 4–12; © **300/593-4855**) is one of the most popular nightspots in town. The international crowd pack into this anything-goes (you can expect some dancing on the bar) American-style bar for fine cocktails (COP$12,000), shots (COP$5,000) and beer (COP$4,000). Revelers spill out onto the sidewalk on the weekend when there's live music or a themed DJ event. **Crabs Bar** (Calle 18 no. 3–69; © **315/796-3636;** Wed–Sat 7pm–3am) tends to what most travelers dream of in a home-from-home kind of bar. With an old pool table (free to play), rock memorabilia, looping rock videos, and irreverent touches such as a bike hanging on the wall and a bath tub masquerading as a chaise, this old school rock 'n' roll bar draws an eclectic, fun-loving clientele of all ages. There's great live music on the small stage on the weekend, as well as games and competitions. **Iguanas** (Calle 19 no. 4–58; © **5/878-5522;** Mon–Thurs 5pm–1am, Fri and Sat 5pm–3am, Sun 4pm–midnight) is a great place to kick off the evening. With tropical murals, lounge seats, and festive lighting, this is a chilled-out place to enjoy awesome cocktails, live music (mostly son or salsa), folk dance shows, and dance competitions.

On a third-floor rooftop overlooking Parque de los Novios, top local DJs spin late night Latin beats at the urban-cool **La Azotea** (above Radio Burgeur; Wed–Sat 5pm–2am) a bar/dance club where elegant locals dress up for cocktails at the cool bar before the whole space turns into a thumping dance floor. **Miko** (Carrera 1 no. 22–93; © **317/359-0784;** Mon–Sat 4pm–3am, Sun 10am–2am) is the closest thing you'll get to Ibiza on this stretch of coast. Right on the waterfront, the tropical, open-air space with stylish lounge seating and stunning marina views draws a cool, international crowd of 20- and 30-somethings with its mixed soundtrack (dance, house, reggae, Latin), potent cocktails, and fun staff.

Side Trips from Santa Marta

ARATACACA ★

Márquez's birthplace, Aracataca, just a 90-minute bus ride south of Santa Marta, has become a place of pilgrimage for Gabo acolytes. With blistering heat year round, dilapidated buildings that date to the Aratacaca's early-20th century boom

GABO'S LINGERING legacy

"The problem is that the Caribbean reality resembles the wildest imagination."
—Gabriel García Márquez, 1982

Soul stirring and utterly spellbinding, the magical realist narratives of Gabriel García Márquez are credited with transforming the literary culture of a continent. Winner of the Nobel Prize for Literature in 1982, Márquez (known affectionately as Gabo) has become a cultural moment; impassioned readers will remember the time and place that Márquez's fantastical prose first captured their imagination.

The most Colombian of Colombian authors, to read Márquez is to be immersed in the omens, tropical sensuality, family histories, superstitions, and magic of the Caribbean Coast. The town of Aracataca, where Márquez was born in 1927, provided the inspiration for the fictional town of Macondo in Márquez's revered masterpiece, *Cien años de soledad*. Raised by his grandparents, the author's political leanings were shaped at an early age by his grandfather, a colonel who fought in the Thousand Days' War. His grandmother inspired his magical realist tendencies. In their home, surrounded by an eccentric cast of relatives, stray guests, servants, and Wayúu Indians, the young Gabo became transfixed by her supernatural tales.

Reading Kafka's *Metamorphosis* stirred the budding author to craft his own intellectual short stories, which were published in the newspaper *El Espectador* in Bogotá. After a nomadic youth, studying law in Bogotá and working as a journalist in Barranquilla, Márquez joined the literary Barranquilla Group and found inspiration in the Lost Generation of American writers. Gabo inhabited the life of a struggling artist, sleeping in brothels and immersing himself in the savagery and the beauty of Colombia's wild Caribbean Coast.

During the 1940s, Márquez worked as journalist, reporting on the period of violent unrest known as La Violencia. When he sympathized with the communist cause, he was vilified by conservatives and forced to flee to Europe. Márquez would spend most of his life in self-imposed exile in Mexico City, returning only sporadically to his home in Cartagena. Later in life, Márquez's enduring relationship with Fidel Castro proved a sticking point for conservatives worldwide.

years, and kids eating fruit off the trees and scampering in the river, the whole town feels like a mirage. Nowadays, the banana groves that filled the coffers of American banana companies have been replaced by palm-oil plantations.

Certainly, Aracataca is not a tourist carousal, which is both its salvation and its damnation. A dusty, forgotten town, selling out hasn't been an option. Any efforts to conjure tourist hotspots and slap on a Márquez placard have failed due to the town's woeful infrastructure and crippling poverty. Still, the ramshackle town is a worthy stop on the Márquez trail and, along with Mompox (see p. 155), it's a curious place that captures the isolation and tropical mysticism that pervades Gabo's best works.

The most compelling Márquez "attraction" is the **Casa Museo Gabriel García Márquez** ★★ (Calle 5 no. 6–35; Tues–Sat 9am–1pm, 2–5pm, Sun 9am–2pm; free; ✆ **5/425-6588**), the home where Márquez was born in 1927, and which has been faithfully reconstructed as a museum. Period furnishings, quotes, and memorabilia relate Gabo's novels to his upbringing (he lived in Aracataca until 1936), and formative years.

In 1950, at age 22, Gabo returned from Europe to Aracataca with his mother and found the town redolent of the seediness, decadence, and oppressive heat that characterized Faulkner. In an interview with *Paris Review* in 1982, he stated, "I felt that I wasn't really looking at the village, but I was experiencing it as if I were reading it. It was as if everything I saw had already been written down and all I had to do was sit down and copy what was already there and I was just reading . . . everything evolved into literature; the houses, the people, and the memories."

In 1957 he wrote his first novella, *La hojarasca* (Leaf Storm), which he would later describe as his means of escape from the political mire that was engulfing Colombia. A year after its publication, he married his childhood sweetheart Mercedes Barcha in Barranquilla, who supported the family financially while Márquez dedicated himself to writing full time. It wasn't until he had published five of his seven novels in 1967, and received critical and popular acclaim with the publication of *Cien años de soledad* (One Hundred Years of Solitude), that he earned royalties.

Throughout his career, García Márquez garnered innumerable awards and honors. While most of his works do not have the improvised, stream-of-consciousness quality of *Cien años,* they are populated with magical characters, peppered with the same fantastical elements, and interwoven with the politics, landscape, and culture of Colombia's Caribbean Coast. The 1985 bestseller *El amor en los tiempos del cólera* (Love in the Time of Cholera) was set in Cartagena and related the author's parents' relationship; it was a huge success and sold millions of copies worldwide.

Following his cancer diagnosis in the late 1990s, Márquez laid bare his own life in his 2002 memoir, *Vivir para contarla* (Living to Tell the Tale), which was well received by critics and readers. Gabriel García Márquez died in Mexico City on April 17, 2014, at the age of 87, bequeathing a beautiful legacy of seven epic novels, 10 non-fiction works, and a dazzling collection of novellas, which have been translated into 21 languages.

Local buses leave from Santa Marta's Terminal de Transportes (every 30 min., 90 min., COP$10,000). You'll need to ask the driver to let you off at the road just outside of town.

MINCA ★★

Just a 45-minute drive from Santa Marta, Minca is one of those salubrious, high-altitude towns that just puts a spring in your step. Nestled in the highlands of the Sierra Nevada, at an elevation of 2,165 feet (660m), Minca's holistic aura, idyllic natural beauty, and thrilling topography lure travelers in search of off-the-beaten track adventure. It's one of those places that travelers plan to escape to for a day or two and end up staying for days, or even weeks. The tiny, pretty town proper has no real sights to speak of. Days are spent hiking, bathing in shallow pools beneath cascading waterfalls, bird-watching, ziplining, or touring a coffee plantation. Here in the mountains of the Sierra Nevada de Santa Marta, indigenous Kogi and Arhuaco tribes have spearheaded the production of organic coffee based on a unique and sustainable farming network that fuses spiritual beliefs with contemporary planting techniques. For seasoned travelers, Minca provides an interesting complement to the coffee plantation tours offered in the Eje Cafetero (Colombia's southwest coffee triangle, see chapter 7).

Getting There

COLECTIVO TAXI   From Santa Marta, the easiest and cheapest way to get to Minca (24km/15 miles) is to take a *colectivo* taxi (regular departures) from the market area (Calle 11/Carrera 12) signed Estación de Minca; COP$7,000 per person, 45 minutes. *Colectivos* wait until there are four passengers before they depart.

TAXI   A private taxi direct from Santa Marta to Minca will cost COP$30,000 to COP$40,000. Ask your hotel in Santa Marta to arrange the taxi and confirm the price before you get in.

MOTOTAXI   From Santa Marta's market, take a bus signed Yucal, and ask the driver to let you off after the train tracks, where mototaxis (motorcycle taxi) will take you to Minca for COP$8,000. A *mototaxi* direct from Santa Marta will cost COP$12,000 to COP$16,000.

Exploring the Outdoors

BIRD-WATCHING   The Sierra Nevada Mountains are the holy grail for avid ornithologists. One of South America's most prized bird-watching destinations, the region is home to more than 1,900 species (that's 33% of all bird species on the planet). Over 600 bird species have been recorded in the mountains surrounding Minca, including the allusive Ruby Topaz, Sapphire-bellied Hummingbirds, Keel-billed Toucan, and the Black-headed Tody-Flycatcher. On the northern slopes of the Sierra Nevada de Santa Marta, **El Dorado Bird reserve** (a 90-min. bone-shaking drive from Minca) provides sanctuary to a rich profusion of endangered birds, including the Santa Marta Parakeet, the Santa Marta Bush-tyrant, and the Santa Marta Sabrewing. The only accessible subtropical-to-montane forest in the Sierra Nevada, the 1,600-acre reserve has six moderate to challenging trails (totaling around 5km/3 miles) that traverse diverse habitats. Excellent bird-watching tours, including visits to the El Dorado Reserve, are offered by tour guides and outfitters in Minca (see "Tour Operators," facing page).

HIKING   Trails right from Minca's town center lead through pristine ecosystems where you can take cool dips in waterfalls, follow pre-Columbian trails, stumble across rock carvings, and marvel at ancient stone work. For longer day hikes into the mountains, I recommend hiring a local guide or taking a tour; see "Tour Operators," facing page.

WATERFALLS   An easy 45-minute hike/mountain-bike ride through pristine forests, where bird life and butterflies abound, leads from Minca to idyllic **Pozo Azul**, two captivating swimming holes with a small waterfall surrounded by massive rocks and lush vegetation. Pozo Azul was a spiritual Kogi site where ceremonial rituals were performed; indigenous people still convene here for purification rituals. An Eden of lush vegetation and pulsating wildlife, it's a lovely place to relax and take a refreshing dip (the water is cold). Try to go during the week when it's quieter; it can get very crowded on the weekend. An hour hike from the village, **La Casada Marinka** offers more drama, with two large drops that plummet into a small pool below. After swimming in the pool, hike up to the top of the first waterfall for the exhilarating views. **To get to the waterfalls**: Follow the main road through Minca until you cross a bridge—you can either go straight or turn right. For Pozo Azul go straight; for Marinka turn right. At the intersection, *mototaxis* will offer to take you to Marinka or Pozo Azul for around COP$7,000. To enter Marinka, you'll need to pay the entry fee, COP$3,000 pesos. There is a cabin here with a bar, bathroom, and hammock space (or you can camp; negotiate a rate with the owner of the cabin).

LONGER HIKES   The hike to **Los Pinos** (1,760m) takes around five or six hours (each way). From here, you can continue on to San Lorenzo and Sierra Kennedy, with breathtaking views of the Sierra Nevada; you can also take a *mototaxi* service to El Campano and walk the final stretch. You'll need to stay overnight at **Hostel Santa Elena** (Carrera 11 no. 2A–25, Cerro Kennedy; www.hostalsantahelena.blogspot.com; ✆ 314/561-9608) which has simple dorms rooms and incredible views of Pico Bolívar and Colon peaks draped in snow. The less trodden trail (comparatively speaking) is from Minca to Bonda, where the **Paso del Mango** takes you into an ethereal landscape of indigenous paths, prehistoric stones, rushing rivers, and abundant fruit trees. If you choose this route, you can overnight (it may be hard to leave) in a simple cabin at the wonderful **Finca Carpe Diem** (Paso del Mango; www. fincacarpediem.com; ✆ **5/420-9610**; double room from COP$94,000), a 50-acre farm with horse-riding, hiking, crystal clear rivers for swimming, and breathtaking views.

COFFEE TOURS   It wasn't that long ago that Colombia's unofficial policy was to export the best coffee. Things have definitely changed. Just outside of Minca, several local coffee farms promote tours and tastings of their high-end organic coffee. One of the best is **Hacienda La Victoria** ★★ (www.lavictoria coffee.wordpress.com; ✆ **317/308-5270**; tours COP$10,000). Between Minca and the town of San Lorenzo, a 20-minute 4WD ride (or 40-min. hike from Pozo Azul), La Victoria provides a fascinating insight into the coffee-making process. Established by Brits in 1892 (hence the name), the hacienda still uses waterpower (part of the tour involves a hike to the waterfall) as well as traditional techniques and equipment, including hand-cranked presses and gravity-driven sorters. Tours take guests through every stage of coffee growing, roasting, and processing followed by the opportunity to try their smooth blends along with a slice of homemade apple pie.

Tour Operators
Expotur ★   This Santa Marta–based agency offers a full-day bird-watching tour (departs at 6am, returns 6pm) in Reserva el Faunal with expert guides, 4×4 transfer from Santa Marta (tours can also be arranged from Minca), entrance to the reserve, breakfast, lunch, and soft drinks (COP$150,000).

Carrera 3ra no. 17–25, Santa Marta. www.expotur-eco.com. ✆ **5/420-7759.**

Fidel Travels Mica Aventura ★   This established, Minca-based outfitter is highly recommended for its full-day coffee plantation tours from Santa Marta (COP$55,000), bird-watching in the Sierra Nevada (departing from Minca, COP$40,000), and bird-watching combined with San Lorenzo and Cerro Kennedy Snow Peaks (COP$150,000). Professional local guides, 4×4 transportation, equipment, and insurance included.

Diagonal to the church. www.fideltravels.com. *℃* **5/321-589-3678.**

Joe Ortiz ★★   The English-speaking owner of the I-center in Minca, "Jungle Joe" offers a range of excellent eco-friendly tours in the Minca area, including tubing, rafting, and canyoning. Joe also offers a full-day (9am–5pm) tour of Minca/Sierra Nevada from Santa Marta (COP$110,000) and a morning bird-watching tour in the Sierra Nevada (customized according to bird-watching experience) from 6 to 9am (COP$25,000).

Minca I-center (opposite Hotel Minca). www.junglejoeminca.com. *℃* **5/308-5270.**

Where to Stay

Casa Elemento ★★   Perched high on a ridge with sublime views of the Sierra Nevada, Casa Elemento is an adventure camp for backpackers young and old. A massive hammock and a small swimming pool with a bar take center stage amid myriad onsite activity stations including a slackline, superman swings, and a climbing wall. Self-guided trails lead from Casa Elemento through a pristine ecosystem. No one takes themselves seriously here, and the nightly bonfires and family-style dinners followed by games of chess and backgammon cultivate a tone of convivial inclusivity. With howler monkeys as the nocturnal soundtrack, this is a great place to feel immersed in nature. Clean, functional dorms sleep up to seven and hammock spaces are available. In 2016, Casa Elemento constructed new "micro cabins" with double beds, electricity, and a private porch. Instead of taking a *mototaxi* to get here, many travelers choose the scenic hike (2 hr.) through coffee plantations and past the Markina waterfalls.

Calle 18 no. 4–70. www.casaelemento.com. *℃* **313/587-7677.** 6 units. Dorm rooms from COP$35,000, double rooms/micro cabins from COP$120,000, hammocks COP$20,000. **Amenities:** Swimming pool (very small); restaurant/bar; onsite activities and tours arranged; no Wi-Fi.

Casa Loma Minca ★★★   Nestled in Minca's lush hills, accessed via a series of steep steps up the side of the mountain (no vehicle access), Casa Loma is one of the most enchanting hostels in Colombia, indeed in Latin America. A series of simple, open-air wooden huts and dorms (no electricity) with beds draped with mosquito nets and clean, shared bathrooms form a large treehouse surrounded by riotous vegetation. Colorful hammocks and beanbags are strewn through the lively communal areas where backpackers, families, and couples read, play cards, bird-watch, and enjoy the glorious sunsets. There's a highly praised, inexpensive Italian-vegetarian restaurant, a yoga platform, and a fire pit. If you are an early riser or light sleeper, avoid the rooms over the communal areas. Be prepared to get off the grid; there's no Wi-Fi here.

Casa Loma also rents a two-bedroom house in Minca, which sleeps up to six (from COP$100,000–COP$200,000 based on number of guests).

No address; *colectivo* taxi from Santa Marta (COP$7,000). www.casalomaminca.com. © **313/808-6134.** 11 units. Dorms (with four beds) from COP$28,000, doubles with shared bathroom from COP$70,000, hammocks from COP$17,000, rainforest camping (bring your own tent) COP$15,000. 10% surcharge for credit card payments. **Amenities:** Restaurant; yoga.

Cocina de Campo ★ Just a few minutes' walk from town, this gem of a hostel run by Californian/Colombian couple Lexi and Jorge offers rooms for all budgets nestled among peaceful, winding pathways lined with fragrant fruit trees and exotic flowers, and populated with rambunctious bird life. Rustic double rooms with private bathrooms are spacious and clean, or for families or longer-stay guests, the spacious apartment with a kitchen/dining room proves highly cost effective. There's a small swimming pool, but the main draws here are the laidback ambience and the onsite organic restaurant with delicious light meals, cakes, pastries, and smoothies.

Calle 1 no. 5–130. www.cocinadecampo.info. © **312/627-0219.** 7 units. COP$80,000 (apartment), COP$60,000 doubles with private bath, COP$50,000 doubles with shared bath, COP$40,000 camping. **Amenities:** Swimming pool; restaurant; free Wi-Fi.

Rancho de la Luna ★★ There's a holistic vibe to this enchanting bamboo home/boutique hotel which blends harmoniously with the lush setting. The spacious, eco-friendly rooms are constructed using indigenous techniques and materials and feature thoughtful design touches: colorful mosaic tiles with indigenous motifs, "floating beds" suspended from the ceiling, and wraparound private porches where you can sit and revel in the transcendent views. The warm, welcoming hosts are adept at skill diversification, with services that extend to Reiki massages and wholesome organic meals. There are also yoga classes and "mystical music" sessions if you need to channel your inner *om.*

400m from Puente de la Acequia in Minca town. www.ranchodelalunaenminca.com. © **317/352-7025.** 4 units. Doubles from COP$90,000. **Amenities:** Yoga; massage; restaurant; no Wi-Fi.

Where to Eat

Minca's cluster of eateries embraces the region's natural bounty with delectable local produce and exotic ingredients finding their way into Latin American classics and international fare. As well as the options listed below, many of Minca's hostels and inns offer organic, home-cooked meals.

Bururake ★ RESTAURANT This lively fusion steakhouse with an open kitchen, walls covered with murals (the owners are artists), and a balcony overlooking the river is the place to head for a gourmet dining experience. While it's not the cheapest option in town, the meat-centric menu has flashes of inspiration with steak doused in chocolate-and-chili sauce and tender filet mignon wrapped in Parma ham. There are also several vegetarian options and hearty local dishes including *ajiaco* (potato and chicken soup).

Calle del Rio 6. © **313/515-3432.** Main courses COP$14,000–COP$35,000. Daily noon–3pm, 7–10pm.

Casa D'Antonio ★★ RESTAURANT One of Minca's more memorable dining experiences, gregarious Spaniard Antonio delivers a fresh and tasty menu of Mediterranean and Iberian classics with a fish and seafood slant. Crowd pleasers include the *paella mariscos* (seafood paella), *camarones al pimpill* (spicy oven-baked shrimp), grilled *pargo* (red snapper), and lobster. Lunch and dinner are served in a casual, traditional dining room with colonial-style furniture, or out on the porch, where you can revel in the sweeping views of Santa Marta amid hummingbirds and heliconia flowers.

2km from Minca. www.hotelrestaurantecasadantonio.com. ✆ **312/342-1221.** Main courses COP$23,000–COP$55,000. Mon–Sat noon–3pm, 7pm–midnight.

Lazy Cat ★ RESTAURANT Named after the restaurant's languorous feline star, the Lazy Cat is a backpacker favorite for its taste-of-home staples. Creative burgers, stir-fried vegetable and chicken creations, and quesadillas are washed down with fresh juices (try the lulo), fruity cocktails (the daiquiris are excellent), and beer. The experience here is all about the setting, with a balcony that makes you feel like you are in the middle of the jungle.

Calle Principal no. 1–460. ✆ **313/506-5227.** Main courses COP$12,000–COP$19,000. Mon–Sat noon–10pm.

Tienda Café Minca ★ CAFE/BAR A village institution, this coffee shop (bar at night) is a great place to hang out and meet locals, expats, and travelers on the relaxed terrace. The caffeine boost comes in a creative repertoire of frappuccinos, lattes, and espresso made from local organic coffee that will raise the bar for your daily Joe. Decadent baked goods include organic chocolate truffles, banana-chocolate bread, and a signature brownie with homemade ice cream. In the evening, beer trumps coffee with craft iterations from the Bogotá Beer Company brand as well as the elusive Apóstol brand. This is also a great place to buy *artesanía* as well as local coffee, homemade jams, and raw cocoa.

Calle 1 no. 3–134. ✆ **312/638-5353.** Daily 8am–10pm.

TAYRONA NATIONAL PARK ★★★

Tayrona National Park is one of Latin America's undisputed highlights. A wild and pristine landscape that feels untouched by time and the human hand, mountains carpeted with dense jungle plummet down to idyllic palm-fringed coves and white sugar-sand beaches. Part of the Sierra Nevada de Santa Marta mountain chain—one of the highest coastal mountain ranges in the world—Tayrona had long been off limits to travelers. During the 1980s and '90s, the park was ground zero for the civil war that erupted between Marxist guerrilla groups (the FARC and ELN) and right-wing paramilitaries. More recently, it has been associated with drug trafficking, as narco lords established camps within the Sierra Nevadas for cocaine processing and distribution. In 2003, in a high-profile case that garnered international attention, eight backpackers en route to Ciudad Pérdida were kidnapped by guerrillas and held for 3 months. In separate incidents, three of Tayrona National Park's directors were murdered when they refused to establish the park as a base for cocaine trafficking.

DIVING taganga

The once paradisiacal fishing village of Taganga, just 3 miles north of Santa Marta, has lost its soul. When beatniks and bohemians came here with visions of utopia, it didn't take much time for a dizzying development of unsightly lodgings, cheap eateries, and sleazy all-night bars to spring up. While the horseshoe bay—backed by mountains and lapped with aquamarine waters—is stunning when viewed from afar, at close range it's dirty and uninviting. At night, a seedy underbelly prevails and a number of violent robberies have occurred over recent years.

So why visit Taganga? Despite its fall from grace, the town provides a convenient launch pad for the sublime Parque Nacional Tayrona, just a short boat ride away. Another of Taganga's draws is its fantastically economical diving courses.

With temperatures hovering between 24 and 28°C and crystalline waters with visibilities of up to 30 meters (best diving conditions are Dec–Apr), and protected and shallow dive sites (ideal for beginners), it's no wonder diving companies run a brisk trade in these parts. Taganga ranks as one of the cheapest places in the world to dive; you can become PADI certified in 4 to 6 days for as cheap as US$200, including accommodation. Professional, inexpensive diving and snorkeling excursions to the azure waters of **Tayrona** will likely reveal moray eels, tropical reef fish, and, if you are lucky, turtles, rays, and dolphins. For more experienced divers, **El Torrin** is an 18m-deep dive site renowned for its visibility and thriving brain corals. Another expert-only dive site is **Barco Hundido**, a sunken boat covered with coral and oysters. **Los Morritos** is a deep dive around two steep rocks covered in black coral and teeming with prolific marine life. Experienced wreck dives can also be arranged near Rodadero.

Tayrona Diving Center (Carrera 1C no. 18A–22; www.tayronadivecenter; ✆ **5/421-5349**) is the established outfitter in the area, offering PADI courses and a full menu of diving trips for all levels. Independent instructor **Reto Müller** (Casa Jaguar, Carrera 2 no. 18–300; www.divetaganga.com; ✆ **5/421-5349**) provides custom group tours (no more than three divers) and PADI certification courses that include hostel lodging and fun-filled BBQs. An expert on the region and a patient, warm instructor, gregarious, multilingual Reto will make even the queasiest beginners feel at ease.

The top accommodation choice in town, **Casa los Cerros** (Carrera 2 no. 1–35; www.casaloscerros.com; ✆ **5/410-9534**), a 5-minute stroll from the beach and town, offers comfortable studios with sun terraces (from COP$170,000), and an inviting swimming pool. A 10-minute walk from town, **Aparthotel El Oasis** (Calle 23 no. 5B–47; www.hoteleloasis.com; ✆ **5/423-3728**) offers studios (from COP$140,000) with fully equipped kitchens, and terraces with expansive sea/mountain view. There's also a small swimming pool. They provide a free shuttle service; the walk home is not advised at night.

With a cozy bistro setting and accomplished French cooking, **A Deriva** (Calle 14 no. 1B–34; ✆ **316/579-1422**; main courses COP$22,000–COP$26,000; daily 11am–11pm) is Taganga's best dining experience. You can dine on one of the best-prepared filet mignons you will get for COP$25,000 (around $8) anywhere at **Pachamama** (Calle 16 no. 1C–18; www.pachamamataganga.com; ✆ **316/667-2819**; main courses COP$14,000–COP$25,000; daily 5:30–11:30pm, closed Sun) which serves gourmet international cuisine in a big tiki hut with live music and free-flowing cocktails.

A taxi to Taganga from Santa Marta will run between COP$10,000 and COP$14,000. *Busetas* leave every 15 to 30 minutes from Carrera 1C and 5 in Santa Marta (COP$1,500). It's generally easy to flag buses down as they head north on Carrera 6.

In response, then President Álvaro Uribe instigated a ruthless military crackdown that killed many of FARC's most important military architects and forced the guerillas to withdraw to Colombia's southern jungles. With the Sierra Nevada now considered a "secured" area, Tayrona has re-entered the traveler lexicon as a pristine, dramatic, and safe landscape ripe for discovery.

A national park since 1964, the 59-mile-long swath of rugged coastline, fringed with coral reefs and framed by colossal, white, sea-sculpted boulders, comprises one of the continent's most biologically diverse coastal enclaves. Amid virgin rainforest, small Tayrona settlements and evocative archaeological relics stud the park. There are few places this accessible where you feel so utterly immersed in nature. From endangered dry tropical forest to equatorial rain forest and cloud forests at higher elevations, Tayrona National Park just bristles with life: iguanas, monkeys, snakes, red squirrels, collared peccaries, jaguars, panthers, sloths, armadillos, jaguarondi, bats, and deer. An estimated 400 species of birds (migratory and resident), including toucans and red woodpeckers, and more than 1,200 plant species find sanctuary here.

In addition to swimming and wildlife spotting, Tayrona offers incredible hiking, along beaches and through majestic forest to the ancient ruins of **El Pueblito**. A network of trails, formed by ancient stones laid by Tayrona's indigenous Koguis, Arhuacos, Arsarios, and Kamkuamos, wend to untamed beaches and idyllic coves (there are more than 30 beaches within the park); a few offer excellent swimming and snorkeling, see facing page.

Essentials

GETTING THERE The eastern section of Colombia's Tayrona National Park (Cañaveral, Arrecifes, and Cabo San Juan) is the most visited, most beautiful, and also most geared toward tourism, but the western section provides a quieter and wilder alternative.

BY BOAT There are daily speedboats (11am, returning at 4pm; COP$90,000 return) run from Taganga to Cabo San Juan (1 hr.). Arrive well ahead of time in high season; boats fill up quickly. The crossing to the west of Tayrona can be very rough, and infrastructure on this remote side is lacking, with few accommodation options or restaurants.

BY BUS *Busetas* run from Santa Marta (central market at Carrera 11 and Calle 11, every half hour, 60–75 min., COP$6,000) to the park's main eastern entrance accessed via the Troncal del Caribe highway (turn off for El Zaíno), 35km from Santa Marta. It's a further 4km to the park's Visitor Centre (© 5/ 421-1732). The main trails begin at Cañaveral (where there is a parking lot), about a 45-minute walk from the gate. A taxi from Santa Marta to El Zaíno will cost from COP$60,000; from Taganga, around COP$65,000. Because taxis are not metered, always negotiate before you get in.

GETTING AROUND Most visitors travel light and hike from Cañaveral to Cabo San Juan. If you are physically challenged, from the car park in

Cañaveral, you can rent a horse to Arrecifes (from COP$16,000) or to Cabo San Juan (from COP$30,000).

VISITOR INFORMATION Plenty of bug spray (mosquitos are vicious), long pants, shirts, and hiking boots are advised. The park can be visited by boat from Taganga, but the most memorable way to experience Tayrona is to hike from Cañaveral and stay overnight. Always try to book accommodation way ahead of time, especially during peak travel periods. **Aviatur** (www.aviatur ecoturismo.com) is the official tour operator within the park and tends to manage the best accommodation options. In recent years, the park has been closed (without much advance warning) for water shortages and in response to complaints by local tribes of "bad energies" emanating from international backpackers. Always check the park's website (www.parquesnacionales.gov.co/portal/en/ecotourism/caribbean-region/tayrona-national-natural-park) ahead of time, and obtain local information on the ground in Santa Marta or Taganga. Tayrona's eastern section is the most visited area of the park and offers better infrastructure and more attractions (and hence gets more crowded).

WHEN TO GO The rainy season is from April to June and September to November. The park can become very crowded during high season (Dec–Feb, Easter week, and during Colombia's school holidays [June/July]). If you plan to visit the park by boat from Taganga, be aware that the sea can be very choppy between December and February.

FEES The park fees are COP$42,000 international visitors, COP$16,000 Colombian residents, seniors, and students.

Beaches

Tayrona (out of high season) is a castaway's fantasia. There are more than 30 paradisiacal beaches backed by dense jungle, each with their own natural charms and breathtaking views, but very little shade. There are several ways to get to the park's main beaches. Most travelers opt to hike from the main entrance. An easy 1-hour hike through coconut groves and thick mangrove forests teeming with wildlife takes you to the long and windswept **Castilletes** beach (which can also be accessed via a paved road; or you can hitch a ride on one of the *camiones* [trucks] which regularly traverse the route [around COP$5,000]). Some 3km (2 miles) farther, **Cañaveral** is a picture-postcard golden beach, lined with palm trees and surreal formations of Jurassic limestone boulders sculpted by the turbulent ocean. A 5km (3-mile) trail farther west leads to **Arrecifes**, a breathtaking sweep of pristine white sand (normally deserted) backed by a vertical wall of jungle. Swimming here is prohibited due to pounding surf, fierce riptides, and dangerous currents. There's also a freshwater lagoon just behind the beach. At **Arrecifes**, basic but comfortable bungalows front the beach, and an open-air restaurant serves simple grilled fish, seafood, ceviche, and Colombian beer. Just 10 minutes farther on foot from Arrecifes, **La Aranilla** is a paradisiacal cove where water crashes onto Tayrona's signature boulders. A 30-minute walk beyond Arrecifes, the sheltered cove of **La Piscina** forms an alluring swimming area, which is great for families and provides fine snorkeling; sand sharks, Blue Tangs, blowfish, and sea turtles can often be seen.

A 20-minute hike farther, where a series of ladders and staircases carved into the rocks afford sublime ocean views, lies the legendary horseshoe-shaped beach of **El Cabo San Juan del Guía**. Here, mountains woven with a thick jungle canopy in every fathomable shade of green rise above a dazzling white-sand beach fringed with statuesque coconut palms and lapped with calm azure waters. Even when it's busy, this is one of the most mesmerizing beaches you will encounter anywhere. A **nudist beach** is a 10-minute walk west from El Cabo. If you want to camp under the stars to the sound of crashing waves, you can rent hammocks here in **El Mirador** (a gazebo sort of structure, from COP$20,000). If you are visiting during high season and would prefer more solitude (relatively speaking), drive or take a taxi (around COP$170,000; 12km/7½ miles from Santa Marta) to **Playa Neguaje** at the park's Zalangana entry point, or **Playa del Muerto** (20km/12 miles from Zalangana). From Bahia Neguaje, you can take a *lancha* to Playa Cristal, where you can swim and then dine at any number of decent seafood restaurants. Just outside of Tayrona's park entrance at Cañaveral, **Playa Los Angeles** is also a beautiful base (and more cost effective) with five new rustic-chic cabins (see p. 137).

Hiking to El Pueblito

One of Tayrona National Park's most memorable experiences is the 3-hour hike from the park entrance at Cañaveral to the pre-Columbian archaeological ruins of **El Pueblito**. The series of well-preserved stone terraces were built by the autonomous Tayrona people, who inhabited the northern portions of the Sierra Nevada massif from A.D. 200 until A.D. 1600–1650. While El Pueblito is the most famous ruin, it is estimated that there are more than 200 ancient Tayrona settlements with rammed-earth architecture and ornate stone masonry dotted throughout the Sierra Nevada; you will find yourself, magically and unexpectedly, just stumbling across relics as you hike through the emerald forest. If you can't make the Ciudad Pérdida trek, El Pueblito makes a good alternative.

Be advised that the steep stone path can get slippery and muddy during the rainy season. A **guide** with a trained eye can help to identify the flora and resident wildlife along the route, including parrots, howler monkeys, hawks, keel-billed toucans, and rare butterflies. Free guided tours of El Pueblito are offered, but you will need to sign up at the park's main entrance. Dressed in ethereal white robes, the Kogi community lives close to the site and still perform spiritual rituals; do not photograph them without their permission.

Most travelers take on El Pueblito hike as part of a multi-day stay in the park; if you are in good shape, you can complete the arduous circuit from Cañaveral via Cabo San Juan in 1 day. Around 40 minutes west of Cañaveral on foot brings you to Arrecifes; from here is a 40-minute walk to El Cabo de San Juan, then 1½ hours inland along La Boquita stream, where a clear path leads to El Pueblito. The site can also be accessed via the park's Calabazo entrance, 24km (15 miles) along the main road (Troncal del Caribe) from Santa Marta, from where it's a good 2½-hour hike (each way). From El Pueblito you can either loop back to Cañaveral, or continue for the 2-hour walk to Calabaza on the Santa Marta-Riohacha road.

Where to Stay & Eat

The closest thing you'll get to "glamping" in Park Tayrona is the **Yuluka Campsite** (run by Aviatur) at Arrecifes, which also offers tents with mattresses (COP$30,000) and hammock spaces (from COP$16,000 pesos). The site is well organized, with clean bathrooms with good showers, lockers, and a very good restaurant that serves fresh fish (daily 7am–7pm; entrees from COP$30,000). Also in Arrecifes, **Finca El Paraiso** (advance bookings through the office in Santa Marta; Carrera 7B no. 28A–103; ⓒ **5/431-3130**) is a little cheaper (camping COP$20,000, hammock COP$13,000, basic *cabaña* COP$125,000) and it's closer to the beach, but its standards are not as high as at Yuluka. Amid banana plantations, a little before you arrive in Arrecifes (a 200m detour from the main trail), **Finca Don Pedro** (ⓒ **322/550-3933**) is another basic but clean option with a decent restaurant; a path through the forest leads to the beach (5-min. walk). On the best beach, **Camping Cabo San Juan de Guía** (www.cecabosanjuandelguia.com.co; ⓒ **571/382-1616**) has the most enviable setting—it's magical during the quiet season—but with a captive audience, standards fall short (half a dozen showers service hundreds of people, and mosquito nets are not provided), and the all-night-party vibe is not to everyone's liking. The most desirable hammock spaces sit on top of a gazebo-like structure (referred to as the "Mirador") perched on a huge prehistoric rock in the middle of the beach with marvelous ocean views by day and dazzling, star-studded nights. There's also a very small restaurant (camping COP$25,000, hammock COP$20,000 or COP$25,000 [Mirador], basic *cabaña* COP$125,000).

Eco-habs ★★   In Cañaveral, just a short walk from the parking lot, these 14 thatched-roof *bohios* are inspired by the traditional dwellings of the Tayrona people. The two-story bungalows sleep up to four people (the bedrooms on the upper floors have sparkling views of the Caribbean). A spa offers massages and treatments. For an overall dining experience, the restaurant is the best (and most expensive) in the park, with a broad seafood menu that includes ceviche, fried snapper with coconut rice, and shrimp glazed with sweet chili (main courses COP$17,000–COP$38,000). The hotel offers tours and transportation, but all services here are very pricey compared to other outfitters. It's the most luxurious place to stay in Tayrona, and guests here certainly revel in the relaxation and amenities, but they often walk away feeling they've been overcharged (US$275).

Playa Cañaveral. www.ecohabsantamarta.com/ecohabs-tayrona.com. ⓒ **311/600-1614.** 14 cabins. COP$803,618, includes breakfast. **Amenities:** Fans (no air-conditioning); pick up can be arranged (COP$75,000) from Santa Marta; no Wi-Fi.

Los Angeles Cabins ★   These eco-friendly cabanas are located on a small hill that overlooks the gorgeous and off-the-radar golden sands of Los Angeles Beach. The rustic chic rooms with terraces are spacious and airy, with locally made wooden furnishings, comfortable beds draped with mosquito nets, and en-suite modern inside/outside bathrooms with showers (cold water). If you bring your own provisions, there's a communal kitchen for guests' use. There are surfboards for rent; this is one of the best surfing beaches in the area. Breakfast is included in the rate, and meals can be prepared to order (COP$15,000–COP$25,000). If you want to be close enough to the park without the crowds of Taganga or pay the high prices within the park, this is a terrific off-the-grid option.

Playa Los Angeles. www.cabanasantamartalosangeles.com. © **321/522-1292.** 3 cabins. From COP$250,000. **Amenities:** Fans (no air-conditioning), communal kitchen, surfboards for rent; no Wi-Fi.

Vila Maria Tayrona ★★ Set amid lush orchards, just 3km (around 2 miles) from the park entrance, this well-run hotel (another fine hotel from the Colombian Kali boutique brand) offers more luxury and value for money than eco-habs within the park. Stylish rooms and bungalows designed with natural materials and local *artesanía*—wood floors, bamboo, colorful ceramics, hand-woven rugs—and with jaw-dropping ocean and jungle views create an inside-outside design aesthetic. Pathways lead through orchards to a small stretch of beach, and there's a decent onsite restaurant and a pool. Breakfast is cooked to order each morning and a broad lunch/dinner menu is served in the open-air restaurant.

Troncol de Caribe. www.kalihotels.com. © **316/257-8858.** 22 units. Doubles COP$406,000, ocean-view bungalow COP$520,000, includes breakfast. **Amenities:** Restaurant; bar; swimming pool; free Wi-Fi.

LA CIUDAD PÉRDIDA ★★★

Hidden amid dense jungle for over a thousand years, the ancient settlement of La Ciudad Pérdida is Colombia's revered archaeological site. Deep in the Sierra Nevada de Santa Marta, less than an hour's drive from Santa Marta, Colombia's "lost city" has become a rite of passage for Latin America's adventure travelers. Built 650 years before Peru's Machu Picchu, the pre-Columbian city (originally called Teyuna) dates back to 800 A.D. At its zenith, it is believed to have been populated by 4,000 to 10,000 Tayrona people. The hauntingly beautiful site is one of the continent's most enigmatic historical treasures and retains an elemental magnetism uncommon to more touristy archaeological sites, such as Chichen Itza or Machu Picchu.

Tomb raiders from Santa Marta "rediscovered" Ciudad Pérdida in 1973. The looters plundered the gold from the graves of the ancient Tayrona without compunction, and it wasn't long before gold and ancient relics began to flood the black market. Even though the site's treasures were the talk of Santa Marta, it would take the government a further 3 years to secure the area and for archaeologists to begin excavating the site. Since 1976, the park has been protected as Teyuna–Ciudad Pérdida Archaeological Park and it is managed by the Colombian Institute of Anthropology and History (ICANH).

The arduous 5-day quest to get to Ciudad Pérdida ranks as one of the world's most exhilarating hikes. Crowning a 1,300-meter-high (4,265-ft.) ridge above the Buritaca River, trails laid with ancient stones traverse vertiginous cliffs, gushing rivers, and cascading waterfalls that pulsate with a cornucopia of wildlife; hummingbirds hover overhead, iridescent butterflies dance around orchids, cartoon-like crabs scurry from pools, and tiger herons stand to attention in rivers. It's a magical place.

The mystical ruins comprise more than 200 stone settlements, which cling improbably to the mountainside. The 170 stone terraces formed the foundations for the Tayrona people's markets, plazas, and religious sites. The nucleus of the settlement is an impressive ceremonial platform—the holy grail for all travelers—accessed by a steep stone stairway comprising some 1,263-stair steps. When the Spanish conquistadors arrived in the mid-16th century, the Tayrona abandoned the city. Additionally, it is believed that the introduction of diseases such as smallpox contributed to the decline of the Tayrona civilization. The Kogi people, who still live in settlements that dot the park, believe they are the descendants of the Tayrona Indians who occupied the Lost City (they refer to the site as Teyuna).

Until recently, the Lost City was closed to tourism due to paramilitary activity that since the 1960s had turned the Sierra Nevada into a war zone. Though the region is now regarded as safe, the Colombian military maintains a strong, visible presence throughout the area.

Essentials

Travelers can only visit the Lost City as part of an organized tour from Santa Marta. There is an official price for tours (COP$700,000 at the time of writing), which includes all meals and accommodation, transport, and insurance. Most guides do not speak English. There are four companies authorized by the park to provide tours:

EXPOTUR   One of the leading outfitters for tours along the Caribbean coast, Expotur provides informative, bilingual guides, boasts eco-sensitive credentials, and has fostered a good relationship with the Kogi.

Carrera 3 no. 17–27. Santa Marta (also an office in Taganga). www.expotur-eco.com. **Ⓒ 5/420-7739.**

GUIAS Y BAQUIANOS   The pioneer in leading guided tours to Ciudad Pérdida since 1980, this is a professional company with lots of experience, extensive knowledge of the region, sound eco-tourism credentials, and efficient, informative guides.

Inside Hotel Miramar. Calle 10 no. 1–59. Santa Marta. www.guiasybaquianos.com. **Ⓒ 5/431-9667.**

MAGIC TOUR   Another highly reputable company with knowledgeable local guides, excellent customer service, and a few more creature comforts. If it's important to you, the food provided by Magic Tour is considered to be the best on the trek.

Calle 16 no. 4–4. Santa Marta. www.magictourcolombia.com. Ⓒ **5/421-9429.**

TURCOL   This established agency has a useful website that outlines their Ciudad Pérdida itinerary in greater detail than other outfitters (hours of hiking per day, drive time, camps, meal schedule, conditions, etc.).

Calle 13 no. 3–13, Centro Comercial San Francisco Plaza. Santa Marta. www.turcol travel.com/index.php. Ⓒ **5/421-2256.**

hiking CIUDAD PÉRDIDA

One thing is for sure, Ciudad Pérdida is no Machu Picchu. There's no train, no sherpas, and there are no custom tours for all ages and levels of fitness—but it's one hell of an adventure. The 44km trek (27 miles) through rough terrain culminates with a 1,263-stair ascent carved into the side of a mountain to the park's centerpiece: a ceremonial stone terrace. Needless to say, this is no cakewalk. While the 4- to 6-day hike (depending on how much hiking per day your group is prepared to undertake) does not require technical expertise, all hikers need a pretty high baseline of fitness and stamina. There are plunging waterfalls, rock scrambles, steep ascents, and river crossings where you'll need to carry your backpack over your head. It's muddy, sweaty, wet, and you'll likely experience a few blisters, bites, and scrapes along the way. December to March is the driest time to visit (although afternoon downpours still occur). May to November, it can be a mud bath.

Logistically speaking, regardless of which tour operator you sign up with, the trek is now a well-oiled operation. Tour operators will collect you from either Santa Marta or Taganga; then it's a 3-hour drive by 4WD to La Mamay, the departure point for the hike. The jungle is a sweltering and bug-infested place. You'll need to pack sturdy hiking shoes, water purification tablets, long-sleeve shirts and pants, a waterproof jacket, a headlamp, insect and sun protection, and emergency medical supplies. Malaria is a low risk here, but the CDC recommends antimalarial drugs. For bathing, swimming holes are located close to campsites, while sleeping arrangements comprise either hammocks or cabins (usually with mosquito nets), which vary from camp to camp.

LA GUAJIRA PENINSULA ★★

A remote, frontier territory that stretches for 25,000 sq. km (9,700 sq. miles) from Colombia's Manaure Bay to the Gulf of Venezuela, the landscapes of La Guajira Peninsula feel untouched by time and disconnected from space. Infused with a mystical aura, this is a world where the stars wink brighter and the land is cast in shades and hues that feel as though they could only come from a child's imagination. Gold sands, rugged cliff faces, and dunes fold into brilliant blue waters to create a surreal and beautiful landscape. Here, indigenous Wayúu communities are defined by tribal laws, pagan rites, and superstitions. Their settlements, or *rancherías*, dot an arid, inhospitable landscape of extreme poverty where children make makeshift toll booths, allowing "foreigners" (known locally as *alijuna*) to pass in exchange for candy or cookies. In this matriarchal society, goats are traded for dowries and beer and gas (obtained from Venezuela) is sold in soda bottles along the roadside.

While hardly a tourist mecca, the city of Riohacha provides a functional base for exploring the Alta Guajira, where the remote enclave of Cabo de la Vela and even remoter Punta Gallinas—the most northerly point in South America—yield a series of astonishing landscapes, topographical features, and activities, from hiking and parasailing to windsurfing and dune surfing.

Certainly, it's a long and arduous journey to what feels like the end of the world, and few travelers make it this far. For those who do, the rewards do not come in box-ticking format. This is a wild land, a place to find solitude, and a place to immerse yourself in the timelessness of the moment.

Riohacha ★

Some 160km (99 miles) east of Santa Marta, Riohacha is a traveler's hub and layover station for epic journeys to the remote and otherworldly landscapes of La Guajira. Riohacha in and of itself lacks charm. Blue collar and gritty with a rather dispiriting, parochial air, there are no big-hitting sights, and accommodation and dining options are very limited. The city had its moment in the sun as a strategic port and center of the pearl trade during the colonial era. Now, it's the smuggling trade from Venezuela that drives the black economy.

City pride rings loud and true with the mention of native son José Prudencio Padilla (his name is everywhere), the commander who founded Colombia's navy and played top dog to Bolívar. As La Guajira has garnered the attention of travelers keen to explore the unbeaten path, Riohacha looks poised to nurture its status as an eco-tourism hotspot, and a buoyant traveler scene promises to bring greater accommodation and dining options to the currently rather lackluster scene. On the bright side, 24 hours here can be an agreeable enough place to regroup, relax, and get your onward travel plans in order. Fringed with palm trees, the white-sand beach is a fun place to stroll, swim, enjoy a drink, and watch Colombian families at play. Within easy reach, a side trip to the Sanctuario de Flora y Fauna Los Flamencos provides a worthy preamble to the natural beauty of the country's northern frontier.

GETTING THERE & GETTING AROUND

BY PLANE   The José Prudencia Padilla Airport is located 3km (1 mile) south of Riohacha. There are daily flights (1 hr., 30 min.) with **Avianca** (www.avianca.com) from Bogotá.

BY BUS   The bus terminal is located at Calle 15 no. 11–38. There are buses from Santa Marta (3 hr.; COP$17,000), Barranquilla (5 hr.; COP$23,000), Cartagena (every hour; COP$35,000; 7 hr.), Bogotá (two daily; 15–20 hr.; COP$40,000), and Uribia (1 hr.; COP$12,000). At Uribia you can change to Cabo de la Vela (2½ hr.; COP$10,000); buses will stop (on request) at the Wayúu *rancherías* (villages). Transport-only options are often available with tour operators.

For the short time travelers tend to lay over here, the city is easy to navigate **on foot**. The standard **taxi** fare from the airport to town is COP$8,000, for short trips within city limits, including the bus station, it should cost around COP$4,000. There are no meters, so always confirm the price before you get in.

There is an informative **tourist information office** on Avenida de la Marina (no. 4–42; 8am–noon, 2–6pm; www.laguajira.gov.co). Tour operators listed below can provide plenty of information for onward travel to Cabo de la Vela and Punta Gallinas (the most northern point in South America).

MAIN TOURIST SIGHTS

Riohacha's main reference points are **Calle 1/Paseo de la Marina** (more commonly referred to as the malecón), which runs parallel to the beachfront.

One block from the waterfront, between Carrera 8 and 9, the centerpiece of **Parque Padilla** is a statue of independence hero and revered native son Admiral José Prudencio Padilla, famed for his seminal victory against Spanish colonial rule during the Battle of Lago Maracaibo in 1823 (the last battle in the Spanish American wars of independence). The prosaic square, a mishmash of mostly modern edifices, finds a dose of colonial splendor in the 16th-century Gothic **Catedral de Nuestro Senora de los Remedios** (Calle 2 no. 7–13; daily 6am–7pm; free admission). The cathedral is Admiral Padilla's final resting place (look for the marble tomb to the right of the entrance) and is worth a look inside for the colonial high altar with its hallowed image of the Virgin de los Remedios and intricate stained glass.

The **malecón** is the place to find yourself at sunset, as locals and travelers gather at the lively bars and restaurants and music fills the air. On the impressive **Muelle Turistíco** (pier), built in 1937, the indigenous Wayúu people in their traditional dress sell their colorful *artesanía*.

EXCURSIONS

If you have time for a side trip, the **Sanctuario de Flora y Fauna Los Flamenco**'s (www.parquesnacionales.gov.co) swamps, dry forest, and mangroves provide refuge for profuse wildlife including anteaters, egrets, opossums, turtles, and an estimated 200 species of bird (the area is a migratory corridor). However, the main draw here is the breathtaking vision of thousands of resplendent crimson and pink flamingos, which congregate by lagoons densely populated with brine shrimp (which give flamingos their pink hue). The best time to visit is from May to November, when there can be as many as 10,000. The flamingo's mud nests, which range between 30 and 60 cm in height, are impressive. The sanctuary is located 25km (16 miles) from Riohacha along Carretera 90. The park entrance is at Guanebucane, 3.5km (about 2 miles) from the town of Camarones; *colectivos* leave from the bus station in Riohacha (40 min.). There is very little infrastructure within the park. Entrance to the sanctuary is free, but you will need to arrange boat transportation with a Wayúu guide to see the flamingos; guides solicit at the park entrance and charge around COP$30,000 to COP$45,000 for the hour ride.

If you want to decompress on a more alluring stretch of sand, **Playa de Mayapo** (20km/12 miles north of Riohacha), forms part of the Wayúu reserve. The Mayapo white-sand beaches and translucent waters are popular with **kitesurfers** and **windsurfers** due to the consistent strong winds. It's also a quiet place to relax and check out the handicrafts purveyed by the indigenous Wayúu. A taxi will cost around COP$70,000 (the driver will need to wait for you) from Riohacha or you can take a *colectivo* (they leave when full) from the market, around COP$7,000.

TOURS

Riohacha is the base for tours of La Guajira. While you can make your own way to Cabo de la Vela and Punta Gallinas via *colectivos* and shared taxis, it's a long, hot, and arduous journey. The benefits of a Wayúu guide with local knowledge cannot be overstated.

Aventure Colombia ★★   Based in Cartagena, Santa Marta, and Bogotá, Aventure runs a 2-night tour (COP$609,000) from Riohacha to Punta Gallinas including all meals, accommodation in a traditional Wayúu *ranchería*, 4WD transportation, and Wayúu guides. The itinerary includes the Taroa Dunes, the beaches of Bahia Honda, and brief stops in Cabo de la Vela, Piñon de Azúcar. A great option if you are short on time.

In Santa Marta: Calle 14 no. 4–80. www.aventurecolombia.com. ✆ **5/430-5185.**

Expotur Adventure Tours ★★   This reputable, extremely professional Santa Marta–based agency (offices in Riohacha and Taganga) with a strong sustainable-tourism ethos offers excellent tours to La Guajira with Wayúu with bilingual guides. The 2-day tour to Cabo de la Vela (COP$250,000) includes Uribia, Manaura salt complex, Playa Dorada, and Pilar de Azúcar. The 4-day Punta Gallinas (COP$450,000) tour roughly follows the same itinerary, with an additional 2 days at Punta Gallinas, Parque Eólico, and the sublime Taroa Dunes. Both tours include comfortable 4WD transportation, all meals, and basic accommodation in hammocks or *chinchorros* (a type of wrap-around hammock/blanket hybrid) in a traditional Wayúu *ranchería* (village). Highly recommended.

Carrera 5 no. 3A–02, Riohacha. www.expotur-eco.com. ✆ **5/728-8232.**

Kai Ecotravel ★★   The first eco-tour company in La Guajira, Kai offers eco-sensitive multi-day tours and day trips throughout the region with an emphasis on community tourism and responsible travel. The company was a trailblazer in eco-tourism in the region and has nurtured close, fruitful ties with the Wayúu people. In addition to well-orchestrated itineraries, Kai will also customize packages according to your needs. Tour prices vary according to the number of travelers in your group. A 3-night/4-day tour of Punta Gallinas costs COP$800,000 based on a private tour for four people, including 4WD transportation, basic accommodation, and meals.

Hotel Castillo del Mar, Calle 9A no. 15–352. www.kaiecotravel.com. ✆ **311/436-2830.**

WHERE TO STAY & EAT

Al Arz ★ MIDDLE EASTERN   Al Arz is a staple among the town's sizeable Middle Eastern population. If you are tired of fish, this friendly locale mixes it up with large, healthy platters of classic Mediterranean and Lebanese dishes, including falafel, fresh salads, wraps, tabbouleh, hummus with pita, chicken shawarma, and fresh juices. It's all served in a welcoming cafeteria-style setting with alcoves, wall tapestries, and a few other decorative nods to Arabian culture. Don't miss the baklava and other intoxicatingly sweet Arabian desserts.

Calle 7 no. 10–115. ✆ **5/728-3760.** Main courses from COP$22,000. Daily 11:10am–9:30pm.

Bona Vida Hostel ★★   There's an intimate, social vibe at this colorful and welcoming hostel that attracts young, intrepid travelers blazing an independent trail in La Guajira. There are two dorms with one shared bath (which sleep between four and eight guests) and one private room (also shared bath).

All rooms are pristine, neat, and well maintained and have individual fans and lockers. There's a communal dining area and kitchen, and a "chill out" zone with honor bar. Breakfast with pancakes, tropical fruit, and great coffee is included in the rate. Convivial Austrian/Colombian hosts Johannes and Katy offer tips and advice on travel in the region. Just a couple of minutes' walk to the beach and Plaza de Padilla, the location could not be better.

Calle 3 no. 1010. ℂ **314/637-0786.** 12 dorm beds, 1 double room. COP$29,000 dorm room, COP$67,000 double with shared bath, breakfast included. **Amenities:** Free Wi-Fi.

Casa del Marisco ★ SEAFOOD Of the seafood restaurants on the malecón, Casa del Marisco tends to pull the crowds for its consistency, broad menu, and pleasant service. The seafood soups, stews, and ceviche are decent, and the catch of the day here is served with more exciting presentations than the typical whole fried fish that dominates most menus in these parts.

Calle 1 no. 4–43. ℂ **5/728-3445.** Main courses from COP$25,000. Daily 11:00am–10pm.

Casa Patio Bonita ★ Three blocks from the beach, this traditional Colombian home, owned by a gracious Canadian/Colombian couple, has been transformed into a great-value B&B with accommodation options for every budget. Thoughtfully appointed double rooms with private bathrooms and dorm rooms all boast air-conditioning, cable TV, and Wi-Fi. There's also a very comfortable two-bedroom apartment, which is a great family option. Full breakfast is included.

Calle 3B no. 1C–74. www.casapatiobonita.com. ℂ **314/763-7221.** 5 units. COP$40,000 (dorm) COP$70,000 (private room), COP$200,000 (2-bed apartment), breakfast included. **Amenities:** Small gym; free Wi-Fi.

Taroa ★★ With an ideal location right on the beach at the center of the malecón, the Taroa is easily the best hotel in town. Tasteful, comfortable rooms offer white linens and drapes paired with minimalist wooden furnishings. The attention to detail extends to plush mattresses, balconies strewn with hammocks (most rooms overlook the ocean) and large modern bathrooms. With a fancy rooftop bar-restaurant, Aliuuka (if you want to go to bed early, request a quiet room on the lower floors), and warm, efficient service—it's staffed with local Wayúu people—the Taroa is the place to enjoy a smattering of creature comforts before you embrace your inner Spartan in the remote recesses of La Guajira.

Calle 1 no. 4–77. www.taroahotel.com. ℂ **5/729-1122.** 48 units. COP$220,000. **Amenities:** Restaurant/bar; free Wi-Fi.

Cabo de la Vela ★★

With its ethereal landscapes and mystical aura, the tiny Wayúu settlement of Cabo de la Vela has assumed the unlikely mantle of La Guajira's eco-tourist hotspot. The 2-hour journey here from Riohacha is part of the adventure. Sure, bouncing around to booming *vallenato* music in the back of a truck is hardly comfortable, but the scenery along the way is utterly spectacular. Some 101km (63 miles) northwest from Riohacha, it's worth a stop at the compelling **Salinas de Manaure**, where blinding white conical stacks of salt are harvested by local workers (including the Wayúu people that have a 50% share in the operation) and loaded into wheelbarrows.

Also known as Jepirra, Cabo de la Vela is considered sacred to the Wayúu, and the place where their souls remain after death. A settlement rather than a town, Cabo comprises a string of Wayúu *rancherías* that front a gorgeous 2-mile bay of golden sands dramatically juxtaposed by waters in brilliant shades of turquoise and aquamarine and surrounded by flat, rocky, arid landscape bristling with shrubs and hirsute cacti. This land feels (and is) truly off the grid. Here, you won't find Internet, hot water, or regular electricity (it's generators only). Instead, you'll encounter a world where goats and cows meander along dirt track roads, where makeshift shacks sell soda bottles filled with gas (technically illegal contraband from across the Venezuelan border) and where you will encounter Wayúu children at "toll booths" who "trade" candy and cookies in exchange for onward passage. A customary phenomenon in any frontier land, smuggling used to be endemic here, as was the violence that generally comes with it. While illicit activities do still happen, they rarely encroach on travelers' experiences.

Several "sights" in the area form part of the standard La Guajira tours. A 90-minute walk (7km/4⅓ miles) from town, **El Faro** is a lighthouse best visited at sunset when skies blaze as the sun drops like a stone into the ocean. The Technicolor vision of bright purple, blue, red, and gold is nothing short of transcendent. The dark-sand beach of **Ojo del Agua** has a freshwater pool that has spiritual significance for the Wayúu. The **Pilón de Azucar** is a shrine to the Virgen de Fátima (the patron saint of Cabo) on top of a hill (it's a 10-min. climb to the top) that affords memorable views of the Alta Guajira. Below, the **Playa de Pilón** is a stunning ribbon of terracotta sand framed by cliffs; from January to April the beach can be busy with Colombian holidaymakers, but otherwise you will likely have it to yourself. Cabo has fast established its reputation as a **kitesurfing** and **windsurfing** destination. **Eoletto** (at Rancheria Utta, see p. 146; www.windsurfingcolombia.com) offers courses and rentals.

GETTING THERE

From just next to the Riohacha bus station, Cootrauri (Calle 15 no. 5–39; ℭ **54/717-7499**) runs *colectivos* to Uribía (COP$15,000; 1 hour); ask to be dropped at the departure point for Cabo de la Vela. From there it's an uncomfortable 2 hours (COP$13,000–COP$16,000) in a pickup truck; last trucks leave at 1pm. Trucks coming back leave Cabo at 4:30am. You can rent your own 4WD with a driver from Cootrauri for around COP$450,000 per day.

A note about safety: Even though the area is considered safe for travelers, La Guajira has long occupied the national consciousness as Colombia's badlands; laws here are few and subject to the whim of armed locals, and foreigners are viewed with suspicion. With coal-mining interests in the region causing strife between multinationals, the Wayúu, and guerrillas, always check on the political situation locally before organizing travel to the region. It's also worth noting that the dynamic between visitors, tour guides, and the Wayúu can, at times, be unsettling for many travelers.

WHERE TO STAY & EAT

Government sponsored eco-tourism projects have taken off here, resulting in around 130 traditional Wayúu *rancherías* that rent out private rooms with bathrooms (bucket showers), hammocks, or traditional Wayúu *chinchorros* (a larger, warmer hammock that serves as a wrap-around blanket). Most *posados* face the beach and serve meals, with a similar menu across the region: fish, goat, and lobster. You may need to bring towels and or even sheets. Electric generators generally only function in the evening, from around 6pm until 10pm.

Hospedaje Jarrinapi ★   Facing the beach, the Jarrinapi is one of Cabo's more organized guesthouses with electricity (from 6am–6pm), fans, clean bathrooms, and quite comfortable beds (for Cabo) in private double rooms in typical *yotojoro* huts. Hammocks and *chinchorros* are also available. The restaurant (with erratic service) is one of Jarrinapi's main selling points, with tasty and creative fish dishes, including fried snapper, "lobster cooked three ways," and Cuban fried rice.

Cabo de La Vela. ⓒ **310/366-4255.** 60 huts. COP$14,000 hammock, COP$35,000 doubles. **Amenities:** Restaurant/bar; no Wi-Fi.

Ranchería Utta ★   One of the fledgling eco-tourism projects in Cabo, this *ranchería* offers various packages/accommodation options (hammocks, *chinchorros*, and private rooms) in clean, indigenous-style *yotojoro* huts made from a cactus heart that proliferates in the deserts of La Guajira. The menu here is broader than most other *posadas* in town, with international dishes served alongside traditional Wayúu mainstays. Tours of the area can also be arranged.

Vía al Faro, Cabo de la Vela. www.rancheriautta.com. ⓒ **312/687-8237.** 11 units, plus ample hammock and chinchorro space. Hammock COP$410,000, chinchorro COP$430,000, double hut with private bath COP$450,000 (per night); prices include transportation from Riohacha, meals, and tours in Cabo de la Vela. **Amenities:** Restaurant/bar; no Wi-Fi.

Refugio Pantu ★   With huts right on the beach about a one-hour walk outside of Cabo de la Vela, Refugio Pantu provides a more intimate, authentic experience than within Cabo proper. Several huts, each with five beds, have private bathrooms and fans, and there are also hammock spaces. The small restaurant serves Wayúu dishes. President Uribe stayed here in 2008 during his quest to launch eco-tourism initiatives in La Guajira.

1-hr. walk from Cabo de la Vela. ⓒ **313/581-0858.** Hammock COP$12,000, huts COP$150,000 (sleep five people). **Amenities:** Restaurant/bar; no Wi-Fi.

Punta Gallinas ★★

Spiritually and geographically, Punta Gallinas really is the end of the road. The most northerly point of South America is a hauntingly beautiful wilderness that feels utterly cut off from civilization as you know it; fewer than 100 Wayúu families inhabit the area. Cast in hues of bright orange, rust red, and ochre, the ancestral lands of the Wayúu are a primordial landscape where winds roar and golden dunes fall into a brilliant blue Caribbean Sea. A place for seclusion and contemplation, you can spend a couple of days here, roaming the beaches, mudflats, and mangroves and experiencing traditional Wayúu culture.

An aura of mysticism permeates the remote lands of La Guajira, where shamans conduct rites, animals are sacrificed, bones are exhumed 5 years after death, and a spiritual force called *Mariewa* (the creator) stands at the center of a paragon of deities. The seminomadic Wayúu (also spelled Wayuu, Wayu, or Wahiro) people (the Wayúu frown upon the term "indigenous") represent an estimated 20% of Colombia's Amerindian population. With ancestral lands straddling both Colombia and Venezuela, they hold dual Colombian and Venezuelan citizenship and freely cross the border, especially during the harsh, dry season when they attempt to find work in Maracaibo (Venezuela).

The Wayúu are an extremely impoverished and marginalized community. Men and women share the task of eking out an existence based on subsistence farming (goats and fishing) and the production of handicrafts; they are famed for their hammocks, blankets, *mochilas* (knapsacks) and distinctive *susu* (meaning "what travels with you") bags. Traditionally, *rancherías* (a settlement of five or six houses) are made out of *yotojoro*, which refers to the heart of the *yosú* cactus. The Wayúu language (*Wayuunaiki*) forms a subset of the Arawak language group that is common to Caribbean regions. A matriarchal society, communities are organized around female clans and the Wayúu women occupy the leading roles in the community; they retain sole parental authority, and *rancherías* are given the matriarch's last name.

A series of rituals accompany a girl's transition to womanhood, which is known as the *encierro* (usually defined by menstruation); their heads are shaved and, in place of a staple diet based on goat and fish, they consume a largely vegetarian diet (known as *jaguapi*). A period of confinement that involves frequent washing/purifying sometimes lasts up to 2 years, during which time the girl must rest in a *chinchorro* (a large hammock with a wrap-around blanket). The liquor *chirrinchi* (a strong liquor/moonshine) is liberally dispensed during each girl's ceremony to celebrate "motherhood."

Less than a decade ago, many areas of La Guajira were considered off limits to travelers due to paramilitary and guerrilla activity. President Uribe created a series of initiatives that encouraged the Wayúu to find alternative sources of income through tourism. Despite the government's overtures, which aimed at enhancing the region's infrastructure and fostering tourism, La Guajira remains extremely impoverished, and Wayúu life expectancy is woefully poor.

The two main features of the area the stunning, untouched **Playa Taroa**, where colossal dunes rise above aquamarine waters (it makes for excellent dune surfing) and to the south **Bahía Hondita**, a gorgeous bay with crystal clear water laced with mangroves. The consistent winds here make this another of Colombia's top kitesurfing and windsurfing spots.

GETTING THERE

Unless the (challenging) journey is part of the appeal, the smoothest option by far is to take a tour from Riohacha (see "Tours," p. 142). If you are set on going it alone, jeeps and pickup trucks depart from Cabo de la Vela at 5am. Or, the most efficient route entails a 2-hour jeep ride followed by a 1-hour 30-minute boat ride; hostels in Cabo can help set up onward transportation with the local Wayúu.

WHERE TO STAY & EAT

For the moment, there are very few places to stay in Punta Gallinas in the Bahía Hondita. Expect to pay around COP$15,000 for a main course for dinner (lobster is more expensive)

Hospedaje y Restaurant Luzmila ★   In an unforgettable setting surrounded by the ocean, Hospedaje Luzmila has clean cabins and hammock spaces. The service and food here are very good, and it's a great place to gain insight into traditional Wayúu customs, rituals, and traditions. They can also pick you up from Cabo de la Vela if you contact them in advance.

Punta Gallinas. ℂ **312/626-8121.** 60 huts. COP$15,000 hammock, COP$20,000 chinchorro, COP$30,000 cabin. **Amenities:** Restaurant/bar; no Wi-Fi.

THE WESTERN CARIBBEAN ★★

West of Cartagena, from the Golfo de Urubá down to the border with Panama, lies a region of startling natural beauty. Serrated mountains plunge into sugary white beaches, clear waters offer excellent diving and snorkeling, and swaths of untamed jungle host a mind-blowing inventory of flora and fauna. A string of earthy, authentic towns, accessible only by boat or dirt paths, has yet to make it onto the tourist radar. They provide fascinating bases for exploration.

Most visitors to the region begin at the rough-around-the-edges town of **Tolú**; with its raucous beach bars, lively plaza, street vendors, and seaside fun, it has long been the preserve of wealthy Colombian families. For clued-up international travelers, Tolú is the launch pad for the dazzling **Islas de San Bernardo**, where you can live out your castaway fantasies on the pristine islands of **Tintipán and Múcura**. You can swim, horseback ride, hike, and even take a yoga class at the **Reserva Natural Veinto Solar**, where howler monkeys, iguanas, sloths, and a rich profusion of birdlife provide captivating viewing.

Beyond the frontier of the Golfo de Urubá, the **Darién** forests are Central America's own heart of darkness. Civilization sings its last hurrah at the Afro-Caribbean towns of **Capurganá** and **Sapzurro**, where Colombia beats to a very different drum. Music courses through a web of colorful ramshackle streets (a loose definition) of low-slung dwellings and makeshift storefronts. Here, quite literally at the end of the road, a rich diversity of ecosystems and a series of mesmerizing topographies are catnip for relaxation and for adventure. You can dine on delicious fish served on the sand beneath star-studded skies; go scuba diving in turquoise, translucent waters right off shore (trips can be combined with island hoping around Panama's much-storied San Blas Islands); and hike to picturesque waterfalls or through untamed jungles teeming with howler monkeys. This compelling stretch of Colombia's western Caribbean summons travelers keen to explore beyond Colombia's more fabled (and populated) attractions.

Getting There

BY PLANE   Tolú's airport is just south of town. There is a daily flight (fares from COP$112,000 one-way) from Medellín with **ADA** (www.ada-aero.com).

BY BUS There are daily buses with **Expreso Brasilia** (www.expresobrasilia. com/en) to Tolú from Bogotá (COP$65,000; 20 hr.), Medellín (COP$40,000, 10 hr.) and every hour from Cartagena (COP$30,000; 3 hr.), Santa Marta (COP$35,000; 7 hr.) and Sincelejo (for transfers to Mompox, COP$6,000; 1 hr.). Tolú's unofficial bus stop is the Zeuss gas station (Calle 16, btw. Since-lejo and Coveñas).

Getting Around

BICITAXI In Tolú, a ride on a *bicitaxi* is the only way to go. The set fare within town is COP$2,000 per person. If you are going to the bus station and have a bag the price can be inflated to as much as COP$6,000, so always establish a price before you get in.

BY BOAT A boat tour from Tolú is the most efficient and low-maintenance way to get to Las Islas de San Bernardo; **Mundo Mar** (Av. 1 no. 14–400; www.clubnauticomundomartolu.com.co; ✆ **5/228-4431**).

Tolú ★

With its lively beach scene and constant soundtrack of salsa and reggaeton, Colombian holidaymakers just go wild for the Afro-Colombian town of Tolú. For travelers, the main reason to come here is to explore the undiscovered white-sand beaches and nature preserves that comprise the Golfo de Morros-quillo, which funnels from Tolú south to Coveñas, or as the launch pad for the picturesque Islas de San Bernardo. Down at the heel and with few sights to speak of, Tolú's charms are not easily apparent. Despite being one of the old-est towns in Colombia, founded in 1535, scant vestiges remain of its colonial past, and the dark-sand beach that forms the commercial nexus for the local fishermen is far from a Caribbean dreamscape.

Still, for a short stay, Tolú is a friendly place to take in the scene from a bench on the main square **Plaza Pedro de Heredia** or from the seat of a *bici-taxi* (the customary mode of transportation in Tolú) as it careens through town. On the *malecón* (boardwalk), food vendors run a brisk trade and reg-gaeton booms 24/7 from ramshackle bars. The neighboring town of **Coveñas**, a 16th-century slave port now distinguished by its oil pipeline, has a more aspiring resort feel, with hotels lining the wide beach. Between Tolú and Coveñas, it's worth a trip to the **La Ciénega de Caimanera** nature preserve, where you can take a canoe trip (COP$20,000) through surreal formations of five species of mangroves that thrive within the brackish bog. To get there, take any bus from Tolú in the direction of Coveñas and ask the driver to let you off at La Boca de la Ciénega (where canoe guides convene; be sure to negotiate your price first).

Islas de San Bernardo ★★

Few visitors come to Tolú without taking a boat tour to the beautiful Islas de San Bernardo, a stunning archipelago just a 1-hour boat ride north of the Golfo de Morrosquillo. Part of the Rosario Island's National Park, and one of Colom-bia's most vaunted natural attractions, this tranquil constellation of ten

Caribbean islands delivers the perfect tourist-brochure formula of palm-fringed white sands lapped by iridescent waters and pristine coral reefs that make for excellent diving and snorkeling. If you can't pull yourself away, there are several accommodation options, including the swish eco-tourist resort of **Punta Faro ★★** (see below). If you are short on time, day trips from Tolú generally include lunch and swimming at either Isla Palma or Isla Múcura Island. The tours can have a cattle-market feel during high season, and be advised that many tours take in Decameron's all-inclusive resort on Isla Palma and include a visit to an aquarium with dubious environmental credentials.

WHERE TO EAT & STAY

Hostal El Velero ★   With a prime position right on the beach at the southern end of town, and a slew of amenities including a terrace with a small swimming pool, a sun deck, and dining area (breakfast is included), El Velero is a comfortable and convenient choice. The small but functional modern rooms feature wooden furnishings and nautical design flourishes, which vitalize the otherwise generic spaces. At this rate, in-room air-conditioning, refrigerators, cable TV, and minibars are a real bonus.

Carrera 1 (Malecón) no. 9–31. www.hostalvelero.com. ✆ **5/268-0058.** Doubles COP$45,000, includes breakfast. **Amenities:** Pool, restaurant (breakfast only); free Wi-Fi.

Punta Faro ★★   This idyllic retreat on gorgeous Isla Mucura has all the prerequisites for a relaxing resort escape, with a beautiful beach, clear waters (great for snorkeling), and lush vegetation. Rooms are designed to blend with the environment and feature handmade wooden furnishings dressed with white linens (standard rooms are a little dated; it's worth paying up for the "luxury" rooms with ocean view). Geared toward families, there are plenty of activities onsite, including kayaking, snorkeling, volleyball, scuba diving, yoga, and windsurfing. The all-inclusive price tag includes expansive Caribbean buffet fare with a focus on local fish and seafood. Compared to other tropical island escapes, Punta Faro is a good deal. As with most hotels on the coast (except Cartagena), there's no hot water. Punta Faro is also accessible from Cartagena (2 hr. by boat).

Isla Mucura. www.puntafaro.com. ✆ **317/435-9583.** 45 units. Doubles from COP$880,000, all-inclusive. **Amenities:** Swimming pool; restaurant; massage; free Wi-Fi.

Villa Babilla ★   While it may not have a lot of bells and whistles (no air-conditioning, no breakfast included, no luggage storage), Villa Babilla is a good-value guesthouse in Tolú run by a German/Colombian couple. Large rooms are well maintained and flooded with light, and private bathrooms are neat, clean, and functional. The main draws here are the communal spaces with a simple kitchen for guest use, a lovely roof terrace strewn with hammocks (perfect at sunset) and lush gardens alive with birdsong (rather than the cacophonous music you'll hear all over town). Bikes are also available.

Calle 20 no. 3–40, Tolú. www.villababillahostel.com. ✆ **5/288-6124.** 5 units. COP$50,000 (low season), COP$80,000 (high season). **Amenities:** Free Wi-Fi.

Capurganá & Sapzurro ★★

South of Tolú, the landscape becomes ever wilder, greener, bluer, denser, and purer. This is a world where the developer's touch is light and ramshackle villages encroached by jungle provide a very different insight into the Colombian way of life. Just a few miles from the Panamanian border, the swamps and lowlands of the Colombian Darién were for many years a no-go zone, a battleground for the FARC and right wing militias in the late 1990s.

With a heavy police presence and a ceasefire on the table, this now tranquil enclave is ripe for an eco-tourism boom. The landscape that envelopes the sleepy but authentic Afro-Colombian village of **Capurganá** remains one of Colombia's best kept secrets, with the exception of gilded Colombians from Medellín and a slowly growing quota of international backpackers. From idyllic coves with translucent waters that offer excellent snorkeling and diving to untamed jungle pulsating with wildlife, Capurganá will overwhelm the senses and keep your attention fully focused on the moment. One of the few places where you won't find any cars, a horse and cart will be your go-to mode of transportation.

The next village before you reach Panama (a short boat ride or a strenuous 2-hr. hike), tucked into a horseshoe bay with coral reefs, lowkey **Sapzurro** is a web of thatched-roof *palapas* that line meandering pathways (there are no roads) where toads the size of rabbits cross your path and howler monkeys provide the nocturnal soundtrack. From Sapzurro, you can hike through the jungle to the village of **Miel** across the border in Panama (take your passport), where the alluring picture-postcard white sands of Playa Blanca are reward enough. From here, Cabo Tiburón (the official coastal border between Colombia and Panama) is another 30-minute walk.

GETTING THERE & GETTING AROUND

This alluring corner of Colombia's western Caribbean remains untouched by mass tourism largely due to the logistical challenges and expense to get here.

BY PLANE There are no longer any direct flights to Capurganá, but there is a daily flight (19-seat plane) from Medellín to Acandí's airstrip (from US$165, one-way) with **ADA** (www.ada-aero.com). From Bogotá there is a daily flight connection to Apartado (around COP$200,000 one-way). From Apartado there are taxi services to Turbo (1 hr., COP$40,000).

BY BUS From Medellín to Turbo, COP$60,000, 8 hours, **Transportes Gomez** (www.gomezhernandez.com). From Cartagena to Turbo, COP$35,000, 10 to 12 hours, change required in Montería, **Expreso Brasilia** (www.expreso brasilia.com/es). Expect to spend the night in the unappealing town of Turbo.

BY BOAT There are between three and four daily boats (schedules are highly subject to change) from Turbo to Capurganá (COP$50,000; 2 hr.) starting at 8am—arrive by 7am if you don't have a reservation. There is a 10kg luggage limit which tends to be strictly enforced (you will be charged for any excess). Boats also depart from Turbo to Sapzurro (COP$55,000; 2½ hr.). In both cases, expect a wet and wild ride: Keep your valuables in plastic bags and

In the unlikely event that you have ever mulled over the notion of driving from Alaska to Tierra del Fuego along the Pan-American Highway, you'll need to think again. The iconic highway comes to an abrupt halt for 87km (54 miles) at the mythical **Darién Gap**. A long, thin corridor (50km wide and 160km long) that connects Central America (Panama) with South America (Colombia), the impenetrable jungles of the Darién Gap have forever loomed large as Latin America's heart of darkness. With rugged, mist-shrouded mountains, wild vegetation (armed with spikes, thorns, needles, and poisons), churning rivers, snakes, and blood sucking insects, this is nature hard core.

While intrepid explorers have always viewed the Darién Gap as the ultimate challenge, their forays into Latin America's wildest and most remote recesses have yielded results ranging from the calamitous to the utterly tragic. In 1960, after 5 months and at an average speed of 200 meters per hour, a Land Rover that went by the moniker of the "Affectionate Cockroach" became the first vehicle to cross the Darién from Colombia into Panama. More than 50 years later, less than a dozen vehicles have traversed one of the least trodden places on the planet. In the 1980s and '90s, the Darién Gap's jungles were populated with FARC guerrillas and armed drug traffickers.

With a staggering biodiversity and indigenous population that has had little contact with the outside world, the risk-reward ratio of entering the Darién has always been heavily skewed for conservationists and anthropologists. Amateur horticulturist Tom Hart Dyke and fellow backpacker Paul Winder were kidnapped in 2000 (they were released without explanation 10 months later) while on a quest to find the rare Stanhopea orchid. Other Darién casualties include three missionaries who disappeared from Pucuro (Panamanian Darién) in 1993, and Robert Young Pelton on assignment for *National Geographic Adventure* magazine in 2003; a right-wing paramilitary organization detained, and then released, him. In 2013, 26-year-old Swedish backpacker Jan Philip Braunisch disappeared while attempting to cross the Darién on foot to Panama. The FARC admitted to killing him and claimed they believed he was a foreign spy.

The vision of building a road through the Darién—occasionally proposed by Colombian presidents—remains a touchy subject. Environmentalist groups in both Panama and the U.S. claim that a road would not only pose a threat to indigenous groups within the Darién, but would also accelerate deforestation and permit diseases prevalent in Central and South America (foot-and-mouth cattle disease) to spread north of the border.

close to hand. Boats leave from the docks, a short walk (cross the bridge) from Turbo's main plaza.

You will need to bring lots of cash. There are no ATMs in either Sapzurro or Capurganá, and small hotels and restaurants usually won't accept credit cards.

OUTDOOR PURSUITS

Just north of Capurganá town, the golden sands of **Playa La Caleta** (the main beach) front a coral reef rich with marine life, and the jungle-covered hills of the Darién mountains provide refuge to a boisterous collection of birds and howler monkeys. To the south of town, the grey-sand beach of **Playa de los Pescadores** gains in local color—fisherman casting nets and children playing soccer—what it lacks in Caribbean beauty. The tiny fishing village of **Acandí** has a beautiful bay with crystalline, azure waters.

Capurganá is engulfed by lowland tropical rainforest where swamps, mangroves, and lagoons harbor an astounding array of birds, frogs, reptiles, and mammals. The 2-hour hike from Capurganá to **Sapzurro** starts at the soccer pitch just south of town; follow the uphill path and wear hiking boots if possible, it's steep in places and can get muddy. One of the most popular day excursions from Capurganá is the 90-minute hike (or 10-min. boat ride) to **El Aguacate**, a secluded bay with aquamarine waters that are perfect for snorkeling. Here, there's a blow hole, known locally as **La Piscina**, which forms a natural pool where you can swim. **Playa Soleded** (only accessible by boat, *lancha*, COP$4,000) is a gorgeous stretch of white sand fringed with palm trees. From Capurganá, you can take a jungle hike (you'll need to cross streams, so wear a bathing suit) to **El Cielo** (3km/1 mile, around 1 hr.), a pretty waterfall where members of Colombia's rich bird inventory put on a colorful show. If wildlife spotting is your game, local hotels or **Capurganá tours** (Calle del Comercio; ℂ 316/382-3665) can set you up with a local guide (COP$12,000), or arrange a half-day tour on foot or horseback. If you want to go it alone, take the path behind the airport and ask directions. Another recommended horse-riding tour is to **El Valle De los Rios**, where an abundance of bird and wildlife, including iguanas, toucans, and howler monkeys congregate along rivers and around waterfalls.

Capurganá is famed for its pristine waters with more than 30 dive sites; vertical wall dives and coral reefs are accessible from the shoreline. The best time to dive is from May to November when the waters are calm and visibility is ideal; always be mindful of strong currents. The PADI-certified **Dive and Green Dive Center** (www.diveandgreen.com) offers two dives with professional, bilingual dive masters and new equipment (COP$190,000). Beginners can take the 5-day Open Water PADI certification courses.

WHERE TO STAY & EAT

Sleepy Capurganá has sufficiently diverse accommodation options to keep visitors happy and comfortable for days.

Gata Negra ★ In Sapzurro, this eco-chic wooden construction, set in gorgeous tropical gardens with fruit trees and colorful birdlife, has two spacious, comfortable rooms with shared bathroom and one cabana with a private bathroom. There's a communal dining area, and the owners can also prepare delicious made-to-order fresh fish and Italian staples. With no Wi-Fi or phone connections, this is a friendly and intimate space to get off the grid, meet fellow travelers, and commune with nature.

Sapzurro. www.lagatanegra.net. ℂ **314/725-0325.** 2 units (shared bath), 1 cabin (en-suite). Cabin COP$50,000, double room from COP$35,000 per person. **Amenities:** Restaurant.

Josefina ★ SEAFOOD A local institution in these parts, just 5 minutes along the beach from the Nautilus hotel (see below), this humble *palapa* with erratic service belies the tiny locale's culinary pedigree. Josefina's is without doubt the top spot (lunch or dinner) for inspired, authentic seafood creations. Expertly prepared dishes, served on the beach beneath a shady tree, vary according to the daily catch. Josefina's signature dish is lobster with garlic and coconut (it's a good idea to reserve your crustaceans in the morning) but every dish from the ceviche to the king crab, the octopus to the grilled shrimp, is intensely flavored and satisfying; the portions here are substantial.

Playa Caleta, Capurganá. ℂ **316/779-7760.** Main courses from COP$28,000. Daily noon–9:30pm.

Nautilos Capurganá ★   Location and friendly service are the main draw for this resort-style hotel set in colorful gardens right on Playa Caleta beach. While the Nautilus offers more amenities than the posadas in town, the spartan rooms (with air-conditioning) are small and dated (beds are in desperate need of replacing). On the bright side, most rooms have terraces overlooking the bay and the sunsets here are outrageous. The small swimming pool and hot tub are a big hit for families with kids. If you are looking to streamline the process and have limited time, the hotel also arranges full-day tours to Sapzurro/La Miel (COP$50,000) as well as Playa Soledad/Aguacate (COP$50,000). Myriad packages/plans, which include decent buffet meals, tours, and unlimited cocktails (local liquors only) are cost effective for families and groups.

Capurganá. www.nautiloscapurgana.com. ℂ **320/596-1477.** COP$465,000 (per room, including breakfast). **Amenities:** Restaurant; swimming pool; hot tub; no Wi-Fi.

Posada del Gecko ★   With a convivial Italian at the helm, this clean, bright posada has five cheerful and spacious double rooms and bungalows in two houses built by the architect/owner using traditional techniques and materials. The lush garden with hammocks and a hot tub is the posada's social hub, and the atmospheric Mediterranean restaurant is one of the best dining spots in the area. The very helpful owners plan and organize local hikes, as well as multi-day tours to Panama and San Blas Islands.

Capurganá. www.posadadelgecko.com. ℂ **314/525-6037.** 3 private rooms, 2 bungalows. COP$80,000 doubles. **Amenities:** Restaurant; free Wi-Fi.

Zingara Guesthouse ★★   For a true end-of-the-road experience, this all-wood guesthouse, located on the final stretch before the Panamanian border, overlooking Sapzurro and the bay, is a wonderful place to escape civilization and immerse yourself in nature. The clean, thoughtfully designed rooms (one sleeps five, the other sleeps three) have private bathrooms, mosquito nets, fans, and decks with hammocks. Gracious owner Clemencia takes exceptional care of her guests: fresh fruits and avocados in the morning, assistance with tours, and fine conversation. The resplendent birdlife, reptiles, crustaceans, and amphibians populating the exuberant gardens provide endless entertainment. Don't leave without buying some of Clemencia's homemade tarts and jellies.

Sapzurro. www.hospedajesapzurrozingara.com. ℂ **320/687-4678.** 2 units. COP$25,000–COP$40,000. **Amenities:** Free Wi-Fi.

Mompox (Mompós) ★★★

Few places live up to their mythology quite like Mompox. Isolated for centuries, on the wetlands of the Colombia's longest waterway—the fabled Rio Magdalena—Mompox's UNESCO-protected streets look much the same as they did in the days of Cervantes. Geographically, culturally, and historically, Mompox is a world unto itself. Founded in 1537 by Son Alonso de Heredia, it's one of the best-preserved and most evocative colonial towns in South America. The romantic atmosphere, the sultry exoticism, and the furtive imaginings that ripple through the pages of Gabriel García Márquez (several of Gabo's novels were set here) find expression on every intensely cinematic street corner. Simón Bolívar's pivotal relationship with this otherworldly town is distilled in Márquez's acclaimed novel, *El general en su laberinto* (The General in His Labyrinth): "Sometimes we dream about her, but she does not exist." Even today, Mompox's rich cultural legacy belies the town's parochial air and soporific languor (due in no small part to the blistering heat). There's a seductive beauty not only in the town's extraordinary architecture, but in Mompox's alignment along the Río Magdalena, the once-mighty river that serves as a poignant symbol of the city's dramatic fall from grace and glory.

ESSENTIALS
History
Established as a key trading port for the transportation of goods from the Caribbean coast to the Andes, for more than 300 years Mompox was one of the richest towns in South America. Due to its isolated, inhospitable location, it was in Mompox that the Spanish crown hid its unfathomable abundance of gold, silver, and emeralds, far from the lusty grip of pillaging British pirates. Mompox's silversmiths are famed the world over for their exquisite jewelry fashioned from delicate strands of silver. Around 70% of Momposinos work out of their courtyards as self-employed *filigranas*, creating designs that still incorporate aspects of colonial Spanish filigree.

Mompox was the first town in New Granada to declare independence from Spain in 1810. It was here, in 1812, that Bolívar raised his army of 400 men, which proved pivotal to the liberator's campaign to end Spanish colonial rule in Latin America. Bolívar's much quoted line, "*Si a Caracas debo la vida, a Mompox debo la Gloria*" (If to Caracas I owe my life, then to Mompox I owe my glory), stands as testimony to the town's fiercely independent spirit.

In the mid-19th century, when the Río Magdalena silted up and changed its course, larger boats were diverted to Brazo de Lobos and Magangué became the region's main port. Mompox swiftly transformed from a prosperous commercial center into a languid backwater. In the 1960s, Mompox's isolation was compounded when a period of unrest followed the brutal decade known as La Violencia. The Magdalena became infamous as one of the most violent places on the planet; the burning of the David Arango Uribe steam ferry in 1961—which Márquez had travelled on at age 15—put an end to paid passenger transport along the Magdalena. More recently, during the 1980s and '90s, as the civil war between paramilitary, guerillas, and narco-traffickers shook the region, travel along the river became prohibited at certain times of the day.

GETTING THERE   Getting to Mompox has long been the preserve of travelers with time, patience, and the belief that an arduous journey is part of the adventure. Mompox is only 125 miles from Cartagena, but getting here takes the better part of a day. **From Cartagena**, you can take a direct bus to Magangué (3½ hr.; COP$35,000) followed by a motorized canoe called a *chalupa* (15 min.; COP$8,000), followed by *colectivo* taxi to Mompox (COP$14,000; 45 min.). Or, the company **Toto Express** (© **310/707-0838**) offers a door-to-door service (4–6 hr., COP$75,000).

From **Medellín**, there are direct (night) buses from Medellín to Mompox (arriving early morning) with **Coopetrans** (10 hr.; COP$110,000). Or you can take the bus to Magangué via Sincelejo (8 hr.) followed by a *chalupa* (they leave when full) to Bodega (15 min.; COP$8,000) and *colectivo* taxi to Mompox (COP$14,000; 45 min.). There are flights with **ADA** (www.ada-aero.com) and **Satena** (www.satena.com) to Corazal; from there you can take the bus/*chalupa* combination from Magangué to Mompox. From **Bogotá**, direct buses from the main terminal with Coopetrans (14 hr.; COP$160,000)

GETTING AROUND   The only way to experience Mompox is on foot. You won't see many cars or taxis here; locals get around mostly on foot, or by bicycle, scooter, or auto-rickshaw. Mototaxis will happily run you around town for around COP$2,000.

VISITOR INFORMATION   Year round, Mompox is hot, seriously hot. Even if you are coming from sultry Cartagena, it feels like a furnace. For the most part, Mompox remains half forgotten. With the exception of an acclaimed jazz festival each October and an austere Semana Santa celebration—one of Colombia's most compelling—few tourists make it here; you can likely wing accommodation reservations and bus tickets.

EXPLORING MOMPOX

The 40 blocks that encompass Mompox's UNESCO-protected (since 1995) historic center unfurl along the Magdalena River. Unlike most Spanish colonial towns, Mompox does not have one main plaza, but rather a series of immaculately preserved squares presided over by baroque churches in pastel shades. There are no major museums or big sights. The pleasure of Mompox resides in wandering its fascinating streetscapes, early morning or late at night, when the temperatures are close to tolerable. Even the most resolute of "morning people" will fall into the town's heat-driven nocturnal rituals and find themselves meandering through the town's ebullient squares, gazing at magnificent churches and ornate palaces, or musing in a rocking chair with a glass of local corozal wine until the very early hours.

The main arteries are **Calle de la Albarrada** (Carrera 1, facing the river) and, 1 block inland, **Calle Real del Medio** (Carrera 2), which is where most of the silversmiths' workshops are located. Mompox's principal squares are: **Plaza de la Concepción** (also known as Plaza Mayor), **Plaza de Santa**

Bárbara, **Plaza de San Francisco**, **Plaza Domingo**, and **Plaza Bolívar** (also known as **Plaza Tamarindo**).

MAIN TOURIST SIGHTS

A soul-stirring tranche of old Andalucía, Mompox's main square, **Plaza de la Concepción** ★★, with its eccentric cast of characters, feels straight from the pages of a Márquez novel. Perhaps because it is. In 1540, the plaza was named Plaza Mayor by the city's founder, Alonso de Heredia, and formed the traditional axis for Spanish colonial towns, around which a tangle of streets unraveled. Early evening, when the sun relents, this is the place to sit in a rocking chair, have a cold beer, and watch events unfold.

Presiding over the action, the monumental **Iglesia de Inmaculada Concepción** stands on the spot where the first chapel was built in 1540 in simple *bahareque* style (mud and bamboo, with a thatched roof). Over the centuries, the church has been restored and rebuilt without compromising its architectural integrity. In 1550, the modest chapel was replaced by a more robust whitewashed stone-and-mortar construction (a style known as *mampostería*) and a red-tiled roof was added. In 1795, the interior was embellished before, in another magical realist move, one of the towers suddenly collapsed. In 1839, then-governor José Duque was spurred to action and ordered the demolition of the ailing structure. The current iteration, which was finally completed in 1934, features a marble representation of Our Lady of the Immaculate Conception. Across from the church, on the waterfront, the yellow Republican-style **Mercado Público** (Market) with its harmonious arcades, whitewashed Doric columns, and red-tiled roof has been restored to its former glory and now provides an evocative setting for Mompox's famed jazz festival.

Cementario Municipal ★★ It's worth strolling for an hour around Mompox's photogenic 19th-century cemetery. Along manicured pathways, troupes of black feral cats roam among whitewashed gravestones—with as many as half a dozen graves at a time stacked one on top of the other—grouped around a central chapel. With elaborate funeral sculptures, luxuriant vegetation, bright flowers, and arabesques of wrought iron, it's a compelling and beautiful vision. Candelario Obeso (born in Mompox in 1849), one of the revered "fathers of Black Poetry" in Latin America is buried here. During Semana Santa (Wednesday), the cemetery is illuminated with thousands of candles. Outside there's a sedate plaza with benches and, in place of religious artifacts and flowers for sale, several local *filigranas* purvey their intricate silver jewelry.

Calle 18. Free. Daily 9am–5pm, 2–5pm.

Iglesia de San Augustín ★ In 2012, the Vatican designated the modest San Augustín church, originally founded in 1606, a Basílica Menor as a result of the temple's "miraculous" image of Jesus that was discovered in Mompox in the 17th century. Now it's Mompox's principal place of worship and a holy pilgrimage site for devout Colombians. The church is also known for its Santo Sepulcro representation.

Carrera 2 and Calle 17. Mass 7pm (daily) and at 9am on Sun.

Iglesia de San Francisco ★★ Dominating its namesake square, the Iglesia de San Francisco is Mompox's oldest church, founded in 1580 by missionary Fray Francisco Gonzaga. The striking burgundy facade and wooden interior has been nipped, tucked, and beautified over the years. If you happen to be here on the rare occasion that the church is open, it's worth a glimpse inside for the distinctive polychrome wooden murals.

Calle 20/Plaza San Francisco.

Iglesia de Santa Bárbara ★★ Mompox's most alluring landmark, this whimsical confection on Plaza de Santa Bárbara was built in 1630. The church boasts Colombia's only octagonal bell tower and is crowned with a baroque dome wrapped with a Moorish balcony with ornate moldings of lions, palm trees, and flowers. Three elaborate gilded altars dominate the rather austere all-wood interior, which is a startling contrast to the vibrant egg yolk–yellow facade.

Carrera 1/Calle 14. Entry to the tower COP$2,000. Mon–Sat 8am–noon, Sun 8am–6pm. Mass Sun 4pm.

Museo del Arte Religioso ★ Mompox's only official museum, the Religious Art Museum is housed in an atmospheric colonial mansion that used to belong to independence leader and hero Vicente Celedonio Gutiérrez de Piñeres. Three galleries display a collection of 17th-century religious artworks along with 320 pieces of gold and silver.

Carrera 2 no. 7–17. ✆ **5/685-6074.** COP$3,000. Mon–Fri 9am–noon, 2–4pm; Sat 9am–noon.

Plaza de la Libertad ★ It was here on August 6, 1810, that the Act of Independence was signed, and the *Grito de Independencia*—the cry to "*Ser Libres o Morir*" (Be Free or Die)—resounded through the streets and echoed across the nation. *La Estatua de la Libertad* (1873) extols Mompox's seminal role as the first town to declare its independence from Spanish colonial rule. On the plinth is inscribed the famed Bolívar quote: "*Si a Caracas debo la vida, a Mompox debo la Gloria*" (If to Caracas I owe my life, then to Mompox I owe my glory). The stately 17th-century **Palacio San Carlos**, complete with colonial dungeons, was built in 1660 as a former Jesuit school/convent and now serves as the Alcadía (town hall).

Carrera 2/Calle 18.

Plaza de Santo Domingo ★★ Deserted by day, throbbing by night, Mompox's most animated square sizzles with a furtive sense of possibility. With its eclectic storefronts; sinewy Momposinos hauling wooden carts loaded with fruit; stalls selling *dulce de limón* (local lemon candy), *casabes* (flatbreads made from cassava), and *butifarras* (a type of sausage); and, not to mention, the odd mule and cart passing through, it's a fine window into Mompox's timeless rituals. At night, you can buy inexpensive wooden slabs loaded with *carne asada* and served with a bowl of *mondongo* (tripe soup) for less than COP$12,000. The 16th-century **Iglesia Santo Domingo** (reconstructed in 1850), features a striking image of the Virgin del Rosario wearing a jewel-encrusted crown.

Carrera 3 at Callejon del Colegio.

Plaza Simón Bolívar ★ Also known as Plaza Tamarindo, this charming leafy square, 2 blocks from the river, is believed to be the location of the original settlement of Mompo (named after its indigenous cacique Mompoj). Beneath the statue of the great liberator, women purvey gourds of *chicha* (a corn-based drink), and *bolas de tamarindo* (sweet tamarind balls) while in the surrounding streets, fastidious *filigranas* sit in the shady courtyards of their homes/workshops fashioning exquisite silver jewelry.

Calle 16 at Carrera 2.

EXCURSIONS

BOAT TOURS ★★ Half a century ago, before ecological damage devastated the Río Magdalena, alligators skulked and manatees swooned in the river's fecund shallows. The grandeur and mystery of Colombia's longest waterway has long intoxicated travelers, writers, and explorers including Alexander von Humboldt and Gabriel García Márquez, who confessed to an obsession with the river; in *El general en su laberinto* (The General and His Labyrinth), Gabo narrates Simón Bolívar's final voyage down the river. The best way to experience the Magdalena's mythical potency is to sign up for an afternoon boat trip on a motorized canoe (*chalupa*) which journeys downriver to remote fishing villages and culminates at the Ciénaga de Pijiño, a huge lake where you can jump out and swim. Along the route, guides with trained eyes point out herons and eagles, as well as more raucous riverside protagonists, including skulking iguanas and howler monkeys, that patrol the marshes where stilted wooden houses teeter improbably along the banks of the river. Local guides can be hired through La Casa Amarilla (see below) and several other hotels in town. Boats depart at 3pm and return around 7pm for magnificent views as the blazing sun drops like a stone into the Magdalena; from COP$35,000 per person.

WHERE TO STAY

Bioma Boutique Hotel ★★ This immaculately restored colonial hotel fuses colonial detail and modern élan with aplomb. Serene, light-filled spaces feature high ceilings and colonial detailing, including wooden shutters with arabesques of wrought iron, beamed ceilings, and original tiled floors. Impeccable white-on-white rooms provide serene hideaways, with contemporary styling, high-thread-count linens, and contemporary artworks. You can cool down in the inviting courtyard pool and enjoy a rooftop Jacuzzi with outrageous sunset views over Mompox. There is a substantial breakfast served each morning, and the service crackles with efficiency and warmth.

Calle Real Del Medio no. 18–59. www.bioma.co. ℂ **5/685-6733.** 11 units. Doubles from COP$190,000, includes breakfast. **Amenities:** Swimming pool; Jacuzzi; spa; restaurant; air-conditioning; free Wi-Fi.

Hostal La Casa del Viajero ★   Housed in a yellow colonial home, tucked away behind the Iglesia de Santa Bárbara, this characterful hostel is decorated with exotic wooden furnishings, wrought-iron window grills, bright murals, and whimsical design flourishes. There are bright, clean dorm rooms (all rooms have air-conditioning) and simple but cheerful double rooms with small but functional en-suite bathrooms. With a shared kitchen, hammocks strewn in the public spaces, and a laidback ambience, this is a great value backpacker choice.

Carrera 2 no. 13–54. www.lacasadelviajeromompox.com. ✆ 5/684-0657. 5 units. COP$30,000 dorm room, COP$65,000 double room with shared bath, COP$80,000 double room with private en-suite. **Amenities:** Air-conditioning; free Wi-Fi.

Hotel Casa de Espana ★   A short walk from the river, this gem of a hotel has character and charm in spades, with eclectically furnished rooms, cozy nooks, grand public spaces, rocking chairs all over, a large courtyard pool, and super-friendly, eager staff. Spacious, spotless rooms feature wooden furnishings, comfortable beds, and robust air-conditioning units. This is one of the best value options in town.

Calle Real del Medio no. 17A–52. www.hotelcasaespanamompox.com. ✆ 5/685-5373. 16 units. Doubles from COP$120,000. **Amenities:** Swimming pool; air-conditioning; free Wi-Fi.

La Casa Amarilla ★★   In a prime location next to the Iglesia Santa Bárbara, Casa Amarilla is housed in a gorgeous 17th-century colonial mansion artfully restored by knowledgeable British-Colombian journalist/author Richard McColl. One of the most emblematic places to stay in Mompox, the charming public spaces—with original features and a social terrace with glorious sunset views—exude faded grandeur. Tasteful rooms (with air-conditioning) open on to a leafy courtyard garden with hammocks and feature wooden furnishings, crisp linens, tiled floors, shuttered windows, and modern bathrooms. There's a chilled-out traveler vibe with a communal kitchen, books to trade, and bikes to rent. The warm and gracious staff are happy to set up excursions, including nature/boat tours of the Magdalena River, and assist with onward transportation.

Carrera 1 no. 13–59. www.lacasaamarillamompos.com. ✆ 575/685-6326. 10 units. COP$135,000–COP$250,000 private room with en-suite. **Amenities:** Air-conditioning; free Wi-Fi.

Portal de la Marquesa ★★   Romantic, chic, and with a real sense of place, the erstwhile Palacio de la Marquesa de Valdehoyos marries style, substance, and attention to detail. The artfully restored palace features restrained decor that brings out the exquisite colonial features. In the elegant public spaces, magnificent studded wooden doors contrast with white painted walls and modern white furnishings; a tranquil patio features a small pool (more aesthetic then recreational); and in the fertile gardens, lemon and orange trees, bananas, and bright sprays of bougainvillea impart a heady exoticism. Airy, spacious rooms with soaring beamed ceilings are the epitome of rustic chic. A generous made-to-order breakfast is served daily (included in the rate).

Carrera 1 no. 15–27. www.portaldelamarquesa.com. ✆ **5/664-3163.** 5 units. Doubles from COP$195,000, includes breakfast. **Amenities:** Swimming pool; air-conditioning; free Wi-Fi.

WHERE TO EAT

Ambrosia Bar-Restaurant ★★ COLOMBIAN   On Parque de la Libertad, this inviting restaurant, housed in a whitewashed colonial building, serves artfully presented Colombian dishes with a gastro twist, fine cocktails, and fresh fruit juices. With a serene courtyard with candlelit tables and attentive service, it's a relaxed setting for seafood-oriented dishes.

Calle 19 no. 1a–59. Parque de la Libertad. ✆ **57/627-6825.** COP$24,000–COP$52,000. Daily 6–10pm.

Café Tinto ★★ CAFE   An obligatory stop for travelers, this evocative, family-run bar/cafe on Plaza de la Concepción is the perfect place to fully inhabit the moment in a rocking chair overlooking the square or the Rio Magdalena as the evening unfolds. With cold beer, wine, fresh juices, loud salsa music into the early hours (on the weekend), big soccer games on the TV, an eclectic crowd, and fine conversation, it's everything a Colombian bar should be.

Plaza de la Concepción no. 1–07. ✆ **304/568-9152.** Mon–Thurs 5pm–11:30pm. Fri and Sat 5pm–3am.

Comedor Costeño ★★ COLOMBIAN   In an atmospheric location, with wooden tables right on the river, this a very popular and earthy spot to try traditional *cocina momposina*, including whole grilled *bocachico* (regional freshwater fish) or *mojarra* (a local fish that tastes like tilapia), liver (entrails are popular in town), and tortoise stew. The whiteboard menu changes daily, but all entrees are served with a bowl of soup, rice, *patacones* (mashed fried plantains) and a small salad. You can also dine in the cheerful yellow-painted dining room (it's super-hot, but fans are robust).

Carrera 1 no. 18–45. Main courses from COP$16,000. Daily 9am–5pm.

El Fuerte ★★★ INTERNATIONAL   A local institution, it's worth timing your visit to Mompox for the weekend to savor the ambience, gorgeous setting, and exceptional home cooking at El Fuerte. Most people come here for the terrific thin-crust, wood-oven pizza prepared in various iterations (Hawaiian, Speck, and zucchini), as well as homemade focaccia and a choice selection of gourmet entrees, including filet mignon, and seafood specials. The traditional Spanish colonial house, with a lush courtyard, tables and chairs fashioned from tree trunks, and an open kitchen, makes for a memorable and authentic setting.

Carrera 1 no. 17A–54. Plaza de la Concepción. ✆ **57/685-5978.** Main courses COP$12,000–COP$16,000. Daily 11am–10pm.

MEDELLÍN & THE EJE CAFETERO

7

by Caroline Lascom

Few cities have rewritten their narrative with quite such bold vision and dazzling ingenuity as Medellín. Just 20 years ago, if you told anyone that you were heading to Colombia's second city, they would think you were crazy. And they had a point. In the 1990s, Medellín was the cradle of drug lord Pablo Escobar, with a murder rate of 435 per 100,000 residents, incessant car bombings, kidnappings, and ruthless gang wars. With the death of Escobar in 1993, followed by a series of inspired reforms ushered in by progressive mayor Sergio Fajardo, the city has been truly reborn from a society on the brink of collapse into a dynamic, creative, and safe city.

The world now talks of the "Colombian Miracle." At the heart of Fajardo's "social urbanism." Blighted *comunas* (shantytowns) that were ground zero during the drug war are now connected to downtown by a flashy *Metrocable* (gondola) system. Library parks, sport facilities, and playgrounds form community hubs for the city's once abandoned neighborhoods.

A new cultural effervescence ripples through the city's verdant streets and avenues. There are steel mills reimagined as flashy modern art museums, lively plazas filled with sculptures, and iconic buildings rising from ramshackle barrios that cling to the mountainside. Each week a sophisticated new restaurant raises the culinary stakes and a hip boutique showcases works from the city's flourishing creative class. But for all its overtures to cosmopolitanism, Medellín remains ever true to its Paisa roots.

You'd be hard pressed to find a more glorious setting for a modern metropolis: nestled in the lush Aburrá Valley, framed by majestic Andean peaks, and reveling in its famed salubrious climate. Just outside the city, the traditional Antioquian lifestyle—unchanged for centuries—holds sway, with whitewashed colonial towns, glistening lakes, and coffee plantations providing rewarding day trips from the city.

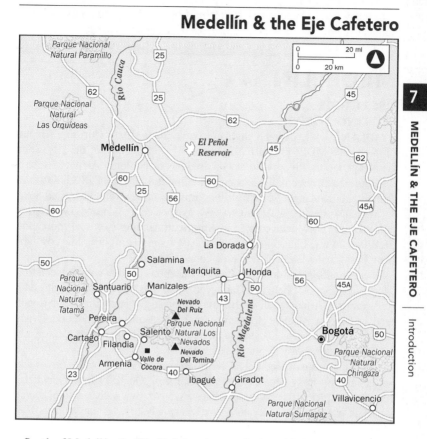

South of Medellín, the **Eje Cafetero** is a magical world. Colombia's impossibly lush coffee triangle combines scenic natural beauty with outdoor recreation, colonial history, and a growing inventory of evocative places to stay.

The industrious cities of **Pereira**, **Manizales**, and **Armenia** provide the commercial hubs and bases for exploration. Coffee plantations and forests of bamboo, *guadua*, and eucalyptus carpet misty mountains that rise above undulating valleys where dairy farms, avocado fields, orange orchards, and rushing rivers stocked with trout speak to the region's incredible fertility; drop a seed here and it will certainly thrive.

The picturesque towns of **Salento** and **Filandia**—where cowboys still ride their horses into town and 1940s Willy Jeeps shuttle travelers and bags of coffee beans along unpaved roads—provide access to one of Colombia's natural treasures, the **Valle de Cocora**. Here, you can hike or horseback ride through mystical cloud forest where the storied wax palm (the world's largest palm tree) adds a dash of the surreal to a bewitching landscape. In the distance, the dramatic snowcapped peaks of **Parque Nacional Natural Los Nevados** summon intrepid climbers to test their mettle scaling the park's five tempestuous volcanic peaks (three are still active).

In many ways, Antioquia is Colombia's beating heart, culturally and economically. Now, with a spirit of peace, openness, and prosperity, you can literally feel, sense, and taste a city and a region that is finally coming into its own.

MEDELLÍN ★★★

Essentials

GETTING THERE

BY PLANE International flights arrive at **José María Córdova Airport** (airport code MDE; ✆ **4/601-212**), about 45 minutes east of the city. Some smaller domestic flights land at **Olaya Herrera National Airport** which is much more convenient; it's located just 7 minutes by taxi (COP$5,000) from Poblado Metro station. Several airlines provide service from the United States to Medellín, including **Avianca** (www.avianca.com), **Copa** (www.copaair.com), **Delta** (www.delta.com), and **American Airlines** (www.aa.com). Both **JetBlue** (www.jetblue.com) and **Spirit** (www.spirit.com) offer low cost fares from Fort Lauderdale with domestic connections.

There are dozens of domestic flight connections per day with Avianca from Medellín to Bogotá, Cali, and Cartagena, as well as three or four flights daily to Pereira and Armenia (all via Bogotá). Domestic Avianca flights via Bogotá tend to be cost-effective, low-stress, and expedient, with comfortable new planes, brisk turnarounds, and a large fleet that helps offset delays, and Bogotá is a super-easy airport to navigate.

Inexpensive direct flights to Pereira are available with **ADA** (www.ada-aero.com) and **Easy Fly** (www.easyfly.com.co), which fly from Olaya Herrera National Airport. Low-cost airlines **Viva Air** (www.vivacolombia.co/co, which is part-owned by RyanAir) and **Easy Fly** offer direct services from Medellín to Cartagena.

To get from José María Córdova airport to Medellín proper, you can take a taxi for COP$65,000 (standard fare), or take a bus for COP$16,000, which will drop you off in the city center close to Plaza Bolívar. Unless you are on a tight budget, it's more efficient to book an airport transfer ahead of time (ideally from your hotel) because most flights from the U.S. arrive into Medellín after 9pm.

BY BUS You can get to Medellín from most major cities and large towns. The journey is breathtaking, and not just because of the scenery: Mountain drop-offs and crazy Colombian drivers will try the nerves of even the most laissez-faire travelers. Nervous travelers, or those prone to car sickness, are encouraged to fly. Medellín has two bus terminals, **El Terminal del Norte** and **El Terminal del Sur**, so check to see which end of town your hotel is closest to before booking your bus trip. *Tip:* If you will be staying in El Poblado, try to arrive at El Terminal de Sur to avoid a long and expensive ride to your hotel.

VISITOR INFORMATION

Medellín's tourism office is located in the **Palacio de Exposiciones** (Calle 51 no. 55–80; www.medellin.travel; ✆ **4/232-4022**), and you'll have to ring

Medellín

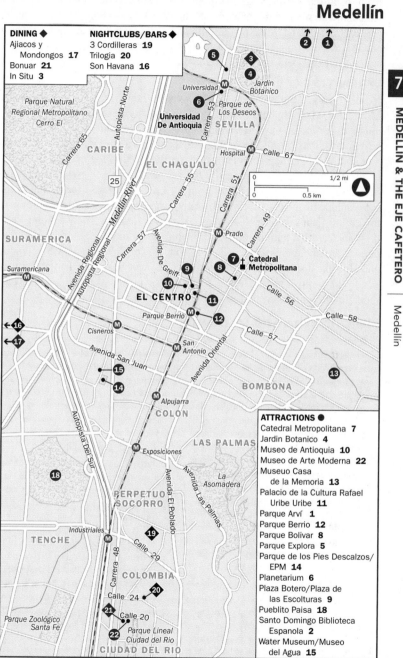

DINING ◆
Ajiacos y
  Mondongos **17**
Bonuar **21**
In Situ **3**

NIGHTCLUBS/BARS ◆
3 Cordilleras **19**
Trilogia **20**
Son Havana **16**

Parque Natural
Regional Metropolitano
Cerro El

Universidad
De Antioquia

Jardin
Botanico

Parque de
Los Deseos

SEVILLA

CARIBE

Hospital Calle 67

EL CHAGUALO

25

0   1/2 mi
0   0.5 km

SURAMERICA

Prado

Suramericana

Catedral
Metropolitana

EL CENTRO

Parque Berrio

Cisneros

San
Antonio

Avenida San Juan

COLON

Alpujarra

BOMBONA

LAS PALMAS

Exposiciones

La
Asomadera

PERPETUO
SOCORRO

Pueblito Paisa 18

Industriales

TENCHE

COLOMBIA

Calle 24

Calle 20

Parque Zoológico
Santa Fe

Parque Lineal
Ciudad del Rio

CIUDAD DEL RIO

ATTRACTIONS ●
Catedral Metropolitana **7**
Jardin Botanico **4**
Museo de Antioquia **10**
Museo de Arte Moderna **22**
Museuo Casa
  de la Memoria **13**
Palacio de la Cultura Rafael
  Uribe Uribe **11**
Parque Arví **1**
Parque Berrio **12**
Parque Bolivar **8**
Parque Explora **5**
Parque de los Pies Descalzos/
  EPM **14**
Planetarium **6**
Plaza Botero/Plaza de
  las Esculturas **9**
Pueblito Paisa **18**
Santo Domingo Biblioteca
  Espanola **2**
Water Museum/Museo
  del Agua **15**

many bells and walk through many doors to find the office. The helpful office is liberal with maps and brochures (including a guide in English and Spanish). The office is open 7:30am to 12:30pm and again from 1:30 to 5:30pm. There are also tourism offices located at José María Córdova airport (© **4/562-2885**) and at Olaya Herrera airport (© **4/285-1048**).

WHEN TO GO

Nestled in the Aburrá Valley, on the western range of the Northern Andes Mountains, Medellín lies at 5,000 feet (1,500m) above sea level. With a balmy climate year-round—average temperatures hover around 24°C/75°F—there's never a bad time to visit Medellín. Sure, it can rain a fair bit (especially during Apr and May, and Sept–Nov) but early morning damp fog usually gives way to sunny skies. August is generally the warmest month. A great time to visit Medellín is late July/early August, during **La Festival de Flores**, one of the most unique festivals in the world, when *campesinos* from Antioquia come to the city to flaunt their brilliant and bold flower designs. The weeklong celebrations feature a number of events, including an antique car parade, a horse parade, and the grand finale: a 3- to 4-hour flower float parade, where young and old alike display their flower designs and dancers, singers, and performers add to the carnival spirit. Be sure to book your plane ticket and hotel accommodation far in advance if you'll be in Medellín during this time.

Neighborhoods in Brief

Centro Most of Medellín's major sights and landmarks are located in Centro, within a 5-block radius of **Plaza de las Esculturas,** also known as **Plaza Botero** for the captivating series of voluptuous sculptures fashioned by native son Fernando Botero. Also on the square stands the city's cultural highlight: **Museo de Antioquia,** with a sublime collection of Latin American art, including a gallery devoted to Botero's signature works. From here, pedestrianized **Carrera Junín**—lined with bakeries, traditional Paisa restaurants, and local brand stores—funnels south. Outside of Centro's historic kernel, a web of ramshackle streets, with improvised storefronts and workshops spilling onto potholed sidewalks, reveals life on the margins: It's messy and it's chaotic, but it's utterly compelling.

North of Centre A 10-minute ride north of Centro, but a world apart from the downtown madness, **Calle Carabono** is the main artery/reference point that links a collection of child-friendly museums and attractions. Families with kids could spend at least a day here. There's the stellar **Parque Explora,** with its aquarium and interactive natural science exhibits; an excellent **Planetarium;** the

serene and architecturally striking **Jardin Botánico;** and **Parque Norte,** a classic theme park with the usual quota of rollercoasters and carousels. Farther northeast, accessed by the iconic Metrocable, **Parque Arví** is a densely forested wilderness with miles of hiking trails and recreational activities, including ziplining, and a butterfly park.

El Poblado A 10-minute metro ride from Centro, the fashionable enclave of **Poblado** is where most travelers should (and do) end up retreating to for the night. It feels rather like a hip California neighborhood dropped into a tropical forest, with an inviting ensemble of fashionable stores, gourmet restaurants, and boutique hotels, crisscrossed by meandering pathways where tropical plants and flowers run amok. Poblado's epicenter is lively **Parque Lleras** with its earthy local Paisa bars, tropical dance halls, international breweries, and wild dance clubs. Up in the hills, Vía de las Palmas leads to **Los Altos de Poblado,** which rich Colombian's have always claimed as their own. Here you'll find gated mansions, fine restaurants, and decadent clubs and casinos that formed the city's nocturnal center of gravity during the drug lords' heyday.

Laureles   This leafy, upscale neighborhood with a decidedly French layout (the rest of the city adheres to a more traditional Spanish grid template) lies just west of Centro. With a lowkey, residential charm, it's also one of the most pleasant places to stroll, dip in and out of designer boutiques, watch the world go by in a funky coffee shop, and party like there's no tomorrow. Some of the city's best bars and clubs are found at **La 70** and around **Calle 33**.

Comunas   On the city's Andean slopes, Medellín's slums were neglected by the government for more than half a century. **Comuna 1 and 13** are two neighborhoods emblematic of Medellín's renaissance. Back in the 1990s, gripped by extreme poverty, isolation, and blight, Medellín's *comunas* (or barrios/shantytowns) nurtured a young, destitute populace ready to find meaning (and money) working for Escobar and the cartels. Now, more than 20 years since the fall of Escobar, Comuna 1 and 13 are barely recognizable.

Getting Around

ON FOOT   While Medellín's safety has dramatically improved, you still need to be mindful of being in the wrong place at the wrong time, and keep track of your belongings at all times. The key areas of tourist interest within the Centro Histórico (outlined below), are considered safe for travelers, and security is bolstered by an imposing, armed police presence, which you may find simultaneously reassuring and intimidating. Unless you are taking a walking tour, you won't want to stray much beyond the several blocks that surround Plaza Bolívar; Centro is chaotic and seedy (especially at night). El Poblado neighborhood is a middle-class haven, made for strolling, and safe to explore day and night. **Real City Tours** (www.realcitytours.com) offers excellent (and free) morning and afternoon city walking tours in English, which cover the city's historic attractions and neighborhoods. Tours book up quickly, so you need to be on the ball; sign up online 1½ days ahead of your desired tour date.

BY METRO   Most of Medellín's tourist attractions are within walking distance of Plaza Berrío in Centro, which is accessible on the fast, clean, and super-efficient Metro system (the only one in Colombia), completed in 2008. Metro tickets cost COP$2,000 per ride. You can buy a card, which saves you having to line up at the ticket booth each time, but it won't save you any money. An integrated (*integrado*) fare system allows you to link with buses and cable cars to the comunas/Parque Aví and the striking Biblioteca Española.

BY TAXI   Taxis in Medellín are cheap and efficient. Most of the hotels listed in this guide will call a cab for you as a matter of course, and most museums will consider it protocol to call a cab for foreign tourists. Beware that taxi drivers drive like madmen, especially on the serpentine roads of Alto Poblado; you might want to make sure your cab has seat belts before you get in (a lot don't). For safety, security, and peace of mind, the best option is to use **Uber** (www.uber.com/cities/medellin), which has been operating in Medellín since 2015, or the award-winning **Tappsi** app (www.tappsi.co), a similar easy-to-use concept with enhanced security features (you can share driver details with family/friends, etc.).

TOUR BUSES   The best way to see the city is to take the hop on/hop off **Turibus** (www.turibuscolombia.com; ✆ **4/371-5054**), which will drop you off at the city's major attractions as well as give you information about Medellín.

Buses depart every 70 minutes. You can catch the Turibus at Parque Del Poblado, Plaza Botero, and Santafé Mall (check the website for full list of stops/*paradas*). A 24-hour ticket costs COP$35,000; a 48-hour ticket costs COP$56,000. Turibus now also offers tours of the surrounding countryside, including Guatapé (7am–9pm, COP$69,900), see p. 189.

Another company that offers tours of Antioquia is **Las Buseticas** (Carrera 43A no. 34–95; www.lasbuseticas.com; ✆ 4/262-7444). The bigger your party, the better the prices. Las Buseticas also offers package tours of El Eje Cafetero and other Colombian destinations. Other bus and car companies offer day tours of the Circuito de Oriente; for more information, contact or visit the **Aviatur** office in Parque de Bolívar, at Carrera 49 no. 55–25, Edificio El Parque (www.aviatur.com; ✆ 4/576-5000 or 576-5002). Your hotel should also be able to provide tour information.

Exploring Medellín

Having shed its violent image, Medellín today is a vibrant new world. The city of 2.5 million people has garnered international kudos for its exemplary model of urban planning; in 2013 it earned the title of "most inventive city" by the Urban Land Institute. Following on the heels of pioneering mayor Sergio Fajardo, Medellín's current mayor Federico Gutiérrez (elected in 2016) has restated his commitment to a policy of urban renewal based on social inclusion.

From the up-and-coming **Ciudad del Rio** neighborhood to posh **Poblado** and gritty **Centro**, an infectious energy and entrepreneurial zeal defines Medellín's cultural zeitgeist. The city's creative class, which languished behind closed doors for decades, has seized the moment and defined its own artistic center. With their signature passion, hardworking ethos, and independent spirit, Medellínenses are blazing their own trail. With contemporary galleries, world-class museums, whimsical parks, striking architecture, gourmet restaurants, hip boutiques, and seemingly a different festival every week, the city feels alive with possibility. Medellín certainly has its flaws, but right here, right now, it's one of the world's most fascinating and innovative cities to explore.

TOP TOURIST ATTRACTIONS

Carrera Junín ★ LANDMARK Behind Parque Berrío, pedestrianized Carrera Junín runs for 5 blocks between Parque Bolívar and Calle 49. A color-ful promenade studded with bakeries, flower kiosks, restaurants (serving the traditional *bandeja paisa*), and eclectic stores, this traffic-free strip boasts an unusual smattering of historic charm. To the south, the promenade is book-ended by the hard-to-miss landmark **Coltejer Tower**. Designed by Esguerra Saenz Urdaneta Samper in 1972, the 574-foot-tall structure is the tallest build-ing in Medellín and the fourth-tallest building in Colombia.

Metro Parque Berrío.

Comuna 13 ★★★ NEIGHBORHOOD Over the last decade, one of Medellín's most progressive and visionary infrastructure projects involved the construction of 1,259 feet of outdoor escalators that connect the citizens of the hillside shanty Comuna 13 to downtown. During the 1990s, Comuna 13 received the notorious distinction of one of the most dangerous neighborhoods on the planet. A battleground for criminal control of Medellín and the Aburrá Valley, guerrilla and paramilitary groups fought over the drugs and contraband that came in and out of Medellín on the San Juan Highway. When the Colombian military launched Operation Orion in 2002, in an attempt to defang left-wing rebels in the area, hundreds of residents of La Aurora were injured in the crossfire.

Today, the San Javier/La Aurora neighborhood has been transformed beyond recognition, with libraries, playgrounds, and cinderblock buildings freshly painted in a rainbow of colors (the local government provided the paint) and emblazoned with dramatic street art and murals. The best way to get to grips with the transformations within the comunas is to take a tour. **Toucan Tours** (Carrera 41A no. 10–28; www.toucancafe.co; ✆ **4/586-9215**) offers fascinating graffiti tours led by co-founders/volunteers of Casa Kolacho: a peace-promoting community organization of hip-hop and street artists who are responsible for most of the graffiti in Comuna 13. Tours (Mon–Sat, 2–6pm; COP$60,000) are in Spanish, but a bilingual tour guide provides English translation and historical context as needed. **Comuna 13 Tours** (www.comuna13tours.com) also offers a 4- to 5-hour daily walking tour, which departs Poblado metro station at 10am (COP$70,000, including metro/gondola ride). All tours should be booked at least 48 hours in advance. If you don't have time for a tour, it's worth taking the escalators (the equivalent of a 28-story building) to the top for impressive views of the city unfurling below. Security here is super-tight and the area is considered safe during the day/early evening for tourists. Still, unless you are going as part of a tour, do not venture a few blocks beyond the Metrocable terminal.

Take the Metrocable from the San Javier metro station (línea B) to La Aurora (línea J), COP$2,000.

Escobar Tours ★★ TOUR   For many Colombians, the notion of leading tourists around Escobar-themed sites (and arguably glamorizing the drug czar's seditious acts) . . . well, it's a touchy subject. For most Colombians, Escobar is the man who terrorized and killed thousands of Colombians, but for some of the city's poorer denizens, Escobar is venerated as a Robin Hood folk hero. Current estimates put Escobar's net worth (in the early 1990s) at US$30 billion, which makes him the richest (as well as deadliest) criminal in history. One thing's for sure: Escobar sells. Several companies now offer tours that contextualize Escobar's role within the country's dark and violent history. **Paisa Tours** (www.paisaroad.com; ✆ **317/489-2629**) pioneered the Escobar Tour, and it's still the best. Balanced, engaging tours (in English) take in key Escobar landmarks, including the cemetery where Escobar is buried, the rooftop where he was shot by military snipers, and his now dilapidated penthouse where you can check out his massive walk-in safe. Informative guides cover the history of the cocaine trade as well as focusing on the personality cult of Escobar.

Tours depart Mon–Sat at 9:30am. COP$50,000. Reservations can be made at the **Black Sheep Hostel** in Polanco, see p. 177.

Jardín Botánico Joaquín Antonio Uribe ★★ PARK   Named after Colombia's famed writer and botanist, Medellín's botanical garden has attained international kudos for its sublime architecture and outstanding conservation credentials. A short metro ride, but a world apart, from the mayhem of Centro, a series of trails and walkways meander through diverse ecosystems. More than 1,000 species of flora and fauna find sanctuary here, including orchids (Colombia's national flower), bromeliad, butterflies, birds, and reptiles; you may spot iguanas basking in the sun beside the lily pond.

Originally conceived in 1972, the garden got a major overhaul in 2005 as part of ex-mayor Sergio Fajardo's grandiose urban investment initiative. In addition to a butterfly farm, a maze, and a flashy new science building, the garden's breathtaking design statement is the award-winning wood-and-steel Orchideorama, designed by Plan B Architects. The 50-foot-tall space features 10 hexagonal structures, which resemble a bouquet of flowers. The garden hosts a spectacular orchid display during the city's famed flower festival (the first week in Aug) and the lively event schedule features yoga classes, outdoor movies, and live music. **In Situ** ★★ (see p. 182), one of the city's most memorable dining experiences, is also located here, and there are two cafes, Café del Bosque (at the entrance) and El Vagón (located in a train carriage) which serve standard cafe fare.

Calle 73 no. 51D–14. www.botanicomedellin.org. ✆ **574/444-5500.** Free. Metro: Universidad.

Museo Casa de la Memoria ★ MUSEUM   Another of Medellín's striking odes to modernity and rebirth, the Museo Casa de la Memoria, unveiled in 2014, dominates what used to be one of the city's dodgier neighborhoods. A series of exhibits present the horrors of Colombia's violent war between the government/right-wing paramilitary groups and leftist guerrillas. Most of the spaces, which aim to be artistic rather than educational, are powerful and compelling in a visceral way. There are interactive maps and screens that allow you to explore specific dates/regions seminal to the civil war, and heart-wrenching videos that feature victims or families of *los desaparcidos* (Colombians who "disappeared" during the civil war).

Calle 51 no. 36–66, Parque Bicentenario. ✆ **4/383-4001.** Free. Mon noon–6pm, Tues–Fri 10am–6pm, Sat 10am–4pm, closed Sun and holidays. The museum is quite a walk from the nearest Metro: Parque Berrío. The best bet is to take a cab (less than COP$6,000) from Centro or from Parque Berrío station.

Museo de Antioquia ★★★ MUSEUM   Housed in a striking Art Deco building on Plaza de la Escultura's west side, this fantastic art museum is Medellín's cultural highlight and the second oldest museum in the nation. More than 100 sculptures and artworks donated by Medellín's native son, Fernando Botero (b. 1932) grace the third floor Sala Botero. With its hushed aura and lack of crowds (except on the weekend), you could easily muse on Colombian art and wander the tranquil patios and inner courtyard for a few hours.

Botero's signature works (Botero has referred to himself as the "most Colombian of Colombian artists") are renowned for their study of rotund people, animals, and objects. According to the artist, his aim was not to satirize his bulbous protagonists but rather to explore shape, proportion, and volume. There are still life canvases of exotic fruits, the lush landscapes of Antioquia, historical characters, and socio-political statements. One gallery is dedicated to a series of watercolors that depict the pomp, pageantry, and bloodlust of bullfighting; Botero's uncle enrolled him in bullfighting school, but he was more interested in exploring the "sport" through art. Botero's sublime sculptures mirror the motifs from his paintings (executed in a figurative style known as *Boterismo*), and include reclining nudes, body parts, and gallant soldiers on horseback.

It's hard to talk about highlights, but the monumental canvases that depict the *Visit of Louis XVI and Marie Antoinette to Medellín* (1990); the sublime *Cabeza* (1981), carved from Siena marble; the chocolaty bronze *Mujer con Moño* (1983); and the luscious 12-foot-tall representations of Adam and Eve embody the themes and style that characterize Botero's seminal works. The violence that took Medellín to the brink of collapse during the 1990s finds expression in *Pablo Escobar Muerto* (2006) with Escobar, lying on a red-tiled roof, his large belly riddled with bullets. The museum also contains a number of other excellent exhibits, including a hall featuring the works of international artists (including Rodin and Rufino Tamayo), and an exhibit featuring religious and colonial art from the period of conquest in South America; don't miss one of Colombia's most famous paintings, *Horizontes*, by Francisco Antonio Cano.

Carrera 52 no. 52–43. www.museodeantioquia.org. ℂ **4/251-3636.** COP$8,000 adults, children under 12 free. Mon 9:30am–5pm, Fri–Sun 10am–4pm. Metro Parque Berrío.

Museo de Arte Moderna de Medellín ★★ MUSEUM

In the energized Ciudad del Rio district, a 1930s steel mill has been reimagined as the avant-garde new home for Medellín's Museum of Modern Art; around 80% of the funds were raised from private industry. A sensitive conversion project retained the industrial character of the mill, with exposed brick, concrete pillars, and a metal roof; the name of its original owners, Talleres Robledo, still appears above the front entrance. A new wing, designed by Peruvian architects 51+1 in 2015, features modern galleries linked by open stairways, which (according to the architects) aim to mirror the barrios that cling to the Andean mountains.

The small but seminal collection of Latin American contemporary talent (60–90 min. usually suffices here) features drawings, videos, paintings and sculptures by Colombia's leading modern artists: Beatriz González (b. 1938), Enrique Grau (1920–2004) and Carlos Rojas (1933–1997). All of MAMM's works were donated by the artists; the museum has not yet needed an acquisitions budget. There's a terrific gift shop, and it is worth framing your visit around lunchtime so you can sample the fine dishes at restaurant/cafe **Bonuar ★★** (see p. 180).

Carrera 44 no. 19A–100. www.elmamm.org. ℂ **574/444-2622.** COP$10,000, children under 12 and students COP$7,000. Tues–Fri 9am–6pm, Sat 10am–6pm, Sun 10am–5pm. Metro Industriales.

Palacio de la Cultura Rafael Uribe Uribe ★ MUSEUM   On the other side of the plaza, this bizarre palace-turned–cultural center is a striking Gothic revival (with nods to Art Nouveau) confection. Designed by Belgian architect Agustín Goovaerts in 1925, the building's massive dome was constructed from iron imported from Belgium. The seat for the Governor of Antioquia until 1987, nowadays it's home to the Rafael Uribe Palace of Culture. Taking up a fair amount of real estate within the palace, the Institute of Culture and Heritage of Antioquia allows visitors to browse fascinating historical, music/sound, and photographical archives (all in Spanish). There's also a small art gallery (rotating local artists), a library, a cinema, and a pleasant cafe. There are great views of the city from the top floor.

Carrera 51 no. 52–03. www.culturantioquia.gov.co. © **4/251-1444.** Free. Mon–Fri 8am–12pm, 2–5pm. Sat 10am–2pm. Metro Parque Berrío.

Parque Arví ★★ PARK   A 15-minute cable-car ride from Acevado metro station leads to the rural enclave of Santa Elena, where you'll find Parque Arví, the country's largest nature park. Within this wild and thickly forested landscape, you'll likely come across cowboys on horseback or farmers herding their cows, sheep, or goats. There are walking trails that crisscross pine and eucalyptus forests, with more than 700 species of flora and fauna, as well as six *núcleos* (themed recreational zones): Núcleo Comforma has a zipline, playground, and musical garden; Núcleo Comfenalco features a nature trail, a hotel, butterfly house, a farm, insectarium, and camping/picnic areas. To fully explore the park, you'll need to allow a full day here. Bikes (available for rent at the entrance) are an expedient way to explore the far-flung reaches of the park.

Santa Elena vía Piedras Blancas. www.parquearvi.org. © **574/444-2979.** Free, with charges for individual attractions. Tues–Sun 9am–5pm. Take línea K/green line (Metrocable) from Acevado to Santo Domingo, then change lines to take línea L/brown line, Santo Domingo to Arví.

Parque Berrío ★ LANDMARK   One of Medellín's oldest squares, dating to 1680, this expansive plaza has always been the city's "front room." Between 1784 and 1892, it was the site of Medellín's lively public market, ceremonial events, and grizzly public executions. A statue of Pedro Justo Berrío (governor of Antioquia from 1864–1873), mounted on a marble pedestal, forms the square's centerpiece. On the west side of the square, the **Basilica Nuestro Señora de La Candelaria** (Carrera 50 no. 50–72; © **574/231-3332**) functioned as the city's cathedral from 1868 to 1931. Dedicated to every Colombian's favorite saint, the Virgin of Candelaria, the eye-catching whitewashed stone and lime church was originally built in 1649, then rebuilt, only to be demolished and reconstructed all over again in 1767 in neoclassical style according to the dictates of then-governor Don José Barón de Chávez. With two symmetrical towers topped by red-tiled domes, the basilica exudes a certain lofty grace; it seems to yearn for an Antioquian village backdrop rather than the hustle, bustle, and architectural mishmash of Parque Berrío. In the southwest of corner the park, Botero lovers shouldn't miss "Torso de Mujer," which goes by the affectionate moniker of *La Gorda*. The headless bronze sculpture was the first work that Botero donated to his hometown in 1987. Carrera 50/Calle 51. Metro Parque Berrío.

Parque Bolívar ★ LANDMARK   The city's main reference point, this revamped square is the best place to begin exploring the city. What used to be hangout for bored old men, prostitutes, and drug addicts now boasts a more salubrious vibe with street vendors selling *agua de panela con limón* (a ubiquitous sugarcane and lime-juice drink that, according to Antiquian matriarchs, fights off the flu), *arepas*, ice cream, and candy. Dominating the plaza, the corpulent **Catedral Metropolitana** (Carrera 48 no. 56–81; © **4/513-2269**), is Medellín's largest church. Designed by French architect Emile Carré, the Romanesque-style edifice with Byzantine flourishes was fashioned from over 1.2 million adobe bricks (one of the world's largest structures created using such materials) which, according to legend, were solidified with bulls' blood. The inside of the massive cathedral is rather somber, but it's worth checking out the stained-glass windows and Italian marble canopy above the high altar. Metro Prado.

Parque de los Pies Descalzos/El Museo de Agua ★ PARK/ MUSEUM   This innovative outdoor play area—dedicated to barefoot frolics in water, sand, and a mini *guadua* forest—is an excellent way for kids to let off steam for an hour or so. The adjacent **EPM Water Museum** is a surprising sleeper hit for young children and teens, with an immersive, multi-sensory, and highly interactive series of state-of-the art exhibits that illuminate water's relationship to evolution, ecosystems, and ancient civilizations. The museum also addresses modern-day consumption and conservation efforts related to global water supplies. All information is in Spanish, but the exhibits are dynamic enough for kids to get a lot out of it. The super-friendly, efficient staff will be more than happy to arrange a (free) guided tour in English; just ask when you buy your ticket.
Parque de los Pies Descalzos. www.grupo-epm.com. © **574/380-6954.** Museum COP$6,000. Tues–Fri 8am–6pm, Sat, Sun and holidays 10am–7pm; last tours at 4pm. Metro San Antonio (a 15-min. walk).

Plaza de las Esculturas ★★ LANDMARK   Also known as Plaza Botero, this is the square where most travelers love to linger, and so they should. A fabulous ensemble of 23 rotund, bronze sculptures created by beloved native son Fernando Botero distinguish this classic South American square. Most of Botero's voluptuous sculptures tell it like it is. There's *Head*, *Man on Horseback*, *Roman Soldier*, and *Eve*, all of which the artist intended to be both admired and touched. Meandering among the statues, sinewy *campesinos* wearing signature woven sombreros heave massive carts loaded with limes, and vendors purvey refreshing *agua de panela*, cups of mango, and Botero replicas in all shapes and sizes.

On Calle 52 (on the south side of the Uribe Palace), you'll see elderly men set up with typewriters composing documents, job applications, and love letters for the city's illiterate population. With plenty of tourists milling around here, you'll notice a beefed up (even more than usual) armed police presence.

Carrera 52/Calle 52. Metro Parque Berrio.

Parque Explora ★★ MUSEUM   Unveiled in 2007, Parque Explora is emblematic of Medellín's civic reinvention. A blighted wasteland just north of Centro has been recast as a dynamic, family-oriented entertainment and learning complex. The striking centerpiece is a postmodern amalgam of five red cubed buildings where a fantastic series of interactive, multi-sensory spaces introduce children and teens to scientific and technological concepts. Within the same complex (admission included), the small but stimulating **aquarium** features coral gardens, sting rays, tropical fish, and crowd-pleasing Amazonian protagonists including the pirarucú—one of the planet's largest freshwater fish which can grow to 4.3 meters (14 ft.)—and marauding piranhas. Whether it's an aerobics class, a salsa performance, a rock concert, an outdoor movie, or a kid's workshop, there's usually something going on at **Parque de los Deseos** (Calle 71 no. 52–30; www.fundacionepm.org.co; ✆ **574/516-6005**), a 5-minute walk from Explora Park (across from Universidad Metro station).

Carrera 50 no. 73–75. www.parqueexplora.org. ✆ **574/516-8300.** COP$23,000. Tues–Fri 8:30am–5:30pm. Sat, Sun, and holidays 10am–6:30pm. Metro Universidad.

Planetarium ★ MUSEUM   Adjacent to Parque Explora (separate entry ticket required), there's no lack of ingenuity at this well-conceived planetarium that packs a lot into a quite small space. Dynamic, child-friendly exhibits encourage visitors to explore space, scientific concepts and phenomena—black holes, gravity, holograms, sedimentation, and sand dunes—through interactive exhibits (with accessible information in English). As well as experiencing what it's like to be caught in an earthquake, children can simulate controlling a space craft as it hovers over Mars, spin marbles into a "black hole" to explore concepts of gravity, and take their own picture orbiting the moon or on Mars. The shows here are well worth it; book in advance, they sell out fast.

Carrera 52 no. 71–117. www.planetariomedellin.org. ✆ **574/516-8300.** COP$12,000 or COP$14,000 (with show included). Tues, Wed, Fri 8:30am–5pm, Thurs 8:30am–6pm, Sat, Sun, and holidays 10am–6pm. Metro Universidad.

Pueblito Paisa ★ ATTRACTION   On the top of the Cerro de Nutibara, 250 feet above the city, the slightly cheesy but free Pueblito Paisa is a miniature replica of a typical Antioquian town complete with church, town hall, and colorful red-roofed colonial-style homes grouped around a lush central plaza with fountains, sculptures, and atmospheric restaurants serving *comida típica*. The main reason to visit is for the 360° views of Medellín and for the profusion of nature; Nutibara is a migratory corridor for birds, and there are more than 60 species of flora on the hill alone. Take a taxi here—ideally on a weekday—when it's less busy. Do not attempt to climb up or down Cerro de Nutibara, because robberies have occurred here over recent years.

Calle 30 no. 55–64. ✆ **4/235-8370.** Free. Daily 5am–midnight (stores and restaurants open from 10am–8pm).

Santo Domingo ★★★ EXPERIENCE   One of the city's highlights, the essence of the new Medellín can be distilled into the compelling Metrocable (cable car) ride from Acevedo metro station to Santo Domingo. During the 1980s and '90s, Santo Domingo held the inauspicious rank as one of the most dangerous barrios on the continent. Now, French/Swiss-engineered gondolas soar over revived neighborhoods that have been at the forefront of the government's scheme to connect the city's slums with downtown. It's hard not to be inspired and moved as you look down on bands playing, bouncy castles, corrugated tin rooftops sporting elaborate shrines and the odd maxed-out paddling pool, and cafes bustling with a mix of locals and tourists.

The three geometric structures that form the now iconic **Biblioteca Española** ★★ (Spanish Library) stand as glorious testimony to the concept that renewal begins with social inclusion. Designed by the Giancarlo Mazzanti (and with a hefty financial contribution from the Spanish government), the "library-park" was completed in 2007. The three massive slabs of black slate, which seem to erupt organically from the mountainside, provide a hub for community programs based on learning and social engagement; resources include a day center for kids and a free Internet suite. The Spanish Library certainly hasn't been without controversy. Due to structural problems, the three buildings have been intermittently covered up with black cloth since 2013.

As you exit the Santo Domingo station, there's a palpable energy and jubilation to the barrio. It's just a 5-minute walk to the new **mirador**, which provides sweeping panoramas of the city below. Even without the noticeable police presence (the area is considered a "secured" tourist attraction), the area is now very safe during the day.

Metro (línea A/blue line) to Acevado, change to línea K (Metrocable [3rd stop] to Santo Domingo). **Spanish Library:** Carrera 33 B no. 107 A–100. www.reddebibliotecas.org. co. Consult the website for schedule of events/hours (which change daily).

Where to Stay

Most travelers, quite rightly, choose to stay in the upscale neighborhood of El Poblado, in close proximity to La Zona Rosa, with its many restaurants/bars and excellent shopping, as well as Vía de las Palmas, Medellín's glitzy party avenue. From Poblado, a 10-minute metro ride will drop you within easy reach of the city's main sights, and you will likely be able to walk (or take a short cab ride) home after bar-hopping at night. If money is tight, a number of midrange establishments orbit Carrera 70, near Medellín's stadium, and there are dozens of super budget options in the city center; it's important to note that this area is rougher around the edges (and seedier at night) than either Laureles or El Poblado. Though the area isn't unsafe, it's worth spending up for location, greater comfort, and facilities—upscale and midrange hotels in Medellín are much cheaper than those in Bogotá and Cartagena and you'll be pleasantly surprised at what just US$100 will buy you. Medellín is becoming an increasingly "hot" tourist destination, and you should always make reservations in advance, especially during holiday weekends and the main tourist season (Dec and Aug).

El Poblado

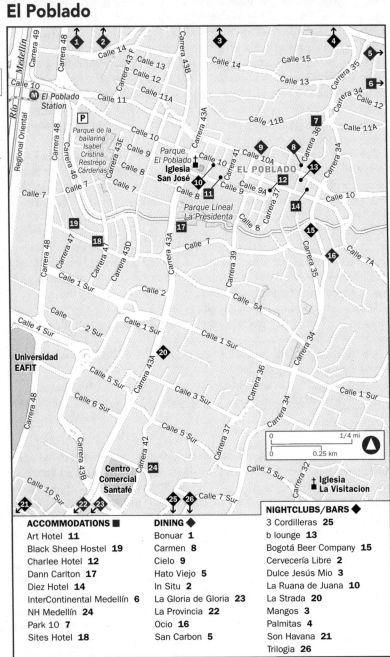

ACCOMMODATIONS ■
Art Hotel **11**
Black Sheep Hostel **19**
Charlee Hotel **12**
Dann Carlton **17**
Diez Hotel **14**
InterContinental Medellín **6**
NH Medellín **24**
Park 10 **7**
Sites Hotel **18**

DINING ◆
Bonuar **1**
Carmen **8**
Cielo **9**
Hato Viejo **5**
In Situ **2**
La Gloria de Gloria **23**
La Provincia **22**
Ocio **16**
San Carbon **5**

NIGHTCLUBS/BARS ◆
3 Cordilleras **25**
b lounge **13**
Bogotá Beer Company **15**
Cervecería Libre **2**
Dulce Jesús Mio **3**
La Ruana de Juana **10**
La Strada **20**
Mangos **3**
Palmitas **4**
Son Havana **21**
Trilogia **26**

Art Hotel ★★　An industrial-chic concept prevails at this cool boutique hotel on a quiet leafy street just 1 block from Parque Lleras. Polished concrete, exposed bricks, and burnished steel are juxtaposed with contemporary Colombian artworks and jewelry (which are all for sale) and plush red carpets. Rooms are grouped around the central atrium, where fire-escape steps lead to minimalist rooms that may be a little small, dark, and moody for some tastes. There's a movie theater (the hotel hosts movie nights that pay homage to venerable film directors), a gym, spa, and a bar/restaurant that attracts the cool cats in town. Sure, there are the occasional snafus here and there, but with its modern élan, creative zeal, and super-friendly, keen-to-please staff, the Art Hotel is emblematic of the new Medellín. And the central Poblado location doesn't get much better.

Carrera 41 no. 9–31. http://en.arthotel.com.co. ℰ **574/369-7900.** 54 units. Double from COP$600,000, includes breakfast. Metro: Poblado. **Amenities:** Restaurant; bar; spa; gym; movie theater; free Wi-Fi.

The Black Sheep Hostel ★★　Tucked away along the calm residential streets of the Patio Bonito neighborhood, a 15-minute walk from Parque Lleras, the Black Sheep is where young international travelers set up for the duration. Run by New Zealander Kelvin Smith, the hostel has a laidback vibe and provides great tourist info for Medellín and onward destinations. There's a fully equipped kitchen, a barbecue area, two TV rooms, and—most Colombian of all—a hammock-filled balcony. Rooms are spacious and comfortable, most featuring en-suite bathrooms, and some rooms have extra-long beds to accommodate tall foreigners. You'll need to reserve in advance for the double rooms with en-suite baths, but dorm beds can usually be booked on the spot. There is a minimum 5-day stay during La Feria de las Flores.

Transversal 5A no. 45–133, Poblado. www.blacksheepmedellin.com. ℰ **4/311-1589.** 21 units. From COP$37,000 dorm; from COP$80,000 double with shared bath. Metro: El Poblado. **Amenities:** TV lounge; free Wi-Fi.

Charlee Hotel ★★　The first upscale boutique hotel in town and still the most fashionable, the Charlee's hip design, edgy ambience, and art-filled spaces court the pretty, party-loving, under-35 demographic. Rooms and suites with large balconies (with hot tubs) channel a minimalist aesthetic that combines textures and colors with aplomb; lots of leather, glass, and bold textiles create striking design statements. This is definitely the place for night owls. At the center of the action, right off Parque Lleras, between the traffic noise and hum of bass—it's loud, really loud. There's a small rooftop pool (more aesthetic than recreational), a decent restaurant, and nightclub Envy, a trendy hangout for gilded locals. The Charlee is one of Medellín's most expensive lodging options, so be sure you are fully in the mood to embrace its spirit of instant gratification before you commit.

Calle 9A no. 37–16. www.thecharlee.com. ℰ **574/444-4968.** 48 units. From COP$475,000 double, includes breakfast. Metro: Poblado. **Amenities:** Restaurant; bar; gym; pool; free Wi-Fi.

Dann Carlton ★　Medellín's grand dame has definitely seen better days, but it still has a classic lobby lavished with marble and crystal chandeliers, a nice pool area, and breathtaking views from the top-floor rotating restaurant. The location is hard to beat; it's just a 10-minute (uphill) walk to the bars and restaurants of Parque Lleras. With dated furnishings and a few maintenance issues to test your patience, rooms are underwhelming and could certainly do with a touch of style and a fresh coat of paint. But the overall experience is comfortable enough, and rates here can be a bargain given the hotel's central location and amenities (especially for families). Service is inconsistent and varies from warm and semi-efficient reception staff and bellboys to downright surly servers in the restaurants/bars and by the pool (don't think to disturb them when they are on their cellphones).

Avenida El Poblado, Carrera 43A no. 7–50. www.danncarlton.com. © **4/444-5151.** Doubles from COP$210,000. **Amenities:** 2 restaurants; 2 bars; outdoor pool; spa; gym; free Wi-Fi.

Diez Hotel ★   A 15-minute walk from Poblado metro, close to lots of shops and bars, Diez works hard to create a sense of place. Each floor is themed according to a different region of Colombia, and the hotel's inviting public spaces are decorated with lashings of bamboo, exotic hardwoods, bright monochrome furniture, and artisanal flourishes. Modern, if rather sparse, angular rooms aren't big on character, but they are clean, comfortable, and well maintained with spacious modern bathrooms. It's worth paying up for a room with a city view. Noise can be a problem here, so if that's important to you, ask for a quiet room at check in. For onsite pampering, there's a spa, a hot tub on the terrace, and two very good restaurants (sushi and traditional Colombian). Service is friendly and brisk.

Calle 10A no. 34–11. www.diezhotel.com. © **4/448-1034.** Double from COP$275,000, includes breakfast. Metro Poblado. **Amenities:** 2 restaurant/bars; hot tub; spa; gym; free Wi-Fi.

InterContinental Medellín ★★   The massive InterContinental is fresh from a major renovation and is now the best resort-style hotel in the city. Up in the hills of Altos del Poblado, it's certainly not front and center of the action, but it's a stone's throw from some of Medellín's fancier restaurants and nightspots (and if you want peace and quiet and amenities galore, this is for you). Guest rooms have shed the nasty old carpets and now boast hardwood floors and appealing wooden furnishings. The hotel still has to work hard to offset the soulless architecture (the building is hardly a beauty), and with low ceilings and small bathrooms, standard rooms can feel claustrophobic. But what you get here is a terrific heated pool, a full-on gym, a spa, tennis courts, a kids' playground, and an expansive daily breakfast buffet (not always included in rate, but worth paying a little extra for). The restaurant, **Fogón de Piedra**, serves excellent wood-oven pizza and decent grilled meat and fish dishes in a tropical poolside setting, and the service gets top marks for effort. Be sure to request a high-floor room overlooking the pool/city—the views are stunning, especially at night. At less than US$100 per night, it's worth putting up with the odd glitch.

Calle 16 no. 28–51. www.ihg.com. © **4/315-4443.** 249 units. COP$290,000 double, includes breakfast. No Metro access; 15-min. ride (COP$6,000 in a taxi to Parque Lleras/Poblado metro). **Amenities:** 2 restaurants; 2 bars; outdoor pool; sauna; spa; free Wi-Fi.

NH Medellín ★★   While it may be a little generic for some tastes, in the context of Medellín's small pond of fine hotels, this sharp, functional hotel scores highly for polished service, bright modern rooms, and a clutch of resort-style amenities, plus a stellar location (at the end of Poblado's Mila de Oro and a short walk from the upscale Santafé mall). Thoughtful in-room touches include coffeemakers, robes, flatscreen TVs, blackout blinds and excellent soundproofing. In the public spaces, heavy ratios of glass and steel, coupled with contemporary lighting and decor, don't tend to foster a warm and cozy vibe, but the large lap pool, gym, spa, cool bar with city views, and manicured outdoor spaces provide a relaxing way to bookend a day in the city. An expansive buffet breakfast is included in the rate.

Carrera 42 no. 5. www.nh-hotels.com/hotel/nh-collection-medellin-royal. ℭ **91/398-5690.** 134 units. COP$320,000 double, includes breakfast. Metro: El Poblado. **Amenities:** Restaurant/bar; swimming pool; hot tub; spa; gym; free Wi-Fi.

Park 10 Hotel ★   This English-style boutique hotel, in a quiet residential neighborhood 3 blocks from Parque Lleras, has a slew of modern amenities, a spectacular outdoor terrace, charming gardens, and fresh, spacious guest rooms, all with views of Poblado. All rooms feature marble bathrooms, orthopedic mattresses, and stained-glass bathroom doors. If you feel like indulging, splash out on the two-level grand suite. The small upstairs gym offers an oxygen bar.

Carrera 36B no. 11–12. www.hotelpark10.com.co. ℭ **4/310-6060.** 55 units. COP$320,000 suites; COP$410,000 grand suites, includes breakfast. Free parking. Metro: 15-min. walk to El Poblado station. **Amenities:** Gym; spa; free Wi-Fi.

Sites Hotel ★★   This superb new aparthotel in the quiet Patio Bonito residential area of Poblado has understated style and great facilities for families and long-stay travelers. The modern spaces channel a literary design ethos (it's tagline is the "writer's hotel") and blends functionality with modern amenities. Pristine rooms are spacious and feature either kitchenettes (in the loft rooms) or full-on kitchen/lounge spaces. The smart, intimate reception area doubles as a library with striking artwork, and there's a small glass-walled pool/hot tub on the rooftop with great city views. A breakfast of fruit, pastries, and made-to-order eggs and pancakes is included in the rate. The friendly and efficient staff will arrange airport transportation (COP$70,000). At less than US$90 a night, this place is a steal.

Carrera 45 no. 5–15. www.siteshotel.com. ℭ **574/605-0006.** 60 units. From COP$243,000 loft, COP$275,000 one-bedroom apartments and suite, includes breakfast. Metro: Poblado (a 15-min. walk). **Amenities:** Restaurant; pool; library; free Wi-Fi.

Where to Eat

If you love *arepas* and beans, you're in luck. Food in Medellín is carb-based and filling, and you're never far from the typical Antioquian *bandeja paisa*, a smorgasbord of soup, rice, beans, avocado, salad, sausage, plantain, shredded beef, eggs, *arepa*, and *chicharrón* (pork rinds). In Centro, and the Envigado neighborhood, you'll find plenty of small restaurants and holes-in-the-wall offering *almuerzos corrientes*, or set-price lunches, which will set you back around COP$7,000 to COP$9,000.

As Colombia's top chefs have returned home from honing their skills at Michelin-star temples stateside and in Europe, a new breed of gastronomic restaurants have invigorated Medellín's traditional dining scene. Smart bistros and fancy gastro-molecular hotspots are cropping up all over town, sporting innovative menus that fuse fresh local produce with exotic ingredients from the Amazon and Colombia's Pacific/Caribbean coasts. For all its embrace of global epicurean styles and techniques, Medellín's haute cuisine still feels firmly rooted in the rich and hearty culinary traditions of Antioquia.

Heading along Avenida Poblado from Centro Commercial Santafé, you'll find the customary onslaught of international and local chain restaurants: Hard Rock Café, Crepes & Waffles, Sushi Light, all with decor (some with outdoor terraces) befitting of their prime real estate setting. Punctuating Vía de Las Palmas, heading into the hills of Altos de Poblado (around COP$6,000 by taxi from Parque Lleras), posh eateries boast terrific views and international menus (but elevated price tags to match). Many of Poblado's chic new boutique hotels are also home to fashionable restaurants with creative menus.

Ajiacos y Mondongos ★★ COLOMBIAN   This family-run, hole-in-the-wall lunch joint strewn with religious artifacts oozes character and local color. It's also one of the best places in town to get acquainted with classic Antioquian dishes; while you may try to resist, no one should leave Medellín without tasting the region's signature tripe soup. Decisions are made fast and easy with just three menu options: tripe soup, *cazuela con frijoles* (beef with beans) and *ajiaco*, every Paisa's favorite type of chicken soup. For dessert, try the classic *tres leches* cake (butter cake soaked in milk and cream) or carrot cake. Liquid refreshment comes in the form of beer and lemonade.

Calle 8 no. 42–46. www.ajiacosymondongos.co. ✆ **574/266-5505.** COP$16,000. Daily noon–3:30pm.

Bonuar ★★ INTERNATIONAL/COLOMBIAN   A stylish appendage to the Museum of Modern Art, Bonuar is a hip bistro/cafe with lashings of dark wood, potted plants, and a convivial bar scene. The outdoor patio is a lowkey place to watch the world go by over solid Caribbean fusion dishes including grilled fish, ceviche, caramelized octopus, and spicy grilled shrimp, as well as hearty soups, salads, and a terrific burger. Weekends are lively here as the energy of the gentrifying Ciudad del Rio neighborhood takes hold, and live jazz and blues fills the airwaves.

Carrera 44 no. 19A–100. www.bonuar.com. ✆ **574/235-3577.** Main courses COP$22,000–COPS$42,000. Daily 11am–10:30pm.

Carmen ★★★ INTERNATIONAL   With California chef Rob Pevitts and his Colombian wife Carmen at the helm (both alumni of Le Cordon Bleu in San Francisco), the chic, elegant Carmen (like it's sister restaurant in Cartagena, see p. 105) is one of Colombia's most memorable dining experiences. Each artfully presented dish is composed of well-curated local meat and fish (flown in daily from the Pacific), complemented with exotic produce that just bursts and pops with flavor. Pevitt's creative combinations and theatrical executions often stray into the realms of gastro-molecular dining, but without the pomp, pretension, and sticker shock you might expect. Asian- and Caribbean-inflected signature dishes include plantain-crusted fish of the day over coconut rice risotto, a seared snapper with coconut curry and candied yams, and plancha-seared duck confit with a wild huckleberry glaze and fried rice. For dessert, try the delicious Maui, a macadamia nut financier coated with cacao ganache, topped with a coconut "cloud," and served with lavender ice cream. You can choose from dining in the serene kitchen-dining room with elegant bamboo furnishings or in the enchanting garden. A five-course tasting menu with wine pairings is also available. Reservations are essential.

Carrera 36 no. 10A–27. www.carmenmedellin.com. © **574/311-9625.** Reservations recommended (even at lunch). Main courses COP$40,000–COP$55,000. Mon–Wed noon–3pm, 7–10:30pm, Thurs and Fri noon–3pm, 7–11pm. Metro: Poblado.

Cielo ★★★ INTERNATIONAL   With sister restaurants in Miami and Bogotá, the Cielo triumvirate is often hailed among Latin America's best restaurants. Here in Medellín, superstar chef Juan Manuel Barrientos brings molecular gastronomy to a captivated local and international crowd. The freshest local ingredients combined with indigenous techniques and a dash of science result in an epic dining experience. Allow 4 hours for the fixed 12- or 15-course tasting menu (or "moments"). There are rose petals to cleanse your hands, an Amazonian "tree of life" made from cassava, chicken marinated in mustard seeds and beer, liquid nitrogen citrus sorbet, and chocolate truffles sprinkled with gold dust. The elegant but exotic dining room provides a serene backdrop for a culinary odyssey (which in NYC, Paris, or London, would be at least five times the price).

Carrera 40 no. 10A–22. www.elcielorestaurant.com. © **314/541-0393.** Daily noon–3pm, 7pm–midnight. Tasting menu of 15 moments: COP$130,000. Metro: Poblado.

Hato Viejo ★★ COLOMBIAN   Even if you are not wild about Colombian food, Hato Viejo is hard not to love. With a colorful dose of kitsch, traditional furnishings, a jukebox playing Latin classics, and courteous waiters dressed in 18th-century Paisa attire, Hato Viejo serves good honest Colombian food at decent prices. Opposite the Hotel InterContinental, set back from a busy four-lane highway in the hills of Poblado, the rambling space features outdoor balconies and terraces (there are wonderful views of the city below, but it's loud), a leafy courtyard, and a separate sports bar. For a true taste of Antioquia, opt for the *Plato Montanero* (ground beef, rice, avocado, *chicharrón*, sausage, egg, salad, beans, and fried *plátano*). The fish here is fresh and well executed with shrimp ceviche, salmon, grilled trout, tuna, or snook; for something a little more exotic, try the *parrillada Caribeña*, Hato Viejo's signature seafood dish with grilled shrimp, mussels, octopus, and *langostinas* (king prawns), served with coconut rice and avocado salad.

Calle 16 no. 28–60, Vía de Las Palmas. www.hatoviejo.com. © **4/268-5412.** Reservations recommended after 8pm. Main courses COP$22,000–COP$50,000. Daily noon–11pm (sometimes later). Taxi from Parque Lleras will cost around COP$6,500.

In Situ ★★ INTERNATIONAL   Located within the botanical garden, In Situ is an alluring atmosphere for a delicious lunch or dinner served in a graceful setting with soaring ceilings and floor-to-ceiling windows that open out onto lush gardens. Exotic wooden furnishings, contemporary decorative statements that pay homage to the landscape of the Aburrá Valley, and natural fabrics create a harmonious inside-outside design concept. The menu features excellent halibut ceviche, innovative salads—try the lychee and gravlax—and imaginative fish and meat entrees; highlights include fish of the day encrusted with nuts and dried fruits and drizzled with passion fruit sauce, grilled tuna with quinoa tabbouleh, and chicken baked with wild berries in a pesto sauce (courtesy of the wild herb garden). The service is polished and discreet.

Calle 73 no. 51D–14. www.botanicomedellin.org. © **574/444-5500.** Reservations recommended (even at lunch). Main courses COP$26,000–COP$52,000. Daily noon–3pm, 7–10pm. Metro: Universidad.

La Gloria de Gloria ★★ COLOMBIAN   Aspiring connoisseurs of *chicharrón* (pork rinds) and lovers of the classic *bandeja paisa* should head to this classic neighborhood joint in Envigado (which nudges up to Poblado). The rib-sticking fried strips of pork rind sprawl across the plate like a T-Rex fossil, with every remaining inch loaded with mounds of rice, *morcilla* (Colombian blood sausage), beans, plantain, and chorizo. There's a homey, welcoming vibe to the place, especially on Sundays, when locals line up for their shots of *aguardiente* as a pre-amble to the feast.

La Provincia ★★★ INTERNATIONAL   Another of Medellín's world-class restaurants, La Provincia serves artfully presented, inventive cuisine in a beautiful setting. The elegant wood-paneled dining room with inspiring city views is one of the city's finest, with tables dressed with crisp white linens and sparkling silver and glassware. The menu is a muse on classic exotic Caribbean and Mediterranean/French dishes, each reimagined with tantalizing results. Menu highlights include risotto with scallops, lobster, and mushrooms; seared salmon steaks with coconut curry and lulo; and tender-as-silk chateaubriand with béarnaise, chipotle, and cilantro. Dessert lovers will enjoy La Provincia's classic repertoire, with heavenly chocolate lava cake, crème brulee, and hazelnut parfait drizzled with strawberry coulis. This is one of those places where you should say yes to everything.

Carrera 42 3s 81. www.laprovinciarestaurante.com. © **4/322-0192.** Main courses COP$35,000–COP$66,000. Reservations highly recommended. Mon–Thurs noon–3pm, 7–10pm. Fri and Sat noon–3pm, 7–12pm.

Ocio ★★★ INTERNATIONAL   Chef Laura Londoño garnered kudos at Michelin-starred restaurants in Europe before returning home to play a leading role in Medellín's evolving culinary landscape. With an industrial-chic setting a short walk from Parque Lleras, and furnishings and decorative objects fashioned from recycled materials, there's a distinctive Antioquian style and spirit to Ocio. The focus here is on slow cooking techniques, hours of tenderizing and enriching the earthy flavors of local meats. Londoño's signature dish is a 12-hour roasted pork shank (*asado de tira*) with caramelized chili and lemon, served with sticky rice. While the menu caters more to carnivorous tastes, memorable appetizers include sushi with seaweed salad and seared octopus bathed in chili butter. For dessert, try the *sandwich de galleta*: a deliciously foofy version of an ice cream sandwich.

Carrera. 33 no. 7–21. www.ocimde.com. ✆ **574/448-8203.** Reservations essential. Main courses COP$39,000–COP$44,000. Tues–Sat noon–3pm, 7–10pm. Metro: Poblado.

San Carbón ★ GRILL/STEAKHOUSE A popular Medellín grill and steakhouse, San Carbón is something of an institution. There's a covered terrace, a chic bar, high ceilings, and an open-air kitchen, all of which make this a very pleasant and atmospheric place to enjoy the energy of Parque Lleras. San Carbón functions as a bar at night, popular with the city's young and hip. The steak and lobster are good, as are the Argentine and Chilean red wines. On the weekend there is usually live music.

Calle 9A no. 37A–13, Parque Lleras. www.sancarbon.com.co. ✆ **4/268-5570.** Main courses COP$26,000–COP$44,000. Daily noon–2am. Metro: El Poblado.

Shopping

One thing's for sure: Medellín is a shopper's city. With an increasingly cosmopolitan and entrepreneurial demographic, the city has fast redefined itself as the cradle of Colombia's rising fashion industry. It's the largest textile producer in the country, and the city's creative young designers are blazing a trail, launching hip (often eco-conscious) brands and labels with a distinctly Colombian sensibility.

In Centro, you will find inexpensive clothing and shoes in local brand stores and markets. For a more designer shopping experience (or just to people-watch and enjoy the scenery), head to the fashion showcase of Poblado's **Mila de Oro** or the Golden Mile (Avenida Poblado/Calle 10). El Poblado's **Vía Primavera** (Carrera 37), an elegant street between Parque Lleras and Provenza neighborhood, brims with funky boutiques, upscale designer emporiums, hip homeware stores, gourmet restaurants, arty cafes packed with digital nomads, and contemporary galleries. From leatherwear to sexy swimwear, you'll soon gain an appreciation for the colors, textures, and feel that is distinctive to Paisa style. In the residential enclave of Laureles, **Avenida Jardín** is another enjoyable place to stroll, with fashionable boutiques and eclectic stores selling unusual one-off items and items of clothing, often signed by up-and-coming designers.

Andres Pajón ★★ FASHION If you have plenty of money, or just want to gain vicarious insight into Colombia's luxury fashion market, check out the elegant, ultra-feminine designs by Andrés Pajón and Felipe Cartagena at the designer duo's flagship store on Vía Primavera. Since establishing his label in 2008, Pajón has taken Colombia's fashion scene by storm with bold colors and vivacious patterns that take their cues from Colombia's tropical landscapes. Calle 8 no. 37A–31. www.andrespajon.com. ✆ **4/352-1051.** Metro Poblado.

The Blue House ★★ HOMEWARE This designer homeware emporium artfully showcases the work of Colombian designers. You'll find unique furniture fashioned from exotic woods, hand woven fabrics, contemporary lighting, and eye-catching decorative objects. For gorgeous handcrafted fabrics and jewelry with an eco-conscious sensibility, check out the Oropendola brand (www.oropendola.co/oropendola); all pieces are designed and produced by local designer Carolina Vélez and her indigenous community collective. Calle 10A no. 38–31. www.thebluehouse.com.co. *C* **4/266-0391**. Metro Poblado.

Centro Commercial Santafé ★★ SHOPPING MALL Wealthier Paisas love to spend a day at the mall. Crowning Poblado's Mila de Oro, the Santafé mall is the biggest, ritziest shopping palace in town and pitches itself as a complete lifestyle experience: movie theaters, restaurants/bars, a kids ball court (the biggest in the world, by all accounts), arcade game rooms, and lots of interactive play spaces for little kids. Stores are a mix of upscale local and international designer chains with high prices that are comparable to the U.S. Avenida El Poblado no. 7. www.centrocomercialsantafe.com/medellin. *C* **800/093-5777**. Daily 10am–9pm. Metro Poblado.

El Hueco ★ MARKET For extremely cheap (and possibly contraband) electronics, clothing, and home goods, head to El Hueco, but be sure to keep your guard up. It might be a good idea to hire a taxi driver for a few hours who can accompany you and offer some protection. Glorieta de San Juan and Avenida del Ferrocarril. *C* **4/512–7273**. Metro San Antonio.

Entreaguas ★★ SWIMWEAR On Vía Primavera, this is one of best places in the country to shop for Colombian beachwear; perfect if you are en route to the Caribbean. Founded by young designer Natalia Botero (born and raised in Medellín), each eye-catching piece, ranging from diaphanous cover ups to sexy bikinis and artfully engineered one pieces (no matter what size or shape you are, there is a bathing suit for you) are handcrafted by a local community collective. Carrera 37 no. 8A–124. www.entreaguas.com.co. *C* **4/268-7007**. Metro Poblado.

Galería Diseño ★ FASHION/HOMEWARES A striking whitewashed building with a corrugated roof and irreverent decorative statements sets the tone for off-beat designs and collections from more than 40 independent Colombian designers, including Dulcinea, Runaway, Oh lala, Maracuya, Reventon Turquise, and Llorona. You'll find bathing suits, casual dresses, shoes, formal attire, and indigenous arts and crafts that you can (pretty much) guarantee someone won't be wearing next to you in line at Starbucks. Carrera 37 (Avenida Vía Primavera), btw. Calle 10 and 36. *C* **4/312-4937**. Metro Poblado.

Makua ★★ JEWELRY An eco-friendly fashion ethos is gaining momentum in Medellín. A dazzling exemplar of the trend, Makua's flamboyant necklaces, bracelets, earrings, and accessories fashioned from gold-plated copper are created using the ancestral techniques of Colombia's Kuna and Embera indigenous people. With pieces starting at COP$60,000, they're a great way to support local communities and take home a beautiful and distinctly Colombian souvenir. Carrera 35 no. 8A–16 (office, 202). www.makua.co. *C* **4/266-6589**.

Parque Comercial El Tesoro ★ SHOPPING MALL   This is another swanky and exclusive mall (and a good place to escape a rain shower) which features all the designer brands (local and international) that you'd expect. Carrera 25A 1ASur–45. www.eltesoro.com.co. ℂ **4/321-1010.** Daily 10am–9pm. Metro Poblado.

Vida Augusta ★★ HOMEWARES   This ultra-hip designer bazaar/workshop is a great place to feel the excitement, creativity, and city pride that defines Medellín's fashion, art, and design scene. You won't find anything generic, clichéd, or passé among the eclectic displays of hand-embroidered linens, custom-made soaps, one-off pairs of glasses, vintage cameras, purses, satchels, shoes, dresses, and books. The workshop also hosts style-oriented exhibitions. Carrera 35 no. 8A–81. www.vidaaugusta.com. ℂ **4/312-8033.** Metro Poblado.

Medellín After Dark

In the 1990s, the drug cartels left their mark on Medellín's decadent party scene, particularly on **Vía de Las Palmas**, the colorful, Las Vegas–style "party row" where, quite literally, anything goes. Medellín's best dance clubs are located on Vía de Las Palmas or La Strada (a mall in Poblado), popular with the area's young and glamorous, national celebrities, and international travelers. If you plan to party here, you'll need to dress the part. **La 70**, centered on Carrera 70 near the stadium (Metro: Stadio), is another popular party area featuring smaller, no-frills clubs and bars. Dotted across the city you'll find salsa bars, ranging from stylish dance halls to makeshift storefronts; regardless, the carnival atmosphere tends to be as welcoming as it is infectious.

The upscale enclave of Poblado is the best place to bar hop. At the center of it all, **Parque Lleras**, in La Zona Rosa, is one of the most vibrant spots in town and a great place to people-watch and try out local spirits and cocktails, or partake of the city's growing passion for craft beers. Avoid the bars and cantinas in Centro, which tend to be seedy at night. Many of the more casual restaurants in La Zona Rosa turn into bars around 9 or 10pm.

Medellín is one of the few places in Colombia that abides by the "must be 18 to party" rule; if you look young, bring a copy of your passport. Drinking and driving has a zero tolerance rule. Even one drink behind the wheel and you run the risk of your vehicle being towed and a very hefty fine. Don't risk it.

3 Cordilleras ★★ BREWERY/BAR   Established in 2008, 3 Cordilleras was one of Medellín's first microbreweries. As well as selling tastings of its six brews in the lively on-site bar, the brewery offers tours (in Spanish). Tours include a meander around the brewery, accompanied by an informative spiel on the beer-making process, rounded off by samples of Cordillera's artisan beers served to a rock/dance music soundtrack; the best night to come is the last Thursday of every month, when there's a live music performance. Tours, held Thursdays 5:30 to 9:00pm, include five beers (COP$21,000). On Fridays, brewery tours also include a music talent showcase from 6:30 to 10pm (COP$26,000). It's a great way to spend an evening. Calle 30 no. 44–176. www.3cordilleras.com. ℂ **4/444-2337.** Daily 5:30pm–midnight. Metro Industriales.

b lounge ★ BAR/NIGHTCLUB   A Zona Rosa nightlife stable, b lounge is a loud bar with deep sofas and a balcony that is packed with locals and visitors on the weekend; the pick-up scene here is far from subtle. B lounge is known for its impassioned karaoke party every Wednesday (which also happens to be Ladies Night), which morphs into Latin pop musical medleys later in the evening. On the weekends, it's electronica, hardcore dancing, and a less chatty vibe. Carrera 36 no. 38–10. ℂ **4/444-7824.** Cover from COP$20,000. Wed–Sat 9:30pm–3am.

Bogotá Beer Company ★★ BAR   In Zona Rosa, BBC's casual Medellín outpost feels rather like an old-school English pub with a long wooden bar, beers by the bottle and on tap, exposed brick, and soccer games broadcast on flatscreen TVs. Popular with an international local/expat crowd, there's pleasant outside seating on the balcony or patio, and the kitchen serves hearty comfort food, including burgers, spicy wings, and nachos (kitchen closes at 11pm). Carrera 34 no. 7165. www.bogotabeercompany.com. ℂ **4/311-5607.** Daily 12:30pm–3am. Metro Poblado.

Cervecería Libre ★★ BAR   Located in the gentrifying Ciudad del Rio neighborhood, this characterful beer hall—in a former car garage—taps into the city's growing thirst for craft beers. As well as offering a variety of IPA and stout brands by the bottle, it serves craft beers on tap from Colombian microbreweries Bogotá Beer Company, 3 Cordilleras, and Apostol. A beer with free snacks will set you back around COP$7,000. There's an international crowd, a chilled-out ambience, classic American rock music, and fun and friendly owner/bartenders. Carrera 44 no. 25–31. www.cervecerialibre.com. ℂ **314/615-4688.** Beers COP$5,000–COP$6,000. Wed–Sat 4:30–11:30pm (later on weekends).

Dulce Jesús Mío ★★★ NIGHTCLUB   A local institution, there's no place on earth quite like DJM. This disco/bar is worth visiting for its sheer bizarreness factor alone. A riotous send-up of a traditional Antioquian village, the decor centers on a kitsch white colonial church, and every remaining inch is smothered with tack, ranging from the shockingly outrageous to the whimsically cartoonish, with blow up dolls, phantasmagoric fairy lights, a giant Woody Woodpecker, Bugs Bunny toilets, and Wonder Woman sinks in the bathrooms. Staff take on their traditional "villager" roles with passion: You will be served by either a priest, a prostitute, the town mayor, or a police officer, and you might even catch a Shakira or Sofia Vergara impersonator making the rounds. The atmosphere is friendly, if a little weird. Everyone here comes to join in the spirit of debauched fantasy, dance like mad, or maybe just limbo; there are some fiercely fought-out competitions. Music is the customary Latin disco soundtrack blending salsa, reggaeton, merengue, electronica, and pop. It's always a madhouse, so be sure to arrive early to reserve a table. DJM has two equally curious locations, one in Las Palmas (a 5-min. drive from Parque Lleras, on the highway that leads to the airport) and the other in Itagui, a 20-minute drive from the Poblado area. Carrera 38 no. 19–255. www.fondadulce jesusmio.com. ℂ **4/444-6022.** Cover around COP$25,000. Tues–Sat 8pm–4am. Metro Poblado.

La Ruana de Juana ★ BAR/NIGHTCLUB   With its festive facade, kitsch decor, disco balls, and random objects dangling from the ceiling, La Ruana de Juana is a distinctively Colombian bar/disco close to the nightlife epicenter of Parque Lleras. Popular with the 30-and-under crowd, the carnival spirit reaches a crescendo with La Ruana's legendary rumba party on the weekend, fueled by a large liquor inventory of imported and national brands, and decent cocktails. Friday is a good night to come: It's two for one drinks all night long. Calle 10 no. 41–75. ℂ **4/266-2965.** Cover around COP$12,000. Wed–Sat 8pm–2:30am. Metro Poblado.

La Strada ★★★ BARS/NIGHTCLUBS   One of the city's most exclusive and glam nightlife hubs, La Strada is basically a posh shopping mall devoted to bacchanalian pleasures—a distinctly Latin American phenomenon. There are 16 restaurants, 15 bars, and three hot nightclubs (Club Crista, Aqua Night Live, and Divina), all aimed at the fashionable under-30 crowd. There's no shortage of high-tech light shows, disco balls, and wild and creative theme parties. If you plan to spend an evening here, you'll need to dress the part. Avendia El Poblado (Carrera 43) no. 1 Sur–150. www.lastrada.com.co. ℂ **4/322-0134.** Cover and hours vary according to the club/bar, from COP$25,000. Metro Poblado.

Mangos ★★ DANCE CLUB   No trip to Medellín is complete without a visit to Mangos, Medellín's best-known nightspot (although it's technically located in the neighboring municipality of Itagüí). Mangos claims to be the largest dance club in Latin America; whether or not this is true, its crazy, over-the-top atmosphere, complete with costumed servers and frequent shows, are the reason why everyone flocks to Mangos. There is a strange American Old West theme (think lots of cowboy hats) as well as an "anything flies" attitude here. Wearing shorts here is frowned upon, and if you wear flip-flops or sandals, you won't get past the style police that guard the door. Carrera 42 no. 67A–151. ℂ **4/277-6123.** Cover around COP$25,000. Wed and Thurs 8pm–3am, Fri and Sat 8pm–5am.

Palmitas ★ DANCE CLUB   Another glitzy crossover restaurant–bar–dance club, located on Vía de Las Palmas, Palmitas hosts raucous salsa, merengue, and even belly-dancing shows. Popular with foreigners out on the town for a night of dancing and drinking, the club also doubles as a restaurant serving international and traditional food, not to mention great views of Medellín. Carrera 38 no. 26–41, Km 2. ℂ **4/232-7199.** Cover from COP$20,000. Daily 11:30am–3:30am (dance club opens at 8pm).

Son Havana ★★★ NIGHTCLUB   On the periphery of the La 70 party zone, in the upscale and trendy Laureles neighborhood, this dark and moody Cuban-themed salsa joint draws dancing duos of all ages and skill sets to its jammed dance floor. On the weekend, Son Havana is famed for its awesome Cuban band. With a great party spirit, dazzling music, and a welcoming vibe, it's impossible not to just get up and dance the night away to salsa, cumbia, and merengue. Carrera. 73 no. 44–56. ℂ **4/586-9082.** Cover from COP$20,000. Wed–Sat 8pm–2:30am. Metro Estadio.

Trilogia Live Bar ★ BAR/NIGHTCLUB   This classic Latin bar/club, a few blocks from MAMM, is a big hit with locals, with a robust live-music-performance schedule that runs the gamut of musical genres, styles, and epochs. Along with crowd-pleasing covers of classic rock, pop, and Latin hits that create an infectious shiny happy people vibe, there's a resident DJ, a revolving stage, and no shortage of high-tech lights, smoke, and glitter effects. If your heart is set on this place, make your reservations online well ahead of time. Carrera 43G no. 24–08. www.trilogiabar.com. ✆ **4/204-0562.** Cover varies, around COP$20,000. Wed–Sat 8pm–3:30am. Metro: Industriales.

Around Medellín

Within striking distance of the city, evocative historic towns and dramatic landscapes provide a dazzling counterpoint to the Medellín's edgy, urban dynamism. A highlight for many visitors, the colonial gem of **Santa Fe de Antioquia** is one of Colombia's most beguiling and best-preserved 16th-century cities. With an enchanting lakeside setting, confectionary-colored colonial homes, and a surreal rock formation (known as "La Piedra"), it doesn't take long for **Guatapé** to seize hold of your imagination. Another popular day trip, known as the **Circuito del Oriente** (offered by many hotels/tour companies in Medellín), comprises a jaunt through traditional Paisa villages, including **Río Negro**, **El Retiro**, and **La Ceja**.

SANTA FE DE ANTIOQUIA ★★

Some 80km (50 miles) north of Medellín, the erstwhile gold-mining town of Santa Fe de Antioquia was founded in 1541 by Jorge Robledo, a conquistador notorious for his unquenchable thirst for blood and gold. Situated on the western banks of the Rio Cauca, at an altitude of 1,000 meters (3,300 ft.), it's much lower in elevation than Medellín; temperatures here can sizzle, and high humidity adds to the city's soporific aura. With the 2006 construction of El Túnel del Occidente—the largest tunnel in South America (through the Andes' central cordillera)—the travel time from Medellín to Santa Fe was reduced by virtually an hour.

From 1584, Santa Fe was the region's capital before Medellín stole its glory in 1826. With its cobbled streets, charming colonial homes, baroque churches, and 400-year-old fountains, the town feels removed from space and time. There's a soul-stirring authenticity and a self-possessed grace to Santa Fe that is palpable, and a fiercely independent spirit still prevails among the city's proud denizens. It was here in Santa Fe de Antioquia in 1813 that Juan del Corral proclaimed Antioquia's independence from Spain.

Santa Fe's central axis is **Plaza Mayor**, one of South America's most evocative and endearing squares. On the square's northwestern flank, Santa Fe's white **Catedral Metropolitan** presides over a cinematic ensemble of single-story colonial buildings with ornately carved lintels, decorative stonework, wooden verandas draped with exotic flowers, and lush courtyards where cats snooze in the midday heat and the steady creak of a rocking chair marks the passing of each hour. The cathedral was built in classic *calicanto* (the city's signature brick-and-stone style) in 1837 by Fray Domingo Petrés (it's the third iteration since the late

16th century). It's worth a peek inside for the ornate high altar with a centerpiece Christ figure, as well as an interesting 18th-century Last Supper sculpture. The centerpiece of Plaza Mayor is a bronze statue of **Juan del Corral**, the President of Antioquia during its few years of independence (1813–1826).

Set in an emblematic 19th-century mansion, the **Museo Juan del Corral** (Calle 11 no. 9–77; ✆ **4/853-4605**; free; Mon, Tues, Thurs, Fri 9am–noon, 2–5:30pm, Sat and Sun 10am–5pm) features a small but engaging collection of historical and archaeological artifacts, gold, and silver, which elucidate the history of Santa Fe de Antioquia and the region, with more than a few nods to the city's Independence movement. Atmospherically set within an 18th-century Jesuit College, the **Museo de Arte Religioso** (Calle 11 no. 8–12; www.santa fedeantioquia.net; ✆ **4/853-2345**; Sat and Sun 10am–1pm, 2–5pm) features a surprisingly lively collection of religious art including seminal works by Colombian artist Gregorio Vázquez de Arce, the leading proponent of 17th- and 18th-century Latin American baroque.

Built in 1721, the baroque **Iglesia de Santa Bárbara** (Calle 11/Carrera 8, mass at 6am and 7am), features a broad *calicanto*-style facade, a rococo font, and Santa Fe's oldest altar. Framed with palm trees, and with whimsical turrets and restrained decorative embellishments, it's Santa Fe's most aesthetically pleasing religious structure.

Some 7km from town, the one-lane **Puente de Occidente**—originally built from wood and steel imported from the U.K.—was completed in 1895. Designed by José Maria Villa (who honed his skills on NYC's Brooklyn Bridge), and just shy of 300 meters, it is hailed as one of the most important civil engineering structures of its time; upon completion it became the longest bridge in South America and third-longest bridge in the world.

Hourly buses (2 hr.; COP$12,000) and *colectivos* (90 min.; COP$15,000, every 20–30 min.) leave from Medellín's Terminal Norte (from 6am–6:30pm) to Santa Fe's bus terminal (Calle 13/Carrera 10), a short (uphill) walk to the Plaza Mayor. The last bus back to Medellín is at 7:30pm; always reserve your seat well ahead of time on the weekend or holidays.

GUATAPÉ ★★

Chances are you won't have spent much time in Medellín before you come across a picture of **El Peñol** (daily 8am–5pm; COP$10,000), a bizarre 200-meter-high granite rock—locals claim it as their very own Sugar Loaf Mountain. El Peñol rises sheer above a beautiful tapestry of turquoise lakes (created by a hydroelectric dam in 1975) known as the **Embalse del Peñol**. If you make the ascent via a spiral staircase of 649 steps (which takes around 35 min.), you will be rewarded with impressive views over the lakes. The "Gu" painted onto the rock face was originally intended to spell "Guatapé"; in 1988, a vehement cadre of Guatapé's denizens attempted to take possession of El Peñol, much to the chagrin of local residents. The painters were swiftly condemned, but the graffiti still remains.

Some 3km (about 2 miles) from El Peñol, the town of **Guatapé** (founded in 1811) boasts all the salubrious trappings of a charming lakeside hamlet, with narrow streets punctuated with rainbow-colored colonial homes, ornate churches, a convivial main plaza, and relaxing boat rides (if you avoid the weekend madness). It's the sort of town where you can happily settle into vacation mode for a day or two, or three. One block from the lake, the main square, **Plaza de Simón Bolívar**, is dominated by the pretty Greco-Roman **Parroquia Nuestra Señora del Carmen** with a distinctive white facade enlivened with decorative red brushstrokes.

Guatapé is famed for its *zócalos*—ornamental relief panels (rather like frescos) painted in kaleidoscopic colors—that adorn a large number of the town's single story colonial structures. The traditional Spanish architectural embellishment has been given a local spin; Guatapé's residents have incorporated fanciful representations of families, folkloric symbols, historical events, and tributes to famed local artists (look out for the homage to Botero) into their designs, with a quite magical effect. The whole town feels like a public art space. While you can happily spend a few hours wandering around the town without an agenda, for the finest examples of *zócalos*, head to Calle de los Recuerdos (Carrera 28), or Plazoleta de los Zócalos, a short walk from the main square.

A standard feature of most tours to Guatapé is a boat ride (around 3 hr.) on the lake. Boat excursions take in **Viejo Peñol**, a submerged town (only a church cross poignantly rises above the water) and/or **La Manuela**, a derelict lakefront *finca* that once belonged to drug kingpin Pablo Escobar. On the lakefront *malecón*, you can sign up for a tour (there are numerous companies with similar prices, around COP$12,000 per person). Boats depart at 2pm during the week and on the weekend boats leave when they are full, which happens fast when Guatapé swells with day trippers, and with music blasting and liquor flowing, it's a party. By far the best time to visit is during the week. For a more thrilling vantage point, there's also a **Cable Paseo** (Mon–Fri noon–6pm, Sat and Sun 9am–6pm; COP$10,000), a zip wire suspended across a section of the lake.

There are hourly bus connections from Medellín's Terminal Norte to Guatapé (2 hr., from 6am–7pm); buses pass through El Peñol en route to Guatapé. Willys run between Guatapé and El Peñol (COP$4,000), and will drop you at the entrance to La Piedra (COP$3,000). Returning to Medellín, the last bus is at 6:30pm or 7:45pm on Sundays and holidays. Weekend buses are always booked solid, so reserve your seat in advance.

EJE CAFETERO ★★★

With its rugged beauty, indigenous history, and independent spirit, there's more to Colombia's coffee triangle than the nation's hallowed red beans. Antioquia's fabled coffee country combines scenic majesty with exhilarating outdoor recreation and fascinating cultural attractions and touchstones. Sculpted Andean mountains and volcanic peaks with crystal-clear lakes rise above emerald valleys where coffee plantations hug century-old *fincas*, and national parks provide close encounters with the region's incredible inventory of flora and fauna. It's a magical place.

Steeped in Antioquian traditions, in the photogenic towns of **Filandia** and **Salento**, narrow streets lined with emblematic *bahareque* (bamboo and clay buildings with red-tiled roofs) lead to sedate plazas. Just a short jeep-ride away, the region's crown jewels are the **Valle de Cocora**, with its skinny wax palms rising above furry grasslands and, for more intrepid travelers, the majestic snowcapped peaks of **Parque Nacional Natural Los Nevados**, a mecca for amped-up hiking adventures.

While hardly destinations unto themselves, the commercial powerhouses of **Pereira**, **Manizales**, and **Armenia** provide the gateway to thermal springs, high-altitude lakes, nature preserves, and haciendas that still employ artisanal processes to produce prized Arabica coffee. As international coffee prices have fallen, enterprising landowners have diversified their crops and opened up their estates to tourism. Restored haciendas, exuding faded grandeur and stuffed with antiques and heirlooms, provide some of the country's most evocative accommodation options.

Pereira ★

211km (131 miles) S from Medellín

Capital of the department of Risaralda, with a population just shy of half a million, Pereira is a lively hub for exploring Colombia's coffee triangle and getting under the skin of traditional Antioquian rituals. Since the city was founded in 1863, it has been repeatedly devastated by earthquakes—the last major earthquake occurred in 1999 and killed more than 1,000 people. Certainly, Pereira is hardly a beauty with its prosaic architectural mishmash of civic and cultural structures. On the city periphery, factories and warehouses testify to the city's thrusting manufacturing prowess, and its status as the region's economic powerhouse.

While it may be low on sights and cultural attractions, there is a buzz and self-confidence to Pereira that's hard not to appreciate. Built on the site of the Spanish colonial city of Cartago Viejo (abandoned in 1691), Pereira prides itself on its spirit of inclusivity; in the 1950s, during the period known as La Violencia, Pereira provided shelter to thousands of Colombians displaced by sectarian violence. The city is also known as the birthplace of César Gaviria, Colombia's 40th president (1990–94), who led the fight against the Medellín and Cali cartels. Gaviria was the target of successive attacks by Escobar; he should have been a passenger on the Avianca flight to Cali, which the drug lord bombed.

GETTING THERE

BY PLANE   Pereira's Aeropuerto Internacional Matecaña (PEI) is located 4km (2½ miles) from the city center. There are domestic flights from Bogotá, Medellín, Cali, and Cartagena with **Avianca** (www.avianca.com; via Bogotá), **Aerolíneas de Antioquia** (www.ada-aero.com), **Copa** (www.copaair.com; via Bogotá), **LATAM** (www.latam.com; via Bogotá), **Easy Fly** (www.easyfly.com.co), and **Viva Colombia** (www.vivacolombia.co). A taxi from the airport to town will cost around COP$7,000.

BY BUS   The bus station **Terminal de Transporte de Pereira** (Calle 17 no. 23–157; ℂ **6/315-2323**) is less than 2km (5- to 10-min. bus/taxi ride, or you can safely walk there in around 20 min.), from the center of town. There are frequent bus connections (hourly at least) to Bogotá (9 hr.), Medellín (6 hr.), Manizales (75 min.), Armenia (1 hr.), and Salento (1 hr.). There are several services daily to Cali (4 hr.).

GETTING AROUND

With **taxis** in cheap and plentiful supply, a cab is by far the easiest way to get around Pereira; standard fares within the city are COP$5,000 to COP$7,000. For local color you can hop on the orange **minibuses** (COP$1,800) that zip around town, the Zona Rosa, along the main Circunvalar, and neighborhood barrios. The flashy (unmistakably green) **Megabús** (which provided the template for Bogotá's more extensive Transmilenio) is a super-comfortable and clean mass transport system which utilizes dedicated lanes and enclosed stations for buses. To use the system, you'll need to buy a *tarjeta* (card), at one of the stations, loaded with a minimum of three fares, at a cost of COP$1,800 each.

VISITOR INFORMATION

There is a small tourist information kiosk with brochures and maps before the taxi rank as you exit the airport. The main tourist office is located inside the Centro Cultural Lucy Tejada (Calle 17/Carrera 10; www.pereiracultura turismo.gov.co; ✆ **6/324-8749**; Mon–Thurs 7:30am–noon, 2:00–6:30pm, Fri 8am–noon, 2–6pm). There are plenty of banks with ATMs on Plaza Bolívar.

WHEN TO GO

The average **temperature** in Pereira is a lovely 72°C, with very little variation. Sunny skies prevail year-round (interspersed with short-lived showers) but the sunniest days fall in January/February and from June to September. Precipitation levels peak in October and November. August is a great time to be in Pereira when the city puts on its annual shindig: **Fiestas de Pereira**, which celebrates the city's founding and cultural heritage with gusto; expect live music, folk dancing, art exhibits, and plenty of opportunity to taste traditional Antioquian street food and regional dishes.

EXPLORING PEREIRA

Pereira's commercial and cultural heart is the expansive **Plaza Bolívar** (Carrera 7/8 and Calle 19/20) with its storied statue of **Bolívar Desnudo**. Unveiled in 1963, to mark the city's centenary, it was sculpted in Mexico by Rodrigo Arenas Betancourt. On the north side of the plaza, the **Catedral Nuestra Señora de la Pobreza** (Calle 20/Carrera 7) dates to the city's founding in 1863, but was reconstructed following the last major earthquake in 1999. Just east of the square, there's an unusual smattering of grace in the ornate, neoclassical **Palacio de Rentas** (Carrera 10/Calle 17), built in 1927, a paradigm for the architectural styles of the Republican period (late-19th and early-20th centuries) when European styles were all the rage. Two blocks west, **Casa Ochoa** (Carrera 7, Calle 22), is the oldest building in the city (built in 1893), and is a fine example of *bahareque*, a clay-and-bamboo framed structure with a central patio and distinctive colorful paintwork and/or stucco.

THE WILD HEART OF eje cafetero

With rolling green valleys and snow-covered volcanic mountains, it's no surprise that Colombia's breathtaking Eje Cafetero (also known as the Coffee Triangle) has made its way onto the adventure traveler's radar. Active families, extreme sport junkies, and wildlife enthusiasts can easily spend a week climbing, horseback riding, hiking, and mountain biking amid a rugged landscape where mass tourism has yet to take hold. Active days can be bookended with restorative pursuits, including dips in thermal springs, a yoga class, coffee-bean picking, or tasting your way through the region's incredible agricultural bounty.

For Thrill Seekers Sign up for a multi-day expedition and mountain bike or climb the five volcanic peaks of **Parque Nacional Natural Los Nevados ★★★** (see p. 202), in the Cordillera of the Andes Mountains. Here, cloud forest and high-altitude *páramo* provide sanctuary to a rich diversity of flora and fauna, including majestic Andean condors, mountain tapir, cougars, and spectacled bear. The mystical cloud forest of **Yarumos Ecological Park** (see p. 206) provides a captivating backdrop for a robust inventory of adventure sports, including rock climbing and ziplining.

For Active Families Combine a cultural immersion in picturesque Salento town with a horseback ride along the moderate trails of the magical Cocora Valley, where rickety wooden bridges traverse rushing rivers and lanky wax palms feel part Indiana Jones, part Dr. Seuss. Within the valley, the **Acaime Nature Reserve** is home to eight species of hummingbirds, and sustenance comes in the form of locally made cheese and chocolate. At **Parque Nacional del Café** (see p. 210), children can hike or horseback ride through the valley, learn about the bean-to-brew coffee process in the Coffee Museum, and visit a mockup of a traditional *campesino* house. At the welcoming **Don Manolo** coffee finca (see p. 194), children can dress up as a mini Juan Valdéz as they simulate the role of coffee picker, operate an antique coffee grinder, take a jeep ride into the mountains, and delight in homemade brownies and guava ice cream.

For Sybarites At **Termales Santa Rosa** (see p. 194) or **Termas Naturales de San Vicente** (see p. 194), you can soak in thermal pools, swim beneath breathtaking waterfalls, indulge in spa treatments, or take a guided hike through the stunning valley. At **Hacienda Venecia** (see p. 207), you can take a morning yoga class, while at **Hotel Sazagua** (see p. 195), you can relax in spaces filled with indigenous artworks, take a Colombian cooking class, or dine on inspired regional dishes beneath star-studded skies.

For Nature Lovers The **Jardín Botánico del Quindío** (see p. 209) is famed for its 850 species of flora, including *guadua* bamboo trees, and its *mariposario* (butterfly farm), with more than 1,500 butterflies (50 species). At the **Reserva Ecológica** Río Blanco, avid birders can expand their logs on trails that meander through a magnificent cloud forest reserve, which is home to around 350 species of birds and more than 50 mammals. The cloud forest of **Recinto del Pensamiento** (see p. 206) has a terrific butterfly garden, lush trails brimming with orchids, and a medicinal herb garden.

Five blocks west, **El Lago Uribe Uribe** (Calles 24–25, Carreras 7–8) is Pereira's prettiest square with charming pergolas, blossoming trees, and the park's centerpiece lake. On the park's north side, the **Iglesia El Claret**, designed by Onel Márquz, has romantic aspirations with its steepled tower and white stones accented with burgundy. Lago Uribe Uribe has always been the city's more bohemian enclave. Orbiting the square is a convivial mix of bars, tango clubs, and traditional restaurants.

Completed in 1997, the **César Gaviria Trujillo viaduct**, which connects Pereira to neighboring Dosquebradas, is one of South America's longest bridges (440m) and is a pretty impressive feat of engineering.

AROUND PEREIRA

A short 10-minute taxi ride (COP$10,000) from Pereira, **Finca Don Manolo** (Vereda el Estanquillo Dosquebradas, Ruta al Alto del Nudo; ✆ 6/332-1831; 4-hour tour COP$30,000) offers welcoming, personalized tours of the family-run coffee finca. Don Manolo and his son Miguel elucidate the history of coffee in Colombia, followed by an interactive immersion into the coffee-production process; kids especially love donning a traditional *chapolera* (*campesino* from Antioquia) outfit, picking and sorting the beans, and operating the traditional roasting/grinding machines and implements. The luxuriant finca is home to countless hummingbird species, a mini *guadua* forest, and banana plantations. Along with coffee tastings, you'll be served homemade brownies and ice cream, and you can pick and taste fruit from the trees of their orchards. Stock up on their deliciously smooth coffee for just COP$12,000 per pound.

Less than an hour drive/taxi ride (COP$25,000) from Pereira, **Termales Santa Rosa** (Km 9.5 Vereda San Ramón, Santa Rosa de Cabal; www.termales.com. co; ✆ 636/365-5237; 9am–11:30pm; entry $36,000 weekend/high season, COP$22,000 during the week;) is a worthwhile half-day trip from Pereira. There are four thermal pools, a breathtaking series of waterfalls which cascade (with unreal, CGI-style precision) down the mountainside, spa treatments (a 60-min. massage costs COP$80,000), and a modern, business convention-style hotel with smart, Alpine-inspired rooms (from COP$240,000, all meals included). There are also guided hikes through the gorgeous valley (COP$13,000 on the weekend/holidays, or COP$9,000 during the week). You can take the bus from Pereira (frequent services from the bus terminal) to get to Termales Santa Rosa, but you'll need to change at Santa Rosa de Cabal; total journey time 90 minutes.

Some 35km (22 miles) from Pereira, and at a much higher altitude, **Termas Naturales de San Vicente** (Km 19 Vía Potreros, Santa Rosa de Cabal; www. sanvicente.com.co; ✆ 634/333-6157; COP$45,000) offers a more multifaceted hot spring/spa experience with therapeutic pools and springs, a zipline, rappel, and guided walking tours through an incredibly biodiverse landscape. Despite the cheesy title, the main attraction is the Pozos del Amor (Wells of Love); enshrouded with primary forest that teems with resplendent birdlife, seven thermal pools create a magical spa experience. If you want to stay the night, **Hotel San Vicente** (on-site) offers basic cabins (which sleep up to six) from COP$160,000 per person. Transport can be arranged from Pereira as part of a package.

WHERE TO STAY

Don Alfonso Boutique Hotel ★ This charming, quite grand boutique hotel oozes charm and authenticity. Built in the late 19th century, the mansion was owned by the richest family in town and is stuffed with colonial antiques, chandeliers, and artworks. Spacious rooms with high ceilings retain their original tiled floors, ornate woodwork, and an eclectic array of traditional furnishings. The lush garden and tranquil inner courtyard provide a soothing escape from the buzz of Zona Rosa; it's worth noting that noise from the nearby bars and clubs can be very intrusive at night.

Avenida Circunvalar Carrera 13 no. 12–37. www.donalfonsohotel.com/en. © **6/340-2486.** Double from COP$231,000, includes breakfast. **Amenities:** Restaurant (breakfast only); free Wi-Fi.

Hotel Sazagua ★★   A 15-minute taxi ride from Pereira, this artfully conceived boutique hotel is one of the region's most characterful choices and is an excellent base for exploring the region. Set amid lush gardens that abound with butterflies, birds, and flowering orchids, it's a haven of tranquility. Rustic-chic rooms with exposed beams are decorated with exotic hardwoods and crisp white linens; the bathrooms are perfectly functional but on the small side, and it would be a stretch to call them luxurious. It's in the romantic restaurant (one of the best in the area) with breezy patios illuminated by candles, and in the labyrinthine lounges and corridors, filled with local art, reliefs, and ceramics, that Sazagua really shines. It's definitely worth spending up for the Junior Suites, which have more space and look out over the lovely heated pool and gardens. Rates include breakfast and a 15-minute complementary head massage in the spa.

Km 7 Via cerritos Entrada 4 Urbanizacion Quimbayita. www.sazagua.com. © **576/337-9895.** Double from COP$350,000. **Amenities:** Restaurant; outdoor pool; spa; tours; free Wi-Fi.

Hotel Sonesta ★   This monolithic hotel, which opened in 2014, won't score any points for local character or charm (you could be anywhere), but it's modern, pristine (there are no bugs, if that's an issue for you), and the staff try really hard, and mostly pull it off. A 20-minute drive from Pereira, it's a fine base for a night or two if you are travelling with kids. There's a large heated pool, a children's pool (complete with a slide and dump buckets), tennis courts, a putting green, and plenty of space to roam. A well-executed international menu is served by the pool (where dance music plays incongruously regardless of the clientele) or in the restaurant; a new rotating restaurant on the top floor was slated for opening at the time of writing. Contemporary rooms with large, design-conscious bathrooms are quiet, comfortable, and flooded with light thanks to floor-to-ceiling windows. An expansive buffet breakfast is included in the rate.

Km 7 Vía Cerritos. www.sonesta.com/co/pereira/sonesta-hotel-pereira. © **576/311-3600.** Double from COP$275,000, includes breakfast. **Amenities:** Restaurant/bar; outdoor pool; gym; putting green; tennis courts; free Wi-Fi.

Movich Pereira ★★   Fresh from a sparkling restoration in 2015, the Movich (part of the InterContinental group) marries style, excellent customer service, and a stellar location. Characterful public spaces are far from generic, with natural hardwood furnishings, black-and-white photographs, lashings of *guadua*, local artworks, decorative nods to the coffee region, and stunning orchids. Pristine rooms are spacious and comfortable with large, inviting bathrooms and all the amenities and features you'd hope for in a hotel sporting a much higher price tag. There's a swimming pool, a spa, and a highly rated on-site restaurant (buffet breakfast is included in the rate).

Cra 13 no. 15–73. www.movichhotels.com/esp/pereira/movich-pereira. © **6/311-3333.** 202 units. Double from COP$320,000, includes breakfast. **Amenities:** Restaurant/bar; outdoor pool; spa; hot tub; sauna; gym; free Wi-Fi.

WHERE TO EAT

The **Corocito** neighborhood (Carrera 12, btw. Calle 2 and 7) is the place to try hearty Antioquian fare, including the typical *bandeja paisa*. The pulsating Zona Rosa is where you'll find Pereira's liveliest bars and international restaurants. Pereira's shopping malls, along with a clutch of hotels, restaurants, coffee shops, and bars can be found on **La Circunvalar**, a circular avenue that orbits the city.

El Meson Español ★ MEDITTERANEAN   This inviting restaurant in the quiet Los Alamos neighborhood just outside town has been a staple on Pereira's upscale dining scene for almost 25 years, and it's still a perennial favorite. The broad menu of Spanish and Mediterranean dishes, with a focus on fish and seafood, features a signature seafood paella (the best thing on the menu), grilled octopus (*a la gallega* style), calamari, and grilled fish dishes, including Chilean salmon and lobster. There are well-prepared meat dishes, and if you want to push the boat out, you can excite your server and opt for colossal surf and turf (COP$72,000). With a thoughtful wine list, friendly (if spotty) service, and tables on the outdoor terrace or in the atmospheric dining room fashioned from bamboo and *guadua*, this is a very good all-round dining choice.

Carrera 14 no. 25–57. www.mesonespañol.com. © **6/321-5636.** Main courses COP$28,000–COP$72,000. Daily noon–3pm, 7pm–11pm.

Leños y Parilla ★★ COLOMBIAN   Widely considered the best place to eat among Pereira's middle and upper classes, this convivial Argentinian-style steakhouse draws carnivores of a more purist ilk. An extensive repertoire of carefully seasoned cuts of Argentinian and Colombian grilled meats are served unadulterated on a sizzling iron plate with a garnish of plantain and potatoes, a side of *arepas*, and a small salad. The service can be erratic, but with a pleasant outdoor terrace, cozy dining room, and upbeat vibe, this is a place where you won't mind lingering.

Carrera 12 no. 2–78. www.lenosyparrilla.com. © **6/331-4676.** Main courses COP$28,000–COP$32,000. Mon–Sat noon–3pm, 6:30–11pm. Sun noon–5:30pm.

Mama Flor ★★ COLOMBIAN   Just outside of town, Mama Flor is a big hit among locals who flock here for good honest cooking that won't break the bank. With rustic wooden furnishings, colorful paintwork, and open-air terrace seating, it's an atmospheric and inviting place to enjoy hunks of meats (filet, pork, chicken, and steak) *a la parrilla* (grilled) or doused with a creamy sauce, and served with the requisite Paisa trimmings; rice, beans, fried plantain, and salad. You can also taste earthy renditions of Antioquian classics including tripe soup and blood sausage. Meat lovers shouldn't miss the signature dish: *parrillada de* *carnes* (a hearty mixed grill for two people, COP$55,000). There is a good range of cocktails, wine, and beer, as well as refreshingly fruity jugs of sangria.

Calle 11 no. 15–12. ✆ **93/325-1713.** Main courses COP$23,000–COP$32,000. Mon–Sat noon–11pm, Sun noon–5pm.

Sazagua ★★ FUSION The Sazagua hotel restaurant certainly offers the most romantic ambience and polished service in the area, with artfully presented cuisine served beneath star-studded skies on the terrace, or in the art-filled open-air dining room. The fusion menu features international fare along with creative iterations of Colombian staples. The simple grilled fish and meat entrees tend to be more successful than complex dishes with gourmet aspirations. For a light appetizer, the green salad served in a Parmesan crust bursts with flavor, while the ceviche trio is tender and fresh but is much too heavy on the onions for my taste. One of the menu highlights, the fresh fish of the day (the grouper is excellent) is served over sautéed vegetables. Service is warm and attentive, and prices are very reasonable for a relaxing fine-dining experience.

Kilometro 7 Via cerritos Entrada 4 Urbanizacion Quimbayita. www.sazagua.com. ✆ **576/337-9895.** Main courses COP$26,000–COP$39,000. Daily 1–3pm, 7–11pm.

Salento ★★

37km (23 miles) SE from Pereira

Larded with otherworldly charms, Salento is one of those towns that feels like walking on to a 19th-century stage set—especially if you have just stepped off the bus from Medellín. With lush foothills that fold into the Andes Mountains, cast in those intoxicating shades of green that only balmy year-round temperatures and consistent rains can yield, the journey here is one heart-stopping pleasure after another. Beyond Pereira's urban sprawl, serpentine mountain roads rise above a tapestry of coffee estates interspersed with eucalyptus forests, fields of avocado and guava, banana plantations, and lemon and orange orchards.

Avid hikers planning to explore the **Valle de Cocora** should consider basing themselves in Salento to have multi-day access the park's trails; most tours from Pereira leave only an hour (two at the most) for hiking or horseback riding in the valley.

GETTING THERE & GETTING AROUND

If you are short on time, day tours from Pereira hit Salento, Filandia, and Valle de Cocora.

From the main terminal in Pereira, there are regular **buses**, around 8 per day (1 hr.; COP$6,500), and buses every half hour from Armenia (1 hr.; COP$4,000). There are three direct buses a day from Medellín (7 hr.; COP$45,000).

Known locally as "Willys," iconic, restored World War II **jeeps** depart from Salento's central plaza at 7:30am, 9:30am, and 11:30am, for the 20-minute ride to the hamlet of Cocora, the Valle de Cocora, and Parque Nacional Natural Los Nevados; COP$6,500. Jeeps return at 12:30pm, 2pm and 5pm; there are a lot more jeeps on the weekend. Chances are that you can hire your own jeep and driver for about COP$26,000 (one-way).

There is a **bank** with an ATM on the main plaza (it can run out of money on the weekend).

EXPLORING SALENTO

Though there are no real must-see sights in town, the allure of Salento resides in a few hours of aimless wandering. In the oldest, and best-preserved, town in the region (founded in 1843), cowboys sit at benches in front of low-slung colorful buildings built in the traditional *bahareque* architectural style and 1940s Willy jeeps shuttle tourists to the Cocora Valley. The **Iglesia de Nuestra Senora de Carmen** (built in 1850) presides over the town's languid central plaza with its manicured topiary and vendors selling fresh juices, local candy, and handicrafts. The main street in town, **Calle Real**, has been recast as a (tasteful) parade of handicraft shores where you can pick up a traditional sombrero for around COP$22,000, a leather wallet for COP$60,000, or a handwoven *mochila* or knapsack for COP$30,000. A 10-minute walk, at the end of the street, you can climb a series of steps marked with the Stations of the Cross to Salento's **mirador** for picturesque views across the town and surrounding valleys. While most visitors come to Salento for only a few hours, it's a wonderful base for exploring the region's coffee fincas, the Valle de Cocora, and Parque Nacional Natural de los Nevados, where you can spend hours, days even, hiking or riding through breathtaking landscapes.

WHERE TO STAY

Betatown ★★   More of a lifestyle concept than a traditional hostel, this fun traveler hub raises the bar on standard backpacker accommodation in the region. Bright, streamlined rooms with comfortable beds, safes, TVs, and private bathrooms are tasteful and comfortable. There's a laidback vibe, with a diverse mix of travelers congregating in the vibrant social spaces, which include a game room, *tejo* court, and a great bar/restaurant (see below). The friendly and efficient staff can organize more intrepid adventures in the area (including paragliding and mountain biking), as well as arrange onward transportation, and they'll happily store luggage. Breakfast is included.

Calle 7 no. 3–45. www.beta.com.co. ℂ **320/485-4760.** From COP$135,000, includes breakfast. **Amenities:** Restaurant/bar; lounge; game room; tejo court; tours; free Wi-Fi.

Boutique Hotel Mirador de Cocora ★   Just a short walk (uphill) from Salento's main plaza, the main draw at this intimate boutique hotel is the terrace, which has outrageous views of the Cocora Valley. Rooms are light, bright, clean, and comfortable, with painted walls and shuttered windows, but they are rather small and too spartan for some tastes. Some rooms look out onto the street, others over the valley; it's worth splashing out on Junior Suite El Qundío for the jaw-dropping views from the private balcony complete with a hot tub. There are plenty of sociable hangouts, and breakfast is included in the rate.

Calle 1A no. 3–01. www.elmiradordelcocora.com. ℂ **315/548-0939.** From COP$180,000. **Amenities:** Lounge; game room; free Wi-Fi.

Hotel Salento Real ★★   Just 4 blocks from the main square, this gem of a hotel is a big hit for its inviting spaces with thoughtful colonial detailing and decorative nods to the region's indigenous traditions. Appealing and comfortable rooms, grouped around an interior courtyard, feature solid wooden furnishings and doors, tiled floors, beamed ceilings, shuttered windows, quality linens, and colorful artworks. The pristine, tiled bathrooms that boast good, hot showers (water pressure/availability can be problematic in Salento) effectively utilize space. There are great-value family rooms available, which sleep up to six. A typical breakfast of eggs, *arepas*, and fruit is included in the rate.

Calle 3 no. 4–31. www.hotelsalentoreal.com. (C) **6/759-3612.** From COP$250,000, includes breakfast. **Amenities:** Free Wi-Fi.

The Plantation House ★★ Five blocks from Salento's main square, this original 19th-century plantation house and newly restored, Don Eduardo coffee finca (tours are available) provide basic but comfortable hostel-style options. Set amid extensive lush gardens with fragrant lemon and orange trees, you can choose from dorm rooms (with bunks) or private rooms with en-suites or shared bathroom. The colorful finca provides the main traveler hangout in town with a very social, international feel; the British owners provide a wealth of local information (it's the town's de facto tourist office) as well as organize standard (as well as more original) regional tours. There are shared kitchen facilities, a bookshop, Wi-Fi, and coffee, lots of it. They also offer a transport service/pick up from Pereira and Armenia.

Alto de Coronel, Calle 7 no. 1–04. www.theplantationhousesalento.com. (C) **315/409-7039.** Dorms from COP$19,000. Double with private bath from COP$55,000. **Amenities:** Bookstore; cafe; shared kitchen; free Wi-Fi.

WHERE TO EAT

Beta Bar/Grill ★★ INTERNATIONAL This super cafe-restaurant seems to have a meal for every mood and moment, and it pulls everything off with aplomb. There are crêpes and waffles for breakfast, chicken sandwiches, salads, or PB&J for lunch, and veal tenderloin or filet mignon for dinner, when an aspiring gourmet mood holds sway. Part of the BETATOWN hotel (see above) with a *tejo* court upstairs, game room, soccer on the TV, and a lively bar, this is a hugely popular backpacker joint and a great place to hang out at night.

Calle 7 no. 3–45. www.beta.com.co. (C) **320/485-4760.** Main courses COP$14,000–COP$25,000. Daily 6am–11pm.

Café Bernabé Gourmet ★★ INTERNATIONAL One of the most popular places in town, and a daily ritual for long-stay travelers and expats, this colorful coffee shop/eclectic restaurant serves excellent coffee and a well-executed repertoire of international cuisine. The traditional 19th-century adobe structure, with a lovely garden, red-tiled roof, beamed ceiling, and outdoor patios with views of the valley, makes for an enchanting, rustic setting. Menu highlights include filet mignon, salmon in a coffee-curacao reduction, and a signature *aubergine parmigiana*, but every dish here is fresh, tasty, artfully presented, and good value.

Calle 3 no. 6–03. (C) **318/393-3278.** Main courses COP$15,000–COP$26,000. Mon and Wed–Sat 10am–9pm.

Restaurante Donde Laurita ★★ COLOMBIAN   With shelves stacked with antique typewriters, sewing machines, and old phones, this eclectic and colorful restaurant is Salento's most atmospheric dining option. It's also a fine place to try fresh grilled trout—the region's specialty—in various iterations: smoked, *a la Criolla* (with tomatoes and onions), *gratinada*, or Hawaiana (aims to turn trout into a pizza, and it's still good), or marinara (with a seafood sauce). *Arepas fritas* with a tomato-and-onion hot sauce are served as a preamble to colossal *platos típocos*, including the epic *bandeja paisa or chuleta de cerda* (pork chops). Rib sticking entrees are accompanied with a *patacón* (a big green plantain toast) and small salad. Try the traditional *mazamorra* (cooked corn and milk) for dessert.

Calle 5A no. 5–36. ✆ **312/772-6313.** Main courses from COP$18,000–COP$24,000. Daily 11:30am–10pm.

Filandia ★★

31km (19 miles) SE from Pereira

Arriving in Filandia feels like you are being let in on a secret. While the town of Salento is firmly on the backpacker trail, Filandia doesn't like to flaunt its charms. From the town's picture perfect central plaza, a tidy mosaic of colorful streets lined with humble low-slung colonial homes trail off into valleys where horses, cows, and sheep graze at century-old fincas and dairy farms. The **Templo La Inmaculada Concepción**, built in 1905, and the oldest house in town, **Droguería Bristol** (Carrera 6 no. 4–07), are the town's only real landmarks. Just outside Filandia, a large, rather bizarre, totally anachronistic **mirador** provides superb panoramic views of the mountains of Parque Nacional Natural Los Nevados and the Cauca River valley. The joy of Filandia resides in a couple of hours meandering its picturesque streets, sitting in a bar, bakery, or cafe, and perhaps sharing a table with a cowboy, a suited politician, and maybe a gaggle of neatly turned out schoolchildren.

Founded in 1876, Filandia's nonchalant air belies its turbulent history. The department of Quindío was at the epicenter of the brutal period known as La Violencia (1948–58), a civil war between Conservative and Liberal parties. Political leaders and right-wing paramilitaries encouraged Conservative-supporting peasants to appropriate the lands of Liberal-supporting peasants, which provoked a bloody civil war that resulted in the murder of more than 200,000 Colombians.

Before the violence of the 1940s, denizens of Filandia and Salento would paint their homes in red or blue to show their party affiliation. This all changed during La Violencia, when peasants would routinely storm rural towns, armed with machetes, to butcher members of the opposing political party; homes and businesses were swiftly repainted in a fanciful rainbow of colors so as not to betray the homeowner's political leanings.

In a culturally egregious (and quite ludicrous) act, a staggering 122 pieces of gold, discovered in a tomb close to Filandia, were gifted to the Spanish Queen in 1893 by then Colombian president Carlos Holguín; it currently forms part of the collection at the Museum of America in Madrid. Colombia's attempts to have the treasure repatriated on the grounds that it comprises cultural and archaeological heritage have, so far, proved futile.

If you are in town for lunch, **Helena Adentro** (Carrera 7a no. 8–01; ✆ **320/665-9612**; main courses from COP$17,000; Sun–Thurs noon–10pm, Fri and Sat noon–1am) serves solid Colombian classic dishes (with a fair few twists) in an eclectic and charming setting with lots of bamboo, flowers, fairy lights, and curious artifacts.

Unless you are coming from Armenia, outside of taking a **taxi** (COP$15,000–COP$20,000 from Salento), Filandia is not the easiest place to get to. There are frequent buses from Armenia (around 40 min.). You can catch a bus from Salento to Armenia and ask the driver to let you out at the main road intersection, where you wait for a bus to Filandia; they run approximately every 30 minutes.

Valle de Cocora ★★

11km (7 miles) SE from Salento

The highlight of a trip to the coffee region, the Cocora Valley, at an elevation of 1,800 to 2,400 meters (6,000–7,800 ft.) is the preserve of the wax palm trees—Colombia's national tree—that dwarf the dairy farms and fincas that nestle within this enchanting emerald valley. The fabled tree, an endangered species, grows to 60 meters (almost 200 ft.) and lives for around 120 years. The palms are named for the wax produced by the tree, which liberally adorned the churches and homes of Spanish colonialists. With their resilient, but gangly bodies—thin enough to hug at the base—and shaggy fronds, the wax palms resemble something plucked from a child's imagination. Colombia's revered wax palms define an otherworldly landscape: radiant light, the interplay of shadows, and swirling mist can utterly transform the scenery from moment to moment. Along with a cornucopia of orchids, butterflies, and prolific birdlife, Cocora also provides sanctuary to puma, deer, cloud-forest sloths, and the spectacled bear.

On the road to the valley, and in the hamlet of **Cocora** (at the entrance to the park), there are several open-air restaurants that serve grilled local fish and meat. *Trucha* (trout) is the area's specialty and is generally served whole and grilled.

Known locally as "Willys," iconic, restored World War II jeeps depart from Salento's central plaza for the 20-minute ride to the hamlet of Cocora, the Valle de Cocora, and Parque Nacional Natural Los Nevados (COP$6,500; 7:30am, 9:30am, and 11:30am, returning at 12:30pm, 2pm, and 5pm; many more on the weekend). You can also hire your own jeep and driver for about COP$26,000 one-way.

HIKING IN THE VALLE DE COCORA

The Cocora Valley's most scenic hiking trail leads to the **Acaime Nature Reserve**, some 2 hours, 30 minutes (5km/3 miles) from Cocora hamlet. A blue gate at the entry to the valley—it's easy to spot but ask any local to point you in the right direction—leads past a trout farm and meanders through mossy grasslands where clusters of sinewy wax palms cling improbably to the mountainside. After traversing a half dozen or so ramshackle bridges that cross the Río Quindío, the trail steadily gains elevation as it weaves through mystical cloud forest. It's certainly worth checking out the Acaime Reserve (Km 11 Valle del Cocora; ℂ **2/893-3052**; COP$5,000), which provides sanctuary to eight species of hummingbird. Here, you can graze on locally made cheese and chocolate (included in the reserve's entry fee) and you have the option of staying the night at the reserve's basic posada (make a reservation ahead of time). When you return from Acaime to Cocora (1km from the reserve entrance), an alternate route follows a steep trail to La Montaña (2,800m/9,000 ft.) where there is a small finca which straddles a razor's edge mountain that stares across at the magnificent Morro Gacho peak (3,450m/11,000 ft.). If you continue on La Montaña trail, you will wind back along a gravel path through the valley to Cocora hamlet. For more intrepid adventures, the Cocora Valley provides access (via Quindío department's entrance; see below) to the snowcapped Andean mountains of Parque Nacional Los Nevados, with its five volcanoes.

Parque Nacional Natural Los Nevados ★★★

With snowcapped peaks, volcanic lakes, and diverse ecosystems that harbor a rich profusion of flora and fauna, including the distinctive *frailejones*, Los Nevados National Park is one of Colombia's most awe-inspiring attractions. Hikers and climbers are lured by the park's challenging multi-day expeditions. In the Cordillera of the Andes Mountains, the 60,000-hectares of Los Nevados National Park encompasses four *departamentos*: Quindío (in the Valley of Cocora); Risaralda; Tolima; and Caldas. Los Nevados' dramatic landscape spans various ecosystems; principally cloud forest, the high altitude *páramo*, and the lunar landscapes of the super *páramo* which hugs the snow line. Emblematic of the *páramo*, the distinctive *frailejones*—plants with massive trunks and a hirsute spiral of dense leaves that blooms with daisy-like yellow flowers—dot the shrubby landscape. The park's rich diversity of birdlife includes majestic Andean condors with a 3-meter (10-ft.) wingspan, yellow-eared parrots, parakeets, and motmots. Mammals that roam the park include mountain tapir, cougars, weasels, squirrels, bats, spectacled bear, the northern pudú, and white-eared opossums.

ESSENTIALS

The best time to visit the park is December through March or July and August, when clear days afford spectacular views. During the rainier months, trails become very muddy. Entrance to the north section (Las Brisas) costs COP$38,000 adults, COP$16,000 children under 12. Entry to La Cueva, Potosí, Nevado de Santa Isabel, and Laguna del Otún costs COP$27,000 adults, COP$5,000 children under 12. For more information about the park, or for obtaining permits, consult the website (www.parquesnacionales.gov.co), or the PNN Los Nevados office in Manizales: Calle 69A no. 24–69; e-mail: nevados@parquesnacionales.gov.co; ℂ **6/887-161**.

Nevado del Ruiz dominates the park's northern sector, which extends south to the (extinct) Paramillo el Cisne volcano and Laguna Verde Encantado (a gorgeous volcanic lake); here there is vehicle access to 4,800 meters (15,700 ft.). The Southern Sector can only be accessed on foot or horseback (usually from Salento); it includes Nevado del Tolima (southeast corner), Nevado Santa Isabel, and Paramillo de Quindío (4,750m/15,400 ft.).

Each of the departments has its own rules and regulations concerning entrance to the park. Currently, all visitors are required to enter the park with a guide, unless your access point is Salento/Cocora Valley where there is no park office/entrance fee. However, if you are planning to enter the park at Cocora, a guide is still highly recommended; the now infamous Valley of the Lost (where Cocora meets Los Nevados) is where rescue operations are often mounted for lost travelers. There are no buses to get to the park from Manizales, Salento, or Pereira; you will need to arrange a taxi or sign up for a tour. There are several *refugios* in the park that will provide basic accommodation, but it's advisable to sign up with a tour operator who will take care of all the logistics.

HIKING & CLIMBING IN LOS NEVADOS

Colombia sits in the "Ring of Fire," a horseshoe-shaped ring of volcanoes that surround the Pacific Ocean. The imperious volcanoes of Nevado del Ruiz, Nevado de Santa Rosa, and Nevado del Tolima loom ominously above the Andean mountains of the Central Cordillera. In 1985, **Nevado del Ruiz** (the "sleeping lion") violently erupted, and lava and mud spewed down the mountain from its three massive craters at a speed of 50km (30 miles) per hour, wreaking havoc for more than 96km (60 miles). More than 23,000 people were killed and more than 5,000 homes destroyed. The town of Armero bore the brunt of the devastation; more than three quarters of the town's 28,700 inhabitants were killed within 4 hours.

Day tours of Nevado del Ruiz, which involves a glacier climb from 2,200 meters/7,200 feet to 5,100 meters/16,700 feet in a day is no mean feat. Multi-day hikes and climbs are also offered that combine Nevado del Ruiz with overnight camps at Paramillo de Cisnes and **Laguno Otún** (see below). At the time of writing, Nevado del Ruiz was closed to climbers and hikers due to volcanic activity; if it's on your bucket list, always obtain up-to-date, on-the-ground information from a reputable outfitter before you sign up for a hiking trip.

Nevado del Tolima, the most scenic but also the most strenuous climb to the summit (5,215m), is also still active, but in recent years, there has been no evidence of seismic activity. **El Rancho** (2,600m/8,500 ft.) is a popular base for climbing Nevado del Tolima, and here you'll find several hot springs. This climb is recommended only for advanced climbers; always go with a reputable guide and the requisite equipment. The inactive **Nevado de Santa Isabel**, the lowest of the three volcanic peaks, can also be climbed and the summit (5,000m/16,400 ft.) is famed for its transcendent views south to Nevado del Tolima and north to Nevado del Ruiz. Captivating **Laguna Otún** (a 4-hour drive from Manizales) is a popular base camp for taking on Nevado de Santa Isabel, and you could spend hours relaxing and fishing for trout here.

DISCOVERING COLOMBIA'S fincas

Colombia's central coffee-growing region holds a special place in the nation's consciousness. Declared a UNESCO World Heritage Landscape for its coffee-growing heritage—Colombia first exported coffee in the early 1800s—coffee plants flourish in this triangle of vertiginous mountains where rainfall, altitude, and temperature strike a delicate balance that allows Arabica beans to thrive. Over the last decade, as coffee prices have fallen, Colombia's coffee families have begun to open up their farms and estates and establish links with a growing network of adventure-tourism companies in order to capitalize on the region's immense tourism potential.

With the same allure as the grand haciendas of Argentina, Colombia's coffee fincas are located in gorgeous settings and combine evocative, authentic places to stay with outdoor recreation, amazing views, prolific wildlife, and compelling history. As well as tours that expound all aspects of the history and production of the coffee-growing business, fincas provide a unique immersion into Paisa history and culture. There are places for every taste and budget, ranging from the intimate and rustic to the utterly luxurious (with polished spaces, manicured grounds, well-conceived amenities, and haute cuisine). There aren't many places in the world where you can wake up amid antiques to the buzz of a working coffee farm, eat breakfast (and drink unlimited coffee) while hummingbirds and butterflies hover and dart, then take a hot air balloon ride, zipline, or hike through the Andes mountains.

Set amid rolling hills, **Hacienda Venecia ★★★** (p. 207) is an award-winning coffee farm with a restored paisa farmhouse that's now a fantastic hotel with diverse accommodation options, a soulful ambience, innovative tours, and a real sense of place. Foodies gravitate toward the swanky **Hacienda Bambusa ★★★** (p. 210), where gastronomic tasting menus are served over candlelight and a swim in the pool caps a day of rugged exploration.

The premier outfitter in the region with knowledgeable, expert guides, **Páramo Trek** (Calle 5 no. 1–37; www.paramotrek.com; ⓒ **311/745-3761**), offers challenging multi-day hiking/climbing trips in Parque Nacional los Nevados, which require a high level of fitness, agility, and some climbing experience.

Manizales ★

51km (32 miles) NE from Pereira, 96km (60 miles) N from Armenia

With its mountain setting, lively atmosphere, proud denizens, and proximity to stunning natural attractions, Manizales makes up for in spirit and location what it lacks in cultural attractions and architectural prowess. Founded in 1848 by Antioquian settlers fleeing civil unrest in the north, Manizales is a modern city that has borne the brunt of earthquakes (most recently in 1979), and fires (1926). To the southeast of the city, the savage peaks of Nevado del Ruiz loom large both geographically and psychologically. Architecturally speaking, the city is, for the most part, a modern glut of behemoth office blocks and drab apartment buildings, and you'll have to cast your net far and wide to experience the city's Republican 19th-century architectural styles.

ESSENTIALS

GETTING THERE There are daily **flights** from Bogotá, Medellín, and Cali to La Nubia (ICAO) airport 8km (5 miles) southeast of Manizales. A taxi from the airport will cost around COP$12,000. There is a comprehensive schedule of **bus** links (be prepared for steep, serpentine roads) to all major cities in the country, as well as frequent services to Pereira (75 min.) and Armenia. Manizales **Terminal de Transporte** is located at Carrera 43 no. 65–100, ✆ **57/878-7858**. To get there, a taxi will cost around COP$5,000, or you can take the super-efficient Cable Aéreo (www.cableaereomanizales.com) which links the bus station (Cambulos) with downtown (Fundadores).

GETTING AROUND The center of Manizales is a pleasant enough place to **walk**. The city's main axis is **Carrera 23** (or Avenida Santander) and you can easily pick up any number of buses (COP$1,600) that ply the route in direction of **Zona Rosa**, where you will find the city's largest concentration of bars and restaurants. If you want to broaden your horizons further, keep riding east to **Barrio Milán**, where there's another glut of bars and nightclubs.

VISITOR INFORMATION The average temperature in Manizales is 65°F. January to March and June to August boast the sunniest skies, warmest temperatures, and the least precipitation. From September to December and April/May, heavy rains can impede road travel (mud slides are a real danger) to Parque Nacional Los Nevados and Cocora Valley. Regardless of the time of year, you should be prepared for some rain; pack a raincoat.

EXPLORING MANIZALES

Plaza de Bolívar forms the city's axis with a customary, and in this case exemplary, homage to the great South American liberator. The magnificent bronze *Bolívar Cóndor* (1991) mounted on a centerpiece plinth presents Bolívar as a condor. The massive wings of the Andean condor are attached to Bolívar's torso, with the legendary freedom fighter's dismembered head/mask thrusting forth into the square. The work of famed Antioquian Rodrigo Arenas Betancourt—one of the most important artists in Colombia and Latin America—the daring sculpture presents Bolívar's spirit, determination, and quest for freedom.

On the north side of the square, the neo-colonial **La Gobernación**, or Governor's Palace, was built following the fire of 1925. With a harmonious paradigm of Republican-style architecture, decorative plant and animal motifs are cast from earthquake resistant cement and plaster. On the south side, the neo-gothic **Cathedral** (daily 8am–8pm) with four towers (the central tower is the tallest of its kind in the nation) and a whimsical spire was built by Italian architects in 1939, after a fire devastated the original structure in 1926. It's worth a quick look inside for the fine stained glass and marble font, and to climb to the top of the tower for great views of the surrounding valleys.

Overlooking **Parque Caldas** (Calle 30/Carrera 22), the early 20th century, neo-Gothic **Iglesia de la Inmaculada Concepción** is worth a visit for its ornate interior with a beautiful vaulted roof, pews, and pillars, all fashioned from cedar wood, and scintillating stained-glass.

Just southwest of the city, in the **Chipre** barrio, a striking 50-ton bronze monument by local artist Luis Guillermo Vallejo commemorates the 22 *Paisas* who founded Manizales in 1849. But what really lures people to Chipre is the incredible views of Parque Nacional Los Nevados from the **Torre al Cielo** (Parque Observatorio, Avenida 12 de Octubre; ✆ 883-8311; daily 9am–10pm; COP$3,000; there are frequent buses from Cable Plaza to Chipre). Locals will proudly tell you that this is the place where Chilean poet Pablo Neruda waxed lyrical about Manizales's "factory of sunsets."

AROUND MANIZALES

Just a couple of miles northeast of town (3km) the **Reserva Ecológica** Río Blanco (Vereda Las Palomas; ✆ 6/870-3810; call 2 days in advance for a permit; 11am–4pm; guided tour: COP$20,000, taxi COP$25,000) is an essential stop for budding ornithologists. Trails lead through this magical and incredibly biodiverse cloud-forest reserve, where an estimated 350 species of bird find sanctuary along with more than 50 mammals (including a spectacled bear that was rescued from captivity), kaleidoscopic butterflies, and stunning orchids. There is also a hummingbird farm and cabins to rent (meals can be provided) within the reserve.

Some 11km (7 miles) southeast from Manizales, the cloud forest of **Recinto del Pensamiento** (Vía al Magdalena; www.recintodelpensamiento.com; ✆ 6/889-7073; Tues–Sun 9am–4pm; COP$13,000; bird-watching tours COP$10,000) has an excellent butterfly garden, *guadua* plantations, short forest trails lined with thousands of orchids, a medicinal herb garden, a modern gondola "ride," and omnipresent birdlife. Buses (around COP$1,600, direction "Sera Maltería") leave every 10 minutes from Cable Plaza, or take a taxi: COP$14,000.

The dense cloud forest of **Yarumos Ecological Park** (Calle 61B no. 15A–01; ✆ 6/872-0420; Tues–Sun 9am–6pm; entry COP$3,200; adventure activities cost extra) is another botanist's wonderland within easy reach of Manizales. Named after the *yarumo blanco* tree, which is not white but green, it's a lush place to wander scenic trails alive with around 40 bird species and a spectacle of endemic flora. You can also make your heart valves squeak with a menu of adrenaline-fueled sports, including rock climbing and ziplining. There's a small but quite interesting natural history museum (information in Spanish only).

WHERE TO STAY

Estelar El Cable ★   In a pleasant, quiet neighborhood but within easy reach of Zona Rosa's shops, bars, and restaurants, this concrete pile may not scream authenticity, but it's one of the most comfortable and convenient options in town. Snappy rooms (with great views of the city and mountains) are spacious, bright, and modern, with desk spaces, mini bars, flatscreen TVs, and good Wi-Fi. Contemporary bathrooms with great, hot showers are flush with amenities. The polished restaurant serves a hot and cold breakfast buffet and light meals/snacks in the evening. The staff are eager to please and there's a small gym.

Carrera 23c no. 64A–60. www.hotelesestelar.com. ✆ **6/887-9690.** From COP$195,000, includes breakfast and snacks. **Amenities:** Restaurant; free Wi-Fi.

Hacienda Venecia ★★★　One of the region's most evocative places to stay, this working coffee hacienda (with excellent tours) has a magical setting, historic charm, and plenty of on-site activities, as well as attractions nearby. With accommodation for all budgets, a diverse mix of travelers adds to the lively, informal ambience. In the characterful Main House (the most upscale options), comfortable, bright rooms are decorated with family artifacts, books, and memorabilia. There are simple, more austere, rooms in the modest Guest House, and dorm rooms with shared baths in the hostel. You can happily spend days swimming in the pool surrounded by birds, butterflies, and lush vegetation; you can take a tour of the coffee farm, or a yoga class in a guadua gazebo, and there's hiking and horseback riding on trails that lead through the property. There's a welcoming family vibe with hearty communal meals, bonfires, and BBQs.

El Rosario Village. www.haciendavenecia.com. ☎ **320/636-5719.** From COP$350,000 in the Main House, from COP$110,000 in the Guest House, dorm rooms (shared bath) COP$35,000 in the hostel, includes breakfast. **Amenities:** Restaurant; coffee shop; outdoor pool; yoga classes; coffee tours; hiking; free Wi-Fi.

Mirador Andino Hostel ★★　There's a dearth of fine places to stay in Manizales, but this super-friendly hostel is the top choice for travelers who want to be close to the city's nightlife/restaurants and maintain easy access to the surrounding countryside. The characterful, traditional home, decorated with colonial antiques, artworks, and exquisite woodwork, is just steps from the city's cable car system. Basic dorm rooms with bunks are pristine (some even have chandeliers and tapestries on the wall), and there are simple double rooms with shared baths. The mountain views from the rooftop bar/terrace are wonderful (especially at sunset) and there's an array of amenities, including a large communal kitchen and a game room. The warm and welcoming hosts are happy to arrange tours of the area.

Carrera 23 no. 32–20. www.miradorandino-hostel.com. ☎ **310/532-8759.** Doubles from COP$145,000. **Amenities:** Bar/restaurant; shared kitchen; game room; free Wi-Fi.

WHERE TO EAT

La Suiza ★★ CAFE/BAKERY　A local institution, this lively cafe fast becomes a ritual if you hang around town long enough. Locals flock here for decadent pastries, cakes, cookies, and ice creams. It's also a great spot for international breakfast fare and hearty Antioquian staples, including fried eggs over a skillet of rice and beans, waffles, and pancakes. For lunch, there's a healthy menu of tasty salads as well as fish and pasta dishes with more gourmet aspirations. Libations come in the form of wine, beer, and fruity house-made cocktails.

Carrera 23 no. 26–57. www.lasuiza.com.co. ☎ **6/885-0545.** Main courses COP$16,000–COP$28,000. Mon–Sat 9am–8pm, Sun 10am–7pm.

Spago Bistro Italiano ★ ITALIAN　A perennial favorite with locals and travelers in the Zona Rosa, Spago boasts an appealing all-things-to-all-men menu. Creative, flavorful Italian dishes—the chef worked in NYC for a while—include homemade pasta, thin crust wood-oven pizza, seafood risotto, chicken parmesan, calamari, and a (generally) inventive fish-of-the-day special. The staff are warm and efficient, and there's a gregarious atmosphere matched by cozy decor.

Vino Y Pimienta ★★ MEDITTERANEAN   The closest thing you'll get to epicurean dining in Manizales, there's a lot to love about Vino Y Pimienta. Each dish is crafted from well-sourced, local ingredients and presented with surprising artisanal flair. Entrees lean toward fish and seafood with creative sauces, preparations, and interesting combinations of flavors. There's a perfectly executed seared salmon, succulent crab claws, a signature creamy shrimp risotto and desserts that are worth saving room for. The wine list is a well-curated ensemble of Latin American wineries with a bottle for every taste and budget. Service is hard to fault, and tables are fitted with crisp white tablecloths and polished silverware. While it's quite expensive for this town, it's a steal by U.S. and European prices.

Calle 7 no. 21–74. © **6/886-5571.** Main courses COP$16,000–COP$55,000. Daily noon–3pm, 7–10pm.

Armenia ★

46km (29 miles) SE from Pereira, 96km (60 miles) S from Manizales

Armenia is the capital of the state of Quindío, and since it was founded in 1889, it has withstood the worst of the region's seismic activity. In 1999, an earthquake with a 6.2 magnitude wiped out more than one third of the city and damaged practically all the buildings in the center. With the enterprising zeal, rugged individualism, and tenacity for which Antioqueños are famed, the city was rebuilt in just 15 years, a feat which led to the city's moniker, "The Miracle City." Now, with its earthquake-proof structures and austere concrete behemoths, Armenia is hardly a gem. Most travelers come here for a brief layover en-route to the region's more scenic pleasures. Still, with its thrusting commercial spirit and several interesting attractions within the city and just a short drive away, Armenia makes for an earthy preamble and urban contrast to the otherworldly landscapes of Colombia's coffee country.

ESSENTIALS

GETTING THERE   It was a pivotal moment for the coffee region when low cost airline **Spirit** (www.spirit.com) launched three non-stop services weekly (Tues, Thurs, and Sun) from Fort Lauderdale to Armenia's **Aeropuerto Internacional El Edén** (AXM), 17km (11 miles) southwest of the city. A great deal, you can book one-way prices (base fares) from as little as US$150. There are seven daily flights with **Avianca** (www.avianca.com) from Bogotá (around COP$372,000, one-way) and with **ADA** (www.ada-aero.com) from Medellín (around COP$225,000, one-way). A taxi to downtown will set you back around COP$35,000.

Armenia's **Terminal de Transportes** is located 2km (1¼ miles) southwest of the center (Calle 35 no. 20–68). Buses ply the route from downtown to the station along Carrera 19 (COP$1,600), or a taxi will cost around COP$4,000.

There are frequent services to: Bogotá (7 hr.), Medellín (5½ hr.), Cali (3½ hr.), Pereira (1 hr.), Manizales (2½ hr.), Filandia (45 min.), and Salento (50 min.).

GETTING AROUND   While it's not a pretty city made for walking, Armenia's main sights are best reached either on foot or by taxi (always take a taxi late at night). Taxis are plentiful and cheap, and most fares within the city limits will cost less than COP$6,000. Always confirm a rate with the driver before you get in. *Busetas* (mini-buses) cost COP$1,600 (COP$1,700 Sun/ holidays) and run from the bus terminal (marked "TERMINAL") to downtown (marked "CENTRO") and covers the city's main arteries.

EXPLORING ARMENIA

It's always worth going out of your way to check out the dramatic works of Colombian sculptor Rodrigo Arenas Betancourt. The ***Monumento al Esfuerzo***, which takes center stage in **Plaza Bolívar ★★**, is no exception. The masterful bronze sculpture embodies the spirit, determination, and resourceful nature of the first migrants to the region and pays homage to Francisco Antonio Cano's seminal (and idealized) work *Horizons*, which is displayed in the Museo de Antioquia in Medellín (see p. 170). Dominating the plaza's eastern flank, fronted by palm trees, the distinctive **La Inmaculada Cathedral ★** (Calle 21 no. 12–20) has an eye-catching triangular facade, which is loved and loathed in equal measure. Whatever your opinion, the modernist church certainly leaves an impression; it's worth a peek inside for the contemporary stained glass windows and bronze statue of Christ. On the northeast side of the square, there's a more traditional bronze Bolívar sculpture by Roberto Henau Buritacá.

The massive **Plaza de Mercado ★** (which spans 3 blocks), 3 blocks northwest of Plaza de Bolívar, is the setting for the **Parroquia de San Francisco ★** (Calle 15 no. 17–24; ✆ **6/745-3230**). The largest church in town is constructed from eye-catching red stone; inside there's impressive stained-glass work. The church, originally built in 1934, was severely damaged by the earthquake in 1999. Five blocks north of Plaza de Bolívar, leafy **Parque Sucre ★** is an agreeable place to watch life unfold, with a 100-year-old ceiba tree, a pleasant cafe, a newspaper kiosk, meandering street vendors, and a fishpond.

At the northern reaches of the city, Armenia's cultural highlight is the **Museo del Oro Quimbaya ★★** (Carrera 14 no. 40N–80; www.banrepcultural. org/armenia; ✆ **6/749-8169**; Tues–Sun 9am–5pm; free). A taxi from Plaza Bolívar will cost around COP$6,000, or take any bus labelled "MUSEO" or "LIMITES." While the collection may be small, it is beautifully curated, and every piece is exquisite. Along with a swift but engaging outline of the region's pre-Columbian history, there are stunning gold statuettes, figurines, and jewelry fashioned by the Quimbaya people, who were revered for their metal working skills.

AROUND ARMENIA

Well worth the short taxi ride south of the city, the **Jardín Botánico del Quindío ★★** (Avenida Centenario no. 15–190; Km. 3 Vía al Valle, Calarcá;

www.jardinbotanicoquindio.org; © 6/742-7254; daily 9am–4pm; COP$20,000) draws the crowds to its world-renowned *mariposario* (butterfly farm), an incredible showcase of more than 1,500 butterflies (50 species). You can happily spend a few hours here meandering through the garden's 10-hectare forest that preserves more than 850 species of flora, including *guadua*, palm trees, ferns, heliconia, and orchid. There's also a bird observatory, an insectarium, a lookout tower, a maze, and a small natural history museum.

Included on many tours of the region, the **Parque Nacional del Café ★** is a rather cheesy theme park which is part-museum (which extols the region's coffee production and heritage) and part-playground (rollercoasters, traditional fun fair rides, sugar-laced treats). You can hike or horseback ride through the valley, learn about the shiny red beans in the interactive (child-oriented) coffee museum, and visit a mockup of a traditional *campesino* house. Don't miss the bizarre Show de Café, an extraordinary (and quite compelling) folkloric extravaganza with music, dance, and acrobatics. The park is at Km 6 Vía Montenegro, Pueblo Tapao (www.parquedelcafe.co; © 6/741-7417; open Wed–Fri 10am–6pm, Sat, Sun and holidays 9am–6pm). Admission is COP$25,000 to COP$59,000 depending on package/rides included; a 20-minute taxi ride will cost around COP$35,000, or buses leave from Armenia's main terminal—destination "Pueblo Tapao"—every 30 minutes at least.

WHERE TO STAY & EAT

Allure Aroma Mocawa ★ With modern, well-designed rooms, a strong emphasis on functionality, and an array of amenities, this well-run, high-rise hotel is downtown Armenia's most stylish choice; although there's not a lot of competition. Neutral rooms with tasteful, streamlined furniture have walk-in showers, large flat screen TVs, blackout shades, comfortable beds, and leather sofas. There's a terrific rooftop pool and hot tub with a poolside cocktail bar, a fine restaurant/grill, a cafe, and tennis courts. An expansive hot and cold breakfast buffet is included in the rate.

Carrera 14a 10an no. 9N–00. www.allurearomamocawahotel.com.co. © **317/572-9275.** From COP$260,000, includes breakfast. **Amenities:** Restaurant/bar/cafe; outdoor pool; hot tub; tennis courts; free Wi-Fi.

Armenia Hotel ★ This characterful hotel may have seen better days, but it exudes a real sense of place and cultivates a friendly vibe. There are plenty of decorative overtures to the region's culture and history, with pre-Columbian ceramics, heavy quotas of bamboo, and plant-filled public spaces. Large rooms could do with a makeover, but they are comfortable, bright, and clean. There's a small pool, gym, and a restaurant (not very good, but breakfast is included).

Avenida Bolívar no. 8–67. www.armeniahotel.com.co. © 6/746-0099. From COP$210,000. **Amenities:** Restaurant/bar; outdoor pool; gym; free Wi-Fi.

Hacienda Bambusa ★★★ With a magical location, gourmet cuisine, and characterful accommodation, this intimate hacienda provides an authentic base for exploring the less-beaten-path of the coffee region. The traditional *guadua* and red-tiled roof structure features seven simple but elegant rooms with high ceilings, tiled floors, white-on-white decor, neat bathrooms, and either an outdoor terrace or patio with hammocks, and mesmerizing views of the gardens/swimming pool or the Andes mountains. The cuisine here is a big part of the experience, with resident chef Vanessa Quintana creating epic nightly tasting menus that showcase Colombia's regional flavors. The impeccable staff can arrange outings and tours across the region, and there are plenty of recreational activities, from hiking through coffee plantations, taking a hot air balloon ride, lazing by the pool, or horse riding in the valley.

30km (18 miles) south of Armenia, 12km (7½ miles) from El Edén airport. www.hacienda bambusa.com. ⓒ **300/778-8897.** From COP$490,000, includes breakfast. **Amenities:** Restaurant; outdoor pool; tours; free Wi-Fi.

La Fogata ★ STEAKHOUSE
A local institution, La Fogata is one of the most atmospheric dining rooms in a city that isn't known for its culinary sophistication. Steak is king in these parts and La Fogata serves Armenia's premier cuts of beef along with hearty stews and meat dishes that span Italian, Argentinian, and Mexican regional classics. Menu favorites include rabbit with tarragon, veal osso buco, and baby beef filet mignon. For less carnivorous palettes, there's a fine grilled trout, sea bass, refreshing salads, and vegetable sides and appetizers. The cavernous dining room features a large open bar, cozy leather and wood furniture, and traditional Paisa artworks. There's often live music on the weekends.

Carrera 13 no. 14N–47. www.lafogata.com.co. ⓒ **6/749-5501.** Main courses COP$24,000–COP$44,000. Mon–Sat noon–3pm, 7–11pm; Sun noon–5pm.

La Fonda Antioqueña ★ COLOMBIAN
For authentic regional flavors served in a prosaic, canteen-style setting just off Plaza de Bolívar, La Fonda is a local institution. The second-floor dining room (above a karaoke bar) packs in the locals for monumental Paisa dishes, including the classic *bandeja paisa* and tripe soup (*mondongo*). There's often live music or a soccer game on TV, but everyone here comes for the sole purpose of eating good honest (filling) food at bargain prices.

Carrera 13 no. 18–59. ⓒ **313/600-0155.** Main courses COP$12,000–COP$22,000. Mon–Sat 8am–7pm, Sun 8am–4pm.

Tierra Morena ★ HEALTHY/VEGETARIAN
If you need to switch gears from the region's traditional meat-centric, artery-hardening menus, Tierra Morena serves creative, tasty, and very colorful dishes—of a vegetarian ilk—in an intimate, arty setting with murals, fanciful lighting, and wooden cafe tables. There are flavorful Portobello burgers, super-fresh salads (which you can load with protein if you desire), zingy seafood ceviche, and noodle/pasta dishes.

Calle 15 no. 12–15. ⓒ **317/685-4656.** Main courses COP$14,000–COP$27,000. Mon–Sat 11am–10pm.

CALI & THE SOUTHWEST

by Nicholas Gill

The southwest of Colombia used to be bypassed by travelers because of security concerns, so it never got the attention of some other regions. Yet this part of Colombia is packed with major attractions. Of course there's Cali, the region's sprawling urban center, home to both grit and glamour that dances to an Afro-Colombian rhythm. There's so much salsa going on that it's considered the world capital. There are unusual landscapes too, like one of the country's only deserts and the mountainous, cloud-covered páramo. History is much deeper here than many other places in the country, from an impressive collection of stone statues and burial chambers to beautifully preserved colonial cities. There are little-known indigenous groups, lakes for windsurfing, and horses outnumber cars in many places.

As long as 5,000 years ago, civilization spread in the Cauca and Magdalena river valleys. In **Tierradentro**, elaborate underground burial chambers were built in the hillsides (they can be seen on a 14km walking loop). At the headwaters of both waterways, in the lush green hills surrounding **San Agustín**, hundreds of stone statues can still be found, best seen on horseback rides that take in towering waterfalls and coffee plantations. Together they provide evidence of a sophisticated, evolving society with artifacts that are unlike anything else in the Americas.

With its 500-year-old Spanish colonial churches and neighborhoods full of whitewashed houses with terracotta tile roofs, **Popayán** is one of Colombia's most intriguing urban settings, with elaborate Semana Santa celebrations that have been going on since the 16th century, attracting thousands for the nighttime processions. Salsa wasn't born in **Cali**, yet it grew up there and is a part of the culture in a big way, from the salsa schools to the late night clubs, though there are also art galleries, fine museums, and marketplaces with a selection of exotic fruits so diverse you are unlikely to ever see something remotely comparable ever again. In **Silvia**, beginning at dawn, the

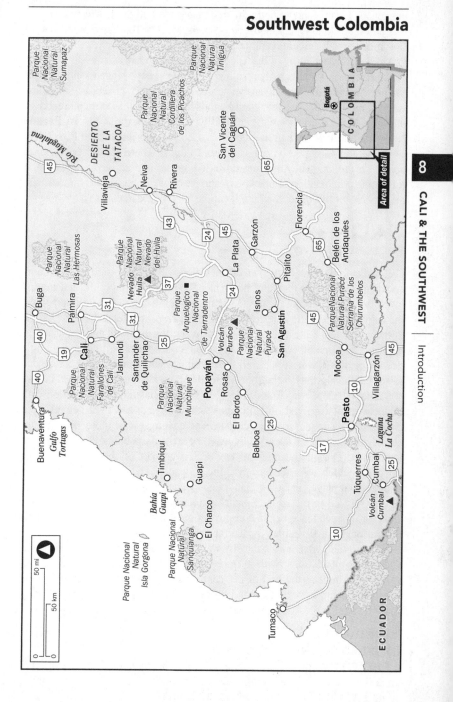

Southwest Colombia

indigenous Guambiano come to the main plaza dressed in their typical bowler hats and blue skirts to sell their goods for the weekly Tuesday market, one of Colombia's most authentic cultural experiences.

Amid the eroded cliffs of the **Tatacoa Desert**, you can see the stars of both the northern and southern hemispheres. In the misty, rugged landscape of **Puracé National Park**, keep an eye out for Andean spectacled bears and tapirs.

On **Lago Calima**, the year-round winds have turned this artificial reservoir into one of the world's great kite- and windsurfing destinations. At **Parque Nacional Natural Farrallones** there's a spectacular 5-day hike to **Pico Loro**.

The region's food is some of Colombia's finest. There are tiny fried *empanadas de pipián*, with their peanut-based sauce, and *salpicón payanese*, a refreshing combination of blackberry and ice. *Cuy* (guinea pig) is famous here in parts closer to Ecuador, where it can be fried or roasted.

CALI ★★

329km (204 miles) S of Medellín, 80km (50 miles) E of Buenaventura

Cali walks to the beat of its own drum. Caleños are quite proud of their home and quick to proclaim their city, not to mention their food, nightlife, and cultural institutions, as Colombia's finest. The magic of the city of 2.5 million people, the capital of the Valle de Cauca department, not to mention the salsa capital of the world, can be lost among some travelers. It's often hot and not nearly as walkable as some other major urban areas. Yet, for those willing to dig a little deeper, or just to wait it out until the evening when there's a cool breeze and salsa fills the air, they'll find one of South America's most underrated cities.

Santiago de Cali was founded in 1536 by conquistador Sebastián de Belalcázar, who first arrived on Columbus's third voyage and later helped Francisco Pizarro conquer the Inca empire. There were several indigenous groups already living in the Cauca Valley when he arrived, including the Calima and Quimbaya. During the colonial era, Cali was part of the gobernación of Popayán, which was ruled from Quito, Ecuador. The city is known for the strong role it played in Colombian Independence. On July 3, 1810, an uprising in Cali refused to recognize Spanish authority, more than two weeks before calls for independence began coming out of Bogotá, and many men from the region fought in the battles for liberation.

Up until the 19th century, the city was quite small, dominated by haciendas and mango plantations, with no more than 20,000 residents. When the railroads were built at the end of the century, everything changed. Coffee and sugarcane could now be exported on the world market, creating a vast new economy and explosive growth that continues today.

Essentials

GETTING THERE & AROUND

BY PLANE Alfonso Bonilla Aragón Airport is 16km northeast of Cali. **Avianca** (www.avianca.com), **Copa** (www.copaair.com), **JetBlue** (www.jetblue.com), **LATAM** (www.latam.com), **American Airlines** (www.aa.com), **Tame**

(www.tame.com.ec), and **Viva Colombia** (www.vivacolombia.co) all serve Cali. Destinations include major Colombian cities like Bogotá, Barranquilla, Cartagena, and Medellín, as well as international cities like Miami, Panama City, Madrid, and Lima. The city center can be reached by bus or taxi (COP$60,000).

BY BUS   Cali's bus terminal (www.terminalcali.com) is 2km north of the center of the city, at Calle 30n no. 2an–29). Dozens of companies offer trips to smaller destinations within the region, as well as direct long-distance buses to places like Cartagena, Medellín, and Bogotá. The mass transit system, called Mio (www.mio.com.co), is an air-conditioned bus network that's similar to the Transmilenio in Bogotá. It runs the entire length of Av. Quinta (Av. 5) and the center. Rides cost COP$1,800 each.

BY TAXI   Taxis are cheap and plentiful, as is Uber. For a reliable taxi service, call **Taxi Elite** (② **320/838-9637**).

USEFUL INFO

There is a **tourist information office** (www.cali.gov.co/turista; Mon–Fri 8am–noon and 2–5pm, Sat 10am–2pm) at the corner of Calle 6 and Carrera 4. There's also a small stand at the airport with brochures and maps.

There are **banks** and **ATMs** all over town, particularly in Barrio Granada. The **post office** (Mon–Fri 8am–noon and 2–6pm, Sat 9am–noon) is at Carrera 3 no. 10–49.

There are English-speaking doctors at **Centro Medico Imbanaco** (www.imbanaco.com; ② **2/682-1000**), at Carrera 38a no. 5A–100.

CITY LAYOUT

Set in the Valle de Cauca, Cali is bordered by the Farallones de Cali Mountains to the west and the Cauca River to the east. It's a mostly flat city, though some parts of the city, such as San Antonio and Loma de La Cruz, are set on hills. Most tourists stick to a few neighborhoods in the northwestern corner of the city, such as the center, Barrio Granada, San Antonio, El Peñon, Versalles, and Santa Monica. Take extreme caution in other parts of the city, particularly in the east.

Exploring Cali

Nearly all of Cali's main attractions, such as colonial churches and museums, are located in **El Centro** and can be seen in a day on foot.

COLONIAL CHURCH ROUNDUP

Iglesia de la Ermita ★   Neo-Gothic La Ermita is Cali's most emblematic church. Built between 1930 and 1948, it's not nearly as old as La Merced or San Antonio, though inside are some of the city's most important religious relics that date to the 17th century, such as the images of the Virgen de los Dolores, San Roque, San Jose, and El Señor de la Caña. Note the musical clock and windows, which were brought over from Amsterdam.

Avenida Colombia and Calle 13. Daily 7:30am–5pm.

Cali

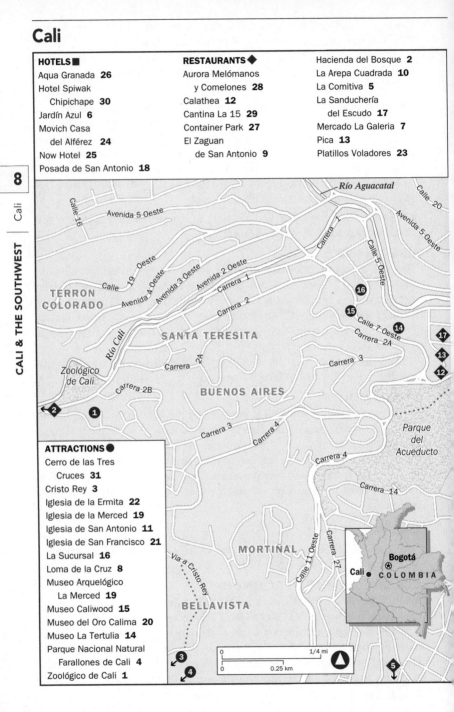

HOTELS ■
Aqua Granada **26**
Hotel Spiwak
 Chipichape **30**
Jardín Azul **6**
Movich Casa
 del Alférez **24**
Now Hotel **25**
Posada de San Antonio **18**

RESTAURANTS ◆
Aurora Melómanos
 y Comelones **28**
Calathea **12**
Cantina La 15 **29**
Container Park **27**
El Zaguan
 de San Antonio **9**

Hacienda del Bosque **2**
La Arepa Cuadrada **10**
La Comitiva **5**
La Sanduchería
 del Escudo **17**
Mercado La Galeria **7**
Pica **13**
Platillos Voladores **23**

ATTRACTIONS ●
Cerro de las Tres
 Cruces **31**
Cristo Rey **3**
Iglesia de la Ermita **22**
Iglesia de la Merced **19**
Iglesia de San Antonio **11**
Iglesia de San Francisco **21**
La Sucursal **16**
Loma de la Cruz **8**
Museo Arquelógico
 La Merced **19**
Museo Caliwood **15**
Museo del Oro Calima **20**
Museo La Tertulia **14**
Parque Nacional Natural
 Farallones de Cali **4**
Zoológico de Cali **1**

Río Aguacatal

Calle 20

Calle 16

Avenida 5 Oeste

Avenida 5 Oeste

Carrera 1

Calle 5 Oeste

Calle 19 Oeste

Calle Oeste

Avenida 4 Oeste

Avenida 3 Oeste

Avenida 2 Oeste

Carrera 1

Carrera 2

**TERRON
COLORADO**

Río Cali

SANTA TERESITA

Calle 7 Oeste

Carrera 2A

Carrera 2A

Carrera 3

Zoológico
de Cali

Carrera 2B

Carrera 2A

BUENOS AIRES

Parque
del
Acueducto

Carrera 3

Carrera 4

Carrera 4

Carrera 14

MORTINAL

Via a Cristo Rey

Calle 11 Oeste

Carrera 27

Bogotá
⊛
Cali ● **COLOMBIA**

BELLAVISTA

0   1/4 mi
0   0.25 km

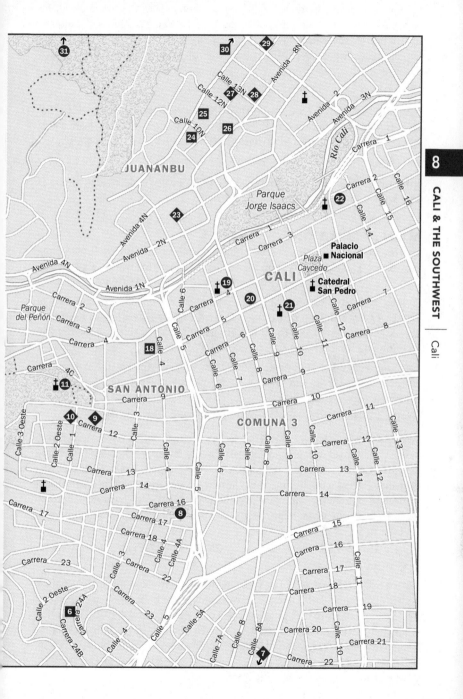

Iglesia de la Merced ★   Cali's oldest church dates to 1545 and was the site of the city's inaugural mass. The whitewashed Spanish colonial building, a national monument, holds the 15th-century carved wooden statue of the Virgen de las Mercedes, Cali's patron saint of the city, on top of the gilded baroque altar.

Carrera 4 and Calle 7. Daily 6:30–10am and 4–7pm.

Iglesia de San Antonio ★   This whitewashed church on top of Colina de San Antonio, a hill west of the city center, dates to 1747. Inside are a collection of wooden statues of various saints that date to the 17th century.

Colina de San Antonio. Daily 7:30am–5pm.

Iglesia de San Francisco ★   This 18th-century neoclassical church is best known for its Mudejar brick bell tower.

Carrera 6 and Calle 10. Daily 7:30am–5pm.

MAIN ATTRACTIONS

Cerro de las Tres Cruces ★   You can walk to this viewpoint with three crosses overlooking the city form Barrio Granada, though it will be a hot, sweaty 2 or 3 hours uphill. A taxi is a better option (COP$40,000–COP$50,000).

Cristo Rey ★   Just like in Rio . . . okay, not quite. This enormous white statue of Christ high up on Cerro las Cristales is less interesting in itself than the view that it provides. You'll need to negotiate a taxi to reach the top and to bring you back down (COP$60,000–COP$70,000).

La Sucursal ★   This contemporary art gallery explores the connection between Cali and the surrounding landscape, with wide-ranging exhibitions on formats such as street art.

Carrera 2 Oeste no. 6-08. www.lasucursal.co. No phone. Free. Mon–Fri 1–6pm.

Museo Arqueológico La Merced ★   In a historic convent attached to Iglesia La Merced, this archaeological museum underwent a major renovation in 2016. Cultures from the region, such as the Tumaco, Nariño, Calima, San Agustín, Tierradentro, Tolima, and Quimbaya, are represented in a permanent collection of ceramics and other artifacts. It's a good collection though the quantity is not overwhelming, so you can probably see the entire museum in an hour or so.

Carrera 4 no. 6–59. www.musa.com.co. ⓒ **2/889-3434.** COP$4,000. Mon–Sat 9am–noon and 2–6pm.

Museo Caliwood ★   The first cinematography museum of Colombia is rather niche, though it will excite movie geeks. The collection encompasses a wide variety of early film projectors that date as early as the 1920s, as well as 19th-century cameras and an exhibit about the film industry in Cali, nicknamed Caliwood, which has a storied history. Audioguides are available at check in.

Avenida Belalcázar 5a–55 Oeste. www.caliwood.com.co. ⓒ **310/473-2282.** COP$10,000. Mon–Fri 8am–noon and 2–6pm; Sat 3–6pm; Sun 10am–6pm.

Museo del Oro Calima ★ Part of the collection of Bogotá's renowned Museo del Oro, the Cali branch is considerably smaller: just one main room, with a focus on the Calima culture. The collection includes gold pieces, as well as ceramics and tools. An adjacent hall also has rotating cultural exhibitions.

Calle 7 No 4–69. www.banrepcultural.org/cali/museo-del-oro-calima. ℂ **2/684-7755.** Free. Tues–Fri 9am–5pm, Sat 10am–5pm.

Museo La Tertulia ★ This modern art museum has one of Colombia's most important collections of more than 1,500 pieces of contemporary artwork, including painting, photography, and sculptures. Additionally, the museum has an independent theater that shows art house, foreign, and award-winning films.

Avenida Colombia 5 Oeste–105. www.museolatertulia.com. ℂ **2/893-2939.** COP$10,000. Tues–Sat 10am–6pm; Sun 2–6pm.

Zoológico de Cali ★★ Without question, Cali's surprisingly modern, sprawling zoo, covering 10 hectares in Santa Ana, is Colombia's best and one of the best attractions in the city. Native Colombian species are well represented with animals like anteaters and monkeys, along with exotic species like Bengal tigers. There's a large butterfly enclosure with more than 800 species, plus 20 or so aquariums, an owl exhibit, and an amphitheater.

Carrera 2A Oeste and Calle 14 Oeste, Barrio Santa Ana. www.zoologicodecali.com.co. ℂ **2/488-0888.** COP$18,000 adults, COP$12,000 children. Daily 9am–4:30pm.

Organized Tours

Cali Tours (www.calitours.co; ℂ **2/305-5309**), Calle 2 no. 10–10, offers bird-watching trips in the surrounding mountains and forests, as well at old sugar-cane haciendas and private reserves. They also offer day trips to the Afro-Colombian village of **San Cipriano** ★★ (see p. 245) and 2-day trips to Salento coffee farms. **Tate Tours** (www.tatetours.com; ℂ **2/371-5727**), at Calle 2 no. 4–126, has paragliding trips, as well as day trips to San Cipriano. **Delta Helicopteros** (www.deltahelicopteros.com; ℂ **2/551-8861**), Calle 9 no. 46–69, has sightseeing trips over the Valle de Cauca, Lago Calima, and the Eje Cafetero, departing from Aeropuerto Alfonso Bonilla Aragón.

Where to Stay

Most of Cali's hotels cluster around a few neighborhoods. You'll find the upscale chains and boutique hotels in Barrio Granada and El Peñon, while hostels and more budget-oriented accommodations can be had in San Antonio and around the center.

Aqua Granada Hotel ★ On a busy avenue just before the Calle 9 bridge to the center, Aqua Granada is close to Barrio Granada's thriving restaurants and nightlife. The rooms here are huge, essentially mini-apartments with kitchens, living areas, and patios. They lack character, but have every amenity you could ask for, such as LCD TVs, stocked refrigerators, and living rooms with sofa beds. Some add balconies or terraces. There's a wine bar and bistro

The Salsa Capital of the World

While salsa was born in Puerto Rican communities in New York City in the mid-1970s, it took on new life in Cali in the 1980s, when drug barons flush with cash began pumping money into malls, real estate, and flashy salsa clubs and orchestras. Local radio DJs began calling the city the "World Capital of Salsa," and the moniker has hung around. Today, salsa is everywhere, blaring out of car windows and filling the void in almost every club. Many of the world's best salsa dancers come from Cali, which is known for a fast-paced, Caribbean-influenced form of the dance. Today the city boasts roughly 200 salsa schools and 80 salsa orchestras. The best time of year to come is during the Festival Mundial de Salsa (www.mundialdesalsa.com) each September, or the Feria de Cali, held every 25th to 30th of December. However, you can learn salsa anytime of the year, and there are dozens of schools and instructors that cater specifically to tourists. Some favorite places to learn salsa include **Arrebato Caleño**, which offers group lessons for adults and children, as well as one-on-one instruction in Barrio San Antonio (Carrera 10 no. 1–47; arrebato cali@gmail.com; © **2/382-1117**), as does **Son de Luz** (www.sondeluz.co; © **2/370-2692**), at Carrera 28 no. 6–118. Or there's the hilariously named **Privateachero** (© **2/713-4903**), at Avenida 6 no. 17a–51 in Barrio Grenada, which offers both Spanish and salsa-dancing lessons.

on the ground floor, plus a small hot tub on a large yet otherwise empty rooftop terrace.

Avenida 8n no. 10–91. www.aquahotelcali.co. © **2/661-0624.** 24 units. COP$195,000 double, includes breakfast. **Amenities:** Restaurant; bar; fitness center; hot tub; sauna; free Wi-Fi.

Hotel Spiwak Chipichape ★ This luxury hotel is built inside the Chipichape mall, which you can see through a glass ceiling. The giant, partially open-air entertainment facility includes shops, restaurants, and movie theaters, not to mention a casino, which helps give it a Las Vegas vibe. The modern suites, all with separate living and sleeping areas, have either wood floors or carpet. Some add terraces with hot tubs. The hotel has extensive meeting facilities, which can bring hundreds of business groups to the hotel during the week, filling up the Mediterranean restaurant and the terrace pool. Weekends tend to be quieter and rates are considerably lower.

Avenida 6D no. 36n–18. www.spiwak.com. © **2/395-9999.** 226 units. Doubles COP$257,000, includes breakfast. **Amenities:** Restaurant; bar; outdoor pool; fitness center; event facilities; spa; free Wi-Fi.

Jardín Azul ★ Jardín Azul sits on a quiet street in the border area of the traditional neighborhoods of San Antonio and San Fernando. Rooms have wood floors and clunky wooden furniture, though they are otherwise quite plain. Four of the rooms add private balconies overlooking the garden, while the others face the street. Lots of extras like a pool and morning yoga make the property a good deal.

Carrera 24A no. 2A–59. www.jardinazul.com. © **2/556-8380.** 6 units. Doubles COP$155,000, includes breakfast. **Amenities:** Restaurant; outdoor pool; yoga; free Wi-Fi.

Movich Casa del Alférez ★★ In a residential area not far from the center, this contemporary hotel, built on the foundations of a colonial townhouse, was inspired by the original architecture, with wrought-iron railings and white marble floors. The rooms have a contemporary feel, with tufted leather headboards, stripped wood floors, and white walls with famous quotes stenciled on them, plus Bose sound systems and rainfall showers. Some have private balconies or loft beds up spiral staircases. There's good restaurant with South American dishes and Pacific coast seafood, as well as a pleasant cocktail and tapas bar.

Avenida 9N no. 9–24. www.movichhotels.com. ℭ **2/393-3030.** 40 units. Doubles COP$480,000; suites COP$664,000, includes breakfast. **Amenities:** Restaurant; bar; fitness center; tour desk; free Wi-Fi.

Now Hotel ★★ Cali's coolest, sleekest hotel towers over Barrio Granada, with the lights from its second-floor disco or the lounge bar beside the rooftop pool cabanas flashing down on the street below during the evenings. The Now Hotel has gone through changes in name and ownership, though it finally seems to have found its footing. A central atrium filled with palm trees is surrounded with terraces and catwalks. The rooms are accented with modish leather armchairs and wall-sized contemporary photography, plus 400-thread-count sheets and state-of-the-art electronics like LCD TVs. Each has a furnished balcony. The property's multiple bars and restaurants have become an anchor for the city's nightlife scene, attracting a well-heeled crowd.

Av. 9AN 10N–74. www.nowhotel.com.co. ℭ **2/488-9797.** 19 units. COP$253,000 double. **Amenities:** 2 restaurants; bar; disco; rooftop pool; business center; salon; free Wi-Fi.

Posada de San Antonio ★ In a charming colonial building in San Antonio, this well-run, small hotel is notable for its plant-filled courtyards, fine woodwork, and wrought-iron window covers. The rooms are airy yet basic, with white tile floors and a painting or two on the walls. Windows open up onto the courtyard.

Carrera 5 no. 3–37. www.posadadesanantonio.com. ℭ **2/893-7413.** 12 units. Doubles COP$220,000, includes breakfast. **Amenities:** Free Wi-Fi.

Where to Eat

Aside from the restaurants below, you should definitely make a trip to **Mercado La Galeria ★**, Calle 8 and Carrera 26, in the Alameda neighborhood. There are dozens of small food stands selling traditional regional dishes, as well as fruit vendors with an incredible variety of seasonal fruits.

Aurora Melómanos y Comelones ★ COLOMBIAN Is this a record shop that serves food or a restaurant that sells records? Either way it's one of the coolest spots in Cali for a burger, *guanabana* juice, or rock album. The menu rotates daily with a list of Colombian and international comfort foods. At night the place livens up with cocktails, especially on the weekends, when there are DJs or live music.

Calle 13N no. 8N–14. ℭ **2/612-3952.** Main courses COP$15,000–COP$25,000. Tues–Thurs 3–11pm, Fri–Sat 5pm–3am, Sun 2–7pm.

Calathea ★★ ICE CREAM This chic little artisanal ice cream shop is possibly the best in a town of surprisingly great ice cream shops. Calathea uses only natural ingredients in their ice creams and sorbets, including a lot of native fruits like lulo and *guayaba*. There are also unique flavors like strawberries with red wine.

Calle 40 no. 3A–50, El Peñon. www.calatheamundo.com. ✆ **2/371-0188.** Ice cream COP$8,000. Mon–Fri 10am–9pm, Sat 10am–10pm.

Cantina La 15 ★ MEXICAN Cantina La 15 isn't just a restaurant. It's a quirky experiment in fine dining that you'll either love or hate. The space is big and loud, with 400 seats and live music playing throughout dinner service. Late nights it feels more like a giant club. The food is for the most part standard Mexican with tacos, quesadillas, and grilled meats and seafood. It's pricey, though you're paying for the overall experience more than anything.

Calle 15n no. 9n–62, Barrio Granada. www.cantinala15.com. ✆ **2/653-4628.** Main courses COP$35,000–COP$55,000. Mon–Wed noon–midnight, Thurs–Sat noon–3am.

Container Park ★ INTERNATIONAL This gated lot on a primary Barrio Granada restaurant and nightlife strip is like the Colombian version of a gourmet food truck court. Instead of trucks, there are a handful of small restaurants selling an array of goods out of recycled shipping containers, with a central patio full of tables running the length of the lot. Prices are moderate for unpretentious offerings of various Colombian snacks, wings, ceviche, and burgers.

Avenida 9n no. 12–31, Barrio Granada. ✆ **2/893-0809.** Main courses COP$15,000–COP$25,000. Mon–Thurs 3–11pm, Fri–Sat 3pm–midnight, Sun 9am–5pm.

El Zaguan de San Antonio ★ COLOMBIAN Traditional *vallecaucana* dishes are the focus of this Cali institution. It's a casual spot serving big, heaping portions of *sancocho de gallina* (hen stew) and *arroz atollado* (meat and rice). There's a great rooftop with views of San Antonio's clay tile roofs.

Carrera 12 no. 1–29, San Antonio. ✆ **2/893-8021.** Main courses COP$15,000–COP$30,000. Daily noon–midnight.

Hacienda del Bosque ★★ CONTEMPORARY Cali's most atmospheric restaurant sits outside of the center, in the Santa Teresita neighborhood near the zoo. The setting is the iconic 19th-century Santa Rita hacienda, with a maze of intimate dining rooms with beamed ceilings and stone floors. The menu is contemporary Colombian, with touches of Peru and the Mediterranean. Dishes include trout cured in panela served with a crunchy focaccia, a Pacific coast seafood risotto with coconut milk, as well as some typical regional snacks like *valluna empanadas* and *pastel de yuca*. On Sundays the vibe is more relaxed, with a brunch focused on home-cooked regional dishes like roasted chicken and *arroz atollado* (meat and rice). Reservations are recommended.

Carrera 2 Oeste no. 14–250. www.haciendadelbosque.com.co. ✆ **2/489-8690.** Main courses COP$35,000–COP$65,000. Tues–Thurs noon–3pm and 6–10pm; Fri–Sat noon–3pm and 6–11pm, Sun noon–4pm.

La Arepa Cuadrada ★ COLOMBIAN   This funky little *arepa* spot near Parque San Antonio is known for dabbling in unique combinations of the favorite corn-based cake. Here they are stuffed with up to six ingredients, which range from bacon and beef tongue to plantains and pineapple. There are even international flavors like chop suey and noisette potatoes, plus an arepa burger.

Calle 8 no. 34–85. © **2/371-4418.** Arepas COP$10,000–COP$20,000; Mon–Sat 6am–12:30pm and 4–10pm, Sun 6am–12:30pm.

La Comitiva ★★ COLOMBIAN   Contemporary Colombian cuisine hasn't really hit Cali the way it has Medellín or Bogotá, though La Comitiva is trying to get there. With a maze of dining spaces and patios, the restaurant is surrounded by dozens of others on a lively circle in San Fernando. The straightforward menu with run-of-the-mill proteins (chicken, pork, and shrimp), stands out by using lots of regional ingredients like *chontadura*, which they add to a ceviche, or *pipian*, which is used to dip chicken rolls in. The gin and tonics are a must.

Calle 4 no. 34–32, San Fernando. © **2/382-7292.** Main courses COP$19,000–COP$57,000. Mon–Thurs noon–11pm; Fri noon–midnight; Sat 1pm–midnight.

La Sanduchería del Escudo ★★ SANDWICHES   This gourmet sandwich shop is run by Chef María Claudia Zarama, the owner of fine-dining restaurant El Escudo del Quijote. She does everything right: bakes her own bread, uses top-quality ingredients, and likes to incorporate lots of unique flavors. Sandwiches include smoked trout or a Peruvian-style *pan con chicharrón* (fried pork), as well as a few burgers. There's even a small wine and cocktail list.

Calle 4 Oeste no. 3–46. www.mariaclaudiazarama.com/restaurante-la-sanducheria-el-escudo. © **2/893-3021.** Sandwiches COP$17,000–COP$20,000; Daily 11am–11pm.

Pica ★★ PERUVIAN   On a chic street in El Peñon, Pica is divided into two spaces: a narrow interior dining room and a large back patio surrounded by a vertical garden. The menu is a combination of standard Peruvian dishes, especially a long list of ceviches and *tiraditos*, as well as some international plates like stuffed crab rolls and rack of lamb. Stick to their seafood dishes.

Calle 4 Oeste no. 3a–32. © **310/388-0901.** Main courses COP$35,000–COP$65,000. Tues–Sat noon–1am; Sun 11:30am–5pm.

Platillos Voladores ★ FUSION   "Flying Plates" is a fusion restaurant mostly dabbling in Asian and Mediterranean fare, though they have gradually been shifting toward more Colombian products and cooking styles. There's a short list of ceviches and carpaccio, plus curries, grilled fish with native fruit sauces, and *posta negra* (black beef). Opt for the patio that's lined with tropical plants rather than the stuffier dining rooms. The wine list is one of the best in the city.

Avenida 3n no. 7–19. www.platillosvoladores.com. © **2/668-7750.** Main courses COP$30,000–COP$50,000; Mon–Fri noon–3pm and 7–11pm, Sat 1–4pm.

The Festival Capital of Colombia

Some of Colombia's liveliest festivals take place in Cali, and many Colombians plan their year around them. Many claim that the vivacious **Festival de Música del Pacífico Petronio** Álvarez is the best party in Cali. The August festival celebrates the African-influenced music of the Pacific Coast through parades and concerts that turn the city into one big dance club. September's **Festival**

Mundial de Salsa isn't technically a global competition, though it's a celebration of Colombian salsa in its epicenter. From Christmas to New Year's, the annual **Feria de Cali** manages to merge with the other holidays, celebrating everything that is Cali with beauty pageants, parades, concerts, and of course lots and lots of dancing.

Shopping

Your first handicraft stop in Cali should be **Loma de la Cruz**, on a hilltop at the edge of the San Antonio neighborhood. It's one of Colombia's best artesanía markets with authentic, handmade goods from most parts of the country that are sold out of a row of small shops and stalls.

La Galeria market in Alameda has a few stalls, though you'll find better quality across the street at **La Caleñita**, Carrera 24 no. 8–53 (www.lacalenita. com; ✆ 2/556-1172), which has been around for decades and has expanded into the surrounding buildings so that it almost takes up an entire block. Packaged food items like panela and sweets are sold alongside woven baskets from La Guajira and other upscale items.

Copias Pre-Colombinas, Avenida 8n no. 15–20 (✆ 2/388-3785), in Barrio Grenada, sells replicas of ceramics from Colombia's ancient cultures like the Quimbaya, Tayrona, and Calima. In El Peñon and Granada, you'll find a slew of high-end fashion boutiques from Colombian designers like **Silvia Tcherassi** (Calle 2 Oeste no. 2–32; www.silviatcherassi.com; ✆ 2/892-0805), **Maria Elena Villamil** (Avenida 9N no. 15N–40; ✆ 2/483-7470), and **Joanna Ortiz** (Calle 18 no. 106–46; www.johannaortiz.co; ✆ 2/373-3483). Also, check out the colorful four-level design and concept store **La Juana** (✆ 2/263-8054), at Avenida 9N no. 17–21 in Barrio Granada.

Nightlife

Cali is home to one of Colombia's most iconic nightlife scenes. Salsa dominates here, and many of the swanky old clubs fueled in the cartel days are still hanging around, most of them staying open until 3am on the weekends. You'll want to plan in advance for **Delirio** (www.delirio.com.co; ✆ 2/405-5300), a wild, monthly salsa party set in a circus tent in the Parque del Amor. Tickets can be purchased at www.tuboleta.com. There are dozens of other great salsa spots that run year-round, however. **Zaperoco Bar**, Avenida 5 Norte no. 16–46 (✆ 3/751-3266), is a classic, with veteran DJs and a high-energy crowd that packs the dance floor until late on Thursday to Saturday nights. Another iconic yet no-frills salsa spot is the second-floor **Tin Tin Deo**, Calle 5 No 38–71 (www.tintindeo.com), also open Thursday through Saturday.

All is not salsa, however. For a modern dance club with all sorts of music that goes beyond salsa, hit **The Lobby Discoteca** at Calle 1 Oeste no. 2–38 (✆ **2/ 892-3206**) in El Peñon. Beer geeks will appreciate **Ritual Cervecería**, Av. 9N no. 10–52, a laidback pub that brews its own beer, amid a sea of other small bars and clubs in Barrio Granada. For cocktails, head to sleek **Roset** (www. roset.co), at Carrera 2 Oeste no. 1–14 in El Peñon, which also has a full menu.

Side Trips from Cali

Long off limits during the civil war, **Parque Nacional Natural Farallones de Cali** is a 1,500-sq.-km national park that is gradually opening back up to the world. Most who come here do so via the park's eastern corner, in the quaint mountain hamlet of **Pance**, which is where many Caleños have fincas and come to relax and get out of the heat on the weekends. It has just one street, with a handful of bars and country-style restaurants that mostly stay closed during the week. The clear river here is great for swimming and there are a few hikes to nearby waterfalls, though you'll need to hire a guide and pay the entrance fee (COP$5,000) back in Cali at the Corporación Autónoma Regional del Valle de Cauca (www.cvc.gov.co; ✆ **2/620-6600**; Carrera 56 no. 11–36). Guides can be found at the visitor center at **El Topocio**, a 30-minute walk from Pance (ask around for directions). Several trails leave from here, including the 7-hour round-trip hike to **Pico de Loro ★**, the famed peak that hovers above the park, as well as the 5-day hike to **Pico de Pance** (ask at the park office in Cali, at Calle 29n no. 6N–43, about setting this up with a guide in advance).

If you don't have your own transportation, getting to Pance requires getting in a minibus outside of Cali's bus terminal, marked PUEBLO PANCE; mini-buses run between 5:30am and 8pm. The trip takes approximately 1½ hours. There are several campsites and cabin facilities in Pance if you decide to stay overnight to get an early start.

About an hour north of Cali is the village of **Buga ★**, a popular Catholic pilgrimage site because of the miracles performed here in the 1500s. There's a large basilica here now, as well as a microbrewery (not in the same location, obviously). It makes a good base for short hikes into the countryside.

LAGO CALIMA ★

86km (53 miles) N of Cali

This man-made lake was created in 1965 when a dam was built on the Río Calima, which flooded the Darién Valley and created a water reservoir for the city of Cali, whose residents then began building fincas and weekend homes in the green hills surrounding it. The weather is cooler here than down on the plains, and there's a steady, year-round wind that brings hordes of wind- and kitesurfers. Most activity is concentrated on the northern side of the lake, with most basing themselves in and around the small town of **Darién**, which fills up on the weekends but is eerily quiet the rest of the week. For just a small grid of streets clustering around the main plaza, the **Parque los Fundadores**, the amenities are quite good with ATMs and supermarkets, plus a handful of restaurants, discotecas, and budget hotels.

Essentials

GETTING THERE

Darién is best reached from Cali, from where there are frequent buses for the 2 1/2-hour ride during the day. If coming from the north you will save time by stopping in Buga and catching a bus from there (1 hr.).

Exploring Lago Calima

Outside of the weekend nightlife, water sports are the primary activity around Lago Calima. Sign up for boat trips on the lake from any of the tour operators around the plaza, or at Entrada 5 outside of town. You can either join a tour for around COP$10,000 or rent an entire boat for COP$60,000 to COP$80,000.

Most of the windsurfing schools are found closer to the dam (catch a mini-bus there from Darién for COP$1,800), and many offer packages with lessons and accommodations. In general, you can expect to pay around COP$60,000 per hour for windsurfing lessons and around COP$100,000 for kitesurfing lessons, plus rentals. You can also rent stand-up paddle boards (SUP) for around COP$60,000 per hour. One of the better surf operations on the lake is **Cogua Kiteboarding** (www.coguakiteboarding.com; © **318/608-3932**), which has a workshop at Calle 10 no. 4–51, where they make custom kiteboards out of coconut fiber.

Where to Stay & Eat

Most restaurants can be found within a block or two of Darién's plaza, with most serving simple dishes like grilled lake trout or *sancocho* (beef stew). Accommodations are mostly rustic hostels aimed at the surf crowd. **La Casa del Viento** (www.lacasadelviento.com; © **315/265-6540**), Carrera 6 no. 12–40, is one of the better options, with a mix of dorms and private rooms for COP$35,000 to COP$65,000. They can also set up kitesurfing lessons and parasailing over the lake.

The only formal hotel near Lago Calima, **Hotel Brisas del Lago ★** (Carrera 7 no. 7–50; www.hotelbrisasdelcalima.com; © **2/253-3460**) has been a go-to weekend retreat for Colombian families since opening in 1995, though during the rest of the week you'll probably have it to yourself. It's right in the heart of Darién, a short walk from the lake. The rooms (COP$104,000–COP$145,000) are smallish but modern and equipped with flatscreen TVs. Bunk beds are added in family rooms so entire families can squeeze in. There's a discoteca open on weekend nights. Rates include continental breakfast and dinner.

POPAYÁN ★★

112km (69 miles) S of Cali

For those enchanted by Cartagena's colonial splendor, just wait until you set your eyes on Popayán. While Cartagena's cobblestone streets are increasingly filled with tens of thousands of cruise ship passengers at a time, Popayán, with architecture that is equally as stunning, remains relatively tourist free. Nicknamed La Ciudad Blanca, or the White City, for its whitewashed facades, the city is home to several universities that sit side by side with historic churches and monasteries that have all been beautifully maintained.

Founded by Sebastián de Belalcázar in 1537, Popayán was once the most powerful city in southern Colombia, strategically located on the crossroads between Quito and Cartagena. Wealthy sugar barons came here to escape the heat in the Valle de Cauca, building elaborate mansions and religious monuments. When the railroads, and later highways, were built in the early 1900s, Cali's population ballooned and the balance of power shifted away from Popayán.

Essentials

GETTING THERE

BY PLANE   Just beyond the city center, behind the bus terminal, Aeropuerto Guillermo León Valencia has multiple daily flights to Bogotá with **Avianca** (www.avianca.com).

BY BUS   Popayán's bus terminal is 1km north of the city center and has frequent service to Cali (3 hr.), as well as San Agustín (5 hr.), Tierradentro (5 hr.), Pasto (6 hr.), and other destinations around southern Colombia. Direct buses to Bogotá and Medellín depart in the evenings, both taking 11 to 12 hours.

USEFUL INFO

Most amenities can be found within a few blocks of Parque Caldas, Popayán's main plaza. Here you will find banks and ATMs, along with the **tourist police office**. There's a **post office** at Calle 4 no. 5–74.

While not known as an outdoor destination per se, Popayán makes a good base for exploring the nature of southern Colombia. **Popayán Tours**

Semana Santa in Popayán

Of all of the traditional celebrations in Colombia, Popayán's Holy Week festivities may be the most famous. The town fills up with both national and international tourists during the event and rooms are reserved months in advance, with dramatically higher prices. The most important processions take place on Maundy Thursday and Good Friday, where tens of thousands of worshipers crowd the city streets. In 1983, a violent earthquake hit Popayán just as the Maundy Thursday procession was about to begin. The roof of the Cathedral collapsed and many other historic buildings were damaged, killing hundreds. While the city has gone on to repair the damages, the tragic event has given the festivities added significance.

(www.popayantours.com) can arrange hot spring and cycling trips in Coconuco, climbs of the still active Puracé Volcano, and visits to the indigenous market in Silvia.

Exploring Popayán

Popayán's historic center is a masterpiece of colonial architecture; many of the most important buildings are within a few blocks of **Parque Caldas** (the main square) and can be seen in a day.

Casa Museo Edgar Negret ★ MUSEUM   The former home of Colombian artist Edgar Negret, who passed away in 2012, now serves as the city's modern art museum. Negret is best known for abstract iron sculptures that are found in public squares around Colombia. Art from Negret's private collection, which he donated to the city following the 1983 earthquake, are also on display, including an etching by Picasso that was stolen in 2011 but recovered a few months later.

Calle 5 no. 10–23. www.museonegret.wordpress.com. © **2/824-4546.** COP$2,500. Wed–Mon 8am–noon and 2pm–6pm.

Casa Museo Mosquera ★ CHURCH   This mansion turned museum once belonged to General Tomás Cipriano de Mosquera, who was the four-time president of Colombia from 1845 to 1867. Documents and photographs, alongside period furnishings, detail Mosquera's storied life. The urn in the wall is said to contain his heart.

Calle 3 no. 5–38. © **2/820-9900.** COP$2,200. Daily 9am–noon and 3–5pm.

Catedral ★ CHURCH   This impressive neoclassical cathedral on Parque Caldas dates to the second half of the 19th century. A former cathedral on the same site was destroyed in an earthquake.

Calle 5 at Carrera 2. Free admission.

Iglesia de San Francisco ★★ CHURCH   If you have time to see only one colonial church in Popayán, make it this one. Iglesia de San Francisco was completed in 1775 and replaced another one that was destroyed in a 1736 earthquake. This church is notable not only for its impressive size, but for its spectacular altars. During the 1983 earthquake a crack opened in the ossuary, which revealed six unidentified mummies. During guided tours of the church, several of the mummies can be seen enclosed in glass.

Carrera 9 at Calle 4. Guided tours COP$2,200.

Iglesia La Ermita ★ CHURCH   Dating to 1610, this is Popayán's oldest church, having survived earthquake after earthquake. There are lovely wood carvings, and the view of the city from the street outside is quite picturesque.

Calle 5 at Carrera 2. © **2/820-9725.** Free admission.

Museo Arquidiocesano de Arte Religioso ★ MUSEUM   Owned by the Popayán archdiocese, this 18th-century house is home to a vast collection of religious art that fills up 10 rooms. The collection, mostly of the Quiteño school, includes paintings, liturgical vessels, and various other pieces.

Calle 4 no. 4–56. ✆ **2/824-2759.** COP$5,000. Mon–Fri 9am–12:30pm and 2–6pm; Sat 9am–2pm.

Museo Guillermo Valencia ★ MUSEUM   Once home of the native poet Guillermo Valencia, whose son later became president, this late-18th-century building is something of a time capsule. Much of the original furniture and paintings still remain.

Carrera 6 no. 2–69. ✆ **2/824-1555.** Free admission. Tues–Sun 10am–noon and 2–5pm.

Museo de Historia Natural de la Universidad de Cauca ★ MUSEUM   The best natural history museum in southern Colombia was founded in 1936. Its collection of flora and fauna here is extensive, revealing the extent of Colombia's rich biodiversity. Birds are well represented, as are species of insects, butterflies, and mammals.

Carrera 2 no. 1A–25. www.museo.unicauca.edu.co. ✆ **2/820-9861.** COP$3,000. Daily 9am–noon and 2–5pm daily.

Puente del Humilladero ★ BRIDGE   At the west end of Calle 2, near the Rio Molino, this 11-arch brick bridge that dates to the mid-19th century is a symbol of the city, connecting the center to the neighborhoods in the north. Nearby is the older Puente de la Custodia, a stone bridge that gave priests access to the sick.

Where to Stay

Camino Real ★   Close to Parque Caldas, this colonial casona that dates to 1592 is defined by lots of fine woodwork and the clay tile floors that run through the common areas. The rooms, some with balconies, surround two courtyards and are a bit kitschy, with shiny tile floors and dark wood accents, though they have been immaculately maintained. The hotel restaurant (see p. 230) is one of the best in the entire region.

Calle 5 no. 5–59. www.hotelcaminoreal.com.co. ✆ **2/824-3595.** 28 units. COP$213,000 double, includes breakfast. **Amenities:** Restaurant; bar; free Wi-Fi.

Hotel Dann Monasterio ★★   Popayán's best hotel is set in a 16th-century Franciscan monastery adjacent to the Iglesia San Francisco. Despite being taken over by the upscale Dann chain, the hotel's historic architecture has been preserved. Throughout the property are fine hand-carved woodwork, gold-framed oil paintings, and elegant chandeliers. The rooms, which have carpeted floors and are decked out with antique furnishings, wrap around a huge stone courtyard. Some add furnished balconies, and suites have dining areas. The sprawling grounds, with beautifully manicured gardens and an outdoor pool, make the property feel like a city within the city.

Calle 4 no. 10–14. www.hotelesdann.com/dann-popayan. ✆ **2/824-2191.** 47 units. COP$436,000 double; COP$555,000 suite, includes buffet. **Amenities:** Restaurant; bar; outdoor pool; fitness center; sauna; event facilities; free Wi-Fi.

La Plazuela ★★   One block from Parque Caldas, this mid-18th-century casona was home to many illustrious residents of Popayán, such as the parents of former Ecuadorian president Carlos Arroyo del Río. After the 1983 earthquake it was turned into a hotel, retaining much of the original atmosphere, as well as antique furnishings and a stone courtyard. The rooms are more straightforward than common areas, with heavy dark wood furnishings and tile floors, plus flatscreen TVs and minibars. Some rooms add balconies. There's a small restaurant and bar on the ground floor. Overall, this is one of the best values in town.

Calle 5 no. 8–13. www.hotellaplazuela.com.co. ✆ **511/824-1084.** 27 units. COP$151,000 double, includes breakfast. **Amenities:** Restaurant; bar; business center; free Wi-Fi.

Where to Eat

Popayán is one of Colombia's gastronomic capitals, with countless traditional dishes originating here and still prepared in much the same way they were decades ago. Keep an eye out for *empanadas de pipián*, fried potato turnovers filled with a mildly spicy peanut sauce; *salpicón payanese*, a refreshing snack of blended ice and blackberries; and *champus*, a corn-based drink flavored with fruits like lulo and pineapple.

The city is host to the **Congreso Nacional Gastronómico** (www. gastronomicopopayan.org), a culinary event held each year in early September. Many of the country's premier chefs descend on the city to cook at special dinners held during the festival. Tastings of traditional dishes, gastronomy themed lectures and forums, and cooking competitions also take place.

Camino Real ★★ COLOMBIAN   The closest thing to what you might call fine dining in Popayán is this classic restaurant at the Camino Real hotel, which is heavily involved in the annual Congreso Nacional Gastronómico. The colonial-style dining room and bar have a clubby feel, with wood floors, lots of dark wood furnishings, and antique knickknacks hung up all over the place. The service here is as good as it gets in southern Colombia, and the menu of Colombian classics and a few modern interpretations is well executed. Try their Pacific-style *sopa de mariscos* or the pork ribs in a spicy pineapple sauce. The COP$55,000 set dinner menu—with several courses and dessert—is a steal.

Calle 5 no. 5–59. www.hotelcaminoreal.com.co. ✆ **2/824-3595.** Main courses COP$25,000–COP$40,000. Daily noon–3pm and 6–10pm.

Doña Chepa ★ COLOMBIAN   Directly beside Mora Castilla is this simple sweet shop in the corner of the house of Josefina Muñoz, better known as Doña Chepa, an iconic cook who has been serving her *aplanchados* more or less the same for some seventy years. Now in her 90s, her kids and grandchildren have taken over the business, producing the typical sweets.

Calle 2 n. 4–46. ✆ **2/824-0071.** Sweets COP$200–COP$500 each. Daily 7am–7pm.

La Cosecha Parrillada ★ STEAKHOUSE   This straightforward Colombian *parrillada* is one of the most popular dining destinations in town. There's nothing particularly Popayán-esque about it, though they have good beef, including a few cuts from Argentina, and serve lots of national plates like bandeja paisa and cazuelas. It's a rustic atmosphere with clunky wood tables and live music on some nights and weekends.

Calle 4 no. 7–79. www.lacosechaparrillada.com. © **2/824-3799.** Main courses COP$10,000–COP$25,000. Mon–Fri 11:30am–4pm.

La Fresa ★★ COLOMBIAN One of Popayán's must-do experiences is coming to this no-frills corner spot and ordering a plate of *empanadas de pipián*. These fried turnovers are made from corn and potatoes and are dipped into a mildly spicy peanut sauce. They're tiny, so ordering at least a half dozen is essential, and a dozen won't seem odd.

Calle 5 n. 8–89. © **2/211-006.** Empanadas COP$200 each. Daily 7am–7pm.

Mora Castilla ★★ COLOMBIAN This small, second-level cafe specializes in traditional Popayán recipes and does them well. At Mora Castilla you'll find *salpicón payanese* (an icy blackberry drink), *champus* (a corn, fruit, and panela drink), *tamales de pipián* (steamed corn dough with a peanut sauce), and *carantantas* (fried corn crisps). The ingredients are fresh and everything is made from scratch.

Calle 2 no. 4–44. www.moracastilla.com. © **2/824-1513.** Main courses COP$3,000–COP$4,000. Daily 9am–7pm.

Taller de Cocina la Escuela ★ COLOMBIAN Part of a school (with locations all over the country) designed to rescue Colombian patrimony, this student-run restaurant serves regional dishes in a lovely colonial building in the same plaza as Iglesia San Francisco. The quality of the food and service is surprisingly great. Set lunch menus with three courses plus a juice are just COP$9,000. The chairs and dining area were all designed by students in the same building.

Calle 4 no. 9–12, Plazuela San Francisco. © **2/429-8248.** Main courses COP$5,000–COP$12,000. Mon–Fri 11:30am–4pm.

Terra Inca ★ PERUVIAN/INTERNATIONAL Most of the food in Popayán comes from very classic, old-school recipes, so this modern Peruvian restaurant offers a nice change of pace. The menu has a few ceviches and seafood dishes, but it's not overwhelming, as many Peruvian restaurants tend to be. Instead they offer a more balanced approach with a lot of meat, potato, and rice based fare like *causa*, a layered potato terrine, and *lomo saltado*, stir fried beef with French fries.

Carrera 8 no. 13n–67. www.terraincarestaurante.com. © **2/836-1615.** Main courses COP$19,000–COP$25,000. Daily 11am–11pm.

Side Trips from Popayán

Popayán makes for a good base for the surrounding region. Up in the mountains about 30km outside of Popayán, on the road to San Agustín, is the village of **Coconuco**, where you will find two thermal springs. **Termales Aguatibia** (www.termalesaguatibia.com; admission COP$16,000), which as the name suggest is more warm than hot, is the more formal of the two and has a restaurant, plus basic lodging and camping facilities. The facility has six thermal pools, a mud bath, and a 53m-long toboggan ride. **Agua Hirviendo** (www.aguahirviendo1.wixsite.com/coconuco; admission COP$7,000), which stays open 24 hours on the weekends and can get wild in the evenings, has two pools and a natural sauna, plus a small restaurant.

About 53km northeast of Popayán is the town of **Silvia**, best known for its indigenous marketplace. The region is home to the Guambiano people, who live in mountain communities such as Pueblito, La Campana, and Caciques, and still retain their own language and traditional customs. Guambiano clothing is particularly distinctive, with men wearing blue skirts and bowler hats, while women wear finely woven *ruanas*, a sort of poncho, plus *chaquiras*, necklaces and wristbands made with elaborate beadwork. The women are known for their weaving, and they bring their work via colorful chiva buses to sell during Silvia's **Tuesday market ★★**, alongside the produce the communities have grown. It's not a tourist market by any means—it's one of the most authentic in all of Colombia. If you don't have your own transportation, you can catch a bus from Popayán's terminal in the early morning for the 1½-hour ride. The market begins at dawn, so it's best to get there as early as you can. It fizzles out by early afternoon. There are some small guesthouses in town, though most come just for a day trip.

The 830-sq.-km national park **Parque Nacional Natural Puracé** is one of the only places in all of Colombia you can see the Andean condor, which has been gradually introduced here from California zoos. Spectacled bears and mountain tapirs can also be seen. Declared a UNESCO Biosphere Reserve in 1979, the park is home to a string of volcanic mountains, called the Serrania Coconucos, which stand as high as 5,000m and form the headwaters of several of Colombia's most important rivers, such as the Magdalena, Cauca, and Patia. The rare páramo landscape seems surreal, with forests of strange-looking cacti and a wet, thick fog hanging throughout the park. Most visitors see Puracé while driving from Popayán to San Agustín, a bumpy route that cuts right through the park. During good weather, usually from December to March, it's possible to ascend the steep summit of Volcán Puracé (4,750m/15,600 ft.), which takes about 8 hours roundtrip. **Popayán Tours** (www.popayantours.com) can set up guided excursions with transportation to and from the trail. Admission to the park is COP$10,000.

SAN AGUSTÍN ★★★

135km (84 miles) SE of Popayán

San Agustín is home to the largest group of megalithic sculptures in South America, making it the most important pre-Columbian archaeological site between Peru and Guatemala. These statues, carved from volcanic rock, representing gods and mythical creatures, are probably the reason you are willing to spend a very long, rough car ride from Popayán to get here, though they

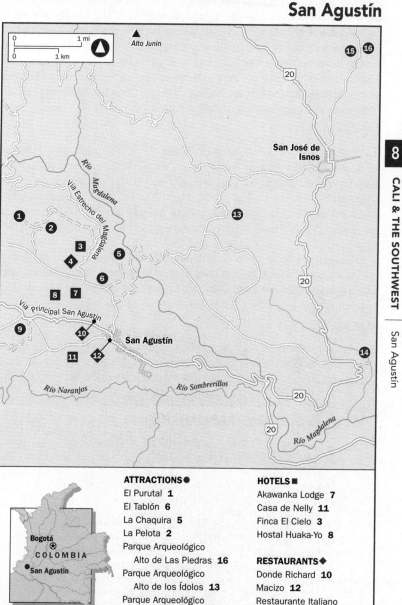

0 1 mi
0 1 km

▲ Alto Junin

San José de
Isnos

San Agustín

Vía Magdalena

Vía Estrecho del Magdalena

Vía Principal San Agustín

Río Naranjos

Río Sombrerillos

Río Magdalena

ATTRACTIONS●
El Purutal **1**
El Tablón **6**
La Chaquira **5**
La Pelota **2**
Parque Arqueológico
  Alto de Las Piedras **16**
Parque Arqueológico
  Alto de los Ídolos **13**
Parque Arqueológico
  de San Agustín **9**
Salto de Borodones **15**
Salto de Mortiño **14**

HOTELS■
Akawanka Lodge **7**
Casa de Nelly **11**
Finca El Cielo **3**
Hostal Huaka-Yo **8**

RESTAURANTS◆
Donde Richard **10**
Macizo **12**
Restaurante Italiano
  da Ugo **4**

Bogotá
⊗
COLOMBIA
● San Agustín

may not be the only reason you decide to stay. The colonial town that forms the base of explorations for the region is rather charming, with cobblestone streets and a lively marketplace. Accommodations are attractive and inexpensive. The weather is like spring every day. Most importantly, the natural beauty surrounding the town and archaeological site is absolutely incredible. There are misty green hills lined with coffee plantations, and steep cliffs drip with waterfalls hundreds of meters high. There are few tourists to be seen, and horses are a primary method of transportation to some attractions.

Essentials

The hardest part of San Agustín is getting there. The road from Popayán, while dramatically crossing the páramo of Parque Nacional Natural Puracé, is rough and slow, taking about five hours. Other options are to come from Tierradentro (5 hr.) or Nieva (4 hr.), though roads can be just as bad to those cities. Bus companies in San Agustín congregate around Calle 3 and Carrera 11 near the market. Several have direct buses to Bogotá (11 hr.) in the early morning or evening.

San Agustín's small plaza is officially the center of town, and the narrow grid of streets runs from the southeast to the northwest. A **tourist information office** is in the Casa de Cultura, at Calle 11 and Carrera 8, while several ATMs can be found in town, though they are often out of cash.

What to Do

Seeing the main archaeology park in San Agustín is relatively simple, because it's close to town and public transportation and taxis can easily get you there. The other attractions require some advance planning. You'll need about 2 days

who WERE THE SAN AGUSTÍN?

Archaeologists are still piecing together the origins of the early culture that developed as far back as 5,000 years ago in Colombia's southern Andes, at the headwaters of the Magdalena and Cauca rivers near present-day San Agustín. The chiefdom society reached its peak from around the 1st to the 9th centuries, leaving behind remnants of large burial mounds surrounded by terraces and connected by walkways. Tombs, often marked by the famed statues ranging between 1 and 7 meters high and some weighing more than a ton, sometimes contained stone columns, sarcophagi, and stone corridors. There are about 600 total statues that have been discovered,

and most of them are found within the archaeological park and its environs. It's believed that the culture abandoned the sites around A.D. 1350, and no one is exactly sure why. There was no written language, and there weren't gold artifacts like with the Tayrona and other important pre-Columbian cultures in the region. Due to the remote location, it wasn't until the 18th and 19th centuries that they were rediscovered. While looters sometimes reached the tombs first, the archaeological park was established early on, in 1931, providing reliable protection and ensuring that someday the mystery of who the San Agustín were might be revealed.

to see everything; with 3 days you'll be able to go at a much more leisurely pace.

Parque Arqueológico de San Agustín ★★★ ARCHAEOLOGICAL SITE

This 78-hectare archaeological park, a UNESCO World Heritage Site, forms the core concentration of stone statues left behind by the mysterious San Agustín culture. More than 130 statues are here, some brought from other sites, and they are spread out in four main clusters called *mesitas*, as well as along a short forest trail called the Bosque de las Estatuas, with statues brought from around the region. One of the most interesting sites in the park is the covered site of **Fuente de Lavapatas**, a ceremonial complex of pools and bas-reliefs (faces, snakes, and lizards) carved into a rocky stream. On a hill above the complex is the Alto de Lavapatas, the oldest archaeological site in the park, which dates back some 5,000 years.

Upon entering the park, walk through the small **Museo Arqueológico**, which has some minor statues and various artifacts found in the tombs. It's a good introduction to the San Agustín and the origins of the statues.

Guides can be hired at the entrance—they'll likely find you first—for around COP$70,000 per group. Plan on spending around three hours in the park. Be sure to bring a rain jacket, sunblock, and water, not to mention good walking shoes. There is parking on site, though you can easily come by taxi or bus from town, which is 2.5km (1½ miles) to the east. Your admission to the archaeological park also gets you into the Alto de los **Ídolos** site either that day or the next, so be sure to keep the "passport" that they give you.

2.5km west of San Agustín. www.icanh.gov.co. COP$20,000 adult; COP$10,000 student; COP$5,000 child. Daily 8am–5pm (last tickets sold at 4pm).

Parque Arqueológico Alto de los Ídolos ★★ ARCHAEOLOGICAL SITE

This impressive site is on the other side of the Magdalena, higher up in the hills outside the town of Isnos. From the entrance, where there's a small museum and a few snacks bars and souvenir stalls, a steep path climbs up to a clearing with several hills set with various statues and tombs, all of which can be seen in about an hour. One impressive anthropomorphic statue measures 4.3 meters (14 ft.), the largest in the area.

The same ticket here gets you into the Parque Arqueológico de San Agustín. Reaching this site is convenient if you have your own transportation and you are on your way to or from Popayán; otherwise, your best option is to join a jeep tour that takes in the park and other attractions. Public transportation is non-existent.

8km (5 miles) SW of Isnos. www.icanh.gov.co. COP$20,000 adult; COP$10,000 student; COP$5,000 child. Daily 8am–5pm (last tickets sold at 4pm).

Parque Arqueológico Alto de Las Piedras ★ ARCHAEOLOGICAL SITE

On the road to the Salto de Borodones waterfall, this small archaeological site has a few statues and tombs, notable for their original red, black, and yellow pigments.

6km (4 miles) N of Isnos. www.icanh.gov.co. Free admission. Daily 8am–5pm.

El Tablón, La Chaquira, La Pelota, and El Purutal ★ ARCHAEO-LOGICAL SITE   In the hills around San Agustín are these four smaller archaeological sites that lack road access and are rather close to each other. While walking to each is possible with a good map, nearly everyone that visits these sites does so on a horseback-riding tour (see below). Each site is unique. La Chaquira, at the edge of a gorge overlooking the Magdalena, features a bas-relief sculpted in rock, while El Purutal has two statues that still have much of their original pigment. There are no facilities at any of these sites, so plan accordingly.

Free admission.

OUTDOOR ACTIVITES

HORSEBACK RIDING ★★   Nearly every hotel and hostel can set up a horseback riding trip to archaeological sites in the hills outside of town, as well as to waterfalls and the Lagunda de Magdalena, a 3-day trip to the birth-place of the Magdalena River. Usually it's just a guy with some horses, so if you are looking for an English-speaking guide, be sure to specify. Prices vary depending on your exact needs, though expect to pay around COP$40,000 to COP$60,000 per half-day per rider.

JEEP TOURS ★   Similar to the horseback riding tours, jeep trips will bring you to the remote archaeological sites, for around COP$150,000 to COP$200,000 per group. If you are a single traveler, you can usually just join a group to cut down on cost. All of the agencies in town tend to pool together.

WATERFALLS ★★   Several stunning waterfalls can be seen near San Agustín, in the upper Magdalena River gorge on the way to Isnos. The 400-meter (1,300-ft.) **Salto de Borodones** is the most impressive, though the 200-meter (650-ft.) **Salto de Mortiño** is also quite spectacular. Both can be seen from the road, though several horseback riding tours will bring you much closer.

WHITEWATER RAFTING ★   **Magdalena Rafting** (www.viajes-colombia.com, ✆ **311/271-5333**), at Calle 5 no. 16–04 offers a range of whitewater rafting excursions on the Magdalena River. Tours range from half-day excursions on Class II to III rapids (COP$75,000 person) to full-day trips on Class V rapids (COP$175,000 person).

Where to Stay

While several hotels can be found right in town, most of the better options are on the road to the ruins or in the surrounding countryside.

Akawanka Lodge ★★   The most formal lodging in the San Agustín area is this resort-style lodge situated in the hills on the outskirts of town. The beautifully landscaped property is surrounded by organic gardens and tropical foliage. Clean, rustic rooms have wood floors, tree trunk tables, and animal skin rugs, plus colorful paintings of local birds and animals directly on the white walls. Each has a balcony or terrace access. After dinner, you can retreat to the fire pit with a glass of wine while telling travel tales with other guests. The tour desk can arrange mountain biking, hiking, horseback riding, and photo expeditions in the area.

Vereda El Tablon. www.hotelakawankalodge.com. ✆ **1/450-1377.** 5 units. COP$350,000 double, includes breakfast. **Amenities:** Restaurant; cafe; bar; tour desk; free Wi-Fi.

Casa de Nelly ★　San Agustín's original backpacker haunt has been luring travelers to southern Colombia since 1982. Rooms are quite basic, with plank-wood floors, thin walls, and windows looking out to a central garden area. The owners will rent out mountain bikes, which are good for getting around the archaeological sites.

Vereda La Estrella. ✆ **1/489-9269.** 11 units. COP$80,000 double w/private bathroom; COP$50,000 w/shared bathrooms, includes breakfast. **Amenities:** Shared kitchen; BBQ area; free Wi-Fi.

Finca El Cielo ★　This family-run, tropical finca with clay-tiled roofs, whitewashed walls, and bamboo railings has spectacular views over the green hills and gorge. An open-air lounge and restaurant sit on the ground level, while the simple rooms, which open from the outside, sit on two floors in an adjacent building. A very chic four-person suite adds cow-skin rugs, an LCD TV, and a large furnished balcony. It's on the road to El Estretcho, a spot where the Magdalena is at its narrowest. You'll need your own transportation there; otherwise contact the owners about the setting up transfers.

Via Estrecho del Magdalena Km 3. www.fincaelcielo.com. ✆ **313/493-7446.** 5 units. COP$140,000 double; COP$350,000 suite, includes breakfast. **Amenities:** Restaurant; bar; tours; free Wi-Fi.

Hostal Huaka-Yo ★　Two-hundred meters down the road from the archaeological park, this beautiful little hotel is in a two-level colonial-style building with a tin roof and wraparound terraces strung with hammocks. It's set in its own gated compound, with a sprawling lawn surrounded by lush plants and a good-sized restaurant that stays open until 9pm with typical dishes. The rooms are rather plain, though well kept, plus they have hot water and decent Wi-Fi.

200m from the archaeological park (take the dirt road that veers right at the entrance). www.huakayo.com. ✆ **1/489-9269.** 12 units. COP$150,000 double, includes breakfast. **Amenities:** Restaurant; bar; free Wi-Fi.

Where to Eat

Donde Richard ★★ COLOMBIAN　Set amid a string of open-sided parrillas on the road to the archaeological park, Donde Richard stands out for its big portions and commitment to local recipes. Meat, in many forms, is the emphasis here. My personal favorite is the *lomo de cerdo ahumado*, the smoked pork, which comes with a side of fried potatoes and plantains.

Vía al Parque Arqueológico. ✆ **2/432-6399.** Main courses COP$20,000–COP$30,000. Wed–Mon 8am–6pm.

Macizo ★ CAFE   This small cafe on the plaza serves *arepas* and light meals, as well as a long list of coffee drinks using local beans. It has a couple of sidewalk seats, while inside there's an earthy vibe with reddish beige tile floors, lots of plants, and chairs made from bamboo.

On the Plaza. Coffees COP$3,000–COP$6,000. Daily 8am–8pm.

Restaurante Italiano da Ugo ★ ITALIAN   The town tends to shut down after sunset, so dinner in San Agustín is usually limited to a few pizza spots and hotel restaurants. One exception is this Italian restaurant about one kilometer from the center. There is a list of standard house-made pasta dishes, as well as bruschetta and some vegetarian plates. On the weekends there is usually live music.

Via Al Estrecho del Magdalena Km 1. © **314/375-8086.** Main courses COP$25,000–COP$35,000. Tues–Fri noon–3pm and 6–9pm; Sat–Sun noon–9pm.

TIERRADENTRO ★★

If you think San Agustín feels empty, wait until you go to Tierradentro. Few tourists make it to this remote archaeological site, Colombia's second-most important. While San Agustín is known for its statues, Tierradentro is known for its more than 100 *hypogeum*, underground tombs that date from the 6th to the 10th century. These burial chambers can measure as much as 12m wide and are carved out of volcanic rock. The walls of many of them are painted with red and black geometric motifs. They are unlike anything else found in the Americas, and the culture that built them disappeared, leaving little record as to who they were. While the tombs show some similarities to the ruins at San Agustín, they are believed to have been built by distinct cultures.

Essentials

The primary route to Tierradentro is from Popayán. Expect a very slow, bumpy 4-hour drive. Buses arrive/depart at the El Crucero de San Andrés, a 20-minute walk from the museums, though some go straight to the tiny town of San Andrés de Pisimbalá, 4km away.

Facilities in Tierradentro and the adjacent town of San Andrés de Pisimbalá are slim. There are no banks or tourist information office. Bring all cash and any other non-basic supplies you might need with you.

What to See

Parque Arqueológico Tierradentro ★★★ ARCHAEOLOGICAL SITE
The archaeological park contains five main burial sites, which are spread out on a 14km loop from the main entrance. All five sites can be seen in 1 day, though most spread it out over 2 (tickets are good for 2 consecutive days). Upon entering and receiving your wristband you will come to two museums: the **Museo Etnográfico** and the **Museo Arqueológico**. The Museo Etnográfico focuses on the Paez culture, an indigenous group that of around 25,000 who are not believed to be related to the tomb builders. The Museo Arqueológico

centers on the tombs themselves, with models of tombs and funerary urns. Both help shed some understanding on what you will soon see, especially helpful since there is practically no information out on the trail.

From the museums, walk counterclockwise toward **Segovia**, which is about a 20-minute uphill hike. This is the most important site in Tierradentro. There are several dozen tombs here, most decorated with red, black, and white patterns and figures. These tombs are some of the best preserved. Continue on another 20 minutes to **El Duende**, which has just four tombs. Another 25 minutes on is **El Tablón**, where there are nine badly deteriorated stone statues that look similar to the ones found in San Agustín (though they were built centuries later). Continue until you reach the restaurant La Portada in town, where you can have lunch or hop on the trail that runs along the side of the restaurant to **Alto de San Andrés**, 10 minutes away. There are six very well-preserved tombs here with still visible wall paintings. The path continues on to **El Aguacate**, the farthest site, about 1½ hours away (plus another 1½ hours to walk back to the main entrance). The views of the valley below are stunning and there are several dozen tombs, which are in various states of ruin but have some unique styles of wall paintings. Keep in mind that very few of the tombs have lighting, so be sure to bring a flashlight.

www.icanh.gov.co. COP$20,000 adult; COP$10,000 student; COP$5,000 child. Daily 8am–4pm.

Where to Stay

Several small budget hotels and eateries are clustered above the museums, though you'll find better facilities in San Andrés de Pisimbalá. **La Portada Hospedaje** (http://laportadahotel.com; © 1/601-7884; COP$50,000 double), right near where the bus stops, has five rooms with modern bathrooms with hot water, and rates include breakfast. They can also set up guides and horses to explore the park. **Hotel El Refugio** (hotelalbergueelrefugio@gmail.com; © 1/811-2395; COP$80,000 double) is rather basic, though at its center is a nice pool and garden.

DESIERTO DE TATACOA ★★

The second-largest desert in Colombia after the Guajira Peninsula is one of the most unique ecosystems in the country. It was named the Valley of Sorrows by conquistador Gonzalo Jiménez de Quesada when he stumbled upon it in 1538. The landscape of eroded cliffs and canyons is home to a rare tropical dry forest that covers some 330 sq. km. Within the desert are a handful of smaller micro-regions like Los Hoyos, which is characterized by gray clay, and the ochre-colored Cusco with its many strange rock formations. Fauna like alligators, eagles, snakes, and scorpions have adapted to the high heat and low humidity here. Cacti can grow as high as 5m. It's an odd place, but because of the dry, clear conditions and little light pollution, the Tatacoa makes for an excellent place to see the stars of both hemispheres.

Essentials

The Tatacoa Dessert is far from anywhere, though it makes a great detour if you are driving between Bogotá and San Agustín. Its best accessed through Villavieja, a 45-minute minibus ride from Neiva on the Magdalena River, the capital of the Huila department. From Villavieja, you can negotiate with taxis and moto drivers to take you out into the desert.

There is very little tourist infrastructure to speak of when visiting the Tatacoa Desert. There is one bank with an ATM, as well as a few basic *hospedajes* and campsites in and around Villavieja, though none are particularly recommended. You will find better options in Nieva.

What to See

Aside from the museum and observatory listed below, most fill their visit here simply driving out into the desert—there's just one main road—to explore the wild scenery. The Cusco area has several viewpoints, like the **Laberintos del Cusco** near the observatory and **Ventanas** 4km on, that look over the red rock formations that seem much more Utah than South America. At **Los Hoyos,** there is a strategically placed swimming hole fed by a natural spring that is the perfect cool-off point during the blazing heat of the day.

Museo Paleontológico ★ MUSEUM   The Tatacoa Desert was filled with lush vegetation millions of years ago, before it dried out. Paleontologists are actively excavating fossils, such as giant armadillos and sloths, plus crabs and fish—the remains of which are on display at this museum on Villavieja's main plaza.

Plaza. ☏ **314/347-6812.** COP$2,000. Daily 8:30am–noon and 2–5pm.

Observatorio Astronómico de la Tatacoa ★ MUSEUM   This small observatory is open to the public every evening when a local astronomer shares several telescopes to look up in the sky.

El Cusco. www.tatacoa-astronomia.com. ☏ **312/411-8166.** COP$10,000. Daily 7–9pm.

Where to Stay & Eat

There are a few basic *hospedajes* and campsites in and around Villavieja, and most are not particularly recommended. One exception is **Hotel Boutique Yarayaka** ★ (hotelyarayaka@gmail.com; ☏ **313/247-0165**), at Carrera 4 no. 4–43. This surprisingly chic 12-room property in the center of town has white-washed walls, a thatched roof, and contemporary rooms. All have private bathrooms and good Wi-Fi. Best of all there's an outdoor pool with lounge chairs, which helps make up for the lack of air-conditioning. Doubles COP$150,000.

Another option is **El Peñon de Constantino** ★ (www.desiertodelatatacoa colombia.com; ☏ **317/698-8850**), a collection of cushy safari-style tents with private bathrooms and running water, as well as basic cabins and thatched-roof *malokas*. There's a simple restaurant on-site and a rock-wall pool fed by a natural spring. They can also help coordinate excursions in the desert. It's about 2km beyond the observatory. Tents costs COP$80,000 for two, while the cabins, *malokas*, and camping are considerably less.

THE PACIFIC COAST

by Nicholas Gill

Off limits to most travelers for decades until just a few years ago, Colombia's Pacific Coast is a natural paradise just waiting to be discovered. This is some of Colombia's most spectacular landscape. It's here that jagged hills covered in dense, tropical foliage meet the Pacific in dramatic fashion. El Chocó, as the northern half of the region is called, is one of the wettest places on earth, though that doesn't stop adventurous tourists from camping out in a growing number of small eco-lodges perched on rocky bluffs or pristine black- or white-sand beaches. They take surf lessons, fish for big game, or go whale-watching. To the south, Colombia's largest port, Buenaventura, once a dreadful place to spend the night, is even coming around with some good places to stay and eat. The vibe up and down the coast is less mestizo and gravitates more toward the Afro-Colombian and indigenous groups that call this region their home. Visiting isolated communities that still cling on to their traditions is just a hop on a canoe or makeshift motorcycle-powered rail cart away.

Much of the human history on the Pacific Coast is relatively recent. Maroon communities of escaped slaves, and later Free Towns, began to appear in the 17th century, setting up in the rugged rainforest where few others would go. It wasn't until the 1930s that reliable road connections reached **Buenaventura**, but after that the port quickly grew and tourism followed soon after. During the Civil War the region was mostly avoided, though it's finally starting to come back.

El Chocó is rich with unique cultures that have changed little in hundreds of years. In the interior, indigenous groups such as the Emberá still live traditional hunting and gathering lifestyles. In Buenaventura, locals play the *marimba de chonta*, an instrument with African origins made from a spiny palm tree, and dance the El Currulao. In **San Cipriano**, far from any roads, locals have created a system of motorcycle-driven rail carts called *brujitas* to zip them through the jungle to the nearest town.

But make no mistake about it, nature dominates here. Many visitors to the Pacific are surprised just how much lush greenery is around them. The mountains and dense jungles, mostly uninhabited and untrammeled, force themselves right to the edge of the Pacific, like at **Parque Nacional Utría**, where you can kayak through narrow canals inhabited by kingfishers and herons, plus search for glow-in-the-dark mushrooms and hike to secluded beaches.

The entire coast is thick with trees teeming with wildlife. Tiny crabs scatter beside your every step. Howler monkeys and green macaws chatter from the treetops. Humpback whales congregate close enough to the shore near **Nuquí** that you can often see them from the beach from late July to October. Join a fishing expedition in **Bahía Solano** and within an hour you'll be trying to reel in marlin, sailfish, and yellowfin tuna.

While many are content to lie on the beach, the adventure contingent runs strong on the Pacific Coast. Most lodges offer hikes into the jungle to search for birds, butterflies, and waterfalls. If it's sportfishing you are after, the sea near Bahía Solano is rich with big game. Whale-watching is best in Nuquí or **Juanchaco**. If you are looking to dive, UNESCO World Heritage Site **Isla Malpelo** is one of the most renowned destinations on the planet. You'll swim with giant grouper, billfish, and hundreds of hammerhead sharks off this remote island some 500 kilometers off Colombia's coast.

BUENAVENTURA ★

124km (76 miles) W of Cali

The largest port city on Colombia's Pacific Coast, mostly contained on the small island of Cascajal, is not the drab place it once was. It's still rough around the edges, sure, but with posh new hotels and hip restaurants it's slowly returning to the days of the 1950s, when the international jet set would swing by. Founded on July 14, 1540 by Juan de Ladrilleros, Buenaventura remained a coastal backwater until the opening of the Panama Canal in 1914 and the arrival of interior connections in the 1930s. The population has ballooned to more than 400,000, and the port accounts for 60% of all exports and imports to Colombia. Still, while some have gotten rich, this is one of the country's poorest cities. While tourist areas are generally safe, the drug trade and gang violence flare up at times in outer neighborhoods. City leaders and business owners are pushing for change, like the construction of pedestrian streets and waterfront parks. Sunbathers are returning to nearby beaches, and whale-watching tours are filling up.

Essentials
GETTING THERE
BY PLANE Buenaventura's small airport, **Gerardo Tobar López** (© 312/8254233) is about 30 minutes outside of the city center. **Satena** (www.satena.com) offers infrequent flights from Bogotá and Medellín.

BY ROAD Buenaventura is the only town of any size with a road connection to it. It's easily reached on good roads and tunnels through mountainous,

The Pacific Coast

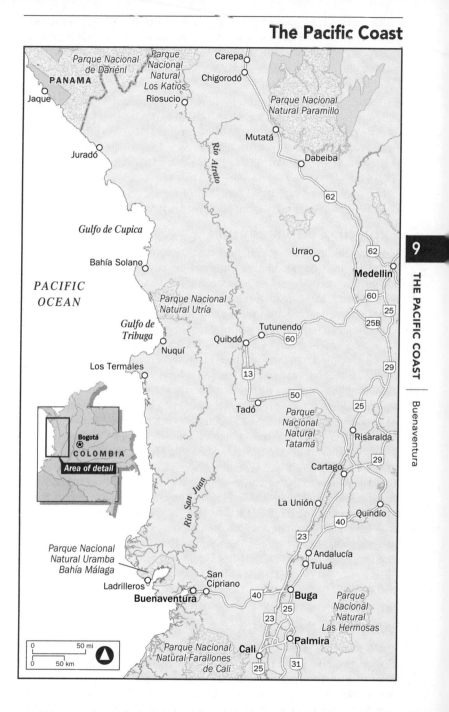

PANAMA

Jaque

Parque Nacional de Dariénl

Parque Nacional Natural Los Katios

Riosucio

Juradó

Carepa

Chigorodó

Parque Nacional Natural Paramillo

Mutatá

Dabeiba

62

Gulfo de Cupica

Bahía Solano

PACIFIC OCEAN

Río Atrato

Urrao

62

Medellin

60

25

25B

Parque Nacional Natural Utría

Tutunendo

Gulfo de Tribuga

Nuquí

Quibdó

60

29

Los Termales

13

50

25

Tadó

Parque Nacional Natural Tatamá

Risaralda

Bogotá

COLOMBIA

Area of detail

Cartago

29

La Unión

Quindío

Río San Juan

40

23

Parque Nacional Natural Uramba Bahía Málaga

Andalucía

Tuluá

Ladrilleros

San Cipriano

Buenaventura

40

Buga

Parque Nacional Natural Las Hermosas

25

23

0   50 mi

0   50 km

Parque Nacional Natural Farallones de Cali

Cali

Palmira

31

25

rainforest-covered terrain on a 3- to 4-hour drive from Cali. Bus and microbus connections with companies such as **Expreso Palmira** (www.expresopalmira. com.co; ✆ **321/890-3597**) and **Corredor del Pacifico** (✆ **2/1701-5633**) run between the two cities throughout the day. The terminal is at the corner of Carrera 5 and Calle 7, in the city center.

BY BOAT   There aren't any cruise ships plying these waters, at least not yet, but cargo boats make the trip north to Nuquí and Bahía Solano, a rough 18- to 24-hour trip. Ask around at the Muelle Turistico (see below) for leads. Here you can also find fast boats to the nearby beach destinations of Juanchaco and Ladrilleros (COP$54,000), a short ride north of the city, or Isla Gorgona (COP$280,000).

There are several **ATMS**, as well as pharmacies, around and within a few blocks of the Bulevar, the central plaza bordered by the city's best hotels.

Exploring Buenaventura

Most tourists in Buenaventura will contain themselves within a few-block area downtown surrounding the **Bulevar**, the city's main plaza. There's the **Muelle Turistico**, the rickety tourist pier (COP$4,500 admission) that makes for a pleasant walk. Artisan stalls hawking handicrafts made from coconuts, honey, and *viche* (the local aguardiente) line the route there.

A 25-minute boat ride away from Buenaventura, outside of the bay, are the towns of **Juanchaco and Ladrilleros ★**. Juanchaco, facing the bay, is less pleasant, while Ladrilleros is directly on the Pacific coast and has better beaches and good waves for surfers (Aug–Nov), attracting weekenders from Cali. Both are within easy reach of **Parque Nacional Natural Uramba Bahía Málaga**, a coastal reserve that was turned into a national park in 2010. Most come here between June and October, when the humpback whales come to breed just off shore. **Whale-watching tours ★★** can be arranged at hotels in Ladrilleros, or from the agencies beside the Muelle Turistico in Buenaventura, for around COP$50,000 per person.

Many visitors to Buenaventura skip the city entirely and opt to stay on the beach in Ladrilleros at the family-friendly **Reserva Aquamarine** (www.reserva aguamarina.com; ✆ **1/728-3213**; doubles COP$110,000, including all meals), with basic but clean rooms with balconies, not to mention a restaurant, pool, and numerous tours options. There's also **Papagayos Beach Hotel** (www. hotelenladrilleros.com; ✆ **2/551-8505**; doubles from COP$114,000, including all meals), or **Hotel Pacific Blue** (www.hotelpacificblueladrilleros.com; ✆ **2/667-6521**; doubles from COP$75,000, including all meals), both with simple rooms and cabins with air-conditioning and private bathrooms.

Where to Stay & Eat

Café Pacifico ★★★ COLOMBIAN   The owner of this excellent second-floor eatery, one of the best regional restaurants in all of Colombia, calls it more of a social experiment than a restaurant. Rarely seen Afro-Colombian recipes like *atollao*, a soulful seafood stew, and *encocao de munchílla*, made with local river shrimp, are immaculately researched and served according to tradition. Be sure to sip on *viche*, the local *uguardiente*, which they have macerating in different regional herbs and fruits, to use in cocktails or to be taken straight.

Calle 1, 5a–15. ☏ **2/241-3428.** Main courses COP$24,000–COP$40,000. Mon–Sat 10am–midnight.

Cosmos Pacifico Hotel ★★   What's this modern high-rise tower aligned with Hilton hotels and filled with cool architectural features—a circular lobby staircase, a glass fronted wave-like facade, and a rooftop infinity pool—doing in the middle of Buenaventura? Surely, they are preparing for the tourist boom that is on its way. The stylish rooms feature light woods and aquatic tones and are equipped with state-of-the-art electronics and mod furnishings. Each has a balcony with harbor or city views. There are restaurants on the ground floor and rooftop, not to mention a fitness center adorning a steam room. Whale-watching packages tend to be a good bargain during the season.

Calle 3, 1a–57. www.cosmospacificohotel.com. ☏ **1/644-4000.** 100 units. COP$290,000 double, COP$350,000 suite, includes breakfast. **Amenities:** 2 restaurants; 2 pools; bar; business center; salon; free W-Fi.

Escuela Taller Buenaventura Restaurant ★ COLOMBIAN   Inside the former rail station beside the square, this student-run restaurant is in a school created to rescue cultural patrimony. It serves inexpensive meals based on regional recipes.

Calle 2, 1a–07. www.escuelataller.org. ☏ **2/414-449.** Main courses COP$8,000–COP$15,000. Mon–Sat noon–4pm.

Hotel Tequendama Inn Estación ★   Dating to the 1920s, the Estación is a throwback to the days when Buenaventura was catching on with the wealthy and fabulous. On the seafront and across from the much more modern Cosmos, the white neocolonial hotel makes for a striking contrast with its hanging chandeliers and wraparound verandas. The rooms feature louvered doors and tile floors, retaining the classic ambience even with LCD TVs.

Calle 2, #1a–8. www.hotelestequendama.com. ☏ **2/243-4070.** 78 units. COP$160,000 double, includes breakfast. **Amenities:** Restaurant; bar; outdoor pool; free Wi-Fi.

A Side Trip to San Cipriano ★★

This Afro-Colombian village with a population of about 450 people sits deep within a lush, green tropical forest reserve, adjacent to a clear river perfect for floating in rented inner tubes. There are small restaurants with typical dishes like *encocadas de jaiba* (coconut crab stew) and *pargo frito* (fried red snapper). Locals sell homemade *viche* from path-side stalls. San Cipriano is a beautiful, pristine place with an atmosphere all of its own. There's only one problem: There are no roads there. However, there is a railroad track that passes right to the edge of town. So, locals figured out how to jerry-rig motorcycles on to rickety rail platforms and these *brujitas* (little witches) zip a handful of passengers at a time through the jungle for the 30-minute ride. When another cart is coming, one of the carts needs to be pulled off the track and everyone gets out as it passes. It's one of the most unique and exhilarating experiences anywhere in South America. To reach the *brujitas*, you need to drive to the town of Córdoba, about 20km from Buenaventura. Once there, you need to go downhill about one kilometer to the tracks. Someone will approach quickly offering their *brujita*. Expect to haggle, though you should be paying around COP$8,000 each way (note: locals pay much less). You can park for around COP$10,000 per day, though again, expect to haggle. Once in San Cipriano, there's a COP$2,000 fee per tourist.

BAHÍA SOLANO ★

59km (36⅔ miles) N of Nuquí; 199km (125 miles) W of Medellín

Many visitors hardly step foot off the tarmac at Bahía Solano's tiny airport before hopping on a fishing boat or going to **El Valle**, about 22km (14 miles) away. It's the sport-fishing capital of Colombia, and a high percentage of the visitors here come for that purpose and that purpose only. But Bahía Solano makes for a good base for surfing and lounging on nearby beaches, joining whale-watching tours, and exploring **Parque Nacional Utría**. The town itself, sitting at the mouth of the Río Jella, is one of the largest in the Chocó Pacific, though without roads leading to it, there's still that frontier vibe running through.

El Valle, a mototaxi (COP$15,000) ride down the area's one paved road, is a laidback beach and surf community on the southern side of the peninsula. The wide black-sand beach of **Playa Almejal** on the western edge of town is home to several small eco-lodges (see p. 248) and makes a good base for exploring the area. Sea turtles nest here from September to December, when the town fills up with volunteers. The surfing here is superb, some of the best in Colombia. Ask around for the trail to **El Tigre**, a waterfall that's a 30-minute hike from town (COP$5,000 admission).

Essentials

Satena (www.satena.com; ✆ 1/605-2222) offers five weekly **flights** to Bahía Solano from Medellín, and less frequently from Bogotá. Fights are often canceled because of weather. Luggage is limited to 15 kilos.

There are speed **boats** twice a week between El Valle and Nuquí on Mondays and Fridays. The trip lasts about one hour and costs COP$65,000. Ask your hotel to arrange a pick up.

There are a few ATMs in Bahía Solano and El Valle, though they are frequently out of money, so make sure you bring whatever money you need with you. Several agencies in town offer a variety of **tours**, including deep-sea fishing, whale-watching, surfing, and hiking. I recommend **Pacifico Tours** (www.pacificotours.com; ✆ 300/513-5916) in town, though most hotels in El Valle will also offer packages if fishing or whale-watching is what you are after.

During low tide you can walk to **Playa Mecana** ★ from town, though it's quicker to take a boat there when the water is high (45 min., COP$60,000 per boat; ask at your hotel to set up). It's a long, wild beach fringed with palm trees and is home to the 170-hectare nature reserve **Jardín Botánico del Pacífico** (www.jardinbotanicodelpacifico.org; ✆ **321/759-9012**), which includes patches of tropical rainforest, mangroves, and a native reforestation project. One-time Emberá hunters are now the guides and give tours (from COP$15,000) ranging from 2 to 9 hours on the four different trails. There are a few rustic cabins, plus packages with transportation from the airport.

Perhaps the most impressive national park—not to mention most accessible—on Colombia's entire Pacific Coast, **Parque Nacional Utría** ★ is situated approximately halfway between Bahía Solano and Nuquí. The 54,000-hectare reserve is home to tropical forest, mangroves, and sheltered coves with untrammeled beaches where whales come to play. Several trails lead from the visitor center, the easiest being a wooden walkway over the mangroves. There are three nice wooden cabins (COP$200,000 per person, including meals and use of kayaks) on site, each with three rooms, which will allow you to stay in the park after closing to search for glow-in-the-dark fungi. From late July to October, Utría is one of the best places to see whales in the Pacific—you can occasionally see them right in the lagoon in front of the cabins.

Costs can add up coming here for a short trip, as transportation costs roughly COP$300,000 per person roundtrip, from either the Bahía Solano or Nuquí. Entrance is COP$37,500. The park is open daily 8am to 5pm. You can contact the visitor center (✆ **310/793-7664**) for any additional information. They will even help you find a boat.

OUTDOOR ACTIVITIES

HIKING ★ There are several waterfalls, such as **Cascada Chocólatal** and **Cascada Cocacola**, within a 30-minute to 2-hour hike from Bahía Solano. Unless your hotel draws you a good map, you're bound to get lost, so it's best to hire a guide through a tour agency. Treks through the jungle to visit indigenous communities can also be arranged.

SPORTFISHING ★★ Bahía Solano is Colombia's premier sportfishing destination, and it attracts big-game fishermen from all over the world. There's good fishing for wahoo, sierra, and yellowfin tuna from March to June. For marlin and sailfish (catch and release), October through December, when the water is rough and choppy, is your best bet. Most fishermen arrange packages through their hotel, though 8-hour excursions can be arranged.

SURFING ★ **Playa Almejal** and environs are some of Colombia's best surf spots. There are both left and right breaks and the swells can get big and fast, which attracts a considerable amount of experienced surfers. You can negotiate rentals from a surf shack or two near the beach, though don't expect great quality. Tour agencies like **Pacifico** (see p. 251) will take surfers to more remote waves.

WHALE-WATCHING ★★ Colombia's Pacific Coast is right on a whale migration route, so from late July to about October, humpback whales come up from the South Pole to breed in the warm waters. In places like El Valle or

Bahía Solano

Parque Nacional Utría, they can sometimes be seen right from the shore. Nearly every hotel or tour operator in the region will offer tours during the season. Prices average around COP$150,000 per person, though they depend on the number of people in the boat.

Where to Stay & Eat

Most visitors here either stay on the beach at Playa Almejal near El Valle or at a fishing lodge in town. Nearly all hotels have restaurants and offer all-inclusive rates, plus packages for fishing, whale-watching, or surfing. For eating outside of the hotels, you are limited to small, local eateries. In El Valle, the best is **Doña Rosalia**, with simple fish dishes.

El Almejal ★★ Eco-conscious El Almejal is the area's best hotel. It's set in the jungle near Playa Almejal. Its well-designed wood cabins have thatched roofs, private bathrooms, and terraces. You won't find Wi-Fi or TVs, but there's a freshwater pool and a sea turtle hatchery program that guests can get involved in. Meals center on whatever the local fishermen bring in that day, and vegetables are from their organic garden. Staff can arrange bird-watching, whale-watching, and hiking trips.

Playa El Almeja, El Valle. www.almejal.com.co. ✆ **4/412-5050.** 12 units. COP$440,000 doubles, includes 3 daily meals. **Amenities:** Restaurant; bar; pool; tour desk; no Wi-Fi.

The Humpback Turtle ★ Owned by Pacifico Tours, this funky beach-front hostel built of local woods and bamboo has a dorm room and four private rooms, plus camp sites. Their bar and restaurant serves as the unofficial meeting point for surfers in the area.

Playa Almejal, El Valle. www.humpbackturtle.com. ✆ **314/766-8708.** 5 units. COP$120,000 doubles; COP$35,000 dorm beds; camping COP$20,000, includes breakfast. **Amenities:** Restaurant; bar; tours; no Wi-Fi.

Playa de Oro Lodge ★ On Playa Huina, a 20-minute boat ride from Bahía Solano, the Playa de Oro has a resort-style set up with a collection of sturdy buildings facing the beach. The simple rooms feature wood floors and walls, as well as private bathrooms and patios. A full range of tours and packages, including diving and fishing, can be arranged.

Playa Huina, Bahía Solano. www.playadeorolodge.com. ✆ **313/651-8457.** 28 units. COP$235,000 doubles, includes breakfast and transfers from town. **Amenities:** Restaurant; bar; tours; free Wi-Fi.

NUQUÍ ★★

59km (36⅔ miles) S of Bahía Solano; 196km (121 miles) W of Medellín

In recent years, Nuquí has become the face of the Pacific's ecotourism trade. Here, within an hour boat ride north or south along the absolutely unspoiled, green, mountainous coast, you will find a dozen or so small eco-lodges, each its own plot of paradise. Don't expect luxury by any means, but do expect pristine nature everywhere you turn. The town itself is not much to look at, with ramshackle houses and a collection of muddy roads between a wide beach and the airport. There are a few simple restaurants and handicraft shops, but little else. All passengers must pay a COP$7,000 fee at the airport upon arrival. Additionally, Nuquí makes a good base for going to **Parque Nacional Utría ★** (see p. 247).

Essentials

Satena (www.satena.com; ✆ 1/605-2222) offers almost daily **flights** from Medellín, and occasionally Bogotá. Flights are often canceled because of weather. Luggage is limited to 15 kilos.

There are speed **boats** on Mondays and Fridays to El Valle, outside of Bahía Solano. The trip takes about one hour and costs COP$65,000 per person. Ask at your hotel to set up a reservation.

There's a small **tourist information office** at the airport with brochures, maps, and contacts for local guides, though hours are sporadic.

OUTDOOR ACTIVITIES

CANOEING ★ Coquí, a rural farming and fishing village founded by escaped slaves about 20-minutes south of Nuquí by boat, is home to some of the best-preserved mangrove forests on the Pacific. Ask at the office of the community-based **Jóvenes Ecoguiás de Coquí** about 1- to 3-hour tours of the mangroves in *chingos*, hand-carved dugout canoes. Prices range from COP$40,000 to COP$100,000. You'll see it just off the beach once you arrive in Coqui.

WHALE-WATCHING ★★ The whale migration season runs from late July to October, and during that period, they come close enough to shore that you can see them from your eco-lodge. Day trips can be organized to Parque Nacional Utría, where humpback whales breed and nurse their young in sheltered lagoons. Every hotel can set up a whale-watching excursion, and most offer packages. Prices average around COP$100,000 per person, depending on the number of people in the boat.

Where to Stay

Unless you have some business in Nuquí, you will most likely get picked up at the airport and immediately head out to a lodge north or south of town. The lodges are anywhere from a 30-minute to a 1-hour boat ride up or down the coast. *Note:* All eco-lodges charge additional fees for transportation to/from Nuquí, which varies considerably by how many people are on the boat. A one-way ride for a single person is around COP$300,000, though the price drops considerably the more people there are on the boat.

Nuquimar Hotel ★ The best spot in Nuquí is this straightforward pair of wood houses near the waterfront. Some of the rooms have private bathrooms, others are shared. The best is the large penthouse room on the third floor of the larger house. It's a 15-minute walk from the airport.

Avenida La Playa, Aguas Calientes. www.hotelnuquimar.com. ✆ 786/514-3636. 9 units. COP$180,000 double, includes breakfast. **Amenities:** Restaurant; bar; tours; no Wi-Fi.

SOUTH OF NUQUÍ

El Cantil ★   This family-run lodge is the most polished in the Nuquí area, even as it limits its carbon footprint with minimal electricity use. Each of the spacious cabins includes a private bathroom, mosquito net, and terrace with hammocks. There's good surfing right in front of the lodge and a thermal spring a short hike away. Whale-watching trips and other excursions can be arranged.

Termales. www.elcantil.com. ℃ **4/448-0767.** 7 units. COP$354,000 per person, includes all meals. **Amenities:** Restaurant; bar; tours; no Wi-Fi.

Pijibá ★   Down the beach from El Cantil, Pijiba is the region's original eco-hotel. The three thatched-roof cabanas are each divided into two rooms, each with a private bathroom and mosquito net over the bed. Amenities include a shaded platform for doing yoga, and meals based around local products and recipes.

Termales. www.pijibalodge.com. ℃ **311/762-3763.** 6 units. COP$256,000 per person, includes all meals. **Amenities:** Restaurant; bar; tours; no Wi-Fi.

Punta Brava ★★   The very last lodge south of Nuquí, just beyond the village of Arusí, Punta Brava is perched on a rocky bluff with ocean on three sides of it. There are two beaches that come and go with the tides, and whales can occasionally be spotted right from the lodge during the right time of year. The open-air lodge with a thatched roof is quite simple, featuring just a few basic cabins on two levels, which all get a nice breeze. There's loads of eco-charm, such as the shared bathrooms opening up to the thick jungle on one side. Meals are lovingly prepared local dishes and, miraculously, there's even Wi-Fi at the staff hut. Rates include short hikes to waterfalls and to beaches, though activities like fishing and whale-watching require boat rides and have an additional fee.

Arusí. www.puntabravachoco.co. ℃ **313/768-0804.** 6 units. COP$215,000 per person, includes all meals and some excursions. **Amenities:** Restaurant; bar; tours; free Wi-Fi.

NORTH OF NUQUÍ

Moromico ★   In a remote bay 45 minutes north of Nuquí, this rustic lodge is in a pristine location, with nothing but the sounds of the birds and howler monkeys to keep you company. The rooms, set on three floors, are open-air with mosquito nets and shared bathrooms. The owners are fond of local recipes and using fruits grown around the property for the meals.

North of Nuquí. www.morromico.com. ℃ **311/762-3763.** 5 units. COP$240,000 per person, includes all meals. **Amenities:** Restaurant; bar; tours; no Wi-Fi.

ISLA MALPELO ★★

400km (249 miles) W of Buenaventura

A barren, volcanic submarine ridge just peeking out of the water way out in the Pacific, Isla Malpelo is a UNESCO World Heritage Site and one of the world's most sought after dive destinations. Other than a military post, the island is uninhabited except for a large colony of Nazca boobies and the mosses and lichens that grow from the guano that has built up there. What Malpelo lacks in amenities it makes up for in sharks, 500 hammerheads at a time, as well as silky sharks and occasionally the rare short-nosed ragged tooth shark. The entire island is a marine park, called the **Santuario de Flora y Fauna Malpelo**, and there are 11 dive sites. In the deep waters around Malpelo you can easily see whale sharks, grouper, and manta rays.

The only way to visit is on a live-aboard dive boat, of which only one has permission at a time. Anchoring is not allowed anywhere within the protected area. The trip by boat from Buenaventura takes at least 30 hours, depending on the weather, and usually makes a stop at **Isla Gorgona**, closer to the coast. Several agencies in Panama and Colombia make occasional trips there and can help navigate the extensive application process, including **Coiba Dive Expeditions** (www.coibadiveexpeditions.com) and **Arrecifes de Pacifico** (www.arrecifesdelpacifico.com). You can also contact **Fundación Malpelo** (www.fundacionmalpelo.org) for additional information.

9

THE PACIFIC COAST | Isla Malpelo

THE AMAZON & LOS LLANOS

by Nicholas Gill

On the other side of the Andes, Colombia takes on yet another new look. This is the most isolated part of the country, a place where few roads are able to penetrate. Colombia's Amazon takes up a full third of the country, yet most Colombians have never even been there. **Leticia,** Colombia's tiny foothold on the Amazon River, adjacent to the borders of Peru and Brazil, is the main point of access to the region, with multiple daily flights from Bogotá. It's so close to **Tabatinga,** the town's Brazilian equivalent, that many residents in both cities speak the two languages and have adapted to both nations' customs, so you might not even notice where you are until the waiter serves you a cachaça instead of rum. Within a short boat ride you can be face to face with capuchin monkeys or spotting pink river dolphins near **Parque Nacional Natural Amacayacu,** home to more than 500 different species of birds, hundreds of mammals, and giant spiders and snakes, fulfilling your wildest Amazon fantasies. In **Puerto Nariño** you will chat up indigenous groups whose culture has changed little in centuries, then dine on typical Amazonian cuisine, like the *mojojoy*, a palm grub that gets skewered and grilled, or *pirarucu*, an enormous freshwater fish.

Many parts of **Los Llanos**, a vast, mostly uninhabited flood-prone grassland that extends into Venezuela, were long off-limits to tourists because of guerilla activity and irregular transport, but now flights reach there regularly. One of Colombia's greatest natural attractions is here: **Caño Cristales**, a river that turns an array of colors several months of the year because of the aquatic plants found within, leading many to call it the world's most beautiful.

HISTORY Conquistador Francisco de Orellana sailed the length of the Amazon River in 1541, though it wasn't until the latter half of the 18th century that the region began to be settled. For many years, Peru and Colombia skirmished over the rights to Leticia,

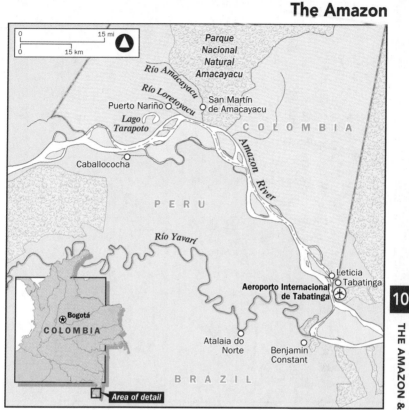

0 | 15 mi
0 | 15 km

Parque Nacional Natural Amacayacu

Río Amacayacu

Río Loretoyacu

Puerto Nariño

San Martín de Amacayacu

Lago Tarapoto

COLOMBIA

Caballococha

PERU

Amazon River

Río Yavarí

Leticia

Tabatinga

Aeroporto Internacional de Tabatinga

Bogotá

COLOMBIA

Atalaia do Norte

Benjamin Constant

BRAZIL

Area of detail

which was founded as a part of Peru; however, in 1934 the League of Nations finally awarded the city to Colombia.

CULTURE Because the Colombian Amazon remains so isolated from the rest of the country, many indigenous groups in the region have managed to maintain many of their traditional customs. While there are nomadic communities that live in voluntary isolation, most of the region's Tikunas, Yaguas, Huitotos, and Boras live in small, mostly self-sufficient agrarian villages, where they preserve traditional cooking techniques, dances, and clothing.

NATURE It's the Amazon rainforest, so yes, nature is a big deal here. The continent's forests act as the lungs of the earth and contain two-thirds of all of the freshwater on earth. You'll want plenty of time to get as far away as you can by riverboats and canoes to see the region's majestic flora and fauna up close.

ACTIVE PURSUITS There is no shortage of adventure in the Amazon. You can fish for piranhas, paddle canoes up remote tributaries, hike along forest trails thick with plants, seek out caimans with a flashlight, and cross off dozens of other bucket-list escapades. In Los Llanos, horseback riding isn't just a tourist activity, it's the primary method for getting from place to place.

Los Llanos

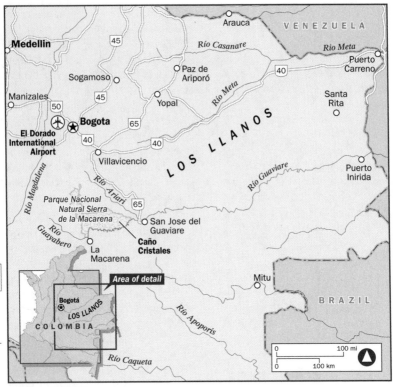

LETICIA ★

1084km (673 miles) S of Bogotá

Colombia's southernmost city, a small port just off of the Amazon River, is the main access point to the Colombian Amazon. It's right on the border with Tabatinga, Brazil and Santa Rosa, Peru, a wider region known as the Tres Fronteras. The city was founded by Benigno Bustamante on April 25, 1867, as a part of the department of Loreto in Peru. Colombia skirmished with Peru over the next 65 years, though the League of Nations finally settled the dispute in June of 1934, officially putting it under Colombian control for good. With a population of less than 40,000, Leticia retains a small frontier-town feel. There's little of the rubber boom architecture that you will find in cities such as Iquitos or Manaus, and the city's biggest economic boom was the drug trade in the 1970s. With no highways leading from the city other than a two-lane road that reaches a few villages and attractions north of the airport, the river is the primary method of transportation.

Essentials

GETTING THERE

BY PLANE   There are two airports in the Leticia area. One is **Aeropuerto Internacional Alfredo Vásquez Cobo**, on the north side of town, which has daily flights to Bogotá with **Avianca** (www.avianca.com) and **LATAM** (www.latam.com). On arrival you will pay a COP$20,000 tourist tax. Taxis shuttle between town and the airport for about COP$10,000. The other airport is **Tabatinga International Airport** across the virtual border in Tabatinga, Brazil. Here you can catch flights to Manaus, where you can connect to Belem, Rio de Janeiro, and Sao Paulo. Both **Trip** (www.voetrip.com.br) and **LATAM** (www.latam.com) have regular flights. *Note:* While you can travel freely within border towns in Peru or Brazil, if you plan on exploring parts farther afield you will need exit and entry stamps, which can be attained at immigration offices in respective airports (or in the case of Peru, at Santa Rosa). U.S. travelers will need to get a visa in advance for Brazil.

BY BOAT   In Leticia, regular high-speed boat service reaches Puerto Nariño (2 hr.; COP$35,000), stopping at countless small villages along the way. Boats depart at 8am, 10am, and 2pm every day. Purchase tickets from Transportes Fluviales, on the riverfront, Calle 8 no. 11.

Boats can also be booked to long-distance cities in Peru and Brazil. For Iquitos, two high-speed companies have boats that depart from Tabatinga several times per week: **Transtur** (www.transtursa.com) and **Transportes Golfinho** (www.transportegolfinho.com), taking about 10 hours and costing COP$150,000 per person. Spots fill up, so be sure to reserve your seat several days in advance. For Manaus, both fast (30 hr.) and slow boats (4 days) depart several times per week from Tabatinga's Porto Fluvial. Check in the offices there for exact prices and departures. *Tip:* Tabatinga is 1 hour ahead of Leticia, so be sure not to miss your boat!

FAST FACTS

There are several ATMS, as well as pharmacies, around and within a few blocks of the Leticia's plaza. There is a tourist office at Calle 8 no. 9–75, as well as a kiosk at the airport.

What to Do

Leticia's main plaza, **Parque Santander**, acts as the center of town. In the afternoons it becomes a hub of activity when thousands of *pericos*, small parrots, flock here for the night, screaming and chattering as the sun sets. During the day the riverfront is more active, with boats full of bananas and other products being brought in from villages from around the region. Everything is unloaded and carried by hand to the **market**, where you'll see giant pirarucu fish and countless exotic fruits.

Mundo Amazónico ★ ECO-PARK   This 29-hectare private reserve is like a mini-Amazon theme park. If you just have a couple of days in Leticia and don't have time to really get out in the jungle, this might quench your needs. The park offers four tours (short walks really) that take less than an hour each and are led by English- or Spanish-speaking guides. The main attraction is the botanical garden, which has hundreds of medicinal plants, though there's also an aquarium filled with Amazonian fish, jungle trails with chances to see some wildlife, and a tea house. Taxi will come here from the center for around COP$20,000; for $1,900, public buses will stop at kilometer 7 north of town, from where you will have a 10-minute walk.

Via Tarapacá Km 7. www.mundoamazonico.com. ☏ **8/592-6087** or 321/472-4346. Tours COP$10,000. Mon–Sat 8am–3pm.

Museo Etnográfico del Hombre Amazónico ★ MUSEUM   Part of the Banco de la República's museum network, which includes Bogotá's Museo de Oro, this small yet good collection is made up of more than 200 objects collected by Father Antonio Jover Lamaña. The collection includes tools, masks, weapons, and various ritual artifacts from the Ticuna, Huitoto, and Yucuna cultures. Everything is labeled in both English and Spanish.

Carrera 11 no. 9–43. www.banrepcultural.org/leticia/museo. ☏ **8/592-7729.** Free admission. Mon–Fri 8:30–11:30am.

Where to Stay

Decameron Decalodge Ticuna ★★   Colombian chain Decameron's Amazonian outpost is less of a rustic jungle lodge than it is a small jungle resort. The leafy compound is right in the heart of Leticia, not far from the riverfront. It is anchored by a large pool area surrounded by lounge chairs and tropical plants. The modern rooms, decorated with indigenous art, feature high ceilings and wood floors, as well as a balcony with a hammock. Every night there is some sort of live performance, such as shamanic chanting or folkloric dances, which keep the caipirinhas flowing in the bar area. Rates include free walking tours of town; trips to a monkey island, to see pink river dolphins, and hikes in the jungle can also be arranged for an additional fee.

Carrera 11, 6–11. www.decameron.com. ☏ **8/592-6600.** 28 units. COP$783,000 double. Rates include breakfast and dinner. **Amenities:** Restaurant; outdoor pool; bar; airport shuttle; Wi-Fi (fee).

Hotel Anaconda ★   Leticia's largest hotel isn't particularly interesting and tends to fill up with business groups from Bogotá, though it's one of the more comfortable options in the city center. There's a large pool area. Offering a respite from the elements, the tile-floor rooms are clean and kept pumped with cold air, though the red-and-white decor scheme is a bit tacky.

Carrera 11 no. 7–34. www.hotelanaconda.com.co. ☏ **311/271-8036.** 50 units. COP$464,000 double, COP$689,000 suite, includes breakfast and dinner. **Amenities:** Outdoor pool; restaurant; bar; free Wi-Fi.

Kurupira Cabaña Flotante ★   A 20-minute boat ride from Leticia, this rustic floating wooden lodge with a thatched roof provides the peace and solitude that many come to Leticia for. Rooms are simple, mostly exposed to the elements, so beds are draped in mosquito nets, though a breeze from the river keeps most bugs away. All rooms have a private bathroom and terrace with a hammock. Keep in mind that you'll be isolated in this hotel, so setting up a more complete package is recommended. The same owners also run a lodge, Heliconia, on a private reserve deeper in the jungle near the Rio Yavari, in the remote border area of Peru and Brazil.

Km 7 Vía Puerto Nariño. www.amazonheliconia.com. (C) **311/508-5666.** 47 units. COP$350,000 double, includes breakfast. **Amenities:** Restaurant; bar; no Wi-Fi.

Reserva Tanimboca ★ This small reserve with a beautiful patch is a good option for seeing a bit of the Amazon without going far from Leticia. Wildlife will be limited, though your hosts make up for it with a canopy tour, kayaking through jungle streams, and nighttime jungle hikes. The rooms are indigenous-style malokas with private bathrooms. Packages can be set up that add on trips to national parks and multi-day hikes in the jungle.

Via Tarapacá Km 11. www.tanimboca.com. (C) **8/592-7679.** 8 units. COP$240,000 double, includes breakfast. **Amenities:** Restaurant; tours; no Wi-Fi.

Waira Suites ★ Waira Suites has the feel of a modern and functional (yet very average) Bogotá midrange hotel with lots of amenities, just dropped into the middle of an Amazonian town. The cookie-cutter rooms have a sort of Ikea set up with light wood shelving and modern tile-floor bathrooms. There's a good-sized pool area and a sometimes lively little restaurant and lounge bar on the ground floor.

Carrera 10 no. 7–36. www.wairahotel.com.co. (C) **8/592-4428.** 47 units. COP$356,000 double, includes breakfast buffet. **Amenities:** Outdoor pool; restaurant; bar; business center; free Wi-Fi.

Where to Eat

In addition to the restaurants listed below, the market near the riverfront has a small bakery and a food court with simple, regional dishes and juice bars.

El Cielo ★ COLOMBIAN El Cielo is the first restaurant in Leticia to even attempt to have some sort of elevated cuisine and nice presentation. They mostly succeed with a menu of international dishes utilizing local ingredients. For instance, they use cassava flour in their pizza dough and slather their pork ribs in an araza BBQ sauce. There's just one simple dining room, with a trippy jungle-painted wall and an outdoor patio. Some of the waiters speak English, which is rare in Leticia.

Calle 7, 6–50. (C) **312/351-0427.** Main courses COP$20,000–COP$55,000. Mon, Wed–Sat 4–11pm, Sun 11am–5pm.

Tierras Amazónicas ★★ AMAZONIAN Think Amazonian tiki bar. While Tierras Amazónicas may seem a bit kitschy—there's a thatched roof, colorful paintings of jaguars, and wood carvings of pirarucus—it's still the most interesting restaurant in Leticia. Regional cuisine is the focus here (and not a lot of other places follow suit), so you'll find dishes like fish steamed in bijao leaves, *mojojoy* (grilled palm grubs), and grilled piranha. Wash it all down with fresh juices like camu-camu or copuazu.

Carrera 8, 7–50. ℂ **8/592-4748.** Main courses COP$18,000–COP$45,000. Tues–Sun 10am–9pm.

Shopping

Handicraft shops are scattered all over town, though the best is **Galería Arte Uirapuru**, Calle 8 no. 10–35, which sells masks from the Matis tribe, wood carvings, blow darts, medical plants, and all sorts of unusual Amazonian souvenirs. There's even a small museum in the back of the store.

Side Trips from Leticia

AMACAYACU NATIONAL PARK ★★

To experience the real Amazon rainforest, you need to get well out of the towns and villages, to a place untouched by man—a place with primary forests that hide more than 500 species of birds, more than 100 species of mammals, dozens of snakes and reptiles, and more types of insects than can even be identified. This place is Parque Nacional Natural Amacayacu, a 300,000-hectare forest reserve that's home to the Ticuna people. Because of irregular flooding patterns in recent years, the visitor center has been closed to the public. The park can still be accessed through communities like San Martín de Amacayacu and Mocagua, though setting up a visit is complicated outside of a stay at Yoi Ecolodge (www.yoiecotours.com).

75km west of Leticia. www.parquesnacionales.gov.co. ℂ **8/520-8654.** COP$5,000 paid in the community of entrance.

RÍO YAVARÍ ★★

In the isolated border area of Peru and Brazil, divided by the Yavarí River, there are several small reserves teeming with wildlife. While access to Parque Nacional Natural Amacayacu remains limited, visits to these private reserves are as easy as just hiring a peque-peque motorized canoe or walking into a tour office in Leticia. **Reserva Natural Palmirí** (www.selvaventura.wixsite.com/amazonas-rc), **Reserva Natural Heliconia** (www.amazonheliconia.com), and the **Reserva Natural Zacambú** (www.amazonjungletrips.com.co) all have rustic eco-lodges with shared bathrooms and all-inclusive packages that include boat transportation, daily tours, and all meals. The lodges set up a variety of activities that include bird-watching, jungle hikes, and visits to indigenous villages. Two-day, three-night packages begin at around COP$850,000 per person.

PUERTO NARIÑO ★

85km (53 miles) W of Leticia

Located where the Amazon River meets the Loretoyacu, the model village of Puerto Nariño is reached only by boat. It's a serene community that maintains its authenticity at every turn. The Ticuna and mestizo village of about 6,000 residents is completely vehicle free, with paved footpaths instead of roads, and where recycling (trash, rainwater, etc.) is a way of life. With regular transportation here, good day tours to explore the area's natural surroundings, and comfortable accommodations, many prefer to base themselves in Puerto Nariño than Leticia.

Essentials

GETTING THERE

BY BOAT   From Leticia, there are regular high-speed boats to Puerto Nariño (2 hr.; COP$35,000) three times a day, departing at 8am, 10am, and 2pm. Make reservations at Transportes Fluviales on Leticia's riverfront, Calle 8 no. 11.

VISITOR INFORMATION

Puerto Nariño's facilities are quite basic. There are a few shops, but no banks, and credit cards are not accepted anywhere. A few Internet cafes provide net access. There is a tourist office inside the alcaldía at the corner of Carrera 7 and Calle 5.

What to Do

Centro de Interpretación Ambiental Natütama ★ MUSEUM   Run by the NGO Natütama, this nature interpretation center helps spread environmental awareness among the community, particularly about the pink river dolphin and highly endangered Amazonian manatee. Wood carvings of Amazonian flora and fauna are on display.

ⓒ **312/410-1925.** Free, though donations are encouraged. Daily 8am–12:30pm and 2pm–5pm.

Lago Tarapoto ★★   This beautiful 37-sq.-km lake—a short peque-peque (motorized canoe) ride from Puerto Nariño—is the area's favorite attraction. There's a trail to hike around the lake where you'll see lots of birdlife in the early mornings and afternoon. In the lake, it's fairly easy to see pink river dolphins, manatees, and giant Victoria Regia water lilies with the help of a guide. Every hotel or tour operator in town can set up a guided visit for around COP$60,000 per person.

10km west of Puerto Nariño.

Where to Stay & Eat

Las Margaritas ★ COLOMBIAN   Puerto Nariño's most popular restaurant is set in a thatched-roof palapa near the soccer field. Regional staples like grilled fish, fried plantains, yuca, rice, and various stews are set out on a buffet and brought to your table by the server.

Calle 6 no. 6–80. No phone. Main courses COP$15,000. Daily 8am–9pm.

Waira Selva ★   The smaller, Puerto Nariño branch of Leticia boutique hotel Waira Suites is as comfortable as this village gets. The rooms are simple, with wooden shutters that open to the outside, but they include modern bathrooms and LCD TVs with satellite channels. There's a pretty good restaurant on site, plus a small terrace with good views of town.

Carrera 10 no. 7–36. www.wairahotel.com.co. © **8/592-4428.** 13 units. COP$143,000 double, includes breakfast. **Amenities:** Restaurants; store; laundry service; no Wi-Fi.

Yoi Ecolodge ★★   Located in the indigenous Ticuna village of San Martín de Amacayacuand within Amacayacu National Park, the Ticuna people make up the staff of the Yoi Ecolodge. The simple thatched-roof cabins have private bathrooms and mosquito nets. There's some electricity to charge batteries, but that's it. Tours include bird-watching, visits to Lago Tarapoto, piranha fishing, jungle hikes, night walks, and visits to a monkey sanctuary.

San Martín de Amacayacu. www.yoiecotours.com. © **310/268-8026.** 6 units. COP$1,105,000 double for a 3-day/2-night package that includes all meals, transportation from Leticia, and tours. **Amenities:** Restaurant; bar; no Wi-Fi.

CAÑO CRISTALES ★

70km (43 miles) W of Villavicencio

From 1989 to 2009, one of Colombia's most spectacular natural wonders, Caño Cristales, was closed to tourism. For the most part, everyone forgot that there was a magical river that turned five different colors in the wilds of Los Llanos, the flood-prone grassland east of the Andes in Parque Nacional Natural Sierra de La Macarena. Even when tourists began to return, they had trouble figuring out how to get there. It required extensive planning to get to the town of Villavicencio and then find a charter flight in a DC-3 to the town of La Macarena. Now, you can just take a flight from Bogotá in the morning and you're exploring this surreal piece of the planet by the afternoon. Welcome to the new Colombia.

Essentials
GETTING THERE
BY PLANE   Satena (www.satena.com; © **1/605-2222**) offers several weekly flights from Bogotá to the town of La Macarena, from where guides can be hired to explore the reserve. Keep in mind that flights are often canceled because of weather. Luggage is limited to 15 kilos.

VISITOR INFORMATION
There's very little tourist infrastructure in place in La Macarena. Cell service barely works, and there is just one very slow Internet cafe.

What to Do
Home to the river called Caño Cristales, the long-lost 629,280-hectare **Parque Nacional Natural Sierra de La Macarena** ★★★ is going to be on everyone's radar in a few years once Instagram sets in. This is the reason anyone comes to this isolated area; there's nothing else around. Caño Cristales is often called the "River of Five Colors" because from around July through November (the wet season), the river bed turns shades of yellow, green, blue,

black, and red because of an aquatic plant named *macarenia clavigera*, which blooms during that period.

From La Macarena, you'll ride horseback or take a boat along the wildlife-rich Río Guayabero—keep an eye out for turtles, iguanas, and birds of prey—before reaching the crystal-clear river system, where you can explore the many swimmable natural pools and waterfalls. It takes about two days to explore all three branches of the river.

All visitors must enter the park with a licensed guide, which can be set up on the ground in La Macarena or through tour operators in Bogotá. Rates are about COP$754,000 per person for a 3-day/2-night package (without flights). Some recommended agencies include **Caño Cristales** (www.cano-cristales.com; ✆ **321/842-2728**), **Aventure Colombia** (www.aventurecolombia.com; ✆ **1/702-7069**), and **Ecotourism Macarena** (www.ecoturismomacarena.com; ✆ **8/665-3870**).

Note: Parque Nacional Natural Sierra de La Macarena is closed to visitors from January to the end of May.

Where to Stay & Eat

While tourism to La Macarena is growing quickly, it will likely be a while before hotels and restaurants will catch up. The best option in town by far is the family-run **Hotel San Nicolas** (www.sannicolas-hotel.com; ✆ **321/300-0802**; COP$50,000 double), 3 blocks from the airport; it has a mix of private rooms (with wood floors, LCD TVs, and private bathrooms with cold-water showers) and basic dorm beds. The friendly owners can help set up excursions into the park. Another decent option is **Hotel Punta Verde** (✆ **314/325-3522**; COP$60,000 double), Carrera 9 no. 4–12, near the waterfront. The hotel has very straightforward rooms with tile floors, LCD TVs, and private bathrooms facing the garden and an outdoor pool. Restaurants in La Macarena do not have tourists in mind. Mixed in with the many pool halls, you'll find several basic panaderias like La Casa de Pan and Pan Unicrema, where you can get arepas and baked goods. Other restaurants serve hearty local dishes, which usually include a big helping of grilled beef or roasted chicken, rice, and yuca.

11 SAN ANDRÉS & PROVIDENCIA

by Caroline Lascom

When Colombians dream of a tropical vacation, they need look no further than San Andrés and Providencia. This remote and breathtaking archipelago is a Caribbean fantasia of blinding white sands fringed with coconut palms, translucent waters cast in unfathomable shades of blue, spectacular coral formations, and a magical abundance of sea creatures. In 2005, UNESCO recognized the islands' immense ecological richness when 25,000 miles were designated as the Seaflower Marine Protected Area. Home to the third-largest barrier reef in the world—spanning some 32km (20 miles)—it's no overstatement to say that the snorkeling and diving here are out of this world.

But there's more to the islands than just sun and surf. San Andrés and Providencia are known across Colombia for their incredible music—a heritage that speaks to the region's fascinating colonial history. Pirates, puritans, and conquistadors have all staked their claim to these strategic islands, which are actually closer to Nicaragua (122km/93 miles) than to Colombia (775km/482 miles). Certainly, there is an eccentric, distinctly Colombian sensibility to the island's ramshackle beauty, yet the islands beat to a very different drum. A third of the population is Raizal: the descendants of British Puritans and African slaves who were shipped to the islands to work on the cotton plantations in the 17th century. On the island's "settlements," you are more likely to hear reggae or gospel than salsa; locals speak English-Creole rather than Spanish, and white clapboard houses tumble down lush green hillsides.

Well established on the Colombian tourist trail, the larger, more developed island of San Andrés is a tarnished gem, and its commercial exploitation of historic sights and attractions has pushed well beyond the boundaries of poor taste. But there is redemption. Just a 20-minute flight away, on the Lilliputian island of Providencia and its satellite island, Santa Catalina, forested mountains crisscrossed with trails plunge into breathtaking isolated coves. Just offshore lies the unforgettable vision of Parque Nacional McBean

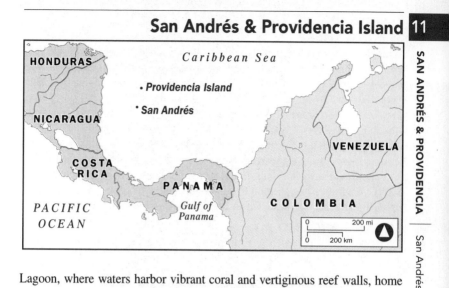

Lagoon, where waters harbor vibrant coral and vertiginous reef walls, home to manta rays, moray eels, hammerhead sharks, trumpet damsel fish . . . the list goes on. On Providencia, daily pleasures come in pure and blissful form: swim, snorkel, sunbathe, hike, eat unadulterated seafood, drink a nice cold beer, and then swing in a hammock as the beats of reggae and the crackle of beach bonfires fill the air.

SAN ANDRÉS ★

Colombia's most commercial Caribbean island, San Andrés is a 12km-long, 3km-wide (7½-mile long, 2-mile wide) seahorse-shaped curl, a 90-minute flight northwest of Colombia's Caribbean coast. San Andrés has long been a mecca for scuba divers in the know and a rite of passage for Colombia's wealthier families, who love their all-inclusive holidays and tax-free. Over the last decade, the island has become a cautionary tale against the Latin American penchant for Cancún-style mass development, with concrete behemoths and any tenuous (or fabricated) excuse to set up a bar or charge an entry fee lending a dispiriting air. Still, with its expanse of multi-hued blue waters that seem to change color from moment to moment—aquamarine, turquoise, green, emerald, navy—and pristine sweeps of white sand on the eastern cays (Johnny Cay, Acuario, and Cayo Bolívar), the island's stunning natural beauty is in no doubt.

Once you hire a golf cart or a *mula* (a powerful, gas-fueled incarnation) and venture off-the-beaten path, the island's less-sanitized Caribbean charms (this is definitely no Barbados or St. Bart's) soon work their magic. Give it a while, and you will soon fall into the seductive rhythms of traditional Raizal culture, a fascinating amalgam of Caribbean, Creole, English, and Colombian customs. In the lush interior, evocative vernacular architecture, homages to Bob Marley (and, bizarrely, Jack Sparrow), surreal landscapes, strange customs, and intriguing cuisine inspires an overwhelming sense of "Where am I?" at every turn.

Essentials

GETTING THERE

Avianca (www.avianca.com) provides connections to Bogotá (from US$120 one-way, 2hr. 10 min.), Medellín (via Bogotá, from US$150), and Cali (via Bogotá, from US$160). **Copa** (www.copaair.com) has direct flights from Barranquilla (1hr. 30 min., from US$210) and Cartagena (1 hr. 30 min., from US$230). Low-cost airline **VivaColombia** (www.vivacolombia.co) flies from Medellín (2 hr., from US$75; base fare) and **Satena** (www.satena.com) operates from most major cities in Colombia and connects San Andrés with Providencia (25 min., from US$80 each way). Located 2km northwest of Centro, the Aeropuerto Gustavo R Pinilla International (ADZ) is a 5- to 10-minute taxi ride (COP$10,000) or 15-minute walk from the town center. There are also direct flights from San José, Costa Rica (Avianca) and Panama City (Copa).

GETTING AROUND

BY BUS   Bus services from El Centro are frequent, efficient, and inexpensive (COP$1,700) and cover the east side of San Andrés.

BY BIKE   There are several bicycle rental shops in El Centro, but quality and maintenance is often an issue. It's wise to select your bike, check it thoroughly, and give it a quick spin before you commit; around COP$25,000 per day.

SCOOTER/MOTOTAXI   Scooters and mototaxis are available to rent, and it's the locals' preferred means of getting around, but with pot-holed roads, insane drivers, and no helmets provided, it's not for the faint of heart.

BY BUGGY   There's no need to rent a car when you can careen around the island in a gas-powered golf cart (around COP$175,000) known affectionately as a *mula*. You can also rent a traditional golf cart for the day (around COP$90,000); discounts apply for multi-day rentals. It's important to remember that neither golf carts nor *mulas* can be driven after 6pm.

VISITOR INFORMATION

The large, enthusiastic tourist office in the center of town (Avenida Newball, opposite Restaurant La Regatta; www.sanandres.gov.co; © **8/512-5058**; 8am–noon, 2–6pm) has limited supplies of maps, brochures, and information on hotels/restaurants/excursions on the islands. There is a **Banco de Bogotá** (Avenida Colón no. 2–86; © **8/512-6363**) with an **ATM**.

Around the Island

While many Colombians come to San Andrés just for the tax-free shopping—as evidenced by the discount warehouses that surround the airport—or to scuba dive, it's well worth getting out of town to experience the island's rugged beauty, rich musical heritage, traditional architecture, and cultural eccentricities. A 30km (18-mile) paved road (Avenida Circunvalar) rings the island, with several unpaved roads connected to the lush, hilly interior where concrete gives way to clapboard stilted houses with corrugated metal roofs.

The northern tranche of San Andrés, **El Centro** is ground zero for the island's hotels, restaurants, duty-free shops, and bars. It's far from pretty and

there are no sights to speak of. The main town beach, **Spratt Bight** (or Playa Centro) is one of the island's most popular beaches and for natural beauty, it ticks the boxes: white sand, coconut palms, clear azure waters, and plenty of on-the-water recreation, including windsurfing, waterskiing and kitesurfing. The town's main promenade (or *malecón*) is punctuated with loud beachfront cafes, a glut of tax-free shops, open-air restaurant-bars, and pushy tour companies. At sunset, it's a pleasant place to stroll among street artists, musicians, and vendors before the island's pulse starts to quicken and a more bacchanalian vibe holds sway.

The island's two other noteworthy towns are: **La Loma** (The Hill) in the central region, and **San Luis** on the eastern coast, with fine examples of Caribbean-English architecture and an opportunity to experience the Raizal way of life that shares few cultural touchstones with the mainland.

MAIN TOURIST SIGHTS

Casa Museo Isleño ★   For an insight into the island's traditional architecture, it's worth stopping for a brief tour at this evocative house with a wide veranda, originally owned by a British family. With antique sewing machines, 265 sepia images, a century-year-old list of families who live on the island, wicker rocking chairs, and quilted beds, there's more than a whiff of Victorian colonial charm. There's also a statue of a pirate (who looks a lot like Johnny Depp) with a cannon in the back garden. The short but sweet tour culminates with a calypso or reggae dance performed by the friendly Raizal guides (tours in English or Spanish) and, of course, there's a souvenir shop.

KM 5 Carretera Circunvalar. ✆ 8/512-3419. COP$8,000. Daily 9am–5pm.

Cueva de Morgan ★   Islanders love to muse on pirate shenanigans, and Morgan Cave is a bizarre expression of this predilection. The cave, connected to the ocean via a 120-meter-long subterranean passage, is one of the spots where the infamous Welsh privateer allegedly hid his stash in the late 17th century. It was from San Andrés that Captain Henry Morgan orchestrated many of his raids against the Spanish galleons loaded with riches from Central America. While locals will say (or sneer) that the Brits swiftly absconded with the treasure, superstition and a healthy dose of wishful thinking lead many to believe that it was hidden here in Cueva de Morgan. You can't enter the cave (it's underwater), but fabricated "tours" take in a replica of the *Sea Wolf* (Morgan's ship), and there's a curious attempt at a **Pirate Museum** with all manner of weird and random artifacts salvaged from shipwrecks in the water of San Andrés and Providencia, and plenty of Jack Sparrow imagery. Next door, the **Coconut Museum** displays some massive coconuts and whimsical artworks fashioned from shells, and there's a small art museum where you'll watch dancers perform.

Km 7 Carretera Circunvalar. COP$15,000. Daily 9am–6pm.

Hoyo Soplador ★   On San Andrés southern tip, the Hoyo Soplador is a blowhole a few meters from the ocean, where, if the wind and tides show willing, a stream of air and gushing water erupts (as high as 20m) through a natural hole. This geyser-like phenomenon—produced by waves crashing against a series of underground tunnels embedded in ancient coral rock—has morphed into a tacky tourist attraction with a glut of makeshift souvenir stores, bars, and loud music.

Km 16 Carretera Circunvalar, frequent buses from San Andrés town.

Jardín Botánico ★★   A research and conservation center, San Andrés's serene botanical garden is well worth an hour visit. Home to a rich profusion of birdlife and butterfly species, over 6 acres of preserved forest crisscrossed with nature trails culminate in a turtle nursery. Informative tours (in English and Spanish) elucidate the properties of the garden's 23 plant species, and guides will impart plenty of informative anecdotes about the island's ecosystems, topography, history, and culture. There's also an herbarium. Don't miss the fantastic views of the island from the lookout tower.

Harmony Hill. www.caribe.unal.edu.co. ✆ 8/513-3390. COP$10,000. Daily 9am–5pm.

La Loma ★★   On the north side of the island, La Loma is the highest point on the island. The second-largest community on San Andrés—in the

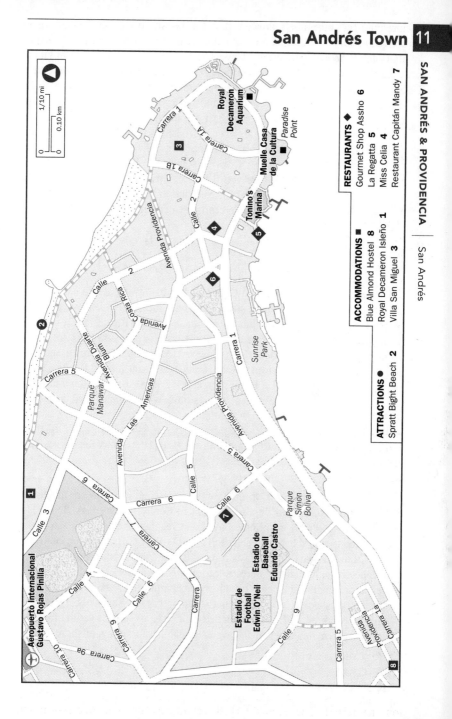

ACCOMMODATIONS ■
Blue Almond Hostel **8**
Royal Decameron Isleño **1**
Villa San Miguel **3**

ATTRACTIONS ●
Spratt Bight Beach **2**

RESTAURANTS ◆
Gourmet Shop Assho **6**
La Regatta **5**
Miss Celia **4**
Restaurant Capitán Mandy **7**

interior—La Loma's traditional English-Caribbean structures provides a more soulful antidote to the concrete mayhem of El Centro. It's here that the majority of the Raizal people (descendants of Afro-Caribbean slaves) that migrated from other Caribbean Islands live; you'll hear more English and Creole than Spanish. Built in 1847, the photogenic Emmanuel Baptist Church with its whitewashed facade, pointy steeple, and red roof, was rebuilt after a storm caused severe damage in 1896. The best day to visit is Sunday, when smartly dressed locals convene from all over the island to attend the impassioned Sunday gospel service (10am–1pm; it's not considered a tourist attraction so you'll need to dress the part). It's worth spending an hour to look around the town's clapboard houses where you'll hear calypso, soca, and reggae music emanating from makeshift bars. You can take in superb views of the island from the church's bell tower, and enterprising locals may invite you take in the view from their rooftops.

Baptist Church. ⓒ **8/513-2042.** Entry to the tower: COP$4,000. Open 9am–5:30pm. La Loma is a 15-min. drive/*mula* ride north from Centro along the Carretera Circunvalar. Or 3 buses per hour from Centro; marked "Cova/La Loma," 35 min., COP$2,000.

La Piscinita ★   Just south of Cueva de Morgan, tropical fish can be seen in abundance at La Piscinita, a small cove with incredibly clear warm water. When you pay to enter—the land is owned by a local Raizal family—you'll be provided with bread to feed the fish; the cove is accessed from the rocky shoreline via a rickety ladder. It's a popular place to snorkel; there are snorkels to rent but they are overpriced (COP$20,000), and you'll need to pay a hefty deposit (COP$100,000). La Piscinita reaches critical mass by lunchtime, so try to arrive early. There's also a restaurant with simple food and poor service.

KM 13 Carretera Circunvalar. Daily 9am–5pm. COP$4,000. From Centro, take bus marked Loma (every 30 min., COP$2,000, 45 min.) and ask the driver to drop you at La Piscinita.

BEACHES

In El Centro, **Spratt Bight**, fronted by the pedestrian walkway (or malecón), is the best beach in town. Just south from El Centro, **Rocky Cay Beach** is a small white-sand cove enshrouded by dense vegetation. Here, you can't miss Hotel Decameron Mar Azul (the beach is public). Just offshore, you can wade out to **Cayo Rocoso** (Rocky Cay), a small island. On the other side of the cay, you can see the remains of sunken freighter *Nicodemus* protruding from the water; more than a few spicy urban myths attempt to explain the wreckage. From the ramshackle former coconut shipping port of **San Luis**, a sweep of white sands dotted with rustic thatched-roof *palapas* unfurls south along the island's eastern flank; when the water is calm, snorkeling offshore can be rewarding.

THE CAYS

Cayo Acuario ★   The main draw to this slip of a sandbank is the tide pools and clear, shallow water that is great for snorkeling (snorkels for rent, but it's better to bring your own). The sandbank can get very busy from 9:30am until around 4pm. Makeshift beach huts sell snacks and drinks. From here, you can cross over to **Haynes Cay**, another picture-postcard islet with dazzling white sand and clear waters where sightings of manta rays are not uncommon.

Frequent lanchas (private) from Spratt Bight beach to Acuario leave from 9am (COP$12,000).

Cayo Bolívar ★★   Some 25km (15 miles) from San Andrés, this beautiful Caribbean dreamscape is where you can flee the crowds and truly unwind. The tiny island—7km (4 miles) from top to bottom and just 3km (about 2 miles) at its widest point—is woven with coconut groves and encircled by white-sand beaches. There is no development on the island, so tours (prices are for the most part standard, but some of the larger hotels will offer discounts) include lunch. There is no shade, apart from palm trees.

Tours (from COP$170,000) include transport via speed boat (1 hr.), lunch/drinks.

Parque Regional Johnny Cay ★★   Less than three miles north of Spratt Blight, Johnny Cay is a beautiful speck of an island with swaying palms, an idyllic white-sand beach, clear waters in every conceivable shade of blue, more than 40 species of fish, and literally hundreds of iguanas. You can walk the perimeter of the islet in 15 to 20 minutes, snorkel, and scuba dive (there are a couple of wreck dives here). During high season (especially on Sundays when it's a total party), it's mobbed with tourists; try to come during the week and walk to the north side for a little more tranquility. Be mindful of strong currents.

COP$5,000. *Lanchas* depart frequently from Spratt Bight beach (round trip COP$15,000) from 9am. Returning from Johnny Cay, the last *lancha* is at 3:30pm. Boat operators all work independently, so keep your return ticket and take a mental note of your boat.

Diving San Andrés

With translucent, warm waters—temperature ranges from 27°C/80°F to 30°C/86°F—all year-round (you'll get by on just a shorty), awesome visibility, and a mind-blowing inventory of sea life, San Andrés offers thrilling and diverse dive sites with excellent visibility—from 30 to 60 meters—and depths, from 3 to 30 meters. There's never a dull moment. Optimum diving conditions prevail from February through May; the winds whip up in June/July and September/October, the rainy season is from January to June. Most of the dive shops listed below furnish a full menu of drift, shore dives, vertical walls, coral reefs, cave sites, and shipwrecks.

DIVE SITES

A UNESCO Biosphere Reserve, San Andrés island forms part of the third-largest coral reef in the world, with more than 50 species of coral and 140 species of fish, including butterfly fish, eels, trumpet fish, damselfish, angel fish, blue tang, and snapper as well as less conspicuous octopus, barracudas, dolphins, turtles, eagle rays, and hammerhead sharks. There are more than 40 dive sites, less than a 30-minute boat ride from shore.

Due to the trade winds from the east, the island's best dive sites are on the island's **west side**. On the **northeast** side, calm shallow waters laced with sea grass are protected by a barrier reef. The more thrilling **southeast** side lures advanced divers to its extensive cave sites, vertiginous wall dives, and vibrant, healthy communities of living coral; the reef's plateau—with an impressive vertical drop—is just a few hundred meters from the rocky shoreline.

Blue Wall   On the east coast, this is an advanced wall dive which drops from 7 meters (23 ft.) to 300 meters (984 ft.). The wall, draped with overhanding yellow tube sponges and gorgeous corals, is populated with prolific marine life, including sharks and sea turtles. At a depth of about 40 meters (131 ft.), a massive cave called Grouper Palace—a misnomer (it's home to durgon rather than grouper)—is surrounded by feathers of black coral and soft gorgonian coral.

The Pyramids   One of the island's top beginner and night dive spots, on San Andrés's north end, this shallow dive introduces divers to gorgeous anemone and marine life including sting rays, French grunts, tiny cowries, snappers, and fascinating macro life.

Wild Life   On the west side, scintillating reef fish and marauding pelagics can be seen at this calm site, which caters to novice divers who can stick to the site's shallow water. More experienced divers can continue on to the precipitous wall.

Trampa Tortuga   On the east coast, this is one of the island's best intermediate reef dives with a 15-meter (49-ft.) shallow reef with fantastic visibility and large schools of tropical fish. On the outer reef, experienced divers can drop to 90 meters (295 ft.), where manta rays, grouper, and sharks are the stars.

DIVE SHOPS

Banda Dive Shop   This reputable, established agency runs well-organized scuba diving excursions as well as the full menu of PADI beginner Open Water certification courses, advanced certification, and dive master courses. With a number of dive packages available—including wall, wreck, and night dives, this is one of the most versatile and most cost-effective outfitters on the island. Hotel Lord Pierre, L-104, San Andrés town. www.bandadiveshop.com. ℂ **8/513-1080.**

Blue Life   Based at the Sunset Beach hotel, this excellent dive school has expert dive masters who are detail-oriented and highly knowledgeable about reef inhabitants. Advanced dives are at 9:30am while more family-oriented, single-tank fun dives start at 11am and 2:30pm. Night dives are usually on Wednesdays. Specialty courses are offered, including night dives and deep-dive instruction (COP$550,000 over 2 or 3 days). All dives depart by boat from the hotel's pier. Sunset Hotel. Avenida Circunvalar Km 13. www.bluelife dive.com. ℂ **8/512-5318.**

Karibik Diver   Karibik is a well-established dive operator with top-notch equipment and superb attention to detail. A two-tank dive costs COP$170,000;

Open Water certification, COP$950,000. You can also rent underwater cameras by the day (COP$40,000), dive computers (COP$50,000), and a full set of equipment (including regulator, BCD, wetsuit, etc.) for COP$50,000. Avenida Newball 1–248, San Andrés town. www.karibik-diver.com. ℂ **8/512-0101.**

Scuba San Andrés   This small outfit, on the west side of the island (inside Playa Tranquilo hotel, see p. 272), is super-organized, competitively priced, and boasts new equipment. Expert, friendly instructors cater to all levels. All courses and dives include transportation from/to the hotel. A 4-day PADI Open Water certification course costs COP$850,000, a Dive Master course COP$3,500,000, a two-tank dive costs, COP$180,000, a Discover Scuba course runs COP$160,000. Avenida Circunvalar Km 8.5, Via El Cove. ℂ **311/257-5511.**

Where to Stay

Top dog on San Andrés is the Colombian Decameron chain (part of the Terranum hospitality platform), which has 10 hotels, including several of their flagship all-inclusive (and affordable by Caribbean standards) resorts, on both San Andrés and Providencia islands. Most of San Andrés's hotels are located within the town center, which, while hardly satisfying misty-eyed visions of Caribbean bliss, does put you at the center of the action.

Blue Almond Hostel ★★   The Blue Almond has everything you'd hope for in a backpacker hostel: terrific communal areas, plenty of amenities—including a communal kitchen, TV/game room, book exchange, Wi-Fi (free), free surfboards and scuba tanks—clean and comfortable dorms, and welcoming, knowledgeable hosts. A 20-minute walk from town, with a chilled-out vibe, the Blue Almond pitches itself as a peaceful retreat for sports/nature enthusiasts rather than a party zone. As well as traditional dorm rooms, there are double/single rooms with private/shared bath.

Barrio Los Almendros Manzana 4 Casa 3. www.bluealmondhostel.com. ℂ **8/513-0831.** 14 units. Doubles from COP$44,000, COP$55,000 with private bathroom, dorm rooms from COP$38,000. **Amenities:** Watersports equipment; bike rentals; TV/game room; communal kitchen; free Wi-Fi.

Casa Las Palmas Boutique Hotel ★★   For a more intimate and romantic escape, this serene property is far from the maddening crowds of Centro. Run by Armando and Gloria (who built the house), a large, inviting swimming pool with a mosaic-tiled waterfall/Jacuzzi forms the centerpiece of well-manicured grounds brimming with tropical plants and flowers. Three large, individually styled rooms, decorated in an eclectic fusion of Mediterranean, Moorish, and Caribbean style, are pristine and characterful. A cooked-to-order breakfast is included in the rate, and lunch/dinner can also be served with advance notice. You'll certainly need to arrange your own transportation (golf cart/*mula* or car) in town before arrival; it's a 15-minute drive to the nearest beach.

Elsy Bar no. 5–64. www.casalaspalmashotelboutique.com. ℂ **315/750-0263.** 3 units. From COP$390,000, includes breakfast. **Amenities:** Restaurant; outdoor pool; spa; hot tub; laundry service; free Wi-Fi.

Playa Tranquilo ★★ A 20-minute drive from San Andrés town, on the west coast of the island, Playa Tranquilo artfully channels its rustic-chic ethos. It's set in a tropical garden with direct access to the ocean (but rocky shoreline). Bright, thoughtfully designed rooms, decorated with natural fabrics and furnishings, feature outdoor showers and balconies or patios with ocean/garden views. Larger villas and apartments (great for families) boast kitchenettes and living spaces. Breakfast is included in the rate, and there's a highly recommended dive shop onsite.

Carrera 15 Sur no. 982. www.playatranquilo.com. ✆ **8/512-5509.** 6 units. Rooms from COP$275,000, includes breakfast. **Amenities:** Restaurant/bar; outdoor pool; dive shop onsite; free Wi-Fi.

Posada San Andrés Ultd ★★ On the laidback west coast, close to the island's best dive sites and beaches, this characterful guesthouse decorated with family heirlooms, eclectic furniture, and colorful fabrics is one of the island's more soulful choices. With cozy double rooms, cottages (with kitchens), and a well-equipped apartment (which sleeps eight), there's something for every budget. Amenities include a communal kitchen, a small swimming pool, and helpful hosts who can arrange tours and snorkeling/diving excursions in the area.

Carretera Tom Hooker no. 8-75. www.sanandresultd.com. ✆ **310/625-2938.** 7 units. Doubles from COP$140,000, cabin COP$200,000, apartment COP$300,000m, includes breakfast. **Amenities:** Restaurant; outdoor pool; free Wi-Fi.

Royal Decameron Isleño ★ In a prime spot on the island's best white-sand beach—Spratt Bight—for location alone this is the best option in El Centro. Well-equipped standard rooms, with tiled floors and colorful fabrics, are bright and functional but are showing their age. Maintenance standards need to be improved; air-conditioning units are noisy, Wi-Fi is spotty, and there's mold and poor water pressure in some bathrooms—be sure to check out a couple of rooms when you check in. The buffet is expansive, with plenty of local produce and fish, but it's hardly gourmet. It's worth reserving a table (you must do it the morning after you check in at 7am) at the Islander Beach Club for higher quality a-la-carte options. But, rules aside (there are a lot), the appeal here is the three swimming pools, a spa, beach club, gym, watersports, lively public spaces, a mini scuba course (included in the rate), and access to all of San Andrés's Decameron hotel amenities. It's a solid choice for families with young children.

Avenida Colón no. 6–106. www.decameron.com. ✆ **8/513-4343.** 224 units. Doubles from COP$850,000 (all-inclusive). **Amenities:** 3 restaurants; 2 bars; 3 outdoor pools; health club; spa, watersports equipment; concierge; babysitting; laundry service; nightly entertainment; laundry service; free Wi-Fi.

Villa San Miguel ★ In the center of town, half a mile from Spratt Bight beach, these functional apartments and compact studios, with kitchens/living rooms, Wi-Fi (reliable and free), air-conditioning, and cable TV, are pleasantly decorated, comfortable, and spacious. Although Villa San Miguel certainly doesn't ooze charm, it's a solid, well-priced option for self-catering travelers and families, with plenty of grocery stores, bars, and restaurants nearby to offset the lack of communal spaces or onsite restaurant.

Avenida Colombia. www.villasanmiguelsanandres.com. © **316/383-3397.** 7 units. Studios from COP$285,000, apartments from COP$330,000. **Amenities:** Bikes (no charge); kitchen; free Wi-Fi.

Where to Eat

Donde Francesca ★ SEAFOOD   On the very popular El Pirata beach, this cluster of Caribbean-kitsch *palapas* has tables on the beach and inside the rustic open-air dining room, strewn with fishing nets, shells, and colorful *artesanía*. There's a carnival ambience—reggae is usually playing and there's live music on the weekend—that serves creative, well-executed seafood, including creative ceviche iterations, *carpaccio de pulpo*, sesame-encrusted seared tuna steaks, and coconut shrimp. The margaritas are excellent. Certainly, it's expensive (relatively speaking), but there are few restaurants this good where you get to jump in and out of warm, crystal-clear water between courses.

El Pirata Beach, Playas de Sound Bay. © **8/513-0163.** Main courses COP$32,000–COP$76,000. Daily 7:30am–8:30pm.

Gourmet Shop Assho ★★ SEAFOOD   With creative gourmet fusion cuisine and an extensive wine list, this eclectic restaurant/bar/store is true to its name. The combination of bottles hanging from the ceiling, distressed wooden tables, green walls, and irreverent photographs and artworks results in a cozy, informal ambience that belies the chef's epicurean flair. Menu highlights include tender grilled octopus, seared salmon, inventive filet mignon preparations, and decadent desserts, all made in house.

The Grog ★★ SEAFOOD   On the sands of Rocky Cay, a 15-minute drive from Centro, the popular Grog is hard to beat for its beachfront location and a chilled-out Caribbean vibe. With your feet in the sand, you can dine on simple fried or grilled seafood dishes served with coconut rice and *patacones* (large deep fried plantain toast), *arroz con cangrejo* (rice with king crab), super-fresh ceviche, or flavorful shrimp laced with garlic, all washed down with an ice cold Michelada or terrific fruit cocktails, including excellent piña coladas. With just a few tables on the beach and scattered under umbrellas by the kitchen, the Grog fills up fast at lunchtime.

Bahía Cocoplum, Playa de Rocky Cay (next to Hotel Cocoplum). © **311/232-3247.** Main courses COP$23,000–COP$36,000. Daily 11am–6pm.

Miss Celia ★★ RAIZAL   For an authentic immersion into the flavors and rituals of Raizal cuisine, Miss Celia's is the place. While the namesake chef has passed away, the kitchen of this traditional wooden shack remains steeped in her traditions. With a festive ambience and chilled reggae soundtrack, you can dine inside the colorful and snug dining room strewn with fishing paraphernalia, on the lush terrace, or in the tropical garden. The classic dishes here are certainly hearty, such as the national dish, *rondón* (a rich stew of fish, meat, cassava, and plantains simmered in coconut milk), stewed conch, and for meat lovers, the classic *bandeja paisa* and *típico montañero*. The specialty of the house, the Miss Celia (COP$65,000), is a feast of grilled fish and seafood served with coconut rice. Try a refreshing *limonada de coco* as you peruse the vast menu.

Avenida Newball/Avenida Raizal. ℭ **8/513-1062.** Main courses COP$30,000–COP$60,000. Daily noon–10pm.

Restaurant Capitán Mandy ★ SEAFOOD   Don't be put off by the location or exterior of this casual seafood restaurant/fish market. Simple white tables and blue chairs, white walls decorated with aquatic murals and artwork create a nautical theme. Each creatively presented and well-executed dish is infused with Caribbean and Mediterranean flavors. There's a fantastic paella, fried coconut shrimp, ceviche, and Mandy's signature *octopus a la estrella*. Service is warm if rather too relaxed. This is a great place for a good-value, high-quality seafood lunch if you are in San Andrés town.

Avenida Rock Hole, Frente Agua Halley. ℭ **8/512-8481.** Main courses COP$22,000–COP$35,000. Daily noon–5pm.

Restaurant el Paraiso ★ SEAFOOD   Just a 15-minute ride from Centro, El Paraiso is another paradisiacal location to relax and dine on a gorgeous palm-fringed white-sand beach lapped by crystal clear waters. The gracious staff will serve you at a table in the restaurant, at a beachside table, or on your sun-lounger, where you can happily hang out for the day. The food is solid with a tasty (if predictable) menu that includes grilled and fried fish of the day, creamy crab soup, paella, lobster tail, and coconut rice with seafood.

San Luis Sound Bay 69–87, San Luis. ℭ **8/513-3881.** Main courses COP$28,000–COP$72,000. Daily 9am–5pm.

PROVIDENCIA ★★★

Some 50km (31 miles) north of San Andrés, Providencia has learned an ugly lesson from its bigger, brasher sibling, and it remains an offbeat Caribbean island that has retained not only its soul but also its glorious natural beauty. While it's just 7km (4⅓ miles) long and 3.5km (2 miles) wide, tiny Providencia packs a punch. The volcanic island boasts a much more dramatic topography than San Andrés, with a mountainous terrain draped in wild tropical forest and dry forest, interspersed with cascading waterfalls, bright sprays of tropical flowers, cotton, and breadfruit trees. The undisputed highlight, and one of Colombia's most compelling natural wonders, Old McBean Lagoon—the world's third-largest barrier reef—is an intoxicating vision of white-sand beaches, kaleidoscopic coral, and inviting waters brimming with marine life: the inspiration for untold numbers of (pretty cheap) PADI Open Water certification courses.

With a series of regulations firmly in place, Providencia has preserved its cultural identity; all hotels must be constructed in traditional Caribbean style

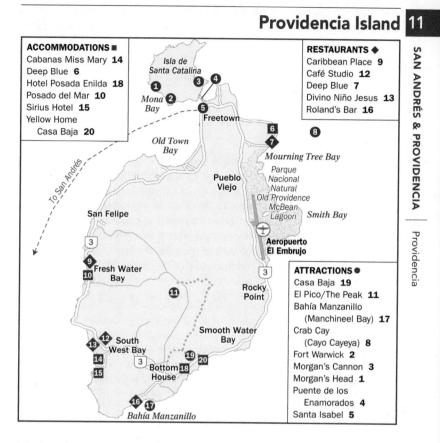

ACCOMMODATIONS ■
Cabanas Miss Mary **14**
Deep Blue **6**
Hotel Posada Enilda **18**
Posado del Mar **10**
Sirius Hotel **15**
Yellow Home
   Casa Baja **20**

RESTAURANTS ◆
Caribbean Place **9**
Café Studio **12**
Deep Blue **7**
Divino Niño Jesus **13**
Roland's Bar **16**

ATTRACTIONS ●
Casa Baja **19**
El Pico/The Peak **11**
Bahía Manzanillo
   (Manchineel Bay) **17**
Crab Cay
   (Cayo Cayeya) **8**
Fort Warwick **2**
Morgan's Cannon **3**
Morgan's Head **1**
Puente de los
   Enamorados **4**
Santa Isabel **5**

Isla de Santa Catalina
Mona Bay
Freetown
Old Town Bay
Mourning Tree Bay
Pueblo Viejo
Parque Nacional Natural Old Providence McBean Lagoon
Smith Bay
San Felipe
Aeropuerto El Embrujo
Fresh Water Bay
Rocky Point
Smooth Water Bay
South West Bay
Bottom House
Bahía Manzanillo
To San Andrés

(clapboard) and must not exceed two stories. Only locals are permitted to own property, and all developers and operators must partner with local owners. All around the island, signposts are in English—the English creole population call the island "Old Providence"—and colorful beach shacks, with a reggae soundtrack form the hub of social activity. All of Providencia's "settlements" are clustered around the island's bays and it's an easy place to navigate without an agenda. Providencia is a world that seems to have transcended all marketing spin—beaches and bays named Smooth Water, Crab Cay, and Rocky Cove speak to the inimitable lure of this beguiling island.

Essentials

GETTING THERE

BY PLANE   It's a 15-minute frog hopper from San Andrés to Providencia's **El Embrujo Airport** (PVA). There are around four flights per day with either government-owned **Satena** (www.satena.com; website in Spanish only) or **Searca** (www.searca.com.co); a return ticket will cost around COP$400,000 and always book well in advance during the high season. Decameron hotels and their affiliates (www.decameron.com) charter Searca flights as part of tour packages, which tends to be the most popular option for Colombian holidaymakers.

BY CATAMARAN   The catamaran boat El Sensation (www.facebook.com/elsensationcom; COP$280,000 return) makes the 2½- to 5-hour journey (depending on the conditions/time of year—in June and July and December/January, conditions reach their nadir) between San Andrés (from Muelle Casa de la Culture) at 8am, returning at 2:30pm.

GETTING AROUND

Providencia is tiny. There is no public transport on the island. It takes no more than 45 minutes to get around the entire island on either a moped or a golf cart. **Taxis** are generally available but can be expensive—around COP$20,000 to get from one side of the island to the other, or anywhere from the airport. **Mototaxis** are a popular way of getting around for locals and relatively inexpensive (around COP$6,000 to cross the island), but with insane drivers, it's not recommended. **Mopeds** are the cheapest rental options (COP$50,000 for 24 hr.) or you can hire a golf cart (around COP$120,000 for 24 hr.) from Santa Isabel. Many hotels can also have scooters, golf carts, and *mulas* delivered or available to rent on their property, but they will charge you a premium for the convenience.

VISITOR INFORMATION

There is a tourist office in Santa Isabel (by the harbor; © **8/514-8054**; open 9am–noon, 2–5pm). The Banco de Bogotá branch in Santa Isabel has an ATM, but you'd be wise to bring cash with you for your stay in Providencia.

Exploring Providencia

Just over 7km (4⅓ miles) long and 4km (2½ miles) wide, Providencia and Santa Catalina combined can be explored within the space of a day. A clutch of sights and natural attractions dot the island's circular coastal road. The island's main "town" and harbor, **Santa Isabel** has a nonchalant Caribbean vibe; colorful wooden buildings line ramshackle streets that trail off into verdant hillsides.

The west coast is where you'll encounter the most alluring stretches of sand. There's a tiny beach at **Freshwater Bay** (Aguadulce) where most of the larger hotels are located. With a smattering of smaller hotels, **Southwest Bay** (Bahía Suroeste) is the poster-perfect image that lures most travelers from the mainland; sugary white sands, almond trees and coconut palms, water so green it looks digitally enhanced, and a couple of restaurants where you can eat unadulterated fresh seafood and chill in a hammock with a rum cocktail in hand. On weekends, you can watch the locals ride horses bareback along the sand.

The smaller and more secluded (relatively speaking) Allan Bay (or Almond Beach) is located between Aguadulce and San Felipe. **Bahía Manzanillo** (Manchineel Bay) is a wild slither of sand—beware of the small fruit produced by the bay's namesake trees: They are toxic (even to the touch). It's a rite of passage to stop in at **Roland's Bar** (see p. 281), a bar with quasi-iconic status on the island.

At the northern tip of Providencia, the miniscule **Santa Catalina Island** is connected to Providencia by a charming, Enamorados pedestrian-only, 100-meter (328 ft.) wooden bridge, referred to locally as the Puente de los Enamorados (Lovers' Bridge). On the island's west side, **Morgan's Cannon** and **Fort Warwick** are the vestiges of a 300-year-old fort (complete with original cannons) built by the English to defend their hotly contested colony. When the Spanish retook the island in the 17th century, it was named Fuerte de la Libertad. Beyond the fort, there's a cave (another rumored treasure trove) and a fine beach, Playa del Fuerte, which is a marvelous place to snorkel and see abundant starfish.

On the southwest of Providencia, a tiny hamlet called **Casa Baja** marks the start of a well-marked hiking trail (very muddy during the rainy season) that weaves through dense rainforest, orchards, and cotton plantations to **El Pico** (The Peak), Providencia's tallest mountain (360m/11,000 ft.). The views of the barrier reef from the summit are nothing short of spectacular. It takes around 90 minutes to ascend and about an hour to come back down. From Casa Baja, there are signs pointed in direction of "The Peak," or any local will point you in the right direction. Once you are on the trail, it's a safe, straightforward climb, but there are standard guided tours offered in Santa Isabel for around COP$45,000.

PARQUE NATURAL NACIONAL OLD PROVIDENCE MCBEAN LAGOON ★★★

Declared a national park in 1996, Parque Natural Nacional Old Providence McBean Lagoon encompasses the beaches and bays of Providencia's northeast coast, including Maracaibo Bay (Bahía Maracaibo). Five vibrant ecosystems, including mangrove forests, dry tropical forest, and a healthy coral reef, provide sanctuary to a rich diversity of flora and fauna, including reptiles, birds (including pelicans and herons), and spectacular marine life. The water here is utterly spellbinding, a psychedelic spectrum of blue that ranges from indigo to turquoise, bottle green to aquamarine, which has given Providencia the alluring moniker of "sea of seven colors."

On land, a moderate 3km (1.9 mile) trail (you will need to take a guide, COP$25,000, from the park office) leads through dry forest and mangrove forest to **Iron Wood Hill** (150m/492 ft.). But the park's jewel in the crown is the Robinson Crusoe fantasy island of **Crab Cay** with its dazzling sands, crystalline waters, surreal coral, and magical sea creatures. You'll need to take a boat tour to get here (see below). En-route to Crab Cay, you can kayak through the mangroves of **Oyster Creek**, home to a prairie of sea grass speckled with coral and numerous wading birds, crabs, and fish.

Park hours: 9am–4:30pm. www.parquesnacionales.gov.co. ℂ **8/514-8885.** COP$14,500 adults, COP$4,000 children.

Tours The beauty of small islands is that everyone knows everyone, so standard prices and outsourcing resources means that you don't need to worry about shopping around. Tours in a speedboat take you around the island and stop at Crab Cay, Santa Isabel, and Southwest Bay; around COP$40,000 per person. Or, you can hire your own boat and skipper (from COP$370,000) for more flexibility.

DIVING

With extraordinarily clear water harboring immense biological riches, spectacular walls, and breathtaking coral reefs, Providencia's 37km (22-mile) barrier reef forms part of the UNESCO-protected Seaflower Biosphere Reserve. With its competitive prices and dramatic, varied dive sites within a very small, accessible area, Providencia has garnered kudos as an excellent, under-the-radar scuba destination for both beginner and experienced divers.

An extensive, steep wall with canyons and an intricate cave system runs along the western side of the reef (more than 182m/600 ft. long) which yields spectacular wall diving (for advanced divers). Popular dive sites include **Tete's Place** (13-m/40-ft. maximum depth), renowned for its large, predictable schools of tropical fish, goat fish, grunts, squirrel fish, and pillar coral. There's the much photographed **Turtle Rock**, with its colossal 10-meter/35-foot-wide rock (from 23m/75 ft.) with distinctive feathery black coral. At **Manta City** (a misnomer, there are no mantas here), Southern Stingrays with spectacular 5-meter (1½-ft.) wingspans convene, along with moray and lobster. Starting at a depth of 10 meters (35 ft.), the wall dive at **Felipe's Place** is another popular spot to see diverse coral species, snappers, groupers, lion fish, turtles, and, if you are lucky, sharks. There are a few wrecks in the area, including *Planchon*, a 90-meter-long (300-ft.) German tanker sunk during World War II.

Local operators on Providencia offer PADI open-water certification courses for around COP$850,000; two-tank dives run around COP$180,000. Recommended dive shops are **Sonny's Dive Shop** (Aguadulce; www.sonny diveshop.com; ℂ **318/274-4524**); **Felipe's Diving Shop** (Aguadulce; www.felipediving.com; ℂ **8/514-8775**) which is run by a local Raizal family; and in the Sirius Hotel, **Sirius Dive Shop** (Bahía Suroeste; www.siriushotel. net; ℂ **8/514-8213**).

Where to Stay

Cabanas Miss Mary ★   On a lovely stretch of palm-fringed white sand, the picture-perfect location is the draw at this traditional, brightly painted Decameron-affiliated hotel. The eight simple but adequate rooms, with orange walls and bright bedspreads, offer more frills than Miss Mary's more lackluster mid-range peers; there's powerful air-conditioning, consistent hot water (a rarity), and large balconies with hammocks and spellbinding views. The grounds and public spaces are vibrant, lush, and well-maintained, and at the popular onsite restaurant, you can dine on fresh fish with your feet in the sand. Southwest Bay. ℂ **8/514-8454.** 8 units. From COP$200,000, includes breakfast. **Amenities:** Restaurant; tours; scooter rental; free Wi-Fi.

Deep Blue ★★   On the edge of a turquoise lagoon, this secluded, intimate boutique hotel is Providencia's most luxurious accommodation choice. The

12 tastefully decorated rooms feature large modern bathrooms and air-conditioning, and revel in glorious ocean views. The chic public spaces are inviting and harness the hotel's in-harmony-with-the-landscape aesthetic. There's a small spa pool, a fine restaurant that sits right over the water with a deck—you can jump in and snorkel; there's no beach access here. The hotel has their own comfortable boat and offers a range of tours; it's COP$400,000 for a 4-hour beach/snorkeling tour (per couple). While this is by far the most upscale option on either San Andrés or Providencia, it's still a very undeveloped island, so you should expect inconsistent hot water and erratic Wi-Fi connectivity. If money is no object, the Luxury Suites have the best views and boast a plunge pool on the large terrace.

Maracaibo Bay. www.hoteldeepblue.com. ℂ **315/324-8443.** 12 units. Doubles from COP$585,000, suites from COP$785,000, includes breakfast. **Amenities:** Restaurant/bar; outdoor pool; spa; hot tub; tours; free Wi-Fi.

Hotel Posada Enilda ★ There's a mellow Caribbean vibe at this characterful mustard-yellow guesthouse, enshrouded by luxuriant vegetation. Gracious Raizal hosts Antonio and Enilda run a tight ship and provide friendly, personalized service. Simple, spotless rooms with white-painted walls, tiled floors, and crisp linens have air-conditioning, TVs, refrigerators and modern bathrooms. Breakfast is included, and the onsite Restaurant Enilda serves tasty regional dishes for lunch and dinner. As with most properties on the island, it's best to rent a *mula*/scooter if you are staying here. The dreamy Manzanillo beach is a 20-minute walk away.

Aguamansa 02. www.hotelposadaenilda.com. ℂ **320/855-4912.** From COP$170,000, includes breakfast. **Amenities:** Restaurant; free Wi-Fi.

Posado del Mar ★ This Decameron-affiliated hotel is a family-oriented posada located at Freshwater Bay (Aguadulce) where most hotels and restaurants are located. The colorful, Caribbean-style complex sits at the water's edge (you take out a kayak and snorkel), but there's no real beach here. The motel-style rooms (no hot water) have plastic furniture and unintentionally retro bedspreads, but they are clean and spacious with air-conditioning and refrigerators (there's a supermarket across the street), and all rooms have beautiful ocean views from balconies strewn with hammocks. While service can be slow, the staff are super-friendly. There is a swimming pool (towels are not provided) with a bar and a small kids' playground. Breakfast (included) is served in the cafeteria-style dining room, but there's no restaurant service for lunch or dinner; there are a handful of dining options within walking distance.

Freshwater Bay. www.decameron.com. ℂ **1/628-0000.** 24 units. From COP$124,000, includes breakfast. **Amenities:** Bar; cafe (no lunch/dinner service); outdoor pool; watersports equipment; free Wi-Fi (spotty service).

Sirius Hotel ★ On beautiful South West Bay, and with a dive school onsite, this modest Swiss/Colombian-owned hotel is scuba-centric, placing a wide menu of tours, equipment rental, and information at guest's disposal. Although some rooms have seen better days (it's worth looking at a couple before you commit) they are comfortable and spacious, with simple wooden furniture, vibrant flashes of color, air-conditioning, mosquito nets, fridges, and TVs. The larger suites have balconies with hammocks. Besides the dive school, the real appeal here is the location, close to the island's best beaches and within walking distance of restaurants and supermarkets.

South West Bay. www.siriushotel.net. ℂ **8/514-8213.** 10 units. From COP$170,000. **Amenities:** Restaurant; dive shop; free Wi-Fi.

Yellow Home Casa Baja ★★   In a great location, overlooking Manzanillo beach, run by gregarious hosts César and Doris, this traditional wooden guesthouse is a relaxed base for exploring the island. Tasteful rooms are pristine and fresh, with white-painted walls, quality linens, stylish black-and-white tiled bathrooms, wooden frame beds draped with mosquito nets, and hammocks on the balconies; there's no air-conditioning, but robust fans are sufficient for most guests. Doris prepares a terrific made-to-order breakfast each morning—the restaurant is one of the island's best—and will happily arrange tours/excursions around the island. There are scooters to rent onsite, a riot of vegetation in the gardens, and a terrace with terrific views.

Entrada a playa Manzanillo. ℂ **310/617-4960.** 3 units. From COP$250,000. **Amenities:** Restaurant; scooter/bike rental; free Wi-Fi.

Where to Eat

Caribbean Place ★★ SEAFOOD   With a cult clientele, this humble shack (decorated with island-theme paraphernalia and a pathway lined with empty wine bottles) is a great place for fresh, imaginative cuisine. The succulent fish dishes are infused with tropical and Asian flavors—try the grouper laced with ginger—and there's black crab, grilled lobster, crayfish, and ceviche. If you are fished out, the very good international fare includes grilled chicken, hamburgers, and pasta; opt for the fettuccini with shrimp over the spaghetti Bolognese. Caribbean Place offers a fine wine selection, delicious fresh juices, and homemade desserts including a memorable coconut pie. There's live music some nights, and the service is friendly and relaxed (albeit slow).

Freshwater Bay. ℂ **8/514-8698.** Daily noon–3pm, 6-10pm. Main courses COP$28,000–COP$68,000.

Café Studio ★★ CAFE/INTERNATIONAL   This cheerful but unassuming Canadian-owned, blue-painted cafe, strewn with holiday lights and nestled among riotous vegetation, belies the culinary pedigree of the kitchen. Inspired dinner entrees culminate with the island's famed black crab, but all the Creole specialties are delicious and served with creative flair. The eclectic menu spans international healthy fare, including salads and conch ceviche as well as copious portions of pasta; the penne pesto and spaghetti with shrimp are excellent. Save room for the cafe's decadent homemade pies—they are the talk of the island—or cheesecake. Excellent value.

Maroon Hill. Southwest Bay. ℂ **8/514-9076.** Mon–Sat 10am–10pm. Main courses COP$22,000–COP$32,000.

Deep Blue ★★ SEAFOOD   Providencia's most chi chi hotel is also home to the island's most elegant restaurant. The romantic setting, with tables on a stylish wooden terrace right over the turquoise waters of Crab Cay, is worth the trip alone. The menu doesn't stray beyond the obvious with artfully presented seafood and fish specials, including lobster with garlic butter, ceviche, coconut shrimp, calamari, and fish of the day bathed in a coconut sauce. There are also a couple of meat (steak and chicken) options for carnivores, and a well-rounded wine and Caribbean cocktail list.

Maracaibo Bay. www.hoteldeepblue.com. ✆ **315/324-8443.** Daily noon–3pm, 6–10pm. Main courses COP$28,000–COP$80,000.

Divino Niño Jesus ★ SEAFOOD   A statuette of the Jesus Child marks the way to this vibrant beach shack with an upbeat Caribbean vibe and reggae soundtrack on the magnificent white sands of Southwest Bay. The large menu features fish of the day (with myriad preparations), conch, seafood casseroles, garlic shrimp, ceviche, lobster, and a colossal seafood platter (the signature dish, for two) served with fish soup and mounds of coconut rice and plantains. You can take a post-lunch siesta in one of the hammocks strewn beneath the palm trees.

Southwest Bay. ✆ **318/791-1356.** Daily noon–10pm. Main courses COP$22,000–COP$50,000.

Roland's Bar ★★★ REGGAE BAR/SEAFOOD   Roland is a local legend on Providencia, and for a true Caribbean Marley vibe, this is the place. This chilled-out Rasta bar/restaurant keeps the reggae playing all day and all night long, and with Roland's signature piña coladas and hammocks swinging between palms by the water's edge, it's something of a ritual to stroll here for a sunset cocktail. The grilled fish and seafood menu (shrimp, conch, fish of the day) is nothing special but it's inexpensive, and it's the atmosphere here—nightly bonfires, dancing at night—that's the trump card.

Manzanillo Beach. ✆ **315/238-5980.** Daily 11am–late. COP$15,000–COP$30,000.

PLANNING YOUR TRIP TO COLOMBIA

by Nicholas Gill

Traveling to Colombia is easier and safer now than at any time in modern history. But it does take some advance planning, especially if you want to hit remote areas of the Amazon or Pacific Coast, or set out on multi-day hikes in the Andes. This chapter provides a variety of planning tools, including information on how to get there and on-the-ground resources.

GETTING THERE
By Plane

Most international planes arrive at El Dorado International Airport (airport code BOG; © 1/413-9053), located about 13km (8 miles) from the city center. El Dorado handles most international arrivals and you'll likely fly into Bogotá. Upon exiting the country, there is a departure tax of $59 (payable in U.S. dollars or the peso equivalent), though all or at least part of this is usually included in your ticket. Other major international airports in Colombia include Rio Negro International Airport in Medellín, Alfonso Bonilla Aragón International Airport in Cali, and Rafael Núñez International Airport in Cartagena.

FROM THE U.S. There are direct flights from New York, Atlanta, Miami, Orlando, and Washington D.C. **Avianca** (www.avianca.com; © 800/284-2622) has several daily flights to Bogotá, as well as one direct daily flight to Medellín and Cartagena. **American Airlines** (www.aa.com; © 800/433-7300) has three daily flights from Miami to Bogotá, two daily flights to Medellín, and one daily from Barranquilla. From JFK in New York, **Delta** (www.delta.com; © 800/221-1212) and Avianca each have one daily direct flight to Bogotá. From Atlanta, Delta and Avianca each offer one daily flight to Bogotá. **Copa** (www.copaair.com; © 800/550-7700) also offers service to Bogotá, though you'll have to connect in Panama. **JetBlue** (www.jetblue.com; ✆ **800/538-2583**) flies direct from Orlando to Bogotá, Medellín, Cali, and Cartagena daily. **Spirit** (www.spirit.com) has daily flights to Armenia, Bogotá, Medellín, and Cartagena from Ft. Lauderdale.

FROM CANADA   Air Canada (www.aircanada.com; ✆ **888/247-2262**) offers a direct flight between Toronto an d Bogotá several times a week. Otherwise, you'll have to connect in the U.S. using one of the carriers listed above, which might actually turn out to be a cheaper option.

FROM EUROPE & THE U.K.   From Paris, **Air France** (www.airfrance.co.uk; ✆ **0870/142-4343**) offers one daily direct flight to Bogotá. Iberia (www.iberia.com; ✆ **0845/601-2854**) flies direct to Bogotá from Madrid. Avianca, American, Continental, and Air France have flights from Madrid to Bogotá, connecting through Paris or in the U.S.; London, Rome, and Frankfurt offer similar options with one connection.

FROM AUSTRALIA & NEW ZEALAND   You'll be connecting in the U.S, and possibly Central or South America as well. Your best bet from Australia is on American Airlines, connecting in Los Angeles en route to Bogotá. From New Zealand, some of your better options are **LATAM** (www.latam.com; ✆ **800/435-9526**) and **Air New Zealand** (www.airnz.co.nz; ✆ **0800/737-000**), though be prepared for at least two stops.

By Bus

Although you can technically enter Colombia via Venezuela to the east and Ecuador to the south, this is not your safest option. It's much safer than it was a few years ago, but flying is not only much more secure, it's quicker and definitely more comfortable. If you insist on traveling by bus, be sure to make your journey during the daytime, and keep an eye on worsening Colombia-Venezuela relations if you're crossing in from Venezuela. You'll probably have to transfer buses at the border.

By Boat

Unless you're going directly to Cartagena, you probably won't be arriving by boat. That said, Cartagena is now becoming a popular stop for Caribbean Cruise liners and private yacht owners. Some of the cruise lines include **Celebrity** (www.celebritycruises.com), **Holland America** (www.hollandamerica.com), **NCL** (www.ncl.com), **Princess** (www.princess.com), and **Silversea** (www.silversea.com). Private yachts and sailing companies also offer trips from the San Blas Islands in Panama to Cartagena, starting at US$300 each way.

GETTING AROUND

Because of its size and natural barriers (including difficult mountain terrain and extensive jungle), getting around Colombia can be arduous. There's a good network of regional airports, so visitors with limited time tend to fly everywhere they can. Travel over land, though very inexpensive, can be extremely time-consuming and uncomfortable. However, for certain routes, inter-city buses or renting a car are your only real option.

By Plane

Flying is the fastest way to get around Colombia. Precipitous two-lane winding roads can make road travel long, tiring, and a bit nauseating. Distances by plane are usually short (between 30 min. and 1 hr.), though prices are relatively steep. Expect to pay about COP$150,000 to COP$500,000 for a 30- to 60-minute flight between major cities. Colombian airline prices are generally fixed and unlikely to vary much between airline carriers. **Avianca** (www.avianca.com; ℂ **018000/123-434**) is Colombia's largest and most extensive carrier, covering both domestic and international routes, while **Satena** (www.satena.com; ℂ **01900/331-7100**) flies to difficult locations such as the Amazon, the Pacific coast, and dozens of other small towns and villages.

Tip: It's important to note that if you will be using an international (non-Colombian) credit card to purchase your airline ticket online, you may need to book your flight at least 3 days in advance, or through a non-Colombian search engine such as Expedia. Another choice if you are short on time is to buy your tickets at the airport, where you won't have any problems using your credit card. Unless you're traveling during Christmas, Easter, or a busy holiday weekend, you shouldn't have too much trouble purchasing last-minute Colombian tickets.

By Bus

Since former President Uribe came to office in 2002, road travel in Colombia has improved dramatically. Most routes between major cities and towns are safe, though remote parts of Colombia can still be dangerous. It's a good idea to check security conditions before you board a long-distance night bus, especially if you'll be traveling through a high-risk area. You can find a bus to almost any city or town in the country from the Bogotá bus terminal, Terminal de Buses. Bus routes from Medellín, Cali, and Barranquilla also cover much of the country. Road conditions are generally good, but it's important to remember that these are two-lane mountain roads, so if there is a back-up or accident, you're stuck in place for at least a couple of hours. Also during the wet season—particularly October and November—the rain can cause mudslides and unpredictable road conditions.

Unless you're taking a route with irregular departures, it's unnecessary to book in advance (the exception being if you are traveling during Christmas or a Puente weekend, both 3-day holiday weekends, when you might want to consider purchasing your ticket a day or two in advance). Bus travel isn't as cheap as in nearby Ecuador or Peru; expect to pay about COP$20,000 per 100km (62 miles), but buses are generally comfortable. *Tip:* Stick to large buses, since small *colectivos* are bumpy and uncomfortable. And avoid taking *corrientes*, which seem to stop every couple of meters. No matter what class of bus, be prepared for onboard entertainment of vallenato and ranchera tunes, as well as ultraviolent movies, at whatever volume your driver chooses.

By Car

Renting a car in Colombia can be either the best idea or the worst. Car accidents are one of the top causes of death in Colombia. In urban areas, Colombians tend to be aggressive and careless behind the wheel, often neither following street signs or traffic lights nor giving pedestrians the right of way. On rural roads and mountain passes, winding roads and near head-on collisions with trucks, as well as the occasional livestock crossing, can be intimidating at best. Also, Colombian car-rental companies examine returned rentals extensively for the slightest dent and scratch. Public transportation options are safer and cheaper. Still, renting a car can give you the ability to investigate entire regions and out-of-the-way destinations where public transportation won't reach. Make sure you and the car are insured, and be aware that gas doesn't come cheap in Colombia—we're talking COP$2,000 a liter. Some companies that rent cars in Colombia are: **Avis** (www.avis.com), **Hertz** (www.hertz.com), and **Budget** (www.budget.com). Some upscale hotels also offer a chauffeur/car service, which can be rented by the hour or by the day, but don't expect any great deals.

TIPS ON HOTELS

Hotels in major cities tend to fill up on weekdays with business travelers and empty out on weekends, when you may be able to bargain up to a 50% discount. The reverse is true in small towns and in the countryside, where you'll pay up to 50% less during the week. One annoying thing about Colombian hotels is that many won't take reservations during holiday weekends or festivals, meaning you'll have to arrive early to reserve a room. Hotels in city centers tend to be dodgier and lower quality than those in outer, more upscale neighborhoods, and many double as pay-by-the-hour establishments—you may want to keep this in mind when making your reservation.

> ### FYI: Breakfast
>
> Most hotels in Colombia include breakfast in their rates. Breakfast may range from a huge buffet (and not only at the largest and most luxurious hotels) to continental breakfasts, or more austere, European-style breakfasts of bread, coffee, and jam.

Safety can be an issue at some hotels, especially at the lower end, and extreme care should be taken with regard to personal belongings left in the hotel. Leaving valuables lying around is asking for trouble. Except for hotels at the lowest levels, most have safety deposit boxes. (Usually only luxury hotels have room safes.) Place your belongings in a carefully sealed envelope. If you arrive in a town without previously arranged accommodations, you should be at least minimally wary of taxi drivers and others who insist on showing you to a hotel. Occasionally, they will provide excellent tips, but in general, they will be taking you to a place where they are confident they can earn a commission.

A final precaution worth mentioning is the electric heater found on many showerheads. These can be dangerous, and touching them while functioning can prompt an unwelcome electric jolt.

SPECIAL INTEREST TRIPS & TOURS

Study and volunteer programs, including Spanish-language programs, are often a great way to travel in and experience a country with greater depth than most independent and package travel allows. Cultural immersion and integration with locals are the aims of many such programs, leading to a richer and more unique experience for many travelers.

Because most travelers have limited time and resources, organized ecotourism or adventure travel packages, arranged by tour operators abroad or in Peru, are popular ways of combining cultural and outdoor activities. Birdwatching, horseback riding, rafting, and hiking can be teamed with visits to destinations such as San Agustín, San Gil, and Santa Marta.

Traveling with a group has several advantages over traveling independently. Your accommodations and transportation are arranged, and most (if not all) of your meals are included in the cost of a package. If your tour operator has a reasonable amount of experience and a decent track record, you should proceed to each of your destinations quickly without the snags and long delays that you might face if you're traveling on your own. You'll also have the opportunity to meet like-minded travelers who are interested in nature and active sports.

In the best cases of organized outdoors travel, group size is kept small (10–15 people), and tours are escorted by knowledgeable guides who are either naturalists or biologists. Be sure to inquire about difficulty levels when you're choosing a tour. While most companies offer "soft adventure" packages that those in decent but not overly athletic shape can handle, others focus on more hard-core activities geared toward very fit and seasoned adventure travelers.

Academic Trips & Language Classes

Consider the local language schools, primarily located in Cusco as well as Lima and Arequipa, and offering both short- and long-term study programs, often with home stays. **International Partners for Study Abroad** (www.studyabroadinternational.com) lists a number of Spanish-study programs in Medellín. **Transitions Abroad** (www.transitionsabroad.com) occasionally lists Spanish-study programs of short duration in Colombia and other South American countries; follow the "Study Abroad" tab on the website for options.

Two standout schools in Bogotá, Cartagena, and Medelllín are **Nueva Lengua** (www.nuevalengua.com; ✆ **315/855-9551**) and **Toucan Spanish School** (www.toucanspanish.com; ✆ **4/311-7176**), which are well organized and can arrange accommodation and other activities. Another school to try in Medellín is **Total Spanish** (www.totalspanishcolombia.com; ✆ **4/311-7049**), which has various levels of classes and a certification program.

Adventure Trips

These agencies and operators specialize in well-organized and coordinated tours that cover your entire stay. Many travelers prefer to have everything arranged and confirmed before arriving in Colombia—a good idea for first-timers and during high season. Many of these operators provide great service but are not cheap; 10-day tours generally cost upwards of US$2,500 or more per person, and do not include airfare to Colombia.

Adventure Life (www.adventure-life.com; ✆ **800/344-6118**), based in Missoula, Montana and specializing in Central and South America, has an interesting roster of rugged Colombia trips, frequently with a community focus, including a 9-day multi-sport tour (mountain biking, hiking, rafting, and coffee fincas), rainforest ecolodge tours, and a 6-day hike in Los Nevados National Park, as well as a 6-day back roads biking trip from Villa de Leyva to the Chichamocha Canyon.

Class Adventure Travel (CAT) (www.cat-travel.com; ✆ **877/240-4770** in the U.S. and Canada, 0207/0906-1259 in the U.K.) is a fine all-purpose agency with Colombia tours ranging from 7 to 12 days. In addition to professionally organizing virtually any kind of travel detail in Colombia, its adventure offerings include rafting, trekking, and jungle tours.

Journeys International (www.journeys.travel; ✆ **800/255-8735**), based in Ann Arbor, Michigan, offers small-group (4–12 people) natural history tours guided by naturalists. Trips include the 11-day "Colombia Kaleidoscope," which includes the Parque Nacional Tayrona along with Cartagena, Bogotá, and the Valle de Cocora.

Overseas Adventure Travel (www.oattravel.com; ✆ **800/955-1925**) offers natural history and "soft adventure" itineraries, with optional add-on excursions. Tours are limited to 16 people and are guided by naturalists. All accommodations are in small hotels, lodges, or tent camps. The 12-day "Colonial Jewels and the Coffee Triangle" includes exploring the colonial architecture of Bogotá and Cartagena, tasting coffee in the fincas of Manizales and Pereira, and cumbia dancing lessons. They also offer frequent cruises through the Panama Canal that begin or end in Cartagena.

Southern Explorations (www.southernexplorations.com; ✆ **877/784-5400**), based in Seattle that specializes in Latin America, offering a variety of Colombia tours, ranging from 6 to 14 days, which include hiking in Parque Nacional Tayrona, mountain biking in Parque Nacional Iguaque, and rafting the Chichamocha canyon.

Wilderness Travel (www.wildernesstravel.com; ✆ **800/368-2794**) is a Berkeley-based outfitter specializing in cultural, wildlife, and hiking group tours that are arranged with tiered pricing (the cost of the trip varies according to group size). In Colombia, they offer a 10-day cruise that includes the Panama Canal, Islas Rosarios, Cartagena, Santa Marta, and other Caribbean islands.

Culinary Trips

While Colombian cuisine hasn't attracted the attention of neighboring Peru, news of its diverse set of ingredients and vibrant cultural traditions, not to mention fine restaurants, is spreading. Several companies now offer food-centric vacations.

Owned by several young Americans and a Colombian, **La Mesa Food Tours** (www.delamesa.com; ✆ **316/530-8590** in the U.S.) offer street food tours of Bogotá and Medellín, as well as day trips to the coffee fincas in the Zona Cafetero. In Bogotá, food bloggers Karen Attman and Peter Corredor of **Flavors of Bogotá** (www.flavorsofbogota.com) run a behind-the-scenes coffee shop tour that puts you in touch with the city's best baristas and roasters.

Guided Tours

BIKE TOURS

Mountain biking is still in its infancy in Colombia, although fat-tire options are growing fast. Several tour companies in those places rent bikes, and the quality of the equipment is continually being upgraded. If you plan to do a lot of biking and are very attached to your rig, bring your own.

U.K.-based **Red Spokes** (www.redspokes.co.uk; ✆ **44/207-502-7252**) offers a 14-day cycling trip from Medellín to Bogotá, stopping at coffee fincas and colonial villages. With offices in San Gil, Medellín, and Cartagena, **Colombian Bike Junkies** (www.colombianbikejunkies.com; ✆ **316/327-6101**) is one of the most professional and best-equipped bike companies in Colombia. They offer specialized day trips, such as the Suarez Canyon or Guatape. **Cyclota** (www.cyclota.com; ✆ **316/833-4072**), based in Bogotá, has bike rentals and offers a variety of cycling tours around the country. There are intense training camps at altitude, downhill day trips, backroads between colonial villages, and just simple day trips around Bogotá.

BIRD-WATCHING

Colombia is the world's richest birding nation and one of the greatest countries on earth for birders. Its bird list includes nearly 2,000 species of resident and migrant birds identified throughout the country, more than any other country on earth, not to mention more than 70 endemics. With so many distinct microclimates, great bird-watching sites abound.

Colombia Bird Watch (www.colombiabirdwatch.com) is a Colombia-based tour operator with fixed-date trips and customized tours in small groups to more off the beaten track birding destinations around the country, such as the Chocó, Putomayo, and the Valle de Cauca.

Field Guides (www.fieldguides.com; ✆ **800/728-4953**) is an Austin, Texas–based specialty bird-watching travel operator with trips worldwide. It features five birding trips to Colombia, including Los Llanos, Andean cloud forests, Bogotá, and the Sierra Nevada de Santa Marta. Group size is limited to 14 participants.

Kolibri Expeditions (www.kolibriexpeditions.com; © **01/652-7689**) offers birding tours across South America, including around Colombia. Their intensive 19-day tour of the Magdalena and Cauca valleys, as well as the west coast of El Chocó. Most of their offerings are no-frills, budget camping trips, but the outfit also offers a few pampered, high-end trips.

WINGS (www.wingsbirds.com; © **866/547-9868** from the U.S.) is a specialty bird-watching travel operator with 3 decades of experience in the field. It promotes several trips to Colombia, including a 20-day trip to the Cauca Valley, the Sierra Nevada de Santa Marta, and Bogotá. Group size is usually between 6 and 18 people.

HORSEBACK RIDING

Lovers of horseback riding will find several areas in Colombia to pursue their interest, as well as hotels and operators that can arrange everything from a couple hours in a saddle to 2-week trips on horseback.

For riding around San Agustín, most local operators can arrange day-long trips to the different sets of statues and in the countryside.

Based in Bogotá, **Riding Colombia** (www.ridingcolombia.com; © **01/9503-14065**), has 1- to 6-day tours on Colombian *criollo* horses, in groups of two to six people.

SURFING

Though it remains somewhat under the radar, Colombia has some superb waves if you know where to look. The swells are best from December through March and July through September. The best spots tend to be on the Pacific Coast, where the waves are stronger, though those on the Caribbean side tend to be more accessible. On the Pacific Coast, most base themselves out of lodges like **El Cantil** (www.elcantil.com) or the **Humpback Turtle** (www.humpbackturtle.com) to surf local beaches or hire boatmen to take them farther afield. **Asta Adventures** (www.astadventures.com; © **310/424-3530** in the U.S.) offers organized tours of Pacific Coast surfing spots out of Nuquí. In Parque Nacional Tayron on the Caribbean side, **Costeño Beach Surf Hostel** (www.costenobeach.com) has a surf camp and can arrange trips to area breaks.

Volunteer & Working Trips

Several institutions and organizations work on humanitarian and sustainable development projects in Colombia. Some international relief organizations, such as **Doctors Without Borders** (www.doctorswithoutborders.org), accept volunteers to work crises and relief efforts. The lingering effects of the civil war, not to mention upticks in tropical diseases like malaria, bring hundreds of volunteers to Colombia. The NGO **Misión Gaia** (www.misiongaia.org) helps develop socio-environmental programs in local communities in the Sierra Nevada de Santa Marta.

Colombia isn't the place to wander off the beaten path, not even in cities. Stick to neighborhoods you know are safe. The following advice is relevant, particularly in large cities.

- Never resist an attempted robbery—Colombian criminals can be armed and unpredictable. Carry at least a little cash on you to avoid angering thieves. There have been cases of tourists being killed for resisting robbery.
- Always call a cab at night, especially if you have been drinking or if you're traveling alone. If your Spanish skills are limited or you are a woman traveling alone, I advise you to always call a cab to avoid being taken on a long and expensive ride. Always make sure the cab door is locked to avoid an armed assailant hopping in at a stoplight. Calling a cab only costs a bit more, and since the cab number is registered by the company, the chances of something happening are much lower. The same goes for Uber, available in large cities.
- Don't accept any drinks, drugs, or cigarettes from a stranger or someone you've just met; they could be laced with an odorless drug called scopolamine that makes you lose your will while you are robbed. Also, it's best not to pick up any papers or cash that someone walking ahead of you drops, because this can also be the same kind of trick. This is especially important for women. These types of crimes are rare but not unheard of, and can happen in taxis as well. If you start to feel dizzy or sick, get someone's attention.
- If you're a man out drinking or partying alone, be very cautious before going home with a Colombian woman or group of women. Although rare, there have been cases of foreigners and even Colombians being drugged with scopolamine and robbed while under the influence. It's always best to go out with a group in Colombia, especially in big cities.
- Many travelers who come to Colombia do so because of the wide variety of drugs available. While you will probably see many locals smoking marijuana, getting high off inhalants, and even smoking crack on the streets, particularly in Medellín, I strongly advise against buying or doing drugs in Colombia. You can easily be set up by the "seller," who then turns you in to the "police," who then extort significant sums of money from you. Penalties for buying drugs are hefty, and the last thing you want to do is spend 10 years in a Colombian prison.
- If someone approaches you claiming to be a police officer and asks for your documents, go to the nearest police station; never give your money or documents to someone claiming to be an undercover officer.
- Women traveling alone may want to dress modestly to avoid unwanted attention from men. Colombia is still very much a "macho" country, and many men think that a woman traveling alone, particularly one dressed provocatively, is fair game. In Bogotá, women tend to dress conservatively, and showing too much skin may attract unwanted attention. As an extra precaution, women should always call for a taxi rather than hailing it on the street.

Other volunteer programs include **Habitat for Humanity** (www.habitat.org; © 800/422-4828), with a base in Bogotá (© 571/235-0090); and **Volunteers for Peace** (www.vfp.org; © 802/259-2759), based in Vermont.

Walking Tours

Colombia is a very underrated hiking destination. While security issues once prevented many of the greatest trails from being seen, most are now open and just waiting to be discovered. The country's most famous trek is the 5-day trail to Ciudad Pérdida, the 1,200-year-old Kogi city in the Sierra Nevada de Santa Marta. The 44km route passes through lush rainforest and through indigenous villages that rarely see outsiders. Other good hikes include the Páramo landscapes near Bogotá, like Chingaza or Sumapaz, as well as the 6-day circuit in the Sierra Nevada de Cocuy. The best months for climbing are during the dry season, between December and March.

Many tour companies based in the United States and elsewhere subcontract portions of their tours, particularly guided hikes and treks, to established Colombian companies on the ground in Bogotá, Santa Marta, and across the country. Though it's often simpler to go with international tour companies, in some cases, independent travelers can benefit by organizing their tours directly with local agencies. Prices on the ground can be cheaper than contracting a tour from abroad, but there are risks of not getting what you want when you want it.

Backroads (www.backroads.com; ✆ **800/462-2848**) is a luxury-tour company that offers upscale, light-adventure trips around the globe, and it has several tours of Colombia on its menu. It specializes in walking, hiking, and biking tours from along Parque Nacional Tayrona and the Caribbean coast, Bogotá, and the coffee triangle. Service is personalized and the guides are top-notch.

In Santa Marta, **Turcol** (www.turcoltravel.com; ✆ **5/421-2256**) is one of the original companies offering guided hikes to Ciudad Pérdida. **The Colombian Way** (www.thecolombianway.co; ✆ **44/20-8099-3506** in the U.K.), based in the U.K., sets up both day hikes and multi-day treks around the country, including Ciudad Pérdida, Caño Cristales, Tierradentro, and cloud forests near Bogotá.

[FastFACTS] COLUMBIA

Addresses Av." (sometimes "Avda.") is an abbreviation for "Avenida," or avenue. "Ctra." is the abbreviation for *carretera*, or highway; cdra. means *cuadra*, or block; and "of." is used to designate office (*oficina*) number.

Business Hours Business hours vary significantly between urban and rural areas. In urban areas,

businesses and banks are generally open between 8am and noon, and then again between 2 and 6pm. In Bogotá, banks are supposedly open all day between 8am and 4pm. Stores are generally open between 9am to 5pm, while department stores and large supermarkets generally stay open until around 9pm. In the countryside, businesses

and stores are generally open fewer hours and don't necessarily stick to their posted schedules. Also, many businesses close down or reduce their hours on Sundays and holidays.

Customs Upon entering Colombia, you will be asked to complete a Customs form detailing your personal effects. There is a regularly updated limit on cash and

shopping **IN COLOMBIA**

Handicrafts are relatively cheap and easy to find in Colombia. In urban areas, you're likely to find the best bargains in city centers; handicraft stores in upscale shopping malls charge at least double the price, though you're generally guaranteed quality. In small towns and rural areas, you can expect to find more authentic and regional crafts at fair prices. At markets and such, you may be able to bargain somewhat, though don't expect a price to drop more than a couple of thousand pesos.

Aside from handicrafts, Colombians are serious about clothing. Bogotá, Cartagena, and Cali are a shopaholic's dream come true. At shopping centers and boutiques in more upscale areas, clothing is generally high quality, albeit a bit expensive. In the most upscale city zones and shopping centers, you'll be greeted by the likes of Louis Vuitton, Desigual, and other designers. Shoes and leather handbags, as well as gold and emerald jewelry, are popular buys and can be purchased at decent prices; it's best to ask around to find the spots with the best bargains.

goods you may take out of the country. Because of strict drug-trafficking laws, do not try to take more money out of Colombia than you claim—at a minimum, this could result in heavy questioning. For more information regarding this limit, call ☏ **1/546-2200** or 1/457-8270. Usually, there's a limit of about US$10,000. When leaving the country, you must pay an airport departure tax of about COP$114,520, though this tax is often included in your airline ticket.

For information on what you're allowed to bring home, contact one of the following agencies:

Australian citizens: Australian Customs Service (www.border.gov.au; ☏ **1300/363-263**).

Canadian citizens: Canada Border Services Agency (www.cbsa-asfc.gc.ca; ☏ **800/461-9999** in Canada, or 204/983-3500).

New Zealand citizens: New Zealand Customs, The Customhouse, 17–21 Whitmore St., Box 2218, Wellington (www.customs.govt.nz; ☏ **04/473-6099** or 0800/428-786).

U.K. citizens: HM Customs & Excise (www.hmce.gov.uk; (☏ **0845/010-9000**, or from outside the U.K., 020/8929-0152).

U.S. citizens: U.S. Customs & Border Protection (CBP), 1300 Pennsylvania Ave., NW, Washington, D.C. 20229 (www.cbp.gov; ☏ **877/287-8667**).

Disabled Travelers

Colombia is considerably less equipped for accessible travel than most parts of North America and Europe. Comparatively few hotels are outfitted for travelers with disabilities, and only a few restaurants, museums, and means of public transportation make special accommodations for such patrons. There are few ramps, very few wheelchair-accessible bathrooms, and almost no telephones for the hearing-impaired.

A helpful website for accessible travel in Colombia is **Access-Able Travel Source** (www.access-able.com), which offers detailed destination articles on accessible travel in Colombia. Within individual reviews, you'll find information on ramps, door sizes, room sizes, bathrooms, and wheelchair availability.

Doctors Skilled doctors and modern health care facilities can be found primarily in Bogotá and other large cities in Colombia. Some of the best hospitals in Bogotá are **Clínica Marly**, Calle 50, no. 9–67 (☏ **1/570-4424**, 1/572-5011, or 1/343-6600); **Fundación Santa Fe**, Calle 119, no. 9–02 (☏ **1/629-0766** or 629-0477); and **Clínica El Bosque**, Calle 134, no. 12–55 (☏ **1/274-0577**, 1/274-5445, or 1/649-9300).

There are a number of pharmacy chains in the country, most with 24-hour locations, such as **Droguerias Olimpica** and **Farmacity**. Ask at your hotel what is the most convenient location according to where you are.

Drug & Drinking Laws

While Colombia is no longer the world's largest producer of coca leaves, the cocaine trade is still a serious issue here. While small amounts of some drugs, such as cocaine and marijuana, have been decriminalized in recent years, it's best to stay far away from drugs in Colombia. Penalties can be severe.

The legal drinking age in Colombia is 18, though laws are lenient. In urban areas such as Bogotá, Medellín, Cartagena, and Cali, you may be asked to show ID to get into upscale bars and clubs. There are no laws against drinking in public, so if you are low on funds, feel free to open up a bottle of aguardiente in the nearby park or plaza.

Electricity
Electric outlets accept U.S.-type plugs. Electricity in Colombia runs at 110 volts, so transformers are not necessary for tourists from the U.S. If you are planning to use anything with a three-prong plug, bring an adapter, as some establishments only have two-prong outlets.

Embassies & Consulates
In Bogotá: **Australia** (consulate): Carrera 18 no. 90–38 (✆ **1/636-5247** or

1/530-1047); **New Zealand** (consulate): Diagonal 109 no. 1–39 Este, Apt. 401 (pearsona@cable.net.co; ✆ **1/629-8524**); **United Kingdom**: Carrera 9 no. 76–49, Piso 9 (✆ **1/326-8300** or 1/317-6423 for visa information); **United States**: Calle 22, Bis. 47–51 (✆ **1/315-0811**); **Canada**: Carrera 7 no. 115–33, Piso 14 (✆ **1/657-9800**).

Emergencies
In Bogotá, the police emergency number is ✆ 112. Another emergency number that works throughout the country is 123. Other good emergency numbers to know: the Security Police (DAS; ✆ **153/0180-0091-9622**); the Tourist Police (✆ **1/337-4413** or 1/243-1175); and the police station in Bogotá (✆ **156**). The fire department can be reached by calling **119**, and information can be reached by dialing **113**.

Family Travel
Colombians are extremely family-oriented, and children arouse friendly interest in locals. Although there aren't many established conventions, accommodations, or discounts for families traveling with children, Colombia can be an excellent country in which to travel, as long as families remain flexible and are able to surmount difficulties in transportation, food, and accommodations. Few hotels automatically offer discounts for children or allow children to stay free with their parents. Negotiation with hotels is required. On buses, children have to pay full fare if they occupy a

seat (which is why you'll see most kids sitting on their parent's or sibling's lap). Many museums and other attractions offer discounts for children 5 and under. Children's meals are rarely found at restaurants in Colombia outside of chains, but sometimes it's possible to specially order smaller portions. Colombian food might be very foreign to many children, though familiar foods, such as fried chicken, pizza, and hamburgers, are easy to find in almost all Colombian towns.

Health
In major cities, you'll have little cause for worry. Water is generally fine to drink, though cautious travelers may want to stick to bottled water. The problem you're most likely to encounter is traveler's diarrhea from inexpensive food. Use common sense—avoid eating unpeeled fruits and vegetables from street vendors, wash your hands frequently, and when trying a new fruit or vegetable, don't overdo it. Remember to wear sunscreen at all times, even in cool cities like Bogotá. You're closer to the sun, and you don't want to let sunburn ruin your vacation. In major cities, healthcare is adequate and professional, as long as you stick to private clinics. Public clinics tend to have long lines and are usually understaffed and underfunded.

If you are visiting the Andean region, altitude sickness is a possibility. Though it generally goes away after 2 to 5 days, it may be helpful to bring

12

along Tylenol, Advil, or another over-the-counter painkiller. Symptoms include headache, shortness of breath, fatigue, nausea, and sleepiness. Try to take it easy the first day or two to avoid worsening your condition. You might experience altitude sickness in Bogotá or Tunja, or when hiking in the high Andes.

Although no vaccines are required to enter Colombia, it's a good idea to consider getting vaccinations for hepatitis A and B, typhoid, and yellow fever if you will be visiting the Atlantic or Pacific coasts, the Amazon region, or any other tropical region. (As a general rule, the more rural your location in the country's tropical regions, the higher your risk of contracting diseases such as malaria, yellow fever, or cholera). Dengue fever is another concern in the tropics, though unfortunately there is no preventative vaccine. You should also consider taking malaria pills if you will be visiting any of the above regions.

North American visitors can contact the **International Association for Medical Assistance to Travelers** (IAMAT; www.iamat.org; ✆ **716/754-4883**, or **416/652-0137** in Canada) for tips on travel and health concerns. The United States **Centers for Disease Control and Prevention** (www.cdc.gov; ✆ **888/232-6348**) provides up-to-date information on health hazards by region or country. If you suffer from a chronic illness, consult your

doctor before your departure. All visitors with such conditions as epilepsy, diabetes, or heart problems should consider wearing a **MedicAlert Identification Tag** (www.medicalert.org; www.medicalert.org.uk in the U.K.; ✆ **888/633-4298** or **209/668-3333**), which will alert doctors to your condition should you become ill, and give them access to your records through MedicAlert's 24-hour hotline.

Insurance   U.S. visitors should note that most domestic health plans (including Medicare and Medicaid) do not provide coverage abroad, and the ones that do often require you to pay for services upfront and reimburse you only after you return home. Try **MEDEX** (www.medexassist.com; ✆ **410/453-6300**) or **Travel Assistance International** (www.travelassistance.com; ✆ **800/821-2828**) for overseas medical insurance coverage. **Canadians** should check with their provincial health plan offices or call **Health Canada** (www.hc-sc.gc.ca; ✆ **866/225-0709**) to find out the extent of their coverage and what documentation and receipts they must take home in case they are treated overseas.

For general travel insurance, it's wise to consult one of the price comparison websites before making a purchase. U.S. visitors can get estimates from various providers through **Insure-MyTrip.com** (✆ **800/487-4722**). Enter your trip cost

and dates, your age, and other information, for prices from several providers. For U.K. travelers, **Moneysupermarket** (www.moneysupermarket.com) compares prices and coverage across a bewildering range of single- and multi-trip options. For all visitors, it's also worth considering trip-cancellation insurance, which will help retrieve your money if you have to back out of a trip or depart early. Trip cancellation traditionally covers such events as sickness, natural disasters, and travel advisories.

Internet & Wi-Fi   The availability of the Internet across Colombia is in a constant state of development. How you access it depends on whether you've brought your own laptop, tablet, or smartphone, or if you're searching for a public terminal. Internet access is plentiful, particularly in the form of free high-speed **Wi-Fi**, which is available in most hotels, cafes in larger cities, and airports. Cybercafes (*cafés Internet*, or *cabinas*) can still be found in some areas, though they are not nearly as prevalent as they once were. Connections are generally fast and cheap. Expect to pay about COP$1,500 to COP$3,000 per hour. Most hotels will have at least one public computer. May public parks also have free Wi-Fi.

If you have your own computer or smartphone, **Wi-Fi** makes access much easier. Always check before using your hotel's network—many charge exorbitant rates, and free or cheap Wi-Fi isn't hard to find elsewhere, in urban locations at least. Ask locally, or even Google "free Wi-Fi + [town]" before you arrive. Savvy smartphone users from overseas may call using Wi-Fi in combination with a **Skype** (www.skype.com) account and mobile app.

Language   Except for a tiny percentage of rural indigenous communities, Spanish is universally spoken in Colombia. It's hard to find Colombians who speak English, even in Bogotá, so it's important to brush up on you skills before your trip. Outside of Bogotá and the major cities, you'll be hard-pressed to find any English speakers, which can make traveling in a non-touristy country quite difficult if you don't speak any Spanish. Learning a few key phrases of Spanish will help immensely. Turn to chapter 13 for those, and consider picking up a copy of the *Frommer's Spanish Phrase-Finder & Dictionary.*

Legal Aid   If you need legal assistance, your best bets are your embassy (which, depending on the situation, might not be able to help you much), which might be able to direct you to an English-speaking attorney or legal assistance organization. Note that bribing a police officer or public official is illegal in Colombia, even if it is a relatively constant feature of traffic stops and the like. If a police officer claims to be

an undercover cop, do not automatically assume that he is telling the truth. Do not get in any vehicle with such a person. Demand the assistance of your embassy or consulate.

Your first move for any serious matter should be to contact your consulate or embassy (see "Embassies & Consulates," earlier in this section). They can advise you of your rights and will usually provide a list of local attorneys (for which you'll have to pay if services are used), but they cannot interfere on your behalf in the English legal process. For questions about American citizens who are arrested abroad, including ways of getting money to them, telephone the **Citizens Emergency Center** of the Office of Special Consulate Services in Washington, D.C. (✆ **202/501-4444**).

LGBT Travelers   Colombia, a predominantly Catholic and socially conservative country, cannot be considered among the world's most progressive in terms of societal freedoms for gays and lesbians. It remains a male-dominated, macho society where homosexuality is considered deviant. Across Colombia, there is still considerable prejudice exhibited toward gays and lesbians who are out, or men—be they straight or gay—who are thought to be effeminate. In the larger cities, especially Bogotá, Medellín, and Cartagena, there are a number of establishments—bars,

discos, inns, and restaurants—that are either gay-friendly or predominantly gay. Outside those areas, and in the small towns and villages of rural Colombia, openly gay behavior is unlikely to be tolerated by the general population.

If you're planning to visit from the U.S., the **International Gay and Lesbian Travel Association** (**IGLTA;** www.iglta.org; ✆ **800/448-8550** or 954/630-1637) is the trade association for the gay and lesbian travel industry, and offers an online directory of gay- and lesbian-friendly travel businesses. Many agencies offer tours and travel itineraries specifically for gay and lesbian travelers. **Above and Beyond Tours** (www.abovebeyond tours.com; ✆ **800/397-2681**) is a gay and lesbian tour operator. **Now, Voyager** (www.nowvoyager.com; ✆ **800/255-6951**) is a well-known, San Francisco–based, gay-owned and -operated travel service.

Mail   The postal system in Colombia is relatively efficient in large cities, though the same can't be said for rural areas. Servientrega, DHL, FedEx, and DePrisa are available in Colombia for local and international shipping services, as is Avianca Airlines. While mail within Colombia is cheap, sending items abroad is extremely expensive.

Mobile Phones   The three letters that define much of the world's wireless capabilities are **GSM**

(Global System for Mobiles), a seamless satellite network that makes for easy cross-border cellphone use throughout most of the planet. If your cellphone is unlocked and on a GSM system, and you have a world-capable multiband phone, you can make and receive calls throughout much of Colombia. (Mobile coverage in Colombia, even in rural areas, is surprisingly good.) Just call your wireless operator and ask for "international roaming" to be activated on your account. Unfortunately, per-minute charges can be high.

Per-minute charges for international calls can be high whatever network you choose, so if you plan to do a lot of calling home, use a VoIP service like **Skype** (www.skype.com) in conjunction with a Web connection. See "Internet & Wi-Fi," above. For advice on making **international calls**, see "Telephones," p. 300.

Money & Costs   On the whole, though prices have risen in the past few years and Colombia is slightly more expensive than its Andean neighbors like Ecuador (but less expensive than Brazil), Colombia remains relatively inexpensive by North American and European standards. To those with strong currencies, Colombia (outside of top-end restaurants and hotels) is likely to seem comparatively cheap. In the bigger cities, prices for virtually everything—but especially hotels and

restaurants—are higher, particularly in Bogotá and Cartagena. In addition, prices can rise in the high season, such as the Independence Day holidays (late July), Easter week (Mar or Apr), or Christmas, due to heavy demand, especially for hotel rooms and bus and plane tickets.

The Colombian peso (COP$) is the official currency. Money is denominated in notes of 1,000, 2,000, 5,000, 10,000, 20,000, and 50,000, and coins of 20, 50, 100, 200, and 500 pesos. At press time, US$1 equals COP$2,930. These rates can fluctuate somewhat, so it's important to check the latest exchange rate at **www.xe.com/ucc**.

Frommer's lists exact prices in local currency (and occasionally in dollars, principally with regard to hotels that list rates in U.S. dollars).

Unlike in other Latin-American countries, the U.S. dollar is not widely accepted in Colombia, except in a few super-high-end establishments. You can convert your currency in upscale hotels, at casas de cambio (money-exchange houses), at most banks, and at the airport. It's not recommended to bring traveler's checks to Colombia. They can be exchanged at some banks and used at high-end hotels, but usually they aren't accepted elsewhere. Make sure your bank or issuer has a representative in Colombia before purchasing traveler's checks.

ATMs (cash machines) are easy to find in urban areas and most medium-to-large-size towns, though they are almost impossible to come across in rural areas. Withdrawing money from ATMs is preferable to exchanging money in banks, which charge a sometimes hefty transaction fee. ATMs also give you the most up-to-date rate of exchange. Thefts at ATMs have been reported, however, so if you are taking out large sums of money, be sure not to put all your cash in one place (spread the bills among your pockets). It's best to use ATM machines located inside a building, as these offer more security.

Warning: If you are having trouble with an ATM, do not accept help from anyone, even if he or she seems friendly and honest. This is the easiest way to wipe out your bank account. Be sure you know your personal identification number (PIN) and daily withdrawal limit before you depart. At some ATMs, your personal identification number (PIN) must contain four digits.

Credit cards, particularly Visa and MasterCard, are generally accepted in mid-range and upscale shops, as well as at upscale restaurants and hotels around the country. In rural areas and small towns, you are unlikely to find establishments that accept credit cards. When booking tours, you're likely to get a better deal when using cash. Travelers should beware of hidden credit- or debit-card fees. Check with your card issuer to see what fees, if any, will be charged for overseas transactions. Recent reform legislation in the U.S., for example, has curbed some exploitative lending practices. But many banks have responded by increasing fees in other areas, including fees for customers who use credit and debit cards while out of the country—even if those charges were made in U.S. dollars. Fees can amount to 3% or more of the purchase price. Check with your bank before departing to avoid any surprise charges on your statement.

Counterfeit bank notes and even coins are common, and merchants and consumers across Colombia vigorously check the authenticity of money before accepting payment or change. (The simplest way: Hold the bank note up to the light to see the watermark.) Many people also refuse to accept bank notes that are not in good condition (including those with small tears, that have been written on, and even that are simply well worn), and visitors are wise to do the same when receiving change, to avoid problems with other payments. Do not accept bills with tears (no matter how small) or taped bills.

Making change in Colombia can be a problem. You should carry small bills and even then be prepared to wait for change.

Packing Outside of a few high-end restaurants

and clubs in Bogotá and Medellín, Colombia is overwhelmingly casual. You should probably be more concerned about packing the proper outdoor gear than the best duds to go out and be seen in. If traveling in rainy season, you'll want to be extra prepared for deluges in the mountains.

For more helpful information on packing for your trip, download our Travel Tools app for your mobile device. Go to **www. frommers.com/go/mobile** and click on the Travel Tools icon.

Passports A valid passport is required to visit Colombia. Visas are not required if you are a citizen of Australia, Canada, France, Germany, New Zealand, South Africa, Switzerland, the United Kingdom, or the United States. You will automatically be granted permission to stay in the country for 60 days upon entering Colombia. If you plan to spend more than 60 days in the country, you will have to get permission from the Colombian Security Department (DAS) office in any departmental capital, though most tourists do so in Bogotá. To receive this 30- to 60-day extension, you will need to deposit COP$60,400 to Bancafé (account #056-99020-3, code 103), and then present your passport, your plane ticket (showing date of departure), four color passport pictures (3cm×4cm), two photocopies of your

passport picture page, two copies of your passport entry stamp page, two copies of the Bancafé deposit slip, and two copies of your plane ticket. The process usually takes 1 to 2 hours, but you will be given the extension on the spot. You can repeat the process until you've been in the country 180 days. The Bogotá DAS office, at Calle 100 no. 11B–27, Edificio Platino (ⓒ **1/601-7200**), is open Monday through Thursday 7:30am to 4pm and Friday 7:30am to 3pm. If you stay in Colombia more than 60 days without a visa extension, you can be fined $60 to $1,600 (depending on how long you overstay).

No immunizations are required for entry into Colombia, although travelers planning to travel to jungle regions should see "Health," p. 293.

Passport Offices:

○ **Australia Australian Passport Information Service** (www.passports. gov.au; ⓒ **131-232**).

○ **Canada Passport Office,** Department of Foreign Affairs and International Trade, Ottawa, ON K1A 0G3 (www.ppt.gc.ca; ⓒ **800/567-6868**).

○ **Ireland Passport Office**, Setanta Centre, Molesworth Street, Dublin 2 (www.foreign affairs.gov.ie; ⓒ **01/671-1633**).

○ **New Zealand Passports Office,** Department of Internal Affairs, 47 Boulcott Street,

Wellington, 6011 (www.passports.govt.nz; ℰ **0800/225-050** in New Zealand or 04/474-8100).

○ **United Kingdom** Visit your nearest passport office, major post office, or travel agency or contact the **Identity and Passport Service (IPS)**, 89 Eccleston Square, London, SW1V 1PN (www.ips.gov.uk; ℰ **0300/222-0000**).

○ **United States** To find your regional passport office, check the U.S. State Department website (http://travel.state.gov/passport) or call the **National Passport Information Center** (ℰ **877/487-2778**) for automated information.

Pharmacies Prescriptions can be filled at *farmacias* and *boticas*; it's best to know the generic name of your drug. For most health matters that are not serious, a pharmacist will be able to help and prescribe something. In the case of more serious health issues, contact your hotel, the tourist information office, or, in the most extreme case, your consulate or embassy for a doctor referral. Hospitals with English-speaking doctors are listed under "Doctors," p. 292.

Responsible Tourism
Sustainable, responsible tourism means conscientious travel. It means being careful with the environments you explore and respecting the communities you visit. Two overlapping components of sustainable travel are ecotourism and ethical tourism. Traveling "green" and seeking sustainable tourism options is a concern in almost every part of the world today. Colombia, with its majestic large expanses of nature, is a place where environmentally and culturally conscientious travel is not something to think about—it's the reality of the present and future. Although one could argue that any trip that includes an airplane flight or rental car can't be truly green, you can go on holiday and still contribute positively to the environment; all travelers can take certain steps toward responsible travel. Choose forward-looking companies that embrace responsible development practices, helping preserve destinations for the future by working alongside local people. An increasing number of sustainable tourism initiatives can help you plan a family trip and leave as small a "footprint" as possible on the places you visit.

The **International Ecotourism Society (TIES)** defines ecotourism as responsible travel to natural areas that conserves the environment and improves the well-being of local people. TIES suggests that ecotourists follow these principles:

○ Minimize environmental impact.

○ Build environmental and cultural awareness and respect.

○ Provide positive experiences for both visitors and hosts.

○ Provide direct financial benefits for conservation and for local people.

○ Raise sensitivity to host countries' political, environmental, and social climates.

○ Support international human rights and labor agreements.

You can find some eco-friendly travel tips, statistics, and touring companies and associations—listed by destination under "Travel Choice"—at the **TIES website**, www.ecotourism.org.

While much of the focus of ecotourism is about reducing impacts on the natural environment, ethical tourism concentrates on ways to preserve and enhance local economies and communities, regardless of location. You can embrace ethical tourism by staying at locally owned hotels or shopping at stores that employ local workers and sell locally produced goods. In Colombia, it's a great idea to pick up crafts such as textiles and ceramics from shops that ensure that the very artisans are well compensated for their labors. Many times those artisans are residents of poor, rural communities and "fair trade" shops are increasingly seen. Many highlight the names of artisans and their home communities on their wares.

Volunteer travel has become increasingly

popular among those who want to venture beyond the standard group-tour experience to learn languages, interact with locals, and make a positive difference while on vacation in Colombia.

Besides sustainable travel to Colombia's wilderness, national parks and reserves, and threatened areas, there are everyday things you can do to minimize the impact—and especially the carbon footprint—of your travels. Remove chargers from cellphones, PSPs, laptops, and anything else that draws from the mains, once the gadget is fully charged. Turning off all hotel room lights (plus the TV and air-conditioning) can have a massive effect; it really is time all hotels had room-card central power switches.

Green trips also extend to where you eat and stay. Vegetarian foods tend to have a much smaller impact on the environment because they eschew energy- and resource-intensive meat production. Most hotels now offer you the choice to use your towels for more than 1 night before they are re-laundered—laundry makes up around 40% of an average hotel's energy use.

Outside of ecolodges in the Amazon and the Pacific Coast, which are careful to ensure that a healthy percentage of jobs and benefits stay local and that the lodges' imprint on their fragile environment is minimal, few hotels in Colombia make much of an effort to be environmentally sustainable. In a country like Colombia, with such a large tract of virgin rainforest and developmental needs, maintaining a balance between income generation/tourism and sustainable development is a huge ongoing challenge.

A source for environmentally sensitive hotels is **It's a Green Green World** (www.itsagreengreenworld.com), which lists green and eco-friendly places to stay. **Responsible Travel** (www.responsibletravel.com; www.responsiblevacation.com in the U.S.) is one among a growing number of environmentally aware travel agents, with dozens of green Peru trips offered. **Vision on Sustainable Tourism** (www.sustainabletourism.net) is another excellent news hub. Carbon offsetting (not uncontroversial) can be arranged through, among others, **ClimateCare** (www.climatecare.org).

Safety While security around the country has improved dramatically over the past decade, Colombia is still far from being among the safest countries in the world. Parts of the rural countryside are still tightly controlled by armed groups and thus inaccessible to tourists. Travelers are advised to stick to well-touristed areas and keep up-to-date with the ever-changing political situation to avoid problems. But if you take adequate precautions, you're more likely to have a run-in with common street thieves than with guerilla or paramilitary factions. The most precautions, as in most countries, are required in the largest cities: principally Bogotá and, to a lesser extent, Medellín and Cali. In most heavily touristed places in Colombia, such as Cartagena, a heightened police presence is noticeable. Simple theft and pickpocketing are not uncommon; assaults and robbery are rare. Most thieves look for moments when travelers, laden with bags and struggling with maps, are distracted. Occasional car-jackings and armed attacks at ATMs have been reported, but they are very isolated incidents. Use ATMs during the day, with other people present. Street crime and pickpocketing are most likely to occur—when they do—at crowded public markets and bus and train stations. You should be vigilant with belongings in these places and should not walk alone late at night on deserted streets. In major cities, taxis hailed on the street can lead to assaults. (Use telephone-dispatched radio taxis, especially at night.) Ask your hotel or restaurant to call a cab, or use Uber, which has security protocol. Travelers should exercise caution on public city transportation, and on long-distance buses, where thieves have been known to employ any number of strategies to relieve passengers of their bags. You need to be vigilant, even to the extreme of locking backpacks and suitcases to luggage racks.

In general, do not wear expensive jewelry; keep expensive camera equipment out of view as much as possible; use a money belt worn inside your pants or shirt to safeguard cash, credit cards, and passport. Wear your daypack on your chest rather than your back when walking in crowded areas. The time to be most careful is when you have most of your belongings on your person—such as when you're in transit from airport or train or bus station to your hotel. At airports, it's best to spend a little more for official airport taxis; if in doubt, request the driver's official ID. Don't venture beyond airport grounds for a street taxi. Have your hotel call a taxi for your trip to the airport or bus station.

Senior Travel   Discounts for seniors are not automatic across Colombia, though many attractions do offer a senior rate. Mention the fact that you're a senior (and carry ID with your birth date) when you make travel reservations; many hotels still offer lower rates for seniors. Many museums and other attractions also offer discounts; if a senior rate (often expressed as *mayores de edad* or *jubilados* [retired] is not posted, inquire and show your passport).

Smoking   In May 2008, smoking in Colombia was banned in public transport vehicles, hospitals, schools, bars, clubs, restaurants, business centers, and airports. Make sure to ask if smoking is allowed before lighting up. Colombians smoke less than Europeans but more than Americans. Smoking is more prevalent in rural towns than big cities.

Student Travel   Never leave home without your student ID card. Visitors from overseas should arm themselves with an **International Student Identity Card (ISIC)**, which offers local savings on rail passes, plane tickets, entrance fees, and much more. Each country's card offers slightly different benefits (in the U.S., for example, it provides you with basic health and life insurance and a 24-hr. helpline). Apply before departing in your country of origin. In the U.S. or Canada, at **www.myisic.com**; in Australia, see **www.isiccard. com.au**; in New Zealand, visit **www.isiccard.co.nz**. U.K. students should carry their NUS card. If you're no longer a student but are still younger than 26, you can get an **International Youth Travel Card (IYTC)**, which entitles you to a more limited range of discounts.

Taxes   There is a 10% tax on hotel rooms, and a 16% tax on food.

Telephones   Colombia's phone system features a standardized system of seven-digit local numbers with one or two digit area codes.

○ To place a call from your home country to Colombia, dial the international access code (**0011** in Australia, **011** in the U.S and Canada, **0170** in New Zealand, and **00** in the U.K.), the country code (**57**), the one- or two-digit Colombian city code (Bogotá 1, Medellín 4, Cartagena 5, Pereira 61, Armenia 67, Manizales 69), plus the seven-digit local number.

○ To place a local call within Colombia, dial the one- or two-digit city code followed by the seven-digit local number. To call within a city, you only need to dial the seven-digit number. If you're dialing from a cellphone to a land line, dial 031, the city code, then the seven digit number. To call a cellphone from a landline, dial the city code plus the 10 digit cell phone.

○ **International operator info:** To reach an English-speaking international operator from within Colombia, dial ✆ **01/800-913-0110**.

Time   All of Colombia is 5 hours behind Greenwich Mean Time. Colombia does not observe daylight saving time.

Tipping   In midrange and expensive restaurants, there is usually a 10% tip included in the bill. It's not common to tip in budget restaurants or in taxis, so there's no need to do so unless you're feeling generous. Taxi drivers are not usually tipped unless they provide additional service. Bilingual tour guides on group tours should be tipped ($1–$2 per person for a short visit, and $5 or more per person for a full day). If you have a private guide, tip about $10 to $20.

Toilets Public lavatories (*baños públicos*) are rarely available except in railway stations, restaurants, and theaters. Use the bathroom of a bar, cafe, or restaurant; if it feels uncomfortable to dart in and out, have a coffee at the bar. Public restrooms are labeled WC (water closet), DAMAS (Ladies), and CABALLEROS or HOMBRES (Men). Toilet paper is not always provided, and when it is, most establishments request that patrons throw it in the wastebasket rather than the toilet, to avoid clogging. Bathroom quality varies. Expensive hotels, restaurants, and shops generally have clean facilities and toilet paper. As long as you're polite, restaurant, hotel, and store owners won't mind if you use their facilities. It's a good idea to bring your own toilet paper and hand sanitizer wherever you go, as budget establishments rarely have these items. Usually, you'll have to pay a small fee (generally under CO$600) to use a public or restaurant restroom.

Visitor Information
Because Colombia's tourism infrastructure is extremely underdeveloped, traveling here can be a bit tricky, especially if you don't speak Spanish. Except for Cartagena and some parts of the Atlantic Coast, many sections of Colombia have seen only a trickle of foreign visitors in the last few decades. Although tourists are generally treated formally and with polite curiosity, don't expect to find an overwhelming amount of tourist information. However, Colombians are generally friendly and your hotel staff will probably go out of their way to help you. Remember that a visit to Colombia requires patience and a sense of humor.

The **Ministerio de Comercio, Industria y Turismo** is Colombia's National Tourism Ministry. The main office is located at Calle 28 no. 13A–15 (© **1/606-7676** or 1/419-9450), but don't expect them to be very helpful or speak much English. In fact, good luck even getting into the building. But if you read Spanish, you may want to check out their website (www.mincit. gov.co).

Colombia's most popular tourism agency, **Aviatur** (www.aviatur.com; © **1/286-5555** or 1/234-7333), will book tours all over Colombia, usually including transportation, lodging, and most meals. The main office

in Bogotá is at Ave. 19 no. 4–62. There are offices throughout Bogotá and all large Colombian cities as well.

Tourism companies frequently come and go, so if you're looking for eco-adventure tours and travel, your best bet is your hotel which can give you information on local tours and tourism agencies, or at least provide some guidance.

One of the best ways to prepare for your trip to Colombia is on the Internet, where you will find plenty of useful information, especially from fellow travelers. The following websites contain useful information about Colombia.

- **www.colombia.travel**: The country's official travel information portal.

- **www.newworlder.com**: Insider foodie articles and guides focusing on the Americas, with lots of information on Colombian restaurants.

- **www.colombiaemb. org**: Colombia's embassy in Washington. A good place to start exploring the country.

- **www.thecitypaper bogota.com**: An English language paper in Bogotá with news from around the country, not to mention guides and event listings.

USEFUL TERMS & PHRASES

13

Colombian **Spanish** is, for the most part, very clean and straightforward, particularly in the capital of Bogotá. However, regional dialects and pronunciations can make it seem as if there are many other languages being spoken here. In Medellín, paisas tend to make a soft *g* sound whenever there is a *ll*. On the Caribbean coast, the African influence mixed with Spanish can make accents seem more Cuban than Colombian.

You'll here some phrases here more often than anywhere else in the Spanish-speaking world. *A la orden*, which essentially means "at your service," is uttered by nearly every taxi driver and shop clerk. *¿Qué más?* is often used instead of "How are you?" which can be confusing to anyone who translates the phrase literally. Instead of the word "sorry," there's *Qué pena!* Then there's the word *rumba* (party), popular everywhere in the country, which can even be used as a verb (*rumbear*).

Diminutives are similar to Cuba and Venezuela, as *ico* and *ica* rather than the more common *ito* and *ita* like in Peru and Ecuador. Slang is quite common, especially in Medellín, where it even has it's own name, *parlace*. Some favorite Colombian slang words include *farra* (party), *barra* (COP$1,000), *chévere* (cool), *guayabo* (hangover), *porfa* (please), and *plata* (money).

In addition to Spanish, there are dozens of indigenous tongues and dialects in Andean and Amazonian regions. Many of these are in danger of being lost as younger generations are not learning them. On the islands of San Andrés and Providencia, creole English, which sounds closer to Jamaican Patois than Colombian Spanish, is the norm.

BASIC SPANISH VOCABULARY

English	Spanish	Pronunciation
Good day	Buenos días	*Bweh*-nohs *dee*-ahs
Hi/hello	Hola	*Oh*-lah
Pleasure to meet you	Mucho gusto/Un placer	*Moo*-choh *goos*-toh/Oon plah-*sehr*
How are you?	¿Cómo está?	*Koh*-moh es-*tah*
Very well	Muy bien	Mwee byehn
Thank you	Gracias	*Grah*-syahs
How's it going?	¿Qué tal?	*Keh* tahl
You're welcome	De nada	Deh *nah*-dah
Goodbye	Adiós	Ah-*dyohs*
Please	Por favor	Pohr fah-*bohr*
Yes	Sí	See
No	No	Noh
Excuse me (to get by someone)	Perdóneme/Con permiso	Pehr-*doh*-neh-meh/Kohn pehr-*mee*-soh
Excuse me (to begin a question)	Disculpe	Dees-*kool*-peh
Give me	Déme	*Deh*-meh
What time is it?	¿Qué hora es?	Keh *ohr*-ah ehs?
Where is . . . ?	¿Dónde está . . . ?	*Dohn*-deh eh-*stah*?
the station	la estación	lah eh-stah-*syohn*
(bus/train)	estación de ómnibus/tren	eh-stah-*syohn* deh *ohm*-nee-boos/trehn
a hotel	un hotel	oon oh-*tel*
a gas station	una estación de servicio	*oo*-nah eh-stah-*syohn* deh sehr-*bee*-syoh
a restaurant	un restaurante	oon res-tow-*rahn*-teh
the toilet	el baño (or servicios)	el *bah*-nyoh (sehr-*bee*-syohs)
a good doctor	un buen médico	oon bwehn *meh*-dee-coh
the road to . . .	el camino a/hacia . . .	el cah-*mee*-noh ah/*ah*-syah
To the right	A la derecha	Ah lah deh-*reh*-chah
To the left	A la izquierda	Ah lah ee-*skyehr*-dah
Straight ahead	Derecho	Deh-*reh*-choh
Is it far?	¿Está lejos?	Eh-*stah leh*-hohs?
Is it close?	¿Está cerca?	Eh-*stah sehr*-kah
Open	Abierto	Ah-*byehr*-toh
Closed	Cerrado	Seh-*rah*-doh
North	Norte	*Nohr*-teh
South	Sur	Soor
East	Este	*Eh*-steh
West	Oeste	Oh-*eh*-steh

English	Spanish	Pronunciation
Expensive	Caro	*Cah*-roh
Cheap	Barato	Bah-*rah*-toh
I would like	Quisiera	Kee-*syeh*-rah
I want . . .	Quiero . . .	*Kyeh*-roh
to eat	comer	koh-*mehr*
a room	una habitación	oo-nah ah-bee-tah-*syohn*
Do you have . . . ?	¿Tiene usted . . . ?	*Tyeh*-neh oo-*stehd*
a book	un libro	oon *lee*-broh
a dictionary	un diccionario	oon deek-syoh-*na*-ryoh
change	cambio	*kahm*-byoh
How much is it?	¿Cuánto cuesta?	*Kwahn*-toh *kwes*-tah
When?	¿Cuándo?	*Kwahn*-doh
What?	¿Qué?	Keh
There is (Is/Are there . . . ?)	(¿)Hay (. . . ?)	eye
What is there?	¿Qué hay?	*Keh* eye
Yesterday	Ayer	Ah-*yehr*
Today	Hoy	Oy
Tomorrow	Mañana	Mah-*nyah*-nah
Good	Bueno	*Bweh*-noh
Bad	Malo	*Mah*-loh
Better (best)	(Lo) mejor	(Loh) meh-*hohr*
More	Más	Mahs
Less	Menos	*Meh*-nohs
No smoking	Se prohibe fumar	Seh proh-*ee*-beh foo-*mahr*
Postcard	Tarjeta postal	Tahr-*heh*-tah pohs-*tahl*
Insect repellent	Repelente contra insectos	Reh-peh-*lehn*-teh *cohn*-trah een-*sehk*-tohs
Now	Ahora	Ah-*ohr*-ah
Right now	Ahora mismo (ahorita)	Ah-*ohr*-ah *mees*-moh (ah-ohr-*ee*-tah)
Later	Más tarde	Mahs *tahr*-deh
Never	Nunca	*Noon*-kah
Guide	Guía	*Ghee*-ah
Heat	Calor	Kah-*lohr*
It's hot!	¡Qué calor!	Keh kah-*lohr*
Cold	Frío	*Free*-oh
Rain	Lluvia	*Yoo*-byah
It's cold!	¡Qué frío!	Keh *free*-oh
Wind	Viento	*Byehn*-toh
It's windy!	¡Cuánto viento!	*Kwahn*-toh *byehn*-toh
Money-changer	Cambista	Kahm-*bee*-stah

English	Spanish	Pronunciation
Bank	Banco	*Bahn*-koh
Money	Dinero	Dee-*neh*-roh
Small (correct) change	Sencillo	Sehn-*see*-yoh
Credit card	Tarjeta de crédito	Tahr-*heh*-tah deh *creh*-dee-toh
ATM	Cajero automático	Kah-*heh*-roh ow-toh-*mah*-tee-koh
Tourist information office	Oficina de información turística	Oh-fee-*see*-nah deh een-for-mah-*syohn* too-*ree*-stee-kah

Numbers

English	Spanish	Pronunciation
1	uno	*oo*-noh
2	dos	dohs
3	tres	trehs
4	cuatro	*kwah*-troh
5	cinco	*seen*-koh
6	seis	sayss
7	siete	*syeh*-teh
8	ocho	*oh*-choh
9	nueve	*nweh*-beh
10	diez	dyehs
11	once	*ohn*-seh
12	doce	*doh*-seh
13	trece	*treh*-seh
14	catorce	kah-*tohr*-seh
15	quince	*keen*-seh
16	dieciséis	dyeh-see-*sayss*
17	diecisiete	dyeh-see-*syeh*-teh
18	dieciocho	dyeh-*syoh*-choh
19	diecinueve	dyeh-see-*nweh*-beh
20	veinte	*bayn*-teh
30	treinta	*trayn*-tah
40	cuarenta	kwah-*ren*-tah
50	cincuenta	seen-*kwen*-tah
60	sesenta	seh-*sehn*-tah
70	setenta	seh-*tehn*-tah
80	ochenta	oh-*chen*-tah
90	noventa	noh-*ben*-tah
100	cien	syehn
200	doscientos	do-*syehn*-tohs
500	quinientos	kee-*nyehn*-tohs
1,000	mil	meel

Days of the Week

English	Spanish	Pronunciation
Monday	**Lunes**	(*loo*-nehss)
Tuesday	**Martes**	(*mahr*-tehss)
Wednesday	**Miércoles**	(*myehr*-koh-lehss)
Thursday	**Jueves**	(*wheh*-behss)
Friday	**Viernes**	(*byehr*-nehss)
Saturday	**Sábado**	(*sah*-bah-doh)
Sunday	**Domingo**	(doh-*meen*-goh)

SPANISH MENU GLOSSARY

General Terms

Bread **Pan**
Cheese **Queso**
Chicken **Pollo**
Coffee **Café/Tinto**
Dessert **Postre**
Eggs **Huevos**
Fish **Pescado**
French fries **Papas fritas**
Fruit **Fruta**
Meat **Carne**
Milk **Leche**

Pork **Cerdo**
Potatoes **Papas**
Rice **Arroz**
Roast **Asado**
Salad **Ensalada**
Salt **Sal**
Seafood **Mariscos**
Shrimp **Camarones**
Soup **Sopa**
Vegetables **Verduras**

Meat

Anticuchos Skewered meat
Cabrito Goat
Carne de res Beef
Chicharron Fried pork belly
Conejo Rabbit

Cordero Lamb
Costillas Ribs
Parrillada Grilled meats
Pato Duck
Sancochado Stew

Seafood

Almejas Clams
Atun Tuna
Bagre Catfish
Calamar Squid
Cangrejo Crab
Caracol Snails
Conchas Scallops
Corvina Sea bass
Langosta Lobster

Lenguado Sole
Mero Grouper
Mojarra Red Tilapia
Pargo Rojo Red Snapper
Pez León Lionfish
Piangua Black clam
Pirarucu Large Amazon fish
Pulpo Octopus

Fruit

Acaí   A small, purple palm fruit, more common in Brazil
Aguaymanto   Cape gooseberry
Camu Camu   Small Amazonian fruit high in Vitamin C
Carambola   Starfruit
Cherimoya   Custard apple
Chontadura   Peach palm
Curuba   Banana passion fruit
Fresa   Strawberry
Higo   Prickly pear
Limón   Lime
Lulo   An orange citrus fruit sometimes called naranjilla

Granadilla   A variety of passion fruit
Guanabana   Soursop
Manzana   Apple
Maracuyá   Passion fruit
Mora   Blackberry
Naranja   Orange
Piña   Pineapple
Pitahaya   Dragonfruit
Plátano   Banana
Sandía   Watermelon
Tomate de Árbol   Tree tomato
Uchuva   Gooseberry
Zapote   Mamey

Vegetables

Arracacha   Root vegetable
Aceitunas   Olives
Lechuga   Lettuce
Guatila   Chayote
Habas   Legumes

Mazorca   Large kernal corn
Papa   Potato
Palta   Avocado
Tomate   Tomato
Yuca   Cassava or manioc

Beverages

Beer   **Cerveza**
Cocktail   **Cóctel**
Juice   **Jugo**
Milk   **Leche**
Mixed fruit juice   **Refresco**

Soft drink   **Gaseosa**
Water   **Agua**
  carbonated   **con gas**
  still   **sin gas**
Wine   **Vino**

Preparation

Cold (temperature)   **Frío**
Cooked   **Cocido**
Fixed-price menu   **El menu**
Fried   **Frito**

Hot (temperature)   **Caliente**
Raw   **Crudo**
Spicy   **Picante**
Vegetarian   **Vegetariano**

Colombian Favorites

Aguapanela   Panela dissolved in water
Aguardiente   Firewater
Ajiaco   Chicken, corn, and potato stew
Arepas   Corn cakes

Arequipe   Sweetened condensed milk
Arroz con coco   Coconut rice
Bandeja Paísa   A platter with beans, rice, eggs, and meat that varies by location

Carimañola   Yuca fritter

Ceviche   Marinated raw fish

Changua   A creamy, egg soup typical in the Andes

Chicha   Fermented maize beer

Chicharrón   Fried pork belly

Churrasco   Grilled sirloin steak

Cocada   Baked coconut cookie

Cuy   Guinea pig. Can be roasted, fried, or cooked in a sauce

Fritanga   Meats, fried plantains, fried pork, and yellow potatoes

Hormigas culonas   Large-butt ants

Leche Asada   Similar to flan

Mondongo   Tripe stew

Morcilla   Blood sausage

Palta   Avocado

Pan de bono   A typical bread from the Valle de Cauca made of cassava starch, corn flour, cheese, and eggs

Patacones   Fried plantains

Salchipapas   French fries and sliced up hot dogs

Sancochado   A meat and potato stew with dozens of regional variations

Suero   Sour cream

Tamal   Ground corn cooked and stuffed with chicken or pork, wrapped in banana leaves or corn husks, and then steamed

Tinto   Coffee with sugar

ETIQUETTE & CUSTOMS

APPROPRIATE ATTIRE   Many travelers to Colombia are dressed in either head-to-toe adventure gear or their beach clothes. This is perfectly acceptable attire for all but the fanciest restaurants, where "neat casual" would be a better solution. In churches and monasteries, err on the side of discretion (shorts, midriff shirts, and anything else that reveals a lot of skin is not usually acceptable).

AVOIDING OFFENSE   In Colombia, be particularly mindful when discussing politics and the civil war, as many wounds are far from healed. Discussion of drugs (and coca-plant cultivation) and religion should be handled with great tact. Many Colombians refer to foreigners as *gringos* (or *gringas*). It is not intended and should be received as an insult.

On the streets of Cartagena and other tourist towns, shoeshine boys and little girls selling cigarettes or postcards can be very persistent and persuasive. Others just ask directly for money. If you don't wish to be hassled, a polite but firm "*No, gracias*" is usually sufficient, but it's important to treat these street kids with respect.

Queries about one's marital status and children are considered polite; indeed, women traveling alone or with other women should expect such questions. Display of one's relative wealth is unseemly, even though much of Colombia will seem inexpensive to many budget travelers.

GESTURES   Colombians are more formal in social relations than most North Americans and Europeans. They shake hands frequently and tirelessly, and kissing on the cheek is a common greeting for acquaintances. Indigenous populations are more conservative and even shy. They don't kiss to greet one another, nor do they shake hands as frequently as other Colombians; if they do, it is a light brush of the hand rather than a firm grip. Many indigenous people from small villages are reluctant to look a stranger in the eye.

Using your index finger to motion a person to approach you, as practiced in the United States and other places, is considered rude. A more polite way to beckon someone is to place the palm down and gently sweep your fingers toward you.

GREETINGS When entering a shop or home, always use an appropriate oral greeting (*buenos días*, or good day; *buenas tardes*, or good afternoon; *buenas noches*, or good night). Similarly, upon leaving, it is polite to say goodbye (*adios* or *hasta luego*), even to shop owners with whom you've had minimal contact. Colombians often shake hands upon leaving as well as greeting.

PHOTOGRAPHY In some heavily touristed areas, such as the colonial center of Cartagena, locals have learned to offer photo ops for a price at every turn. The ladies with the fruit or the cigars aren't posing so spectacularly by coincidence. Some foreigners hand out money and candy indiscriminately, while others grapple with the unseemliness of paying for every photo. Often it's more comfortable to photograph people you have made an effort to talk to, rather than responding to those who explicitly beg to be your subject. I usually give a small tip (COP$2,000–COP$5,000) if it appears that my camera has been an intrusion or nuisance, or especially if I've snapped several shots.

Photographing military, police, or airport installations is strictly forbidden. Many churches, convents, and museums also do not allow photography or video, or they may charge a fee to take photos.

PUNCTUALITY Punctuality is not one of the trademarks of Colombia or Latin America as a whole. Colombians are customarily a little bit late to most personal appointments, particularly in rural areas, and it is not considered very bad form to leave someone hanging in a cafe for a half hour. It is expected; so if you have a meeting scheduled, be prepared to wait.

SHOPPING Bargaining is considered acceptable in markets and with taxi drivers outside of major cities, and even hotels, but only up to a point—don't overdo it. Also bear in mind that many shops in large and small towns close at midday, from 1 to 3pm or 2 to 4pm.

USEFUL TERMS & PHRASES

Etiquette & Customs

Index

RESTAURANT INDEX

Photo Credits

Map List

Published by
FROMMER MEDIA LLC

Frommer's Easy Guide to Colombia, 1st Edition
ISBN 978-1-62887-284-2 (paper), 978-1-62887-285-9 (ebk)

Editorial Director: Pauline Frommer
Editor: Elizabeth Heath
Production Editor: Erin Geile
Cartographer: Roberta Stockwell
Photo Editor: Meghan Lamb
Cover Design: David Riedy

For information on our other products or services, see www.frommers.com.

ABOUT THE AUTHORS

Writer and photographer **Nicholas Gill** is based in Lima, Peru and Brooklyn, New York. He travels extensively throughout Latin America, and his work appears in publications such as *The New York Times, Wall Street Journal, Bon Appétit, Draft, Saveur, New York Magazine,* and *Roads & Kingdoms.*

Travel writer/editor **Caroline Lascom** has spent over a decade living, working, and traveling in Latin America. She has written and contributed to more than 25 guidebooks for market-leading publishers in the U.S. and U.K. and is a regular contributor to travel websites, blogs, and print publications. As well as being the co-author of *Frommer's Colombia*, Caroline has also penned chapters for *Frommer's Chile*. She is based in Chicago.

ABOUT THE FROMMER TRAVEL GUIDES

For most of the past 50 years, Frommer's has been the leading series of travel guides in North America, accounting for as many as 24% of all guidebooks sold. I think I know why.

Though we hope our books are entertaining, we nevertheless deal with travel in a serious fashion. Our guidebooks have never looked on such journeys as a mere recreation, but as a far more important human function, a time of learning and introspection, an essential part of a civilized life. We stress the culture, lifestyle, history, and beliefs of the destinations we cover, and urge our readers to seek out people and new ideas as the chief rewards of travel.

We have never shied from controversy. We have, from the beginning, encouraged our authors to be intensely judgmental, critical—both pro and con—in their comments, and wholly independent. Our only clients are our readers, and we have triggered the ire of countless prominent sorts, from a tourist newspaper we called "practically worthless" (it unsuccessfully sued us) to the many rip-offs we've condemned.

And because we believe that travel should be available to everyone regardless of their incomes, we have always been cost-conscious at every level of expenditure. Though we have broadened our recommendations beyond the budget category, we insist that every lodging we include be sensibly priced. We use every form of media to assist our readers, and are particularly proud of our feisty daily website, the award-winning Frommers.com.

I have high hopes for the future of Frommer's. May these guidebooks, in all the years ahead, continue to reflect the joy of travel and the freedom that travel represents. May they always pursue a cost-conscious path, so that people of all incomes can enjoy the rewards of travel. And may they create, for both the traveler and the persons among whom we travel, a community of friends, where all human beings live in harmony and peace.

Arthur Frommer